MYSTERIES
of ANCIENT CHINA

NEW DISCOVERIES FROM THE EARLY DYNASTIES

Edited by Jessica Rawson

Published for the Trustees of the British Museum
by British Museum Press

Chinese names and terms are romanised according to the *pinyin* system,
the standard form of transliteration used throughout China today.
Pronunciation of some consonant sounds is described below:

c = *ts* (*cong* = *tsoong*)
q = *ch* (*qi* = *chee*)
x = *sh* (Xi'an = *Shee-an*)
zh = *j* (Zhou = *Jo*)

Chinese place names are generally given in three parts, ordered from
smallest to largest as in normal English usage (site, county, province).
Sometimes, however, the Chinese system is used, in which the largest area
is given first and the smallest last (province, county, site).

Cover Detail of life-size bronze standing figure from pit 2,
Sanxingdui, Guanghan county, Sichuan province,
c. 1200–1000 BC (no. 22). Photo Ray Main, The Times

Frontispiece Detail of bell set from tomb M2, Leigudun,
Sui county, Hubei province, Eastern Zhou period,
Zeng state, 5th century BC (no. 62).
Photo Ray Main, The Times

Exhibition sponsored by
THE TIMES

© 1996 The Trustees of the British Museum

Published by British Museum Press
A division of The British Museum Company Ltd
46 Bloomsbury Street, London WC1B 3QQ

ISBN 0–7141–1472–3

A catalogue record for this book is available from the British Library

Designed by John Hawkins Book Design

Typeset in Monotype Garamond by Wyvern Typesetting Ltd, Bristol
Printed in Italy by Grafiche Milani

CONTENTS

FOREWORD

When conceived with thought and intelligence, a museum exhibition can profoundly affect our understanding of its subject. *Mysteries of Ancient China* is one such, bringing together the most important archaeological finds from China of the past two decades, and it will transform our ideas about ancient Chinese society.

The origins of China's exquisite craftsmanship in ceramic, jade, bronze, lacquer and textiles can be traced back seven thousand years. This exhibition brings to the British Museum a selection of outstanding objects, many of which were preserved as burial goods in the tombs of emperors and nobles. Among these, the highly wrought bronze vessels and finely tuned bells, lacquer chests and the garments they contained are sources with which we can reinterpret the civilisation and beliefs of the ancient Chinese.

The eerie bronze figures, heads and monster mask from the sacrificial pits at Guanghan, dated to about 1200 BC, represent the rich creativity of the people living in south-western China and challenge us to explain this new material evidence of their religious world. This is the first time that the key objects from this site have been shown outside China. Many rarely seen pieces from later periods are also displayed here, including the magnificent bronze crane with antlers from the tomb of the Marquis Yi who died about 433 BC, one of the terracotta warriors from the tomb of the First Emperor, and a jade suit belonging to the imperial prince Liu Sheng of the late second century BC. These remarkable objects bring us closer to understanding the religious attitudes of the ancient Chinese when they built their tombs and prepared themselves for the afterlife.

An exhibition of this nature could not have been realised without help from many quarters. Our first and greatest debt is, of course, to our Chinese colleagues in the China Cultural Relics Promotion Centre in Beijing, and to their Director Tong Zhenghong and Deputy Director Professor Lei Congyun. Without the support of the many museums which generously lent objects and of the State Bureau for Cultural Relics this exhibition would have been impossible to organise. The British Museum is one of five European museums to host these treasures from China, along with the Kulturstiftung Ruhr in Essen, the Hypo-Kulturstiftung in Munich, the Kunsthaus in Zurich and the Louisiana Museum of Modern Art in Humlebaek, Denmark. I am grateful for the help of colleagues in all these institutions who took part in the initial negotiations and brought the exhibition to Europe. We are especially in the debt of Professor Paul Vogt, Chairman of the Kulturstiftung Ruhr, Essen, and Professor Roger Goepper, former Director of the Museum for East Asian Art, Cologne, who fostered the project from the beginning and brought it to fruition.

For the fact that this exhibition has come to the British Museum we must thank Dr Jessica Rawson, a former Keeper of Oriental Antiquities and now the Warden of Merton College, Oxford, who has worked tirelessly to ensure that it has had a London showing. Among the many members of staff of the British Museum who have contributed to this exhibition I would especially like to thank Dr Oliver Moore, one of the Chinese curators in the Department of Oriental Antiquities.

Finally, I would like to thank Times Newspapers Ltd, especially Sir Edward Pickering, Executive Vice Chairman, and Peter Stothard, Editor of the Times, for their support of the exhibition. Without their enthusiastic help this undertaking would not have been manageable. This is the second occasion on which the Times has collaborated with the British Museum on a major exhibition, and we are grateful for our continuing relationship.

R.G.W. Anderson
Director

CONTRIBUTORS AND LENDERS

Authors of the essays

Lei Congyun, China Cultural Relics Promotion Centre, Beijing

Yang Yang, China Cultural Relics Promotion Centre, Beijing

Zhao Dianzeng, Institute of Archaeology and Cultural Relics, Sichuan Province

Zheng Zhenxiang, Institute of Archaeology, Chinese Academy of Social Sciences, Beijing

Jessica Rawson, Warden, Merton College, Oxford

Yu Weichao, Historical Museum, Beijing

Chen Lie, China Cultural Relics Promotion Centre, Beijing

Roger Goepper, University of Cologne

Lenders to the exhibition

Historical Museum, Beijing

Institute of Archaeology, Chinese Academy of Social Sciences, Beijing

Institute of Cultural Relics, Beijing

Hebei Provincial Museum

Institute of Cultural Relics, Hebei Province

Henan Provincial Museum, Zhengzhou

Institute of Archaeology and Cultural Relics, Henan Province

Guanlin Museum of Stone Sculpture, Luoyang, Henan Province

Luoyang City Museum, Henan Province

Cultural Relics Bureau, Luoyang City, Henan Province

Hubei Provincial Museum, Wuhan

Jingzhou Regional Museum, Hubei Province

Suizhou City Museum, Hubei Province

Hunan Provincial Museum, Changsha

Nanjing City Museum, Jiangsu Province

Institute of Archaeology and Cultural Relics, Sichuan Province

Sichuan Provincial Museum, Chengdu

Cultural Relics Bureau of Xindu County, Sichuan Province

Institute of Archaeology and Cultural Relics, Zhejiang Province

PREFACE

The Times has the longest connection with China of any British daily newspaper. Our two centuries together, however, form but a brief span for the civilisation that invented the journalist's daily tools of paper and ink when ancient Britons were still unable to read.

In the early days of our association England was already fascinated by chinoiserie, but Chinese culture still awaited deeper Western understanding. In 1817 we reported the Prince Regent's Eastern fantasy, Brighton's Royal Pavilion, his Chinese–Indian domed palace at the English seaside. We grumbled, of course, about the public cost: we were amazed by the exoticism and glamour.

Our forefathers at the Times and the British Museum knew as much about Chinese porcelain and poetry as any Westerner. But only recently has there begun a proper mutual understanding between the thought of Europe and the thought of Asia. Through the work of British and Chinese scholars and through access to collections such as those on permanent display in the British Museum, the true richness of the spiritual and aesthetic world of Chinese art has become more widely known. Its exquisite craftsmanship, delicate colours, deep respect for scholarship and vivid observations of nature and the human condition are now justly famed.

The Times is proud to have played a part in that process of discovery, not only through our reporting but through helping to make it possible for the British public to gain a wider direct experience of China's artistic wealth. In 1972, the then proprietor of the Times, Roy Thomson, visited China, where he and his party were received at length by the Chinese premier, Zhou Enlai. Lord Thomson offered to buy the People's Daily, an offer that Zhou politely declined, but the two old men happily discussed capitalism and culture.

The interest of the Times in modern China led to its sponsorship, in 1974, of *The Genius of China* exhibition at the Royal Academy, a virtuoso display of the diversity of Chinese art down the ages. Among its treasures were the 'flying' horse of Gansu, as remarkable as the bronze horses that ended their long journey on St Mark's in Venice, and the magnificent jade burial suit of the Princess Dou Wan, whose husband's suit visits the British Museum this year.

Since then, there have been astounding new archaeological discoveries, finds that have both enriched understanding of China's distant past and exposed hitherto unknown and still mysterious Chinese civilisations to the tantalised eye. From the astonishing burial pits in Guanghan, south-west China, discovered in 1986, an imposing ten-foot-tall bronze figure reaches sternly out to us across 3000 years.

The Times is honoured to be associated with the British Museum's enthralling exhibition of these *Mysteries of Ancient China*. This is an exhibition that not only shows the richness and sophistication of Chinese states in remotest antiquity; it allows us to glimpse the hidden 'soul' of successive Chinese civilisations. For two centuries, the Times and its readers have been fascinated by China. It is more important today than it has ever been for the United Kingdom and China to understand each other's cultures, ways of thought and 'souls' expressed in art.

Peter Stothard, Editor
THE TIMES

ACKNOWLEDGEMENTS

In preparing this catalogue I was very fortunate to be able to make use of the catalogue edited by Professor Roger Goepper for the exhibition as shown in Germany and Switzerland. The order of the exhibits has been changed and the presentation of the catalogue reflects this. I am grateful for the illustrations and information supplied in the German catalogue, on which I have drawn in part in the writing of the present text. In particular I would like to thank Professor Goepper, Dr Jeonghee Lee-Kalisch and Dr Peter Wiedehage. The entries on textiles and associated items draw heavily on the contributions to the German edition of Professor Dieter Kuhn. Entries 90–94, 99 and 108–116 were written by Carol Michaelson, and Oliver Moore has contributed entries 76, 95 and 117. He has also been responsible for the Bibliography, and I am grateful for his help at all stages of the preparation of the catalogue. Carol Webb in the Warden's Office at Merton College was indispensable to the production of the text, and I thank her especially for her help and interest. In the British Museum, Carol White and Mandy Pearson have kindly assisted with the text, Annie Searight drew the maps and David Gowers and John Williams have provided supplementary photography, as has Ray Main for the Times.

As ever I am grateful to Susan Leiper for her thoughtful editing and for the enthusiasm and support of Emma Way, Head of British Museum Press, Nina Shandloff, Senior Editor, and their colleagues Julie Young, Simona Borroni and Catherine Wood. The catalogue was designed by John Hawkins and the index prepared by Susanne Atkin. The exhibition was designed by Graham Simpson with the help of many members of the British Museum Design Office, directed by Margaret Hall, including Teresa Rumble, Jude Simmons, Suzanne Haberfeld and Andrea Easey. Much help on the installation was given by the Museum Assistants in the Department of Oriental Antiquities led by David Bellamy. Many others in the British Museum have, of course, assisted with a project of this magnitude, including Chris Jones and other members of the Administration, Marjorie Caygill and others in the Director's Office, Geoffrey House and his colleagues in the Public Relations Office, John Reeve and other members of the Education Service, and Sarah Carthew and Patricia Morison of the British Museum Society.

Work on this exhibition started before I left the British Museum in 1994 and I would like to thank the Director, Robert Anderson, for his support from the very beginning and Robert Knox, my successor as Keeper of Oriental Antiquities, for carrying to fruition this large-scale endeavour.

Jessica Rawson
Merton College, Oxford

INTRODUCTION

Jessica Rawson

This introduction and the catalogue cover a formative period of China's history, from about 4500 BC, when diverse neolithic societies occupied the landmass of present-day China, to the second century AD, by which time the country had experienced almost three centuries of strong rule following the unification of the country in 221 BC by the First Emperor – King Zheng of Qin, or Qin Shi Huangdi. Objects of ceramic, jade and bronze illustrate this period of development from diversity to unification. In about 4500 BC each region of China had its own distinctive ceramics and types of ornament, indicating widely different religious and social values. By the third century BC, China's material culture mirrored the new political unity: similar types of ceramics, jades and bronzes were used in areas as far apart as a thousand kilometres.[1]

The two hundred or so pieces illustrated come from many different regions. They show how the customs and practices of different peoples contributed to a culture that, by the periods of the Qin (221–206 BC) and their successors, the Han (206 BC–AD 220), we recognise as Chinese. The catalogue is divided chronologically into three sections. The first, Unknown China (*c.* 4500–*c.* 1000 BC), covers periods and places that have not been described in China's historical writings. From the time of the conquest by the peoples known as the Zhou, in about 1050 BC, the Chinese self-consciously recorded their own history in some detail. These accounts describe the predecessors of the Zhou, known as the Shang (*c.* 1500–*c.* 1050 BC) (nos 36–50), but not the neolithic peoples whose remains are now being discovered in most parts of China (nos 1–21). Nor do these early records enable us to identify the other bronze-using peoples contemporary with the Shang. Thus one of the most striking groups of objects, the bronzes and jades from the sacrificial pits at Sanxingdui, in Sichuan province in western China (nos 22–35), was made by peoples who are as yet not known to be described in any early Chinese text. For this reason, these finds are grouped within the section on Unknown China, before the better known bronzes and jades of the Shang.

The second section, the Great Dynasties (*c.* 1500–221 BC), covers the periods dominated by the ruling houses of the Shang and the Zhou (nos 36–77). Large cities and great tombs constructed by these states have been explored by archaeologists for more than half a century, yielding prolific discoveries, such as the possessions of the royal consort Fu Hao, wife of a Shang king, who lived about 1200 BC. Her magnificent bronzes, which were used in rituals, and her rare jades (nos 39–50) continued the neolithic tradition of high craftsmanship, which was to become the hallmark of Chinese culture. Moreover, these objects are complemented by the earliest textual evidence in the form of oracle bone inscriptions (no. 37) and inscriptions in the bronze vessels.

The Zhou, successors to the Shang, inherited and adapted a considerable amount of Shang material culture. However, they also established a new ideological framework, which was to hold true for the following thousand years or more. Only a few items from the early Zhou period are illustrated (nos 52–57), but these were essential to the political claims made by the Zhou. The first half of the Zhou period, known as the Western Zhou, contrasts with the second half, known as the Eastern Zhou, when much of present-day China was subdivided into competing states. In the Eastern Zhou period, bronzes and jades served both the religious rituals of the day and the competing ideologies of the time (nos 58–77). The great philosophical theories of Confucius, Laozi (the putative founder of Daoism) and the Legalists, advisers to the Qin state, were expounded in attempts to grapple with the political turmoil.

The third section, Imperial China, explores the unification of the competing states under the Qin and Han empires (221 BC–AD 220). Diverse contending states were thrust together into a unified polity, whose control of military and civil affairs was expressed in a unified material culture. The collation of varied religious, ritual and magical practices within a single state resulted in enriched notions about the universe, the cosmos and the fate of mankind. Craftsmen produced a wealth of fine objects and equipped sumptuous tombs. These tombs, and the objects found in them, reflect new interests in a hierarchy of celestial deities (no. 68), in a bureaucracy of the underworld (no. 95), in deathlessness through transformation to a jade-like state (no. 81), and in lands of the immortals (nos 82, 86, 87). The tomb of the First Emperor, accompanied by the terracotta warriors (no. 78), is only the most renowned of these.

One of the central themes of the catalogue is the way in which objects can represent ideas, and changes in ideas. Contrary to general belief, texts are not essential for the generation and transmission of ideas. For the early period of China's history no texts survive, and it is likely that extensive writing appeared only in the Shang period, from which time a highly developed script is known (no. 37). Therefore, in place of documents, we have to make use of excavated monuments and their contents. Once their potential is recognised, material remains provide a direct route to an understanding of the past, which sometimes complements, sometimes differs from, and is often as reliable as the textual tradition. It is in the later periods, with the benefit of a number of different types of writing (nos 95, 117), that material and textual sources begin to complement one another to advantage.

Texts are additionally important because the ancient Chinese expected to communicate with the world of gods and spirits in writing, as well as by other means. Inscriptions on ritual vessels (fig. 9) were probably addressed as much to the ancestors as to the living. Inventories placed in tombs, such as that displayed at no. 95, were certainly addressed to the underworld bureaucracy.

Many of the objects in the exhibition appear to be primarily functional: containers, cups, stands and lamps. First and foremost they offer us information on the specific uses to which they were put, on the technologies with which they were made, and on the artistic styles of their day. But we can look at them in a wider context. Many, if not all of them, were used in groups, possibly in rituals for the living and the dead. From these functional groups we can investigate the beliefs that informed ritual and religious practices. These practices and the beliefs that the objects presented are central to any understanding of ancient China.

Other objects were far less obviously functional. Figures of terracotta warriors (no. 78) and fittings in the shape of immortals (no. 86) are images; boxes (no. 64) and mirrors (no. 88) may depict images. These images are often combined to present complex pictures, both of daily life and of the spirit worlds. From such pictures we gain different insights into ancient China.

However, these two categories of object – the functional object and the object that is either itself an image or depicts one – cannot always be completely separated, and, in the case of the boxes and mirrors, for example, they overlap. Each category presents ideas in a different way. On the one hand, a group of functional objects suggests actions, or a series of actions, that might take place in a ritual affirming a religious belief. On the other hand, an image, or a group of images, is in itself a representation of an idea or a belief.

Unknown China: the neolithic period, *c.* 4500 BC–*c.* 2000 BC

The neolithic period is represented in the catalogue by two distinct groups of objects: ceramics (nos 1–15) and jades (nos 16–21). These serve to illustrate not only the diversity of ancient China's neolithic societies, but also certain recurring threads, which can be woven together to create a nascent, if somewhat hazy, tapestry of ancient beliefs and practices.

Among neolithic ceramics, and even the most finely made ones, the great majority were functional. The first ceramic techniques were unassuming: coils of clay were built up to make basins, jars and large containers. Yet even in some of the earliest neolithic cultures, such as that of the Yangshao, which occupied the regions of present-day Shaanxi province near Xi'an, the masses of pieces found in any one grave indicate a large industry (fig. 1a). The exquisite painting on some of the Yangshao pieces shows too that there was a desire to make certain pieces that went beyond the everyday (no. 1).

A few of the ceramics illustrated in the catalogue bear images, and have indeed been chosen for this reason. Such pieces were presumably exceptional: the human-headed fish (no. 1), the reptile-like forms (no. 6) and the coiled snake or dragon (no. 7) are great rarities. Such images hint at other worlds, and are different from the more common ways of embellishing functional vessels to indicate that they surpassed the everyday, that they were special.[2] Vessels played an important role within society and for this reason they were beautifully made, with fine shapes and exquisite abstract ornament, but their designs seldom incorporate identifiable creatures or beings. Peoples in Gansu province, to the west of the main Yangshao culture, developed a range of linear patterns composed of lines, circles and scrolls, the kaleidoscopic variety of which indicates an interest in making individual and visually intriguing pieces (fig. 1b).

In eastern China, potters made wheel-thrown cups and dishes on high stands in sections, and lobed tripods by joining together three or more moulded parts. Such

Fig. 1 *Drawings illustrating neolithic ceramics from three distinct areas of China:*
a *Yangshao culture, Shaanxi province, c. 4500 BC*
b *Majiayao culture, Gansu province, c. 3500–2500 BC*
c *Dawenkou culture, eastern China, c. 4500–3000 BC*
After Beijing 1984e, p. 44, fig. 12:1; p. 90, fig. 28:3; p. 112, fig. 35:2.

elaborate pieces (fig. 1c) were probably for particular purposes, perhaps ritual, for many of the exceptionally slender stands appear quite impractical. Although we do not know how the potters were organised, it seems likely that complex vessels were made in large workshops.[3]

A characteristic eastern neolithic burial is illustrated on page 251, fig. 3. Small cups on very high stems suggest a drinking ceremony rather than simply the provision of liquor. Indeed, the stems involve more clay and more workmanship than do the cups. Graves contain more of these fine pieces than would have been required by the tomb occupant on a single occasion. Their position at the centre of the tomb implies their importance to the individual or to a particular rite, perhaps even a banquet in the afterlife. Indeed, the many different groups of neolithic peoples may already have believed, as did their successors, that the dead required the finest of cups and dishes for the victuals to sustain them in the afterlife.

Just as ceramics could be made special by the use of painted decoration or unusual forms, so too could items of stone by the choice of fine, translucent materials. For the neolithic peoples produced not only ceramics but also stone objects. Indeed, the use of stone distinguishes the neolithic period from the subsequent Bronze Age, when items of bronze predominated. The peoples of north-eastern China, known as the Hongshan culture (fig. 2; Lei, figs 1–5), and those of the south-east, known as the Liangzhu culture (nos 16–20), employed exceptional stones, primarily nephrite (or jade, as it is known colloquially), for their finest stone implements and ornaments.

Over the past few decades archaeologists have been amazed by the extent to which the Hongshan and Liangzhu peoples used nephrite. Nephrite is the name given to metamorphosed varieties of two rather different minerals – actinolite and tremolite; these have been changed by great pressure and heat over geological time, transforming their fine crystalline structures into hard, compact semi-translucent stones. This structure is difficult to carve, and must be ground with abrasive sands. Although the Chinese word *yu*, which we translate as jade, is less specific than our term nephrite, the ancient Chinese seem to have developed considerable expertise in identifying nephrite, and much ancient so-called jade carving is of this mineral.

As with good clays, the search for nephrite and related gem-like stones presumably required special skills, and so too did working the pieces. Some of the early stone carvings of the Hongshan culture were simply special versions of everyday objects: arrow heads were chipped from agate and fine axe heads ground from nephrite. In tombs of the Hongshan culture jade implements and ornaments are almost the sole burial goods.[4] This practice differs from that of most Chinese neolithic peoples, who seem to have believed that food and vessels were essential to the afterlife. The exceptional jade ornaments found in Hongshan tombs were perhaps indicators of status and harbingers of well-being. One such ornament is a coiled creature, known as a pig-dragon (fig. 2), that was buried on the chest of the tomb occupant.

These pig-dragons are approximately circular, and often substantial. They have few distinct features apart from a blunt head with oval eyes held within a figure-of-eight pattern of finely modulated ridges and a pair of rounded ears. Although these features are thought to bear a slight resemblance to those of a pig, the creature could not be said to represent a real animal. As the Hongshan peoples carved these substantial creatures from valuable materials, such as jade, they must surely have valued the image. Moreover, as the creature is not part of the everyday world, we can argue with relative security that here we have a reference to something beyond the everyday, that is, to something spiritual or

Fig. 2 *Pig-dragon carved in jade. Neolithic period, Hongshan culture, c. 3000 BC. Height 14 cm. After Beijing 1993b, pl. 38.*

religious. It is impossible to identify the creature, or understand the associations it probably carried, but we can recognise its value to the peoples of Hongshan.

A similar situation occurs in the other major jade-using neolithic culture, the Liangzhu. As discussed and illustrated in the essay by Yang, jade, while in relatively short supply in the north-east, was more readily available in the south-east (Yang, fig. 2). Here it was used not only to make ornaments, but also for special versions of axes, which were too fine to be functional. In this they resemble the tall-stemmed ceramics of the east coast (fig. 1c). Yet, like the jade dragons of the Hongshan, other jades from the Liangzhu area (nos 16–20) are beyond our comprehension and seem to refer to realms beyond the everyday.

Among such objects whose functions we cannot guess are the jade tube (no. 16) and disc (no. 17). Both are beautifully worked from fine stones and were buried in large numbers, indicating their value. But as we have no idea of their functions, we cannot begin to suggest their meanings. This difficulty is compounded by the 'eye' motifs that occur on many of the tubes. These are abbreviated forms of a highly complex motif, the full version of which can be seen in figure 3, drawn from the jade tube (no. 16).

Even more than the coiled Hongshan pig-dragon (fig. 2), this strange human-like figure, with what appears to be some sort of feathered headdress, grasping the eyes of a large monster with fangs, suggests an imagined world peopled with strange deities. The motif is repeated on other jades of the Liangzhu culture, and abbreviated forms are standard on the jade tubes, known by the name of *cong*. An interest in such images was shared by peoples of a relatively large area although the associations of the image may have varied from place to place.

The very rich tombs in which such jades occur are relatively few in number and suggest that their owners were a small priestly or élite class, whose power involved the monopoly of fine materials and craftsmanship. Huge numbers of jade pieces in particular tombs (Yang, fig. 2) indicate a high concentration of wealth. Jades were probably an indication of status and identity, and they may also have been considered to offer some kind of protection to the tomb occupant.

Even at this early date, the unchanging, permanent nature of the stone may have been attractive. At later times the material qualities of jade were applied metaphorically to those who owned it, and it is possible that the Liangzhu peoples believed that, by burying large quantities of jade with the deceased, the permanent qualities of the stone would be transferred to the indi-

Fig. 3 *Detail of a human-like figure with a feathered headdress holding the eyes of a monster in his hands. From the centre of a jade* cong *(no. 16) from Fanshan in Yuhang county, near Hangzhou, Zhejiang province. Neolithic period, Liangzhu culture, c. 2500 BC.*

vidual. In other societies, especially in the West, the qualities of gold were thought to be transferred to those embellished with it. Indeed, peoples throughout the world use objects and materials to express analogies: gold may indicate purity and brilliance; jade may represent permanence.[5]

Before the end of the neolithic period, therefore, several recurring features of Chinese religious beliefs and practices had been established. Ceramic vessels seem to have been made both for everyday and ceremonial use, and individuals were buried with vessels that would contain nourishment for their afterlife. People adorned their bodies, and those of the deceased, with fine jades, probably to indicate status and perhaps to absorb the enduring and permanent qualities of the stone. And finally, both ceramics and jades show evidence of imagery that appears to refer to a world of spirits or other beings.

From Unknown China to the Great Dynasties: the sacrificial pits at Sanxingdui and the tomb of Fu Hao

The catalogue illustrates large groups of bronzes and jades from two very different regions of China, made by two very different societies (nos 22–50). These differences are evident in the pieces themselves. The bronzes from western China have been included in the section on Unknown China because we do not know who made them, nor can we guess what purposes or religion they

served. The other group comprises the bronzes of the Shang dynasty, the first dynasty for which there is both textual and excavated evidence. The two groups of objects fall very neatly into the two categories of object mentioned above: objects which suggest a meaning through their use in a group, and objects which appear to be a visual image of an idea or belief.

The Shang inhabited Henan province from about 1500 BC and established large cities. Their principal bronzes were food and wine vessels for making offerings to their ancestors, such as the magnificent pieces (nos 39–45) buried with Fu Hao, the consort of one of the most renowned Shang kings, Wu Ding, who lived about 1200 BC. Fu Hao's bronzes may be slightly earlier than the group from western China (nos 22–32), but both belong to much the same era.

The technology by which the two widely separated groups of bronzes were made was also similar.[6] Moreover, it was a casting method peculiar to China. The Chinese developed a system of casting with moulds of multiple sections. The casters of Fu Hao's vessels made use of section moulds to emphasise vessel forms and to match decoration to them. Such technology served rituals that demanded highly distinctive vessel types, each reserved for a particular food or wine. The appearance of an unusual form at a banquet, such as Fu Hao's vessel shaped as a tiger and a bird (fig. 4a), would have attracted attention and highlighted the food served in it.

We know that these bronze vessels were employed for food both from traces of bones and liquids discovered in them and from somewhat later texts that describe ritual meals. Inscriptions both in the bronzes and on oracle bones reveal that offerings were made to the ancestors in these vessels. The use of bronze rather than ceramics for this purpose emphasises the importance of the practice.

The ancestors, it seems, were deemed to contribute to the lives of their descendants. Their goodwill and support were sought to intervene with the other denizens of the spirit world. For, in addition to the ancestors, the Shang seem to have revered gods, among whom Di, the High God, was all-powerful.

But we have no visual picture of this spirit world. While the Hongshan and Liangzhu peoples employed a few images, the Shang do not seem to have provided visual images of their ancestors, gods or spirits. A great number of the bronze vessels carry fine cast designs of a monster face (fig. 4b), known today as a *taotie* from a term given in later texts. But the significance of this image is not known; it is impossible on present evidence to establish to what it refers.[7] It seems unlikely to refer to the Shang ancestors or to the High God. Variations

Fig. 4a *Bronze ritual wine vessel, gong (no. 45), from the tomb of Fu Hao at Anyang, Henan province. Shang dynasty, c. 1200 BC. Height 22 cm. The vessel is shaped and decorated as a tiger at the front and a bird at the rear. These creatures are rare on Shang bronzes and may have been introduced to the Shang area from further south. Much more usual is the decoration of an animal face known as a* taotie, *shown in fig. 4b.*

in its shape and features seem less likely to be connected with the depiction of a variety of spirits than with the wish to create ornamented vessels of different proportions, which thus required images whose proportions could be easily changed. Craftsmen could vary the motif to make both highly decorated and also less well

adorned vessels, presumably for individuals of different status. The ways in which scholars have attempted to interpret the *taotie* ornament betray a Western concern with images and iconography. What probably mattered most was the practice of the ritual and the ways in which the vessels contributed to its proper performance.

The ritual vessels of the Shang thus present not so much a picture of a spirit realm as a model of society, structured by rites in the form of ceremonial banquets. The vessels belonging to a particular individual mirrored his status with respect to his contemporaries. In addition, the banquet presented the relationships of the living to their ancestors, as they made offerings and showed their respect for the older members of the family. Such banquets thus confirmed the hierarchy of generations. As the banquets were prepared on a fixed cycle, these rites presumably regularly reminded the Shang kings and nobles of the most enduring relationships of their society, which bound together not just the whole living world, but the whole known universe.

Today we find it difficult to read the functions of the individual vessel types and to imagine the gestures with which they were used, or the sequences in which they came. We do not always know to whom particular vessels belonged, or the status of the owner. But all these features would have been immediately intelligible to the owners of the bronzes and to the priests of the day, in other words to the experts. In our own time, we are experts in our own religions: Christians readily recognise the communion cup and plate of their own parish churches and through them can call to mind the members of their congregation with whom they share the

Fig. 4b *Decoration of a* taotie *face from a wine vessel,* pou *(no. 43), from the tomb of Fu Hao, at Anyang, Henan province. Shang dynasty, c. 1200 BC. The features of the* taotie *vary from vessel to vessel. It does not, therefore, appear to represent a specific creature. Its associations with ritual may have helped to define ritual vessels and the categories within them. It probably contributed to the implicit ranking of vessels through references to their functions and to their owners.*

Communion Service and envisage the relationship between their priest and this congregation. All Christians are familiar with the references to the Last Supper and to the Crucifixion that these objects convey.

An analogy can be made with a set of bells of a somewhat later period, from southern China (fig. 5). These were made in graded sizes and, when struck, produced two notes, one at the centre of the bell and one at the corner. It is impossible for us to imagine, just by looking at the bells, what notes they would have produced.[8] But skilled Chinese musicians of the late fifth century BC would have known from the shape of individual bells and their position on the rack what their tones would be. In the same way the Shang would have recognised the precise function of each vessel type. In addition, the musicians of the day would have known precisely in which sequence the bells should be struck to produce the correct music, exactly as the Shang nobles and their priests would have known in which sequence to use the individual vessels in a banquet. Finally, the musicians and their audiences would have been familiar with the rituals in which the music was played, and with how the music was used to communicate with the ancestors and spirits. Thus the Shang, too, would have recognised the significances of the ritual offerings of food and the images of society that these reflected and reinforced.

Fu Hao's bronzes came from her tomb, where they were neatly arranged as though they had been used in the funeral rite and perhaps laid out for future offerings in the afterlife. The bronzes discovered at Sanxingdui in Sichuan province present us with a very different situation. They were found in two pits, astonishing for their mass of bronze, gold and jade buried beneath a layer

of elephant tusks and charred and burned animal bones (Zhao, fig. 3). These two pits were not carefully prepared burials, but rather deliberate destructions of the highly valuable paraphernalia of an unknown society.[9] Ritual vessels were few and too restricted in type (nos 27, 28) to have contributed to ritual performances such as those practised by the Shang at their religious centres at Anyang. Some of the jade sceptres were similar to those known from the Shang state, but so varied in detail that, once again, they cannot have had the same functions or meanings as their Shang counterparts (nos 33, 34). But what most astonished the archaeologists were the human-like figures that were found in the pits, in particular a complete figure on a tall square base, the centrepiece of the exhibition (no. 22; fig. 6). In addition to the figure, large numbers of heads were also found, the majority with rather similar features, but differing hairstyles (nos 23, 24). These heads have a surreal quality, with large slanting eyes framed by bold outlines, strongly curled nostrils and tight-lipped mouths.

Some of the same facial features occur on even more extraordinary finds: several enormous masks (no. 25). The largest of all is 134 cm wide (fig. 7). Its nose and mouth are similar to those on the human-like heads. In addition, the masks have enormous ears and long pupils projecting from their eyes. On the largest mask of all, the pupils are more than 10 cm in length. While the human-like figures might be kings, priests or man-like gods, it is almost impossible to imagine what these masks represent. Equally intriguing are sections of bronze trees, the largest of which is over 4 m high (fig. 8). Its curving branches carry small birds and tufts of leaves; around the foot are kneeling figures. To this fan-

Fig. 5 *Set of bells, on reconstructed stand, from a tomb of the Zeng state (no. 62), in Sui county, Hubei province. Eastern Zhou period, 5th century BC. Largest bell, height 96.3 cm.*

Fig. 6 *Side view of the head and arms of the standing figure in bronze (no. 22) from pit 2 at Sanxingdui, Sichuan province.* c. 1200–1000 BC.

Fig. 7 *Bronze mask with projecting pupils, from pit 2 at Sanxingdui, Sichuan province.* c. 1200–1000 BC. *Width 134 cm.*

tastic complex of images can be added elephants. Masses of tusks in one of the pits (Zhao, fig. 3), schematic elephant heads on the base supporting the standing figure (fig. 22.3) and perhaps also the large ears of the masks (fig. 7) indicate a preoccupation with the creatures. It has even been suggested that the principal figure (fig. 6) held an elephant tusk in his massive hands.

The peoples of Sanxingdui did not stint on valuable precious resources – bronze, jade and ivory tusks – thus indicating the great importance of the objects. But equally impressive is the picture of a fabulous world created by these striking pieces. The immense bronzes probably stood in some sort of building – a temple or palace – where they may have been seen by an audience, for whom they would have carried meanings and associations. Rather than being the props for the performance of a ceremony, as were the vessels of Fu Hao, the Sanxingdui bronzes were stage settings depicting spiritual worlds, of great import to those who participated in the drama.[10]

Few traces of this world seem to have survived. Miniature replicas of the large figure have been found in much later burials in the realm of the later Zhou peoples in Shaanxi province (fig. 22.1). It has also been suggested that much later tree-like creations found also in Sichuan province (such as no. 87) have some tenuous connection with these immense early trees. But as yet such speculations merely indicate how little is known about the peoples of Sanxingdui and their beliefs.

The Great Dynasties

Zhou unified, c. 1050–771 BC

One of the reasons why so little is known about the peoples who made the bronzes at Sanxingdui and those of other unusual contemporary cultures (among which were the peoples who made the strange faces from much further east at Xin'gan in Jiangxi province, fig. 52.4) is the overwhelming impact of the successors of the Shang, the peoples known as the Zhou. The Zhou seem to have emerged in the west, from Shaanxi province or an adjacent area, and to have overthrown the Shang in about 1050 BC. They put forward their claims to be legitimate successors to the Shang in both texts and ritual practice, and they ignored all other powers that might have coexisted with the Shang.

In their texts the Zhou created a narrative that described the Shang as the successors to a dynasty by the name of the Xia. The Zhou declared that they had overthrown the Shang righteously, just as the Shang had deposed their predecessors. It is as yet uncertain

whether the Xia actually existed among the neolithic and early bronze-using peoples who preceded the Shang (the peoples of the Erlitou culture are frequently called the Xia by today's archaeologists), or whether they were created by the Zhou to justify their own deeds.[11]

In their wish to appear the legitimate successors to the Shang, the Zhou emulated Shang methods of warfare, ritual and burial practices; for their rituals they employed vessels similar to those of the Shang, adopting and adapting Shang vessel shapes and ornament including the *taotie*. The Zhou also used Chinese, the language of the Shang. Indeed, the Zhou combined ritual and language by inscribing their bronze vessels with long texts and incorporating their political ideology into their rituals. Both the Shang and the Zhou relied upon ritual practice and ceremony, rather than images in paintings or sculpture, to proclaim their powers and view of the universe.[12]

The inscriptions in vessels frequently commemorate an honour granted to a noble by the Zhou king[13] and thereby celebrate the relationship between the owner of the bronze and the king. The inscribed vessel thus described a change in status, which may have been remembered each time the vessel was used. The food basin known as the Kang hou *gui* (fig. 9) was given by the king to one Mei Situ Yi to commemorate a military campaign. Other bronzes describe more elaborate occasions and celebrate complex relationships, thereby drawing kings and other noble families into the rituals of a family. Bronzes inherited within a family, or acquired from another, contributed to this commemoration of relationships. Thus the Zhou extended Shang use of ritual bronzes, with the result that the deeds not only of the family but also of society were projected into the afterlife.

An impression of how the Zhou foresaw the afterlife can be gained from tombs of the period, which represent an abbreviated picture of the real world. For the Zhou, as for the Shang, the pre-eminent burial goods were the ritual vessels, although they also buried some weapons and jades near the bodies of the dead (nos 56, 57). Chariots were frequently interred in adjacent pits, creating a separate section to the tomb. Clearly chariots were essential adjuncts to Zhou life (no. 53). In the tombs of both the Shang and the Zhou, the bodies of concubines and servants, guards and charioteers were also buried, so that the tomb occupant would have had not only objects but also a retinue of people to accom-

Fig. 8 *Reconstructed tree in bronze from pit 2 at Sanxingdui, Sichuan province.* c. *1200–1000* BC. *Height approx. 4 m.*

Fig. 9 *Bronze ritual vessel, known as the Kang Hou* gui, *and its inscription. Western Zhou period, 11th century* BC. *Height 21.6 cm. British Museum.*

pany him or her in the afterlife. This practice was, however, shortly to undergo considerable change, prompted perhaps by the radical political upheavals experienced by the Zhou in the eighth century BC.

Zhou divided, 770–221 BC

In the second part of the Zhou period China was not ruled as a single state, but divided into smaller entities. After a century or more of threats from their western borders, the Zhou fell victim in 771 BC to invasion by a people known as the Quan Rong and perhaps also to rebellion by other peoples under Zhou control. The Zhou territory in the west, with its capital at present-day Xi'an, was taken over by the founders of the Qin state, the eventual unifiers of the whole of China. The Zhou themselves moved eastwards to Luoyang, and central China split into diverse states, both large and small.

The history of this period is complex. During the first centuries after the fall of the Zhou capital, lords and rulers still depended on their families for support in controlling their territories and in fighting off their neighbours. Rulers of the central state continued making sacrifices to their ancestors, which reinforced family unity. In addition to sets of ritual vessels, massive sets of bells (fig. 5) became important adjuncts to the ceremonies, as music had become an integral element in communicating with the spirits. But during the latter

part of the period, both the social and religious tenor of the times changed. States became more tightly organised, with extensive bureaucracies and armies; battles might now involve many tens of thousands of men. Rulers were thus dependent not so much on the strength of ties within their family network as on a bureaucratic state. The states of Chu in the south and Qin in the west were to have a particularly strong influence. Concepts of the nature of rulership changed, and so too did attitudes to the gods and spirits. In this period, long and varied as it was, there seems to have been a gradual move, driven from several directions, towards a new understanding of the spirit world, and hence also to a new understanding of the afterlife.[14]

The tomb of the Marquis Yi, ruler of the petty state of Zeng (on the northern border of the state of Chu), a few of whose possessions are included in the catalogue (nos 63–65), illustrates some of the changes that began to take place at this date. Large ritual vessels and sets of bells, beautifully cast (Rawson, fig. 18; p. 133, fig. 2), illustrate continuity with earlier practice. These exceptional pieces consumed even more resources than earlier vessel sets, evidence that ceremonies in honour of the ancestors were still a major part of ritual and religious life.[15]

However, changes in both the structure and contents of the tomb suggest a new direction. The tomb was immense and comprised four rooms, each with a clearly defined function. A central chamber was for ceremony (p. 132, fig. 1). A retiring chamber held the coffins of the marquis (fig. 10) and eight female attendants, and a side room the coffins of a further thirteen young women. At the rear was a small armoury, and hatches between the rooms were presumably to enable the marquis to circulate. This was a veritable underground palace. The notion of living in the tomb, or at least of spending some time there, had become a much more elaborate matter.

The tomb was also equipped in much more detail than earlier ones had been. For example, the diverse types of vessel and musical instrument implied not simply the ceremonial banquet for the ancestors, but other types of ceremony, possibly both religious and secular. Further, the tomb contained boxes for the marquis's clothes as well as objects, such as incense burners, that indicate new practices and beliefs. The marquis was thus provided with the means to live a fuller and more realistically equipped life after death than had been offered to his predecessors.[16]

But the ambition to offer the marquis a complete life did not stop at the provision of all the necessary functional utensils, instruments and dress. He was also given a more complete universe than his predecessors in terms of images, especially pictures. The inner coffin (fig. 10) was painted with windows and doors, extending the concept of a dwelling or a palace, and with patterns of intertwined snakes, monsters and birds. The most telling images are those of strange monsters holding weapons, presumably to deflect malevolent demons. We know from somewhat later texts, found in the same part of southern China, that the peoples of the area attributed many forms of misfortune to the intervention of strange demons, and developed many methods of exorcising them and defending themselves against attacks.[17] These images on the coffin, and perhaps others as well, were directed to an audience of spirits.

Other images in the tomb reveal further aspects of the intellectual world of the time. A clothes box (fig. 11) carries the earliest representation of the Green Dragon of the East and the White Tiger of the West, two of the creatures that were to become the standard icons of the four directions. The other two are the Red Bird of the South and the Black Warrior of the North (a turtle entwined with a snake). Inscriptions on the box name the twenty-eight lunar mansions and the Northern Dipper (the Big Dipper or the Plough and Pole Star). A similar box in the catalogue illustrates legends connected with the archer Yi or Houyi, a figure whose activities were thought to account for the sun and moon and their cycles (no. 64).[18]

Fig. 10 *Lacquer painted inner coffin of the Marquis Yi of Zeng in Sui county, Hubei province.* C. *433* BC.

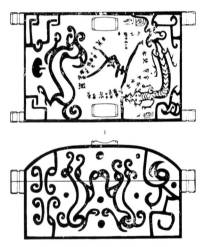

Fig. 11 *Drawing of the design on a clothes box from the tomb of the Marquis Yi of Zeng in Sui county, Hubei province.* C. *433* BC. *On one side is the Green Dragon of the East and on the other the White Tiger of the West. At the centre is the Pole Star and around it are the characters for the twenty-eight lunar mansions. After Beijing 1989c, p. 356, fig. 216.*

While the coffin and clothes boxes offer pictures that filled out and expounded contemporary views about the spirits and heavens, a sculpture in the form of a large bird with antlers (no. 63), from the same area as the tomb of the marquis, was another sort of image or picture. As yet no texts have been discovered that might cast light on its significance. It was succeeded by a large group of wooden carvings in tombs of the same area, often of monsters with antlers, and sometimes of birds and snakes (figs 63.2, 63.3, 71.1). All of these seem to have had a protective function, perhaps to deter demons that might have attacked the tomb occupants. Alternatively, it has been suggested that the bird might conceivably have been a mount for the tomb occupant on journeys to other spiritual worlds.[19] Whatever its function, like the figures on the coffin (fig. 10) or the great figure from Sanxingdui (fig. 6), the bird was part of a vision of the imagined spiritual world of the time, a vision that was to be seen by the dead and by the spirits themselves. In other areas, equally striking (though often smaller) images of mythological creatures and figures were made, as in the case of the lamp from the tomb at Zhongshan (no. 74), where the figure of a man is shown holding snakes wound around dishes, which would have supported lamps. Indeed, in the later part of the Zhou, lamps were a favoured utensil for the display of images that have recently been recognised as having had mythological or cosmological import.[20]

The élite of the Qin state employed another form of depiction for use in the afterlife. Here tombs were often supplied with pottery replicas, sometimes of bronze ritual vessels. This was by no means a new development. From the Shang dynasty, the lower echelons of society had ceramic copies of the bronze vessels of the élite. However, the Qin state potters seem to have developed these copies to a high art, incorporating elaborate appendages and painting, to give a thoroughly realistic appearance. Of special importance among Qin replicas are the models of granaries, made for burial. By including replicas of structures in the tomb, the Qin were creating an image, or in effect a picture, of something that would otherwise have been impossible to take to the afterlife.[21] As with the tomb of the Marquis Yi of Zeng, the landscape of the tomb and the world of the tomb occupant were thus symbolically enlarged.

Models were by no means confined to the Qin. In some areas, wooden models of servants were buried in the same tomb as the bodies of real men. This change, from the sacrifice of living people to the use of wooden, stone and pottery models, is sometimes attributed to the exhortations of philosophers. The move is more likely, however, to have been part of a much more wideranging change from the deployment of real objects and people to the use of depictions.[22] While early tombs were limited extensions of the real world, much fuller representations of the universe became the norm during the latter part of the Zhou. Indeed, there seem to have been two rather different reasons for elaborating these pictures, both of which continued to be relevant: first, a wish to include within tombs items such as granaries that were actually too large to fit inside; and second, a

need to address an audience of spirits reaching beyond the spirits of the dead.

Unified China: the empires of the Qin (221–206 BC) and the Han (206 BC–AD 220)

During the centuries of divided rule, many rulers had sought to claim supremacy and recreate the Zhou empire under one ruler. King Zheng of Qin, who took the name of First Emperor, achieved this ambition. While his fame rests primarily upon his political success, the energy that the First Emperor devoted to his tomb, and the extraordinary finds brought to light in the last two decades, demonstrate the overwhelming importance of the religious beliefs of his time to the most powerful ruler of his day. The armies of terracotta warriors (fig. 78), the bronze chariots, and the maps of the world – said to have been laid out within the tomb – were not simply the toys of overweening vanity, but were vital parts of the Emperor's existence in the afterlife.

The Han, successors of the Qin, and especially the great Emperor Wu, or Wudi (141–87 BC), were equally preoccupied with the afterlife and indeed with the pervasive spirit world. While the tomb of Emperor Wu has not been excavated, the burials of the contemporary imperial prince Liu Sheng and his consort Dou Wan convey to us some of the beliefs of his day (no. 81). In addition, the great Han dynasty historian, Sima Qian, writing during the reign of Wudi, is an invaluable source of information on the beliefs of both the Qin and early Han periods.[23]

Three tombs serve to illustrate the different types of representation within the tomb and a variety of interpretations of the afterlife. These are the tombs of the First Emperor (c. 210 BC), of Liu Sheng (c. 113 BC), and of Lady Dai (c. 168 BC) at Mawangdui near Changsha.[24] The major transformation from tombs equipped with functional objects, such as those found at the time of Fu Hao, to tombs containing pottery models (nos 108–116), which are pictures or images, is reflected in this catalogue.

The desire to create a universe within a tomb, realised by the First Emperor with his terracotta warriors (no. 78), had its origins in diverse forms of representation employed from at least the sixth century BC, in the later part of the Zhou. In addition, varied beliefs in gods, spirits and demons evolved in the different states to form the basis of the views held in the Qin and Han periods. Excavations and research have only recently revealed evidence for some of these beliefs.

Hitherto, writers have tended to concentrate on the

classical philosophies of Confucius, Laozi and the Legalists and their followers in their study of late Zhou, Qin and Han intellectual history. This tendency has been encouraged by the later Han choice of Confucianism as the ruling orthodoxy. But such orthodox canonical texts obscure the multitude of beliefs that inspired and fed the imaginations of the majority of people, including the emperors themselves.[25]

Documents discovered in tombs, and the objects found with them, have brought these quite different preoccupations to light in recent years. A pioneer in their elucidation has been Anna Seidel.[26] These beliefs belong to several rather distinct categories, all of which had some influence. Primary was the view that the other world was ruled by a Celestial Deity, often known as Huangdi, the Yellow Emperor or the Yellow Thearch. The Celestial Deity kept the registers of the living and the dead and possessed a powerful messenger. Another group of notions concerned an underworld bureaucracy which controlled the fate of all who died. Information from the registers was transmitted to the bureaucracy. As a counterbalance to this not exactly friendly underworld, there developed the concept of deathlessness or the avoidance of death and its penalties. Immortals lived in distant magical lands where they kept secret drugs that might confer deathlessness on human beings.[27] Yet another strand comprised abstract concepts about the nature of the world: the forces of *yin* and *yang*, the Five Elements (Earth, Wood, Metal, Fire and Water) and what is known as correlative thinking, by which all material and phenomena were classified in accordance with these Five Elements. These latter notions had been developed by some of the experts who presented themselves, like the other philosophers, as advisers to the courts of the petty states. With these ideas came the notion of *qi*, translated as breath or vapour, seen literally as the vital force of the cosmos, whose energies had to be captured and retained. Artefacts of the Han often depict swirling cloud-like forms that may be representations of *qi* (fig. 13a).[28]

Conquest by the Qin of the diverse states brought their beliefs and practices within its purview, resulting in some measure of synthesis. The First Emperor, and in his turn the Han emperor Wu, were both concerned to mobilise the forces of the great gods and spirits in their own support. Thus the Qin emperor made journeys to the cardinal directions and ascended the most revered mountains of his realm.[29] The Han seem to have formalised the notion of five sacred mountains, matched with five celestial deities who dwelt in the constellations.[30] The central deity was the Yellow Emperor, who had been a supreme deity with martial powers in

Fig. 12 *The summit of Mount Tai, Shandong province. Photograph Helen Espir.*

the Qin state and who could confer immortality. The Qin emperor made an expedition to Mount Tai (fig. 12), which later became the principal peak and the point of contact with the Highest Deity. Mount Tai had been the most potent mountain for the peoples of the Qi state in the east, and it came to absorb the mystical mountains of the immortals, originally thought to lie in the eastern seas. Famous sacrifices were also performed at Mount Tai by Emperor Wu.[31]

As the Yellow Emperor was deemed to rule not only the celestial realms but also those of the underworld, in due course the entry to these lower realms was thought to be near Mount Tai. Although the principal classical texts do not mention the underworld bureaucracy, its presence seems to have been universally felt; documents buried in tombs were addressed to its officials and give clear evidence of its existence in the minds of the people of the time. It would seem that, just as notions of the role of the ancestors had existed in parallel with the aristocratic military society of the Shang and Zhou, deriving from and in turn reinforcing that society, so views about the bureaucratic nature of the underworld followed upon development of large state bureaucracies.[32] Bamboo manuscripts dating to 297 BC, found in a tomb at Fangmatan in Gansu province, tell of the experiences of a man named Dan who, having killed himself, entered the underworld but was released by the authorities and returned to life. The phrases used in this account and its references to documents indicate that the peoples of the time believed that an underworld bureaucracy operated with the same officials, documents and procedures as those of the real world. Thus

Dan's release was effected by a bureaucratic document of a type familiar to the people of his own time.[33]

Further evidence of an underworld bureaucracy is found in many tombs. The catalogue includes, for example, some inscribed bamboo strips from an inventory of funeral goods in the tomb of Sui Xiaoyuan (no. 95). The contents of his tomb are shown at nos 92–94. Such inventories were addressed to the bureaucracies of the underworld to give them evidence of the identification and status of the tomb owner. Indeed, all documents buried in tombs should be understood as being presented to underworld officials. Thus, well before the Qin and Han periods, the architectural plan of structures to be built over a tomb (see p. 156), buried in one of the Zhongshan tombs of the fourth century BC, was probably intended for such officials. Documents found in later tombs include land contracts with the underworld, attesting to the deceased's ownership of the land on which the tomb was built; documents, provided as passports by the highest celestial deity, to ward off evil and introduce the tomb owner to the underworld administration; and talismans, often to control demons.[34] As so many of the documents in tombs were explicitly addressed to spirits and to the officials of the underworld, we can imagine that they too formed an audience to whom the entire contents of the tombs were addressed. If the dead had to account to the underworld officials through documents, such as inventories,

the actual possessions were equally valuable evidence of their status. Completeness was, perhaps, therefore highly desired.

Pictures of the world and the cosmos through possessions, either real or in replica, had existed for some time and can be seen at their most extreme in the underground palace of the Marquis Yi of Zeng (nos 63–65) and in the ceramic replicas of Qin state tombs. A convergence of these two latter trends – the burial of the real and the replica – seems to have produced the tomb of the First Emperor himself, accompanied by his terracotta army (no. 78). The tomb was designed as a complete representation of the world, addressed to the spirits. In the tomb proper were reproduced the rivers of the country, together with palaces, pavilions and offices for ritual, leisure and administration. Around the tomb were grouped essential aspects of the Emperor's power, including his stables, his army, his concubines and his zoo. Different objects – some real, some in replica – were employed as appropriate to the type of subject depicted. Thus real horses were buried in the stable, but ceramic was used for the soldiers. To bury ten thousand men would have been impracticable, but a complete replica, it would seem, was necessary if a complete army was to be available to the Emperor in the afterlife.[35]

The Han may thus have been under pressure from their beliefs in an afterlife (complete with an underworld bureaucracy) to provide for the spirits and the dead ever fuller descriptions of their worlds, both in documents and in replicas of their possessions. Other demands are also evident in the changes in tomb structure and content. The tomb of Lady Dai at Mawangdui, near Changsha, within the former territory of the Chu state, perpetuated and extended the tradition exemplified by the tomb of the Marquis Yi of Zeng. Her tomb, like that of the marquis, was constructed of several wooden compartments, but perhaps because her status was lower, they were neither as spacious nor as sumptuously equipped as his had been. In place of real female attendants, Lady Dai was accompanied by a retinue of servants carved in wood. Although the compartments of her wooden tomb were rather compressed, they represent rooms symbolically and were equipped appropriately.

While the household of the lady was somewhat abbreviated, more attention was given to representing a universe of spirits and the position of the woman in the afterlife.[36] These are shown on a famous painted banner and in the paintings on the lady's coffins. Two of her three coffins, the middle and the inner one, are particularly beautifully painted (fig. 13). One is black, with whirling, cloud-like patterns on it (fig. 13a) which

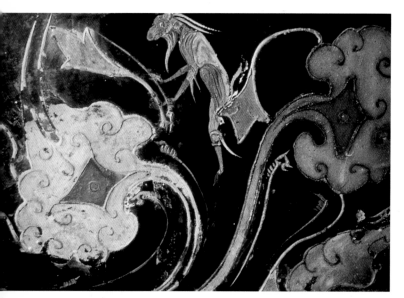

Fig. 13a *Detail of the middle coffin of Lady Dai from tomb MI at Mawangdui, near Changsha, Hunan province. Western Han dynasty, c. 168 BC. The coffin shows the swirling clouds of qi vapour, among which are strange protective spirits, some devouring snakes, a sign of evil. Author's photograph.*

represent the *qi* vapours of the cosmos. Among the vapours are tiny figures of spirits and miraculous creatures which ward off and devour evil, often depicted in the form of snakes. In this case the coffin is the visual equivalent of documents that were buried in tombs, describing methods of demolishing demons. This coffin imagery can also be interpreted as a more comprehensive form of the protection afforded to the Marquis Yi of Zeng by the paintings of birds and snakes and of figures with weapons on his coffin (fig. 10).[37]

The inner coffin of Lady Dai presents a much brighter magical world (fig. 13b). At the centre of one side and at one end stand mountains, surrounded by long curling dragons and deer. At the other end of the coffin, dragons weave through a *bi* disc of jade. These creatures are denizens of the upper celestial worlds and were sometimes depicted as jade pendants, the precious and immortal stone contributing to an image of a powerful creature. The mountains, in particular, suggest the mountains of the immortals.[38]

A famous painted banner was also included in the tomb (Yu, fig. 3). The import of this painting has been

Fig. 13b *Drawings of three sides of the inner coffin of Lady Dai from tomb M1 at Mawangdui, near Changsha, Hunan province. Western Han dynasty, c. 168 BC. The mountains are those of the immortals and miraculous animals. The dragons and the jade disc tied with a silk ribbon are auspicious. After Beijing 1973b, vol. 1, figs 23, 24, 25.*

disputed, but it appears to depict the universe. At the bottom is the underworld and above that a picture of the lady in her shroud. She then appears again at the centre of the painting, accompanied by attendants. Here she stands above another jade *bi* disc and, as on her coffin, two dragons (whose appearance is again jade-like) weave through it. Presumably the woman was protected in the afterlife by the discs and the dragons, both as a body in a coffin and as an image in the painting. At the top of the banner are the heavens, with dragons swirling below the sun and the moon. Debate has revolved around whether this is a picture of sequential incidents, showing the lady's route to heaven, or whether the painting should be viewed as a single consistent whole, each part contributing to a complete picture of the lady in the afterlife. In the more likely second case, the painting suggests an afterlife viewed as similar to her daily existence, for the woman is shown not at the top in the heavenly world of the immortals but at the centre, accompanied by her attendants. It would appear that Lady Dai was to remain in her tomb surrounded by her symbolical household, which would perhaps be brought to life by spiritual powers.[39]

If in the Qin and early Han period people did not expect to ascend to the heavenly world of the immortals after death, then an alternative explanation has to be sought for this world. Perhaps the peoples of the Qin and Han, and indeed those of earlier times, developed notions of immortals and the worlds they inhabited as remedies for their anxieties about demons and the power of an underworld bureaucracy. The immortals and their skills may have been sources of help rather than providers of future paradises for the deceased. Two main regions were revered: the islands of Penglai in the eastern sea and the western mountainous regions of Kunlun, where dwelt the Queen Mother of the West (Xi Wang Mu).[40] In vain the Qin emperor had sent men and youths in search of the immortals thought to inhabit islands far out in the eastern sea.[41] During the Han some of the aura of the mountains of the immortals at Penglai accrued to Mount Tai in eastern China (fig. 12). Interest in western areas also grew in the Han period, and envoys were sent there as well.[42] The accounts by Sima Qian suggest that people in Han times viewed these mysterious realms as repositories of potions and recipes that might assist them in their travails, rather than as places in which they could aspire to live.

Philosophical texts of the fourth century BC mention the Queen Mother of the West, and her cult developed during the Qin and Han periods. The catalogue includes a number of objects that depict her and her consort, the Lord of the East (nos 87, 88, 101). Beliefs that the

Fig. 14 *Bronze weight in the form of a mysterious mountain, surrounded by dragon-like creatures. Han dynasty, 2nd-1st century BC. Height 5.5 cm. British Museum.*

immortals of Penglai and the Queen Mother inhabited mountains gave rise to a more generalised notion of sacred mountains, inhabited by miraculous animals and immortals cultivating plants from which to brew their elixirs (no. 86).[43]

Images of dragons and other creatures and mountains, seen on the coffin of Lady Dai, or in much smaller format, such as bronze weights, are evidence of this interest (fig. 14). Incense burners in the shapes of mountains were a particular manifestation (no. 82).[44] Very fine incense burners have come from the tombs of Liu Sheng and his consort Dou Wan. Their peaks are the peaks of the immortal worlds, and the incense rising from them presumably resembled the *qi*, the vital force of the cosmos. These incense burners appear analogous to religious icons in the West, being, it would seem, objects on which their owners might focus their attention, to imagine and realise those spiritual worlds. Mirrors, too, seem to have had a similar function, as they also carry images associated with the cosmos and immortal worlds, including the animals of the four directions and the Queen Mother of the West (no. 88). They may also have been protective, to ward off demons and evil spirits.[45]

Both the Qin emperor and Wudi, the powerful Han ruler, are renowned for their search for recipes for eternal life and for their interest in mountains, and the deities associated with them, to reinforce their authority. Sacrifices were offered at Mount Tai (fig. 12), in particular, in the hope that the highest celestial deity, the sacred mountains and the forces of the cosmos would act favourably towards the state. The writings of Sima Qian also testify to the preoccupation with omens and portents, including the appearance of miraculous creatures, especially in connection with the good governance of the state.[46]

While texts that mention omens and offerings and images that depict the lands of the immortals might suggest to us that the ancient Chinese aspired to reach these immortal worlds, in so thinking we may be applying Western notions of heaven inappropriately. The avoidance of death was probably of greater importance than the expectation that the dead would be able to attain the spiritual worlds. In the quest for deathlessness, the metaphor of jade is a key element. The first recorded descriptions of immortals, which appear in about the fourth century BC, describe them as white and pure, and from this description we can imagine jade: 'His flesh and skin were like ice and snow. His manner was elegant and graceful as that of a maiden. He did not eat the five grains, but inhaled the wind and drank the dew. He rode on clouds, drove among the flying dragons, and thus rambled beyond the five seas.'[47]

In the poem 'The Distant Journey' in *The Elegies of Chu (Chu ci)*, a Han dynasty poet describes how he rides like an immortal through the heavens:

My jade-like countenance flushed with radiant colour;
Purified my vital essence started to grow stronger;
My corporeal parts dissolved to a soft suppleness;
And my spirit grew lissom and eager for movement.[48]

The miraculous animals of the universe are sometimes described as being white, like jade, and so too are the maidens who assist mankind and wait on the Yellow Emperor or the Queen Mother of the West. The poet Sima Xiangru (179–117 BC) describes a fantastic journey to the gates of heaven, where the travellers enter the palace of the Celestial Emperor and invite the jade maidens to return in their chariots.[49]

It is to this context that the Han use of jade belongs. Pictures of jade maidens occur as amulets, and wonderful creatures such as winged horses ridden by immortals were carved from this white, translucent stone (fig. 15). Indeed, from at least the fifth century, long sinuous dragons had been carved in jade as pendants. Their shapes, and presumably their functions and associations, were similar to those of the dragons on the coffin of Lady Dai (fig. 13b).[50] If jade was the substance of immortals and immortal creatures, jade suits worn by princes were chosen to ensure that their bodies too became as jade-like as those of the immortals (no. 81). Jade coverings of the body had by that date had a long

Fig. 15 *Jade carving of a winged horse mounted by a feathered immortal. From the area of the tomb of Yuandi (r. 48–33 BC). Height 7 cm. This is one of a group of five fine carvings of creatures, of which two are imaginary beasts with wings. After Hebei 1992–3, vol. 4, no. 147.*

history (fig. 57.1; no. 72). The early examples were probably sewn on to textiles. Only in the Han period were complete suits with tightly fitting plaques developed.[51] There has been considerable discussion as to the purpose of the jade suits (no. 81). In that debate Chinese notions of the soul have been expounded, namely the view that everyone has two souls, a spiritual soul (*hun*) and an earthly soul (*po*). But, as Anna Seidel has shown, it is by no means evident that the view was so clear cut. Nor is it certain that the spiritual soul was destined for the heavens and that the earthly one was to remain in the tomb.[52] The dwelling of the dead seems to have been the tomb, with offerings to both souls made there. But perhaps the dead as much as the living could gain the help of the immortals through contemplating hill censers and wearing jade. They might thus avoid the perils of the demons and the prisons of the underworld officials. Moreover the transfer of the essence of jade to their bodies would perhaps ensure that they would, in the afterlife, become jade-like, even if in life all other means to achieve deathlessness had failed. The elaborate tomb fashioned for Liu Sheng and Dou Wan indicates that they expected to continue to live there in their jade-transformed state.

These tombs constructed in the mountainside employed the eternal qualities of the stone, as well as of the jade of the suits, to ensure the eternal existence of their occupants. Such interest in the permanence of stone had many manifestations in the Han period. The last piece in the catalogue, a mysterious animal with wings (no. 118), exemplifies another important use of stone, that is for carvings of the creatures of the universe to adorn roads to tombs. Just as jade was used for the winged horse ridden by a feathered immortal (fig. 15), stone was chosen for the larger creatures to suggest their eternal presence through the physical permanence of the material.[53]

Despite all precautionary measures, the underworld officials probably remained a constant threat throughout the Han. Perhaps for this reason, as the ideas described coalesced into the beliefs we call religious Daoism, the possibility of attaining other, higher worlds seems to have grown more attractive in the later Han.[54] But for much of the Han, the concept of the tomb as the home of the dead remained dominant. Thus tombs were increasingly constructed to offer complete representations of the everyday world of the tomb owner and of the miraculous worlds of the immortals. Essential to our understanding of the way in which later Han period tombs were composed and equipped is the development

of two separate beliefs: belief in the underworld and its officials, and in the higher realms of the Celestial Deity and the immortals.

The underworld required proof of status through inventories and even material possessions for which they were the audiences. Ceramic replicas of buildings and vessels thus became very common (fig. 16; nos 106–116), and seem to have been deemed more appropriate, or, perhaps more helpful, than the real items. Many of these assume absolutely standard forms, as though they were prepared and issued by a government office. Models frequently replicate the buildings, equipment and animals typical of the great estates in Henan province, on which many of the Han officials depended for their wealth and influence. If such people, when deceased, were to present their credentials to the underworld, such replicas would have provided easily recognisable evidence of their standing.[55] Further, later texts suggest that pottery burial items could be brought to life through the intervention of spirits and ghosts.[56]

Fig. 16 *Drawings of pottery models from tombs M1037 and M23 at Liujiaqu in Shan county, Henan province. Eastern Han dynasty, 1st–2nd century* AD. *After Kaogu xuebao 1965.1, pp. 107–68, figs 19:2; 20:8; 23:2; 26.*

Thus the fuller the representation of the world, the more easily perhaps the bureaucrats would be placated and the more satisfactory life would be.

At the same time scenes depicted on the walls of tombs illustrated in great detail not only the everyday lives of the tomb owners, but also the spirits of the higher realms (nos 100–105). Images of the guardians of the four directions, of the Queen Mother of the West, and of other spirits seem to have been intended to represent their support of the tomb occupant.[56] Just as in this life help might be sought from the Queen Mother, so in the afterlife the tomb owners would dwell in their tombs enjoying a life similar to their earthly existence, and assisted by the Queen Mother and other spirits.[57]

The objects in the catalogue provide for us, as they were intended to also for their owners, a picture of an ideal universe. That universe embraced both the real world and the other worlds of the ancestors and spirits. But over time these concepts changed and, therefore, so too did the ways in which these worlds were presented.

The catalogue begins with real objects used in daily life, and especially in ceremonies, and it ends with replicas and models, and even pictures to embellish walls. In practice, both categories of object, the functional and the representational, help us to build up complex images of the lives of their owners. These objects are the props and stage settings of the dramas enacted from day to day by their owners, and the dramas aspired to in the afterlife.[58] However, the changes both in the types and styles of the objects and images are measures of the transformation of Chinese culture in the several thousand years illustrated here. Both daily life and the intellectual and religious frameworks underwent major shifts. Although the images are perhaps easier for us to comprehend than the functional objects, we should not forget that at all periods discussed here, the Chinese valued religious practice and ritual as highly, or more highly, than religious imagery. Thus the wine vessels (fig. 4a) and the lacquer cups (no. 92) were as valued in their own day as the images of the bronze trees (fig. 8) or the antlered crane (no. 63). Moreover, for all periods described we should envisage a universe that was alive, not static. The terracotta army was not to remain frozen as clay, but to march and defend the First Emperor in the afterlife. Utensils and representations both had essential functions. Although much remains to be understood, the exhibition and the catalogue bring us closer than ever before to an understanding of the Mysteries of Ancient China.

1 The jade suits of Prince Liu Sheng from Mancheng, Hebei province (no. 81), and of the King of Nan Yue, buried near Guangzhou, both dating from the second century BC, are evidence of the unified culture of the day (Lam 1991, pls 5–7).

2 For a discussion of the use of special qualities in objects see Dissanayake 1988, chapter 4.

3 For a discussion of the subdivision of labour and resulting mass-production see Ledderose 1992; Bagley 1993b; Keyser 1979.

4 For burials of the Hongshan culture see *Wenwu* 1994.5, pp. 37–52; *Wenwu* 1984.6, pp. 1–5; *Wenwu* 1984.11, pp. 1–11, 12–21; *Wenwu* 1986.8, pp. 1–24.

5 Interest in light as a metaphor for the good is more fully developed in the West than in China and may perhaps have something to do with the Western interest in the reflective qualities of gold. For discussion of the ways in which metaphors create ideas see Johnson 1981; Lakoff and Johnson 1980. With relevance to works of art see Hausman 1989.

6 For a discussion of bronze technology see the essay by Rawson in this catalogue; also Bagley 1987, pp. 37–64; Barnard 1990.

7 For some of the possible interpretations of the *taotie* see the essays in Whitfield 1993 and Kesner 1991. Many of the papers react to Chang Kwang-chih 1983. Most authors take insufficient note of the role of practice, such as the actual movements of the vessels, in the establishment of the references and associations of a rite and hence of the objects and peoples involved in it.

8 For the role of bells in Bronze Age society and their musical features see Falkenhausen 1993.

9 For the finds at Sanxingdui see Bagley 1988 and 1990.

10 A wide variety of interpretations of the find have been made. For some of them see essays in this catalogue and also Sichuan 1989 and 1992.

11 As Bagley points out (1992), much effort has been expended by Chinese archaeologists in work on Erlitou sites with a view to establishing the history of the Xia dynasty. As yet, insufficient attention has been given to the assumptions on which this endeavour is based. For the ways in which perspectives on ancient China have been affected by the Zhou view of their own roles see Rawson 1989b; Bagley 1992.

12 The absence of political sculpture is noted by Trigger 1978, p. 165. I am indebted to Robert Bagley for pointing out this observation.

13 For an account of Zhou bronze inscriptions and their import see Shaughnessy 1991.

14 For an account of ritual vessels of the Eastern Zhou see So 1995; Falkenhausen 1993 gives the authoritative account of Eastern Zhou bells. For changes in military and political structure see Lewis 1990.

15 The report on the tomb is Beijing 1989c.

16 Discussion of the tomb and aspects of Chu culture are found in Thote 1991, 1993, 1995; Mackenzie 1991; Rawson 1989a.

17 The demonography found in Qin tombs at Shuihudi, Jiangling, Hubei province, is discussed by Harper 1985.

18 The lunar mansions are the constellations where the moon lodges during a sidereal month and they define a celestial equator. The chest with the animals of the directions is discussed in *Wenwu* 1979.7, pp. 40–5; Harper forthcoming. The tale of the archer Yi is considered in entry no. 64 and Allan 1991, chapter 2. See also Birrell 1993, pp. 138–45. For a neolithic site with a dragon and tiger recovered in shells, often considered the precursor of the animals of the directions, see *Wenwu* 1988.3, pp. 1–6, pl. 3.

19 For wooden figures with antlers, see references in entry no. 63; Goepper 1995, no. 62, records the view that the bird may have been a mount.

20 For illustration of lamps from Chu see *Wenwu* 1966.5, pp. 33–55; *Wenwu* 1988.5, pp. 1–14. For lamps from Zhongshan see *Wenwu* 1979.1, pp. 1–31.

21 For an account of pottery replicas in Qin tombs see Ledderose and Schlombs 1990, pp. 164–77.

22 A combination of real people and tomb figures is seen at Changzi in Shanxi province (*Kaogu xuebao* 1984.4, pp. 503–30). See also Paludan 1994.

23 The biography of the Qin emperor is translated in Yang Hsien-yi and Gladys Yang 1979, pp. 159–204. For information on the beliefs of the

time of Emperor Wu, see the translation of the chapter on the Feng and Shan sacrifices from the *Shi ji* (Watson 1961, vol. 2, pp. 13–67).

24 For the report on the excavation at Mawangdui see Beijing 1973b.

25 For the development of different philosophies in the Han see *The Cambridge History of China Volume 1, The Ch'in and Han Empires, 221 BC–AD 220*, chapters 12, 14, 15, 16. See also Lewis 1990; Loewe 1974; consider also Major 1993 for the views set out in the *Huainanzi*.

26 See especially Seidel 1987; also Seidel 1982; Lewis 1990; Jan 1977; Loewe 1977. Harper forthcoming is an important synthesis.

27 For descriptions of immortals see Erickson 1992 and 1994b.

28 For correlative thinking see Bodde 1991, pp. 97–133; Bodde 1975, pp. 37–41; and especially Graham 1989.

29 The journeys of the Qin emperor are recorded in the *Shi ji* (Yang Hsien-yi and Gladys Yang 1979, pp. 159–96).

30 See the chapter on the Feng and Shan sacrifices by Sima Qian (Watson 1961, vol. 2, pp. 13–67).

31 For notions of the Yellow Thearch and Mount Tai see Seidel 1987, p. 707; Lewis 1990, pp. 165–7, 199–205, discusses the martial qualities of the Yellow Emperor under the Qin.

32 The notion of the underworld bureaucracy is absent from much discussion of the Han period views of the afterlife. This has been rectified by Anna Seidel 1987. See also Lewis 1990; Harper 1994.

33 Harper 1994 gives a full account and references to further discussions.

34 For documents buried in tombs see Seidel 1987; more elaborate texts are described by Jan 1977 and Loewe 1977.

35 For the tomb of the First Emperor see Ledderose and Schlombs 1990 and references given there; see also Ledderose 1992 and Kesner 1995.

36 For the tomb of Lady Dai at Mawangdui see Beijing 1973b; Wu Hung 1992.

37 Protection of the dead could be achieved by imagery of spirits, and by talismans and texts of incantations (Harper 1985; Bodde 1975, chapter 4). Texts discovered in tombs illustrate preoccupation also with medicine and divination, and early aspects of Daoism. Further, military texts and maps perhaps suggest that after death their owners might continue to hold official positions in the underworld.

38 Interpretation of the inner coffin is given by Wu Hung 1992.

39 For contrasting views see Loewe 1979, who favours the interpretation of the soul ascending to paradise, and Seidel 1982, who discusses the difficulties of supporting the view that after death people expected a future life in a paradise. Wu Hung 1992 carries Seidel's line of argument further, arguing that Lady Dai was expected to inhabit a universe within her tomb.

40 For the role of the Queen Mother of the West see Loewe 1979, chapter 4; Seidel 1982, pp. 99–106; Erickson 1994b; Cahill 1993.

41 Yang Hsien-yi and Gladys Yang 1979, p. 173.

42 Watson 1961, vol. 2, pp. 264–89.

43 Wu Hung 1984.

44 For a discussion of incense burners of the Boshan *lu* type see Erickson 1992.

45 Because they are inscribed, mirrors have been widely discussed. The discussion most relevant here is Cahill 1986; see also Karlgren 1934; Loewe 1979.

46 Wu Hung 1984; Watson 1961, vol. 2, pp. 13–67.

47 Quoted from Erickson 1994b, p. 21, based on a translation by Fung Yulan.

48 Hawkes 1985, p. 196.

49 Erickson 1994a discusses jade maidens. For the poem by Sima Xiangru see Watson 1961, vol. 2, p. 334.

50 Finds of jade animal carvings are very rare. They appear to make use of the stone to signify the miraculous character of the creatures (Rawson 1995, pp. 351–4).

51 Jade suits are derived from coverings in jade that go back at least to the ritual revolution in the Western Zhou (Rawson 1995, pp. 44–53; see also nos 14, 72).

52 Seidel 1982, pp. 106–8.

53 For a discussion of the qualities of stone see Paludan 1991, pp. 29–31.

54 Seidel 1982 discusses Han notions as the prelude to the development of religious Daoism.

55 The role of ceramic replicas has been too little discussed. If the dead were to be examined in the underworld, they were in effect to be in exile, and their goods and possessions too would be required by this underworld, or so it would seem from the inventories. The usefulness of replicas to the underworld bureaucracy has yet to be investigated. For an account of Han tombs and their contents see Pu Muzhou 1993; Los Angeles 1987.

56 For accounts of the ways in which burial replicas were brought to life in stories of the Tang period see Dudbridge 1995, appendix.

57 Wu Hung 1994 describes the imagery in a tomb in Shandong. Although he records a poem inscribed in the tomb, which, together with the representations, illustrates encounters with officials, he does not consider, it would seem, the possibility that these might be officials of the underworld.

58 Goffman 1990 discusses the notion of roles and dramas to describe human behaviour and activity.

59 Walton 1993 considers the use of representations to convey and elaborate ideas.

PART I

UNKNOWN CHINA

The neolithic period

In the neolithic period, from before 6000 BC, farming was practised across much of the landmass we now know as China. The early, complex societies of China were sustained by highly fertile soil. Neither the names nor any detailed histories of these farming people are known to us, because there survive only fragments of any writing system they may have had. This is 'Unknown China' – unknown because, without a writing system, these peoples have left no names or other references to help us reconstruct their lives. Legends recorded later are many and are sometimes invoked to explain the distant, unrecorded past. But it is unlikely that such myths and stories give any sort of reliable information about the neolithic period. What they do indicate, however, is how later Chinese viewed their unrecorded past.

Until the excavations of recent years little was known about the neolithic period in China. These excavations have unearthed remains – villages and small cities, with houses, walls and workshops, ceramics, tools and ornaments in bone and jade – which enable us to distinguish the many different neolithic peoples. Even though we cannot know their names, nor have much inkling of their ideas or beliefs, we can learn a lot about them from the material they have left behind. Moreover, there is some advantage in being without texts, as texts can so often bias our understanding of the past. Texts can only tell us what their writers wanted their audience to know. Our entry into unknown China may, therefore, bear certain restrictions, but we also have a certain freedom that is not available with later periods.

We are not, for example, bound by later judgements as to where the heart of ancient China lay and which of the many peoples or cultures whose remains are now known contributed most to the formation of the dynastic power described in the next section. What is now clear is that all parts of northern and central China supported advanced societies by about 5000 BC.

The principal northern and central neolithic cultures are generally grouped into two main complexes: those of the Yellow River basin and westwards along the Wei River into Gansu province; and those of the east coast. There were also groups of peoples in southern China, but they will not be further considered here.

Evidence of early cultivation and settled farming life, now known as the Peiligang and Cishan cultures, has come to light in Henan province, either side of the Yellow River. This area of China is generally seen as divided into several major regions during the neolithic period, all of which were inhabited by peoples who produced exceptional ceramics. Many of these ceramics may have been used for ceremonial and ritual purposes.

Further west, along the Wei River, ceramics decorated with painted designs are used to define one large area of activity known as the Yangshao culture (c. 5000–3000 BC) (nos 1, 2). Later cultures in Gansu province, to the west, are known as Majiayao, Banshan, Machang, Qijia and Xindian. In the area of the Wei River, the Yangshao was followed by the Miaodigou and then by cultures that made local versions of unpainted pottery borrowed from further east. Indeed, in this part of China a division is evident between the early period, in which the most striking artefacts were painted pottery, and the later period, in which east-coast vessel types with lobed forms predominated. We do not know whether these ceramics came to the area of the Wei River because people moved there from the east, or through warfare and trade.

Recent research has revealed astonishingly complex societies further north in eastern China. In the northeast, in Liaoning province, developed the Hongshan culture (c. 3500–2500 BC) (Lei, figs 1, 2). The ceremonial centres of this culture are represented here by a small figurine (no. 10). Further south, in the provinces of Shandong and Jiangsu, were peoples now known collectively by the name of Dawenkou (c. 4500–3000 BC), whose remains include very fine and elaborate pottery and some jades. They were succeeded by the Longshan culture (c. 2500–1700 BC). The ceramics of these peoples, as mentioned, seem to have exerted some influence further west. Another area that has presented considerable surprises in recent years is that around Shanghai. The existence of a remarkable rice-growing culture has been discovered south of Hangzhou Bay, at Hemudu (c. 5000–4500 BC), where evidence of rice and remains of wooden piled buildings have been found. To the north of Hangzhou Bay was a sequence of cultures matching those of the Dawenkou and Longshan. These peoples, the Majiabang (c. 5000–4000 BC), the Songze (c. 4000–3000 BC) and the Liangzhu (c. 3000–2000 BC), were equally active and produced not only highly specialised ceramics but also some of the most astounding jades known (nos 16–21).

Contemporary with these sophisticated societies of the east coast, related groups of people lived along the middle reaches of the Yangzi River and created what are described as the Daxi (c. 5000–3000 BC) and Qujialing (c. 4000–3000 BC) cultures. Tall stands for offering vessels, which, on the east coast, were made in elaborate pierced shapes, were in this region painted. A feature of this area is the combination of some of the elaborate vessel shapes of the east with the painting that was more highly developed in the west.

All of the archaeological evidence available to tell us about neolithic China is material, whether artefacts created by the peoples, traces of crops or the remains of domesticated and wild animals. From such evidence we must infer their ways of life and grope towards an understanding of their beliefs and social practices.

Although it is possible to argue that these many different peoples all created highly developed and diverse societies, in the absence of writing it is difficult to be more specific. Strong social organisations seem to have allowed various building styles and stimulated a division of labour which, in turn, would have permitted the development of specialised craft industries. Without such division of labour, neither the jades nor the fine pottery could have been made. In addition, these exceptional élite goods were made for specialised functions: there are jars made for the burial of children, ceramic objects that were probably drums, and jades whose uses are not known but which were certainly not used in daily life.

In the absence of written evidence, when we ponder why such fine items were made and used within a complex society, we are in fact forcing ourselves to understand how societies develop and elaborate themselves. Were we to have a written text explaining the religion within which the fine jades (nos 16–21) were employed, we might assume that they were made for use in cere-

monies. We would not be inclined to think further. But, deprived of such evidence, we must be more rigorous and start from first principles.

Thus the first point to be made about the fine ceramics and jades is one that we have already noted: they must have been made by craftsmen with a considerable degree of specialisation. But if such specialisation were to be supported by a society's resources in terms of food and protection, its results would probably have been highly valued by the society. These neolithic societies (as with many in other parts of the world) would therefore probably have deployed their exceptional craftsman-made objects in highly valued activities. We can begin to decipher a process at work: the use of an ordinary object in a ceremony stimulates a need for a special variety, one that is distinguishable from the everyday. We know, for example, that banquets and funeral rites require better or more unusual ceramics than those used for simple meals. These special ceramics can only be made if sufficient ceramic skills are developed to produce them. But as the objects themselves become elaborated, they in turn enable further distinctions to develop within those ceremonies and rites. Then the whole process continues, with the new ceremony or rite requiring new versions of special ceramics. In other words, one type of specialisation invariably leads to another. Religious beliefs and practices and their associated objects do not emerge fully formed in any society, but are elaborated as a society grows and as its resources, among which are skilled labour and the products of that labour, evolve.

The objects presented here do not illustrate the growth of any single society or the chronological development of single ceramic or jade types. Rather the pieces suggest various ways in which ceramics and jades of exceptional forms and designs may have been used for purposes quite distinct from the everyday. This first section illustrates unusual ceramics from several different parts of China, providing a few pieces of a huge and colourful mosaic of activity and industry.

The Yangshao culture and the painted pottery cultures of Gansu province

The first items in the catalogue belong to the central and western neolithic cultures in which painted pottery predominated. The principal area of the Yangshao culture extended from Xi'an eastwards into present-day Henan province and westwards to Baoji. All parts of this relatively large region saw the development of sizeable village communities. The Yangshao culture is well known for its fine painted ceramics, especially bowls.

The pieces have been chosen not because they are typical but rather because they are unusual and somewhat atypical. Thus, although many of the peoples in this area used abstract, almost geometric designs to embellish their ceramics, the pieces included here show rare instances of the representation of fishes, reptiles and human-like figures. It is the rarity of such figurative representations that makes them interesting. An extension of the Yangshao culture flourished to the north-west, in Gansu province, and gave rise to further elaborately decorated ceramics, many of them with particularly beautiful abstract patterns, and a very few with designs of figures and animals (Introduction, fig. 1).

1 Painted bowl, used as a coffin cover

Neolithic period, Yangshao culture, Banpo type, *c.* 5000–4000 BC
Reddish brown clay with pigment
Height 16.5 cm; diameter at rim 39.5 cm
Excavated in 1995 at Banpo, near Xi'an, Shaanxi province (P4691)
Historical Museum, Beijing

This bowl was made by peoples living in a large fortified village, known as Banpo, on the banks of the Wei River.[1] Not only are the remains very impressive in themselves, but the site was one of the first to be excavated after Liberation in 1949 and is now well known on the tourist route. About 12,000 square metres were examined, about a fifth of the

1

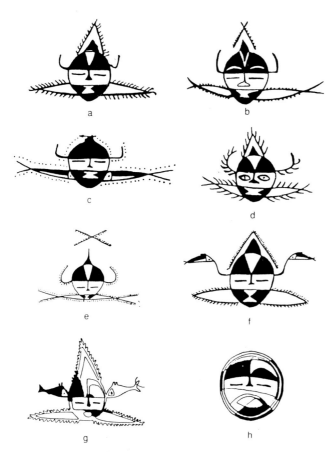

Fig. 1.1 *Drawings of various forms of human-like face combined with fishes from sites in Shaanxi: Banpo (a–c), Jiangzhai (d–f) and Beishouling (g–h). After Beijing 1963a, Beijing 1988a, Beijing 1983c.*

original area. The groundplans of forty-six houses were identified, and ninety hearths, two hundred storage pits, numerous clay vessels, imprints of textiles, ornaments, and utensils of every sort were discovered. It has, therefore, proved possible to gain some insights into the social structure and economic base of the site.[2]

Banpo was occupied over several hundred years, but was abandoned from time to time, perhaps because the soil became impoverished through intensive farming. The people cultivated millet, kept pigs and dogs and practised fishing. Their buildings developed over time, and at the village centre was a large hall. A hall of these dimensions (over 20 m long

and 12.5 m wide) implies a large group gathering or audience.

The painted bowl is one of the best known and most famous of all early Chinese ceramic types. But its function is little regarded. It was placed over the opening of a jar that served as a coffin for a child, the burial of children in jars being a feature of several neolithic societies. A number of such coffins have been found at Banpo, buried beneath houses and within the walls of the habitations rather than in separate burial grounds.

In keeping with its function, the bowl is completely rounded on the underside and has a wide mouth with a flat rim. The principal painted motifs are two human-like faces. A triangle rises from the top of each head and has small extensions that suggest the fins of fishes. Further fishes are indicated on each side of the face by triangles drawn from the cheeks. Each face is subdivided horizontally into three parts, the lowest one suggesting not only part of the human face but also making the heads of the fishes.[3] The ways in which these faces are formed are as intriguing today as they probably were in their own time. Our attempt to read them was probably paralleled in the society of the day by an understanding of what these composite figures referred to. As the bowls had such an important function, it is unlikely that any aspect of their design is fortuitous, and thus the painted motifs probably had some religious or social reference. However, we do not know what that was, and there is no easy answer to be found in a search for origins and descendants. It is possible that the interest in fishes arose simply from the fact that the village of Banpo is sited near a large river, and there is evidence of fishing in the hooks and traces of nets discovered at the site.

Published: *Kaogu tongxun* 1956.2, pp. 23–30; Beijing 1963a; Müller-Karpe 1982; Beijing 1992a, p. 65, no. 50; Wagner 1992; *Kaogu yu wenwu* 1992.6, pp. 55–71; *Huaxia kaogu* 1993.3, pp. 55–65; Cheng Zheng and Qian Zhijiang 1994; Goepper 1995, no. 1.

1 For a discussion of the Yangshao culture see Chang Kwang-Chih 1986a, pp. 107–55.
2 The site report is Beijing 1963a.
3 The mask motif is only found on neolithic ceramics of the Yangshao culture. For the Banpo site see Beijing 1963a (P4666, P4421, P1002). Other examples come from Jiangzhai (Wu Shan 1982, p. 42, fig. 1; *Wenwu* 1975.8, p. 84, pl. 6; Beijing 1988a, p. 255, pl. 181: 1). For Beishouling see Beijing 1983c, pp. 40–50, figs 47, 48.

2 Human face

Neolithic period, Yangshao culture, *c.* 5000–3000 BC
Reddish clay with painting in red and black pigment
Height 7.3 cm; width 9 cm
Excavated in 1977 at Beishouling, near Baoji, Shaanxi province
(T3: 3: 5)
Institute of Archaeology, Beijing

This human face in ceramic comes from another important neolithic site of the Yangshao period, Beishouling, which is a long way west of Banpo, within the present-day city of Baoji. The hinterland of this site embraces not just the long Wei River valley, but also the upper reaches of its tributaries, the Qian and the Jing, which arise in present-day Gansu province. The site occupied about 60,000 square metres near the Wei River. The remains of houses found here, as well as the ceramics and stone implements, are similar to those from Banpo and from the site of Jiangzhai, also in Shaanxi province.[1] The pottery face illustrated here, however, is unlike anything found at either of the other two settlements.

The slightly rounded ceramic face seems, from its strong eyebrows and beard, to be that of a man (fig. 2.1). Paint added to the face to highlight the features is rare in the context of other Yangshao period representations. The small eyes and mouth are pierced into the clay, and the holes in its flat ears were probably intended for ear ornaments.

Almost all the other surviving representations of the human face from the Yangshao culture are unpainted and generally form parts of vessels. Examples of bottle-shaped containers whose upper parts or mouths carry such faces have been found at three places in Gansu province: Chajiaping in Tianshui county, Gaositou in Li county and Dadiwan in Qinan county (fig. 2.2).[2] A connection between vessels and face ornament is thus clearly established. We do not know why these faces should have been used in this way, but they certainly draw attention to the particular containers and suggest that they were of considerable importance. Moreover, given the extraordinary rarity of representations of human-like figures, these examples stand out. We do not know what the present plaque was for or on what it was placed. It is very unlikely to have existed in isolation.

Human figures played a much more important part in other and later neolithic cultures, especially the Hongshan culture of the north-east (no. 10) and the Liangzhu culture of the south-east (nos 16–20).

Published: Beijing 1983c, p. 75; Yang Xiaoneng 1988a, no. 5; Goepper 1995, no. 3.

1 For discussion of Yangshao culture sites see Chang Kwang-chih 1986a, pp. 107–56; *Wenwu* 1989.9, pp. 1–12; Beijing 1963a; Beijing 1988a; Beijing 1983c.
2 For bottles and other pottery containers decorated with human heads see Yang Xiaoneng 1988a, pp. 64–7; *Kaogu yu wenwu* 1983.3, p. 52, figs 9: 2, 9: 4; *Wenwu* 1979.11, p. 52, fig. 1, p. 53, figs 2–3, p. 54, fig. 8.

2

Fig. 2.1 *Drawing of the human face. After Beijing 1983c, p. 75, fig. 57: 1.*

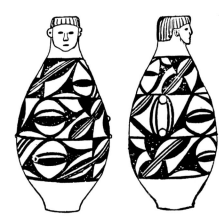

Fig. 2.2 *Drawing of a ceramic bottle capped with a human face from Gansu Qinan Dadiwan. Neolithic period, Gansu Yangshao culture (c. 3000–1500 BC). After* Wenwu *1979.11, p. 53, figs 2, 3; see also Yang Xiaoneng 1988a, p. 43, pl. 2.*

3

3 Jar decorated with human features

Neolithic period, Majiayao culture, *c.* 3800–2000 BC
Loam clay with painting in black and red pigment
Height 21.7 cm
Excavated in 1982 at Shizhao, near Tianshui, Gansu province
(*cai* 01)
Institute of Archaeology, Beijing

The Majiayao culture, from which this vessel comes, produced some of the most elegantly painted of all decorated ceramics in neolithic China, some of them bearing unusually complex spiral designs.[1] This rounded jar with two small handles at the belly has a design in black on a red ground. Its principal motif is unique in the context of Chinese neolithic ceramics. On the shoulder is a small pointed head, modelled from a plate of clay, with a roll at the top which might represent hair. Both the eyes and the mouth are small, suggesting a female. The ears are missing, but small holes remain in the sides of the jar, which may have held ear ornaments. The face is surrounded by a bold black line and the body is also painted in black, in a sketchy, schematic manner that contrasts with the accentuated ribs. The arms are rather short, with small fingers, and the legs are indicated by curved lines which disappear into the registers of abstract patterns around the lower half of the belly (fig. 3.1).

It is generally suggested that the figure is female. This has given rise to a variety of explanations, namely that the jar may have been a storage vessel in some fertility rite or that it was in some way connected with shamanism. It is difficult

to provide evidence that would support these interpretations.

Other Majiayao culture ceramics carry related designs in which rather small relief heads project from vessels covered in dense painted patterns, most of which do not relate closely to the human depictions. Two beakers, or *bei,* recovered at Yuanyangchi, Yongchang county, in Gansu province, bear only the heads.[2] A related, but later, piece belongs to the Banshan phase of the Majiayao culture. These pieces, taken together with the Yangshao ceramics discussed in the first two entries, give us some, if not very extensive, evidence of the representation of human figures among the western neolithic cultures. It is almost certain that the figures had some ceremonial significance, but we cannot work out what it was. It is unlikely that their significance was the same as that of the figures employed by the north-eastern Hongshan culture (no. 10) and the south-eastern Liangzhu culture (nos 16–20). In later periods, human figures were very rarely incorporated into vessel decoration, the bronze vessel (no. 51) with its large staring face on each of its four sides being an oddity in the Bronze Age tradition.

Published: *Wenwu* 1978.10, pp. 62–76; *Wenwu* 1979.11, pp. 52–5, *Kaogu* 1990.7, pp. 577–86; Goepper 1995, no. 6.

1 For discussion and illustrations of Majiayao ceramics see Chang Kwang-chih 1986a, pp. 138–50; Beijing 1979d; Zhang Xuezheng 1980.
2 Yang Xiaoneng 1988a, pls 69, 70.

Fig. 3.1 *Detail of the human figure.*

4 Shallow bowl decorated with a painted reptile

Neolithic period, Majiayao culture, *c.* 3800–2000 BC
Clay with black pigment
Height 5 cm; diameter 16.5 cm
Excavated in 1982 at Shizhao, near Tianshui, Gansu province
(T244.3: 16)
Institute of Archaeology, Beijing

The painted black reptile within this shallow bowl dominates the relatively slight and fragile ceramic. The bowl itself is quite simple, with a rounded underside and no decoration on the outer surface. Inside, a frog or some species of reptile, possibly a turtle, lies across the bottom. It is composed of a circle filled with cross-hatched lines divided vertically down the centre. A further pair of arcs on either side of the circle extends the body, and from these appear four small legs with tiny claws. The head is black and filled in in such a way that the eyes and mouth appear in reserve.

While the neolithic ceramics of western China were decorated with many lively motifs, this explicit decoration of a reptile is very rare. Much more common are various abstract arc, roundel and zigzag designs that bear little or no resemblance to animals.[1] Water creatures appear, it is true, on the ceramics of the earlier Yangshao tradition in Shaanxi at Banpo and

a   b   c

Fig. 4.1 *Drawings of representations of frogs on ceramics of*
a *Banpo phase*
b *Miaodigou phase*
c *Majiayao phase*
After Wenwu *1978.10, p. 65, fig. 4.*

related sites,[2] but the highly abstract designs of the Majiayao culture rarely include explicit representations of creatures. On the other hand, ceramics described below, belonging to a later stage of the western painted ceramic tradition, sometimes display rather abstract versions of four-legged creatures, some of which may descend from reptile-like motifs.[3]

Published: *Kaogu* 1990.7, pp. 577–86; Goepper 1995, no. 7.

1 For ceramics of the Majiayao culture see Beijing 1979d; Zhang Xuezheng 1980; Introduction, fig. 1b.
2 Frog-like motifs are found with fish on bowls from the site of Jiangzhai in the Shaanxi Yangshao area; see *Kaogu* 1973.3, pls 1, 2; Wu Shan 1982, fig. 11.
3 Wu Shan 1982, figs 84: 1, 2.

4

Fig. 5.1 *Drawing showing the three sides of the jar. After Beijing 1984h, p. 117, fig. 82: 1–3.*

head is shown at the neck of the vessel and it is flanked by continuous, intersecting, painted diagonal lines. The face has a large open mouth, small slit eyes, a nose and long ears. Arms and legs are formed from curved rolls of clay. Clearly modelled sexual organs lie below a rounded belly, and the breasts are prominent. This figure is unique among the painted neolithic pottery of western China discovered so far and has therefore excited very varied interpretations.

The figure is interpreted by scholars as either male, female or androgynous, with arguments for each case. At stake are the broader social and religious ideas implied by the various interpretations. If the figure is viewed as a woman, then the notion of an early matriarchal society might be supported.[2] There are a number of other vessels with representations of women, but they come mainly from quite separate neolithic societies and cannot be used to support or refute claims about the present figure. Those scholars who argue that the figure is a man claim that the society was patriarchal.[3] If, as Marxists have tended to argue, a patriarchal society was the inevitable successor to a matriarchal one, then this vessel might mark the change from a matriarchal to a patriarchal society. Others have argued that the figure is androgynous, on the grounds that this would reflect the development of a marriage system of one man to one woman. Claims have been made that this view is confirmed by recent excavations of graves.[4] The vessel is undoubtedly extremely unusual, and further similar finds are needed to support or refute the varying interpretations of it.

Published: *Wenwu* 1978.4, pp. 88–9; *Wenwu* 1978.10, pp. 62–76; *Wenwu* 1979.11, pp. 52–5; *Kaogu yu wenwu* 1983.3, pp. 48–57; *Gugong wenwu yuekan* 1983.5 (5), p. 1; Beijing 1984h; *Wenwu* 1987.1, pp. 54–65; *Wenwu tiandi* 1991.3, pp. 39–40; Zhang Xiaoling 1992; *Kaogu yu wenwu* 1992.6, pp. 55–71; Goepper 1995, no. 5.

1 Beijing 1984h, pp. 56–7, figs 38a, 38b, pl. 7; Palmgren 1934, p. 125; Wagner 1992, pp. 94–111. See also Zhang Xiaoling 1992, pp. 81–2, fig. 7; *Wenwu* 1978.10, p. 72.
2 The most recent opinions have been that the figure is a woman: *Kaogu yu wenwu* 1983.3, pp. 48–57; *Wenwu* 1987.1, pp. 54–65; Zhao Guohua 1990, p. 181; Wagner 1992, p. 108.
3 The view that the figure was a man was taken when the piece was first discovered: *Wenwu* 1976.1, pp. 67–70; *Kaogu* 1976.6, pp. 365–77.
4 For the view that the figure is androgynous see *Wenwu* 1978.10, pp. 62–76; *Wenwu tiandi* 1991.3, pp. 39–40.

5

5 Vessel with relief decoration of a naked figure

Neolithic period, Majiayao culture, Machang type, *c.* 2350–2050 BC
Loamy brownish clay with painting in red and black
Height 33.4 cm; diameter at mouth 9.2 cm
Found in 1974 at Liuwan, Ledu district, Qinghai province
Historical Museum, Beijing

This vessel has a substantial rounded body, a narrow neck opening at the lip and, on the sides, two small loop handles, placed at the point where the decoration begins. In general terms the decoration of the jar is typical of neolithic ceramics in western China. On one side is a design consisting of strong zigzag lines, which some Western scholars have identified as anthropomorphic, and which Chinese scholars usually describe as a frog. The two rows of zigzag lines are joined by a vertical bar, and at the tips of some of the vs are small finger-like strokes. This ornament and the large roundels filled with hatching, to each side of the zigzag pattern, are well known from many ceramics.[1] Much more unusual is a figure modelled in relief on the other side of the vessel. Its gender is not clear, although the sexual organs are emphasised. The

6 Vessel with anthropomorphic or frog-like decoration

Neolithic period, Majiayao culture, Machang type, *c.* 2350–2050 BC
Brownish clay with painting in black pigment
Height 35.2 cm; diameter at lip 10.9 cm; diameter at base 12 cm
Provenance unknown
Historical Museum, Beijing

This vessel, like the previous one, is boldly decorated with thick black lines. The body is rounded and it has two small loop handles. The neck is tubular, opening to a small shallow lip. The principal decoration comprises bold zigzag lines that have been interpreted both as frogs and as sketchily drawn human beings. Such interpretations have then been linked with notions of fertility and shamanism. Chinese scholars have also related this design with an early frog motif seen on a basin of the Miaodigou period (fig. 4.1), where the animal has a rounded, almost semicircular head, a large round body divided by a straight vertical line, and feet terminating in fringes like those seen on the zigzag lines of the present jar. By comparison, it is argued that the zigzag lines on the present jar are abstracted forms taken from the earlier Miaodigou pieces. In addition, some jars dating from the Machang phase of the Majiayao culture bear the zigzag design combined with large roundels that seem to suggest reptilian heads (fig. 6.1).

Although it is difficult, if not impossible, to say what the design signified, it was clearly very popular and occurs on many neolithic ceramics from Gansu province. In tomb 564 at Liuwan in Qinghai province eighty-nine of the ninety-five ceramic pieces carried this painted motif.[1]

All ceramics of the Majiayao and its later Banshan and Machang phases seem to follow strict rules as to which parts of the different vessel types were decorated, and how. In the

6

case of jars, the ornament was confined, as here, to the upper half of the vessel body, whereas bowls tend to have the most important motifs placed inside. In general, it seems as if the craftsmen were taking into account the angle from which the pieces were to be viewed.

Published: *Kaogu* 1976.6, pp. 365–77; *Wenwu* 1978.10, pp. 62–76; *Wenwu* 1979.11, pp. 52–5; *Kaogu yu wenwu* 1983.3, pp. 48–57; Beijing 1984h; *Wenwu* 1987.1, pp. 54–65; Zhang Xiaoling 1992; *Kaogu yu wenwu* 1992.6, pp. 55–71; Goepper 1995, no. 2.

1 Beijing 1984h.

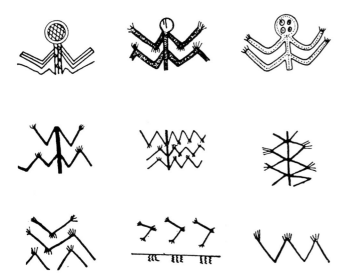

Fig. 6.1 *Drawings of different forms of the so-called frog motif on Banshan and Machang type pottery. After Beijing 1984h, pp. 152–4, figs 1: 8–9.*

Taosi and the later neolithic cultures of northern central China

The later neolithic period in northern central China, that is, the area of the Yellow River, is represented here by two ceramics from the site of Taosi in Xiangfen county in southern Shanxi province. This is a very large site. Although some houses, storage pits and kilns have been found, the principal excavations have been concerned with a large cemetery, thought to contain several thousand burials, of which over a thousand have already been investigated. The ceramics at the site are typical of those of the later neolithic of Henan province and include lobed tripods and other types characteristic of this period.[1]

The cemetery shows signs of considerable social stratification. Among the many graves were nine that were outstanding for their size and contents. These burials were about 3 m long and more than 2 m wide and contained wooden coffins that showed traces of cinnabar, an oxide of mercury that in later times was associated by the Chinese with immortality. These rich graves held as many as two hundred items, among them pottery containers, specially painted wares such as the dish (no. 7), and drums (no. 8). There were also musical stones, wooden furniture, stone and even jade rings and other ceremonial items. Graves of individuals of slightly lower status were somewhat smaller, but they too had rich furnishings. The large graves comprise 1.3 per cent of the total and the medium-sized ones 11.4 per cent, representing a very high concentration of wealth in the hands of relatively few members of the élite. The tombs at Taosi thus demonstrate the growing preoccupation of marking status with an accumulation of high-quality and finely made material possessions.

1 Chang Kwang-chih 1986a, pp. 275–7.

7 Large dish with painted decoration of a dragon

Neolithic period, Longshan type, Taosi phase, *c.* 2500–2200 BC
Brown earthenware with red painting on black ground
Height 8.8 cm; diameter at rim 38.5 cm; diameter at base 15 cm
Excavated in 1980 at Taosi, Xiangfen county, Shanxi province
(M3072:6)
Institute of Archaeology, Beijing

This large shallow dish is made of a low fired earthenware. It is painted with a serpent-like creature, its long jaw filled with tiny serrated teeth, from between which emerges a long spiked tongue. Its body has scales of red which alternate with areas left black. The main area of the ground is black and the vessel has a red rim.

It is always assumed that this is a depiction of one of the dragon-like creatures venerated in early China. Coiled reptile forms occur in several other neolithic cultures, including the Yangshao and the Hongshan. From the Yangshao type culture at Baoji Beishouling in western Shaanxi, an area far removed from Taosi and a culture that is much earlier in date than that of Taosi, is a sherd painted with a dragon and bird (fig. 7.1). Also from a very different area and in a quite different material are the coiled jade dragons of the Hongshan culture (Introduction, fig. 2).

One element shared by these three reptiles is the curved form of the body. This can also be seen in the graph for dragon, *long* (fig. 7.2).[1] But, despite a similarity in general form,

Fig. 7.1 *Painted design on the shoulder of a ceramic vessel. From Shaanxi Baoji Beishouling. Neolithic period, Yangshao culture, c. 4500 BC. After Beijing 1983c, fig. 86: 1.*

Fig. 7.2 *Oracle bone graphs for dragon,* long. *Shang period. After Gugong wenwu yuekan 1988.12, p. 22.*

there is no reason why such creatures represented in three quite separate cultures should have had significances or associations that were in any way related. Nor is it likely that they were related to the large snake-like creatures with heads resembling *taotie*, seen in *pan* of the Shang period.[2] On the other hand, the representation of creatures in basins suggests that they were in some way connected with water, an association that was to become more consistent in later centuries.

There is every reason for treating this basin as a very specially valued item. In the cemetery at Taosi very few graves contained burial goods, the present dish coming from one of the largest tombs that had over two hundred burial items in it. There were fourteen ceramic vessels, of which this basin was one. As the piece was fired at a low temperature it may have been intended specifically for burial in a tomb, for use after death. As illustrated by the drum in the next entry, the burial goods from the Taosi cemetery are highly unusual and included many now vanished wooden pieces, some decorated with lacquer, which have been reconstructed from the traces that they left in the ground.

Published: *Kaogu* 1980.1, pp. 18–31; *Kaogu* 1983.1, pp. 30–42; *Wenwu* 1986.6, pp. 55–6; Beijing 1990a, no. 27; Beijing 1992a, p. 74, no. 61; Osaka 1993, p. 137, no. 1; Goepper 1995, no. 13.

1 For discussion of the origin and history of the graph and representations of dragons see You Rende 1981; Yang Meili 1993; Rawson 1990, no. 93.
2 Another snake-like creature is illustrated in Rawson 1990, fig. 62.

8 Gourd-shaped object with a long neck

Neolithic period, Longshan type, Taosi phase, *c.* 2500–2200 BC
Dark brown earthenware
Height 83.6 cm; diameter at opening of neck 11.6 cm
Excavated in 1980 at Taosi, Xiangfen county, Shanxi province
(M3002:53)
Institute of Archaeology, Beijing

Several examples of this type of tall-necked vessel have been found in the neolithic cemetery at Taosi. They all consist, as here, of a round-bodied vessel with a tall neck, but opinions on their use vary. The neck of this example has twelve bosses around the top, and, further down, two loop handles. On the underside of the body of the vessel are a large central hole and three smaller ones, which make it clear that the object cannot have been for holding food or wine (fig. 8.1).

One of the most plausible suggestions is that it was a drum, with some sort of skin stretched over its mouth and attached

Fig. 8.1 *Underside of the object.*

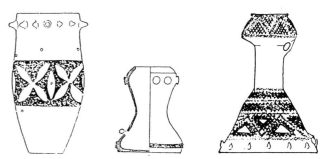

Fig. 8.2 *Drawings of various types of ceramic drum from the lower, middle and upper reaches of the Yellow River. After* Kaogu xuebao *1991.2, pp. 126–9, figs 3: 3, 1: 1, 2: 1.*

by means of the knobs around the neck. Evidence for such notions comes from the use of wooden drums in the Taosi area. These have mainly decayed, but from their traces it has been possible to infer that they were covered with crocodile skin.

Clay drums have been found at various sites ranging from the Dawenkou culture in the east to Gansu in the west (fig. 8.2).[1] Such ceramic drums do not appear to have been made in later periods in the Yellow River area. However, a bronze drum now in the Sumitomo Collection in Kyoto, and probably made in southern China in Hunan province, has patterned ends, possibly imitating crocodile skin.[2] Because musical instruments have often been made of perishable materials their early history has not been easy to reconstruct. However, the drums from Taosi and other neolithic sites, taken together with the evidence of drums in southern China in about 1200 BC, indicate, perhaps, a continuous tradition that culminated in the great orchestra of the Marquis Yi of Zeng (pp. 132–5).

Published: *Kaogu* 1983.1, pp. 30–42; *Kaogu xuebao* 1991.2, pp. 125–41; Osaka 1993, p. 137, no. 3; Goepper 1995, no. 14.

1 For a discussion of ceramic drums see *Kaogu xuebao* 1991.2, pp. 126–9.
2 For a discussion of bronze drums from the south see New York 1980, no. 18.

9 Jar coffin

Neolithic period, *c.* 3000 BC
Reddish earthenware
Height 65 cm; diameter of aperture 30.5 cm
Excavated in 1960 at Dazhang reservoir, Linru county, Henan province
Henan Provincial Museum, Zhengzhou

This pottery coffin was discovered during the excavation of a reservoir in Henan province. Unfortunately there is little or no information on the circumstances of the find, and so we do not know whether there were bones in the jar when it was found. Indeed it is by no means certain that the piece was intended as a coffin, or solely as a coffin. However, large jars were employed in the neolithic period as coffins for children, particularly amongst the Yangshao culture. Although many have been found at sites in Shaanxi, the custom was not confined to western and central China, but was also practised in the south-east at Hemudu, south of Hangzhou bay.[1]

Many of the ceramic jars used for such purposes were simply utilitarian storage jars, turned to a new function. This may have been the case with the present jar, but it also displays certain features of a drum. Most striking is the row of knobs around the neck of the large opening. Such knobs could have been used to secure a skin, as indeed did perhaps the knobs on the previous ceramic from Taosi (no. 8). The shape of the container is distinctive. It has a slight waist

9

between a lower bulbous section and a wider, almost conical, upper part. There is a hole in the lower section. If the jar was indeed used as a coffin, the hole would probably have been intended to allow the spirit of the dead to leave the coffin from time to time to visit his or her relatives in the real world.

Published: Kaogu 1976.6, pp. 356–60; *Kaogu* 1989.4, pp. 331–9; *Huaxia kaogu* 1993.1, pp. 69–73; Goepper 1995, no. 15.

1 *Kaogu* 1973.3, p. 140; Beijing 1983c, p. 80, and pl. 18; *Wenwu* 1981.12, p. 80; *Kaogu* 1989.4, p. 337; *Kaogu xuebao* 1978.1, pp. 39–94.

The Hongshan culture

The small figure described in the next entry was made by a group of peoples who lived to the north of what is today the Great Wall, in Liaoning province and Inner Mongolia. The Hongshan culture (*c.* 3500–2500 BC) is renowned for quite exceptional jade carvings and for complex stone structures, some in the areas of their cemeteries. Large ceremonial sites have been excavated at Niuheliang (Lei, figs 2, 3) and Dongshanzui, and cemeteries at, for example, Hutougou.

Many aspects of the religious beliefs and practices of these north-eastern peoples must have differed from those of their contemporaries in other parts of China. Their remains are distinguished by burials known as cist tombs, lined by stone slabs, and by other stone buildings often reinforced by rows of earth-filled ceramic tubes acting as caissons to prevent the buildings from being eroded by water. At Niuheliang was another remarkable structure, built of clay, in which clay figures of women were installed.

The peoples of Hongshan do not seem to have passed on their beliefs or practices directly to their successors, and their elaborate stone structures and representations of women are without direct parallels in later Chinese cultures. Their jade carvings endured for much longer periods. Indeed, the large and small curved dragons (Introduction, fig. 2) that figure so prominently among the surviving jades were to inspire later copies in the Shang period. This could only have happened if stray examples had survived into these later times.

10

10 Torso of a naked woman

Neolithic period, Hongshan culture, *c.* 3500 BC
Ceramic
Height 7.8 cm
Found in 1982 at Dongshanzui, Kezuo county, Liaoning province
Historical Museum, Beijing

This small, naked torso was found near a structure identified as an altar at Dongshanzui in Kezuo county, Liaoning province.[1] The figure is missing its head, but is clearly female, with slightly enlarged breasts and belly, perhaps indicating pregnancy. The figure, and a similar one from the same site (fig. 10.1), have excited great interest, and it has been assumed that such figures were part of a fertility cult. Indeed they have been compared with ceramic figures from the Palaeolithic cultures of France.[2] There is scant evidence to suggest specifically a fertility cult amongst the Hongshan, although the stone structures and representations of women, mentioned above, do suggest some kind of religious cult. The notion that women figured prominently in the beliefs and ceremonies of

the Hongshan culture is given further weight by the discovery of large clay images of women at one of the sites at Niuheliang, about 50 km from Dongshanzui.[3]

The present figure was found in one of the complex stone structures typical of the area, at Dongshanzui. This site was obviously carefully situated on an artificial terrace, further defined by stone structures. One is circular and the other square, and both are on the same axis. Such careful positioning suggests that the structures served a ritual rather than an everyday purpose.[4]

Published: Zhang Xuqiu 1992, pp. 224–30; Goepper 1995, no. 4.

1 *Wenwu* 1984.11, pp. 8–9, pls 2: 2–3.
2 *Wenwu* 1994.3, pp. 46–51.
3 *Wenwu* 1986.8, pp. 1–17.
4 Nelson 1995, pp. 37–9.

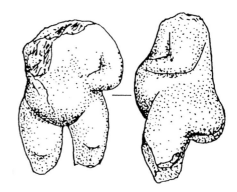

Fig. 10.1 *Drawing of a second female torso from Liaoning Kezuo Dongshanzui. After* Wenwu *1994.3, p. 46, fig. 1: 7.*

The cultures of the middle Yangzi and the surroundings of Nanjing

The next group of pieces has been chosen from the neolithic cultures of central southern China, an area much less fully investigated than the regions of Henan and Shaanxi and the east coast. The items do not illustrate the consistent interest in the representation of humans and creatures witnessed in the previous three sections, but they show, instead, a considerable diversity of approach and suggest that, with further excavation, groups of peoples with varied beliefs and practices may be revealed.

11 Phallus-like object

Neolithic period, Qujialing culture, *c.* 3000 BC
Red ceramic
Height 157 cm; diameter at base 31 cm
Excavated in 1987 at Dengjiawan, Tianmen county, Hubei province
Jingzhou Regional Museum, Hubei province

This very tall cone-shaped object is slightly thickened at the centre with projecting spikes, and the lower part has rows of small notches. It is made in two parts. This item, together with six further sections, together make four large cones. Ever since these four impressive clay constructions were found together in a pit in 1987, they have been the subject of lively debate.[1] As they are so very large and not obviously utilitarian, it is suggested they represent phalli. To support this suggestion, the character for ancestor is invoked, the oldest surviving form of which, employed in oracle bone script, is shown in figure 11.1. On the right is a man in profile offering obeisance to a large phallus on the left. As this phallus is similar in shape to the present object, Chinese scholars have interpreted the object as a phallus.

The present object and its three companions were found in a pit at Dengjiawan in the area of central Hubei inhabited by peoples of the Qujialing culture during neolithic times. Similar items were found nearly forty years ago in other pits in the area of Liujiawan. One of these lay in an ash pit with traces of fireplaces along the edge. Chinese archaeologists have argued, despite insubstantial evidence, that such remains are evidence of a fertility cult, as fertility cults involving the worship of phalli existed in later centuries. Shang period items

Fig. 11.1 *Graph of the character* zu, *meaning ancestor, in oracle bone script. After He Xin 1986, p. 132, fig. 58.*

11 ▶

in stone and wood have been so identified.[2] What is remarkable about these clay phalli from the Qujialing culture is not so much that some sort of continuity with later times might be postulated, but that in the neolithic context and later they stand out as rare and exceptional.

Published: Zhang Xuqiu 1992, pp. 224–30; Goepper 1995, no. 8.

1 Zhang Xuqiu 1992, pp. 224–5.
2 He Xin 1986, p. 137; Wang Binghua 1990, pp. 20–1; *Gugong wenwu yuekan* 1988.12, p. 27; Song Zhaolin 1983a, p. 133.

12 Group of figures of humans and animals

Neolithic period, Shijiahe culture, *c.* 2400–2000 BC
Loamy reddish clay

a Pig
Height 6 cm; length 7.5 cm (H4: 12)

b Sheep
Height 7.5 cm; length 10 cm (H4: 51)

c Cockerel
Height 9 cm (H4: 6)

d Dog
Height 5 cm; length 11 cm (H4: 2)

e Elephant
Height 6.8 cm; length 10.5 cm (H4: 15)

f Tapir
Height 4 cm; length 8.8 cm (H35 2: 7)

g Bird
Height 4 cm; length 6.4 cm (H67: 30)

h Two human figures
Height 9.5 cm (H67: 50 and H67: 56)

Excavated in 1987 at Dengjiawan, Tianmen county, Hubei province
Jingzhou Regional Museum, Hubei province

When figures such as these were discovered in 1955 near the banks of the Shijia River in Hubei province, the archaeologists were convinced that they belonged to the Han period (206 BC–AD 220). They were surprised enough by the initial discovery; they were yet more astonished when forced to revise their opinions and to date the figures to the latter part of the neolithic, before 2000 BC. Since the first discovery, further finds have been made and the number of these small figures is now known to run into the thousands. The largest concentration is in Hubei province.[1] It has been suggested that these figures were either traded with neighbours including peoples in Hunan and Henan, or copied by them.[2]

The animal figures are relatively lively and varied. They include large numbers of birds, such as chickens and perhaps swallows. Among the domestic animals dogs predominate, although sheep and pigs also appear. In addition to the domestic animals there are monkeys, hares, turtles and numerous elephants. The figures of humans belong to the later phase of manufacture and are relatively stereotyped. All are between 5 and 10 cm in height and were formed by kneading small sections of clay and joining them together. We have no idea what purpose they may have served.

Published: Yang Xiaoneng 1988a, figs 132, 134–46, pls 8–11; *Wenwu* 1990.8, pp. 1–16; *Jianghan kaogu* 1991.3, pp. 56–7; Zhang Xuqiu 1992, pp. 283–93; Goepper 1995, no. 9.

1 Zhang Xuqiu 1992, p. 284.
2 *Kaogu xuebao* 1982.4, p. 440, fig. 12, p. 454, fig. 22; *Kaogu* 1983.11, pp. 1039–41.

13 Human face

Neolithic period, *c.* 3000 BC
Clay
Height 9.98 cm
Excavated in 1982 at Yingpanshan, Pukou district, near Nanjing, Jiangsu province
Nanjing City Museum, Jiangsu province

This human face or mask was discovered in the area of a neolithic cemetery at Yingpanshan. The circumstances of its discovery have not been published. Unlike the faces in clay

13

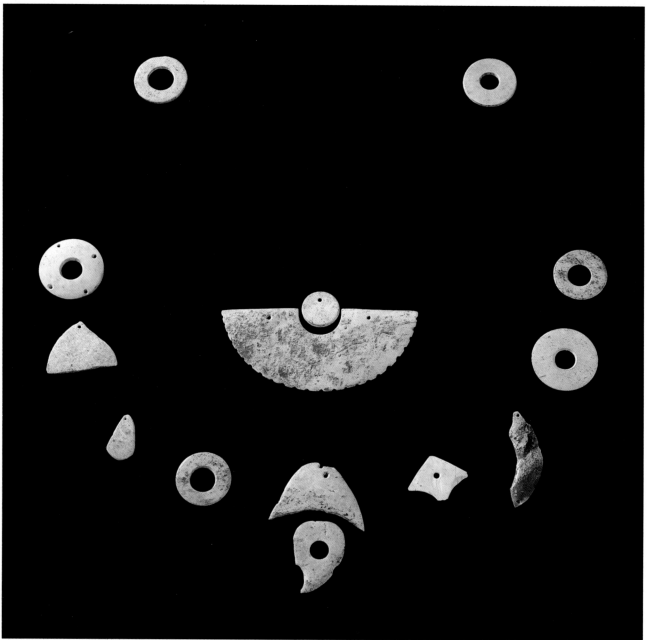

14

of the early neolithic period employed in Shaanxi and Gansu and illustrated above, this face was not part of a vessel or some other object, but was integral in itself.

Made of finely levigated clay, it is the wide and angular face of a human being with narrow, sickle-shaped slit eyes. Below a short nose with bulging nostrils is a narrow, angular, open mouth, which gives the face a slightly grim appearance. The cheeks widen towards the base, creating a shape reminiscent of the stone axe type known as *yue*. Such axes are found in some numbers in the tombs of the cemetery of Yingpanshan and the resemblance may not be entirely fortuitous. The suggestion of an axe shape may have highlighted the fearsome associations of the face.

Published: Wei Zhengjin 1993, pp. 169–72; Goepper 1995, no. 10.

14 Head and neck ornaments

Neolithic period, *c.* 3000 BC
Jade
Width of largest, semicircular piece 14.2 cm
Excavated in 1982 at Yingpanshan, Pukou district, near Nanjing, Jiangsu province (M30)
Nanjing City Museum, Jiangsu province

These jade ornaments are included at this point in the catalogue because they come from the same site as the ceramic face described in the previous entry.[1] The use of jade in China is discussed in the essay by Yang and in the next section of the catalogue and will not be further considered here.

The principal interest of this set of jades is that a precious and durable stone, probably already associated with spiritual and earthly power, is here used to form ornaments to emphasise and cover parts of the upper body and the face of the dead. The exceptionally fine and even workmanship demonstrates the craftsman's superb control of his material.

Jade, too hard to be carved by any form of metal, has to be ground with an abrasive sand. These ornaments, each consisting of a thin slice, were probably made by first cutting a large pebble or block into slices, which were then carved along the edges to shape them. The circles may have been produced by drills as both their inner and outer edges seem very carefully formed.

The small perforations in some of the jades may mean that they were sewn onto clothing. Many of the jades from Yingpanshan have these perforations, suggesting that jades were well established as ornaments. The range of different shapes used at Yingpanshan is unparalleled in other parts of China, even among the peoples of the Liangzhu culture to be discussed below. This diversity suggests a very highly elaborated series of conventions for the display of rank or status by means of these jades.

Published: Wei Zhengjin 1993, pp. 169–172; Goepper 1995, no. 11.

1 For a discussion of the site see Wei Zhengjin 1993, pp. 169–70.

15 Two spindle whorls

Neolithic period
Ceramic

a Whorl with mythical creatures
Diameter 6 cm; thickness 1.2 cm

b Whorl with animal-headed figure
Diameter 5.8 cm; thickness 1.8 cm

Excavated in 1989 at Chengqiao Yangjiaoshan, Liuhe district, near Nanjing, Jiangsu province
Nanjing City Museum, Jiangsu province

Spindle whorls such as these would have been used in conjunction with hand spindles and distaffs to make yarns, but only whorls have been preserved from the early phase of Chinese civilisation.

Our knowledge of the first textiles is gleaned from the impressions of woven and plaited mats or fabrics left on ceramic sherds of the neolithic Yangshao culture (*c.* 5000–3000 BC). Some of these sherds also provide us with information on the precursors of textiles, that is woven cords of plant fibres, which were used to imprint decoration on pottery.[1] Rare archaeological finds of cloth tissues, such as those from

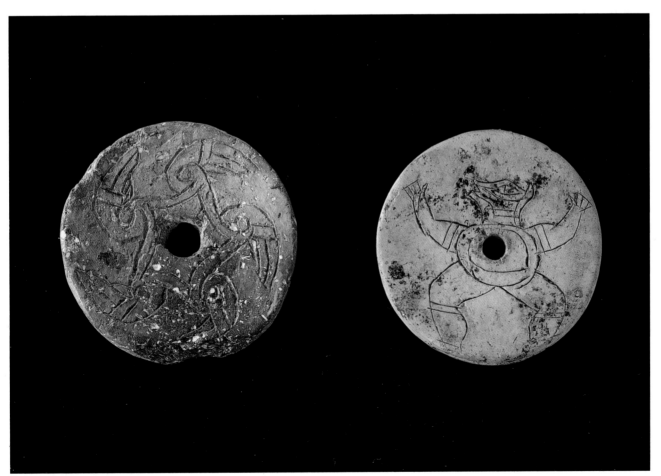

15a,b

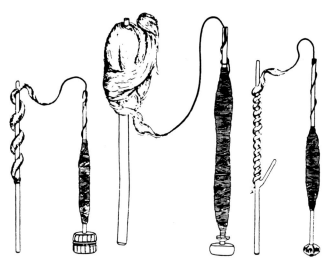

Fig. 15.1 *Three types of 20th-century hand spindles and distaffs from Gansu province. After Kuhn 1988a, fig. 25.*

Caoxieshan in Jiangsu province,[2] which are dated to *c.* 4000 BC, prove that the fibres of the bean-creeper (*ge*) were spun into yarn even earlier than hemp (*dama*) or ramie (*zhuma*).[3] However, the large number of spindle whorls found at neolithic sites confirms the gradual spread of spinning and weaving, which had their beginnings about 5000 BC in the Yangshao culture on the middle reaches of the Yellow River and in the Hemudu culture in Zhejiang, to most parts of China by about 1000 BC.[4] By then the Chinese could produce strong, uniform yarn of the desired thickness. With this they could make fishing nets resistant to tearing, and light fabrics that were superior to skin, pelt and leather because they could be dried quickly without hardening.

To understand the procedure of hand spindle spinning, which involved the use of the whorl, we are dependent on Chinese descriptions of the spinning of inferior quality or waste silk. Good silk did not need to be spun, but was reeled directly from the cocoon of the silkworm. The first step in the hand spinning process was to attach the waste silk, which was sometimes roughly pretwisted, to a stick known as a distaff which was either held in the spinner's left hand or tucked under her left arm. The starting material was then attached to the spindle, which was simply a rod, and the spindle inserted in the whorl. The purpose of the whorl was to regulate, by its weight, the quality of the resulting yarn. For example, a wooden whorl would have been used for a light woollen yarn, and a stone whorl for flax. The spinner would turn the spindle with the fingers of the right hand and the yarn would wrap itself round the spindle, above or below the whorl (fig. 15.1).

It is to be assumed that most spindle whorls were carved in wood, although only specimens in pottery, stone, jade and bone are preserved from neolithic times. In his typology of the Chinese spindle whorl, Dieter Kuhn differentiates

between nine different types of whorl, which can, however, all be taken back to the most widely distributed prototype, the flat disc.[5] Their diameter varied between 2.6 and 11.2 cm, their thickness between 0.4 and 3.2 cm, and their weight between 12 and 100.3 g.[6] Many of them are decorated with fine geometric scratched decor or polychrome painting suggesting rotational movement, but on extremely rare occasions there are zoomorphic motifs, such as on the spindle whorls shown here. These whorls are representative in size and weight.

One whorl has star-shaped decoration of five spirals, which open out into the heads of birds or mythical creatures with long beaks. This design is reminiscent of a geometric pattern on the inside of a clay dish that was excavated in tomb 4 at Hemudu, where it was possibly connected with a bird and sun cult.[7]

A stocky composite being is scratched in fine lines into the underside of the other whorl (b). The limbs of the creature also create a star shape radiating from the almost circular torso in the middle of the whorl. Its head, presumably shown in profile, has a horn which allows us to conclude that it is an animal. The upper side of the whorl is slightly concave and without decoration.

Whether the neolithic settlement of Yangjiaoshan is to be counted in the sphere of influence of the Hemudu culture, or of the later Liangzhu culture, which also depicted birds, is debatable until more precise data are available for the dating of the find site.[8] Cross-shaped patterns are engraved on the underside of one whorl (a). These were commonplace on spindle whorls and are often identified as sun symbols.[9]

Published: Song Zhaolin 1983b, pp. 163–70; Kuhn 1988a, pp. 60–155; Kuhn 1988b, pp. 249–51; Goepper 1995, no. 12.

1 For the botanical identification of the different plant fibres see Kuhn 1988a, p. 63. On the different weaving patterns see Kuhn 1988b, pp. 150–1.
2 They are now in the possession of the Nanjing City Museum and are illustrated and described in detail in Shen Congwen 1992, p. 23, fig. 20.1. For the excavation report on Caoxieshan see *Wenwu ziliao congkan* 3 (1980), pp. 1–14.
3 Kuhn 1988a, pp. 15–59.
4 See the three maps on the distribution of neolithic hand spindles in Kuhn 1988a, pp. 138–40.
5 Kuhn 1988a, pp. 151–5.
6 Kuhn 1988a, p. 151.
7 *Wenwu* 1980.5, p. 10, fig. 7:11.
8 According to information supplied by the Nanjing City Museum, the Yangjiao Mountain was known by the 1960s to be of archaeological interest.
9 He Xin 1986, pp. 1–19.

The Liangzhu culture

The cultures of the Hongshan (Lei, figs 1, 2; no. 10) and the Liangzhu have in recent decades revealed the exceptional skill of neolithic period jade carving, although only Liangzhu jades are represented here. The Liangzhu culture, located in the area north of Hangzhou Bay, extending around Shanghai and into southern Jiangsu province (see map p. 282), was contemporaneous with cultures such as the Taosi, described in the previous section. The Liangzhu peoples belonged to the group of east-coast cultures defined by archaeologists as those who used ceramics distinguished by their complex shapes rather than by their painted decoration. The Liangzhu are renowned first and foremost, however, for their outstanding jade carvings.

Jade is a tough, translucent stone that can only be worked with abrasive sands. In both the Hongshan and Liangzhu cultures jade carving was highly advanced and evidently depended on many centuries of development. In the south-east less elaborate jade carvings were made by the cultures that preceded the Liangzhu, known as the Majiabang and the Songze. The majority of such early pieces were ornaments, often worked from very small pieces of jade.

The three principal categories of jade used in the later Liangzhu culture were ornaments, fine-quality ceremonial weapons and what are now described as ritual carvings, *cong* (no. 16) and *bi* (no. 17). The weapons are not represented here, but this section includes fine examples of the other two types. Unlike the small earlier jades mentioned, the selected pieces include items that must have been carved from large blocks, especially the tube known as a *cong* (no. 16) and the disc or *bi* (no. 17). Not only were supplies of material plentiful, but the techniques of carving were varied. Thick and thin slices were employed, and large and narrow holes were made. Surfaces were polished smooth and some pieces had very fine incised designs. Standardised motifs were employed, particularly the complex design of a human-like figure grasping a monster in its hands, seen at the centre of each side of the *cong* (no. 16, fig. 16.1). This design was adapted, and often abbreviated, for many different uses and positions on various jade types. The full form is illustrated in figure 16.1, but abbreviations can be seen at the corners of the two *cong* (no. 16) and on the plaques (nos 18, 19). The use of both standard shapes and standard motifs capable of intricate and, it would seem, almost infinite variety would have made the jades adaptable to different functions and presumably for owners of varying status. Not just the techniques of carving jade, but also the forms of the pieces

and their implied uses all indicate a complex society.

A number of large tombs containing a mass of jade grave goods have been found in the area north of Hangzhou Bay. Some of the most beautifully made pieces, including the items exhibited here, have come from Fanshan, site of one of two major tomb groups in the county of Yuhang; the other site is at Yaoshan (Lei, fig. 4). There were significant differences between the two tomb groups. For example, while tubes of the type illustrated at no. 16 were found at both Fanshan and Yaoshan, discs similar to no. 17 were discovered only at Fanshan. Thus, if these two jade types had some function in religious beliefs or practices, the beliefs and practices of the two communities living only a few kilometres apart seem to have been different. In addition, there are subtle variations between the different categories of plaque (nos 18, 19). These plaques almost certainly served different functions, and their allocation to specific tombs presumably indicates the rank, status, or possibly even gender of the person buried in the tomb.

All tombs containing fine jades are remarkable for the large quantities found in them. Such finds have been made in the major burials excavated in the Shanghai area and in southern Jiangsu. For example, the tomb at Wujin Sidun, described by Yang (fig. 2), held twenty-four *bi* and thirty-two *cong*, as well as many axes and larger numbers of small jades. Several tens or even hundreds of carved jades represent an ownership of huge resources in terms of both the value of the material and the skilled workmanship required to make such pieces. If the élite owned such carvings, clearly the ordinary people did not. Thus not only were there distinctions within the élite, but there were also huge differences between the élite and the ordinary people. This large social gap suggests a concentration of resources in the hands of a few, and is also a sign of a highly developed society.

But perhaps the most telling features that indicate a complex society are the objects whose uses we cannot guess and the motifs whose significances we cannot fathom. For the tubes and discs refer not to ornamental or everyday objects but suggest purposes with no obvious everyday equivalent. Thus they seem to have had significance for their owners within a universe of ideas, suggesting complex religious beliefs, developed far beyond the everyday. As described in the Introduction, such developments indicate considerable elaboration in the society. In the same way, the motif of a man grasping a monster in his hands is much more than a depiction based upon experience in daily life. It also implies an imagined world. Both the social and intellectual aspects of Liangzhu society were thus far from simple and suggest a complicated and successful society.

While we can suggest the sources of some elements of Liangzhu society, it was very unusual both in its own time and in the context of later neolithic societies. No other people developed jade carving to such a high level or used the material in such abundance. Indeed, between the period of the Liangzhu culture and the Han period very few individuals seem to have owned as many jades as did the élite of Yuhang. It appears that the Liangzhu concentrated on jade and developed its uses to spectacular levels.

16 Two ritual jades, *cong*

Neolithic period, Liangzhu culture, *c.* 3000–2000 BC
Yellowish white jade

a Wide, squat *cong*
Height 8.8 cm; width 17.6 cm; weight 6.5 kg (M12:98)

b Taller, narrow *cong*
Height 10 cm; diameter 8.4 cm (M12:97)

Excavated in 1986 at Fanshan, Yuhang county, Zhejiang province
Institute of Archaeology and Cultural Relics Bureau, Zhejiang province

In modern Chinese these two tube-like objects are known as *cong*.[1] There is no reason to believe that this is what they were called in their own day. Indeed, it is highly unlikely that their makers or users spoke any language that we would recognise as Chinese. The name *cong* was given to the object by the writers of later ritual texts who were attempting to make sense of both earlier and contemporary jades.

The object known as a *cong* consists of a tube of varying length, with an approximately square cross-section and a circular bore. The larger of the two pieces exhibited here is the most magnificent of all excavated *cong* known to date. It is carved from a large block and is much wider than it is high. A small central bore is surrounded by a large circular area on the top and bottom and the cross-section is completed by the four slightly bowed corners which, because they do not extend to the full height of the tube, leave a circular base and rim. There is the impression of a circle contained within, or rather projecting above and below, a square.

The corners of the piece are decorated with two pairs of faces. The upper one of each pair comprises a finely drawn pair of circular eyes with tiny dashes suggesting the corners. Pairs of bands embellished with intaglio lines suggest headbands, and the mouth or nose consists of a much smaller bar, also incised with fine lines. The face in the lower half of the pair of faces has much larger disc-shaped eyes joined by an angled bar, and a small bar acts as nose or mouth. To the left and right of the eyes of this second face is a small bird-like figure, in which the eye shape of the monster has been redeployed as the body of the bird.

The full form of the motif appears at the centre of the *cong* (fig. 16.1). It consists of a human-like figure with a large plumed headdress holding the eyes of a monster in its hands. The monster has a broad nose and a small, rounded, ridge-shaped mouth with projecting fangs. Below the mouth, on each side, are crouching legs and feet with claws. Much of the detail of this motif has been omitted from the designs at the corners of the *cong* and on the middle register of the second *cong*.

While the large *cong* is a completely exceptional piece, the smaller one is of a rather more standard character. It consists of a circular tube much wider and thinner in proportion to the overall width of the whole carving than the previous piece. This relatively thin, tube-like appearance is probably derived from bracelet-shaped jades, which may have been one

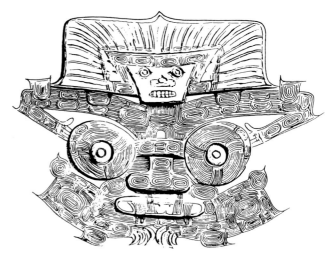

Fig. 16.1 *Drawing of a human-like figure holding the eyes of a monster in his hands, from the centre of the wide* cong. *After* Wenwu *1988.1, pp. 1–31, fig. 20.*

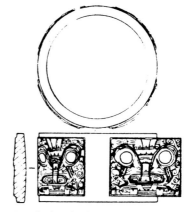

Fig 16.2 *Drawing of a bracelet-shaped* cong *decorated with a single tier of faces within panels, from Zhejiang Yuhang Yaoshan. Height 4.5 cm. After* Wenwu *1988.1, pp. 32–51, fig. 15.1.*

16a

of the sources of the *cong*. A few of the *cong* from the Yuhang area consist of thin rings with panels, rather than sharp angular projections, on which the faces are carved (fig. 16.2). *Cong* may have been an elaboration of such simple jades. The tombs at Fanshan and Yaoshan have shown that a considerable number of types of *cong* were in use at one time.

Further north, in tombs such as that at Sidun in Jiangsu (Yang, fig. 2), much taller *cong* – many carved in a dark stone – were widely used.[2] Here the faces were abbreviated yet further, to little more than a pair of circles as eyes, a bar for the nose and incised lines on the headband. These summary faces were probably a long way removed from the original designs on the Fanshan *cong*, and they may have had quite different significances for their users.

As mentioned above, neither the shapes of these jades nor the motifs on them can be related to objects or decoration of everyday use. Their use and meaning remain elusive.[3] We can but suggest that from the fact that they were carved from such a valuable material and with such precision, and because they were buried in elaborate tombs, they were of great importance to their owners and thus to the society in general.

Published: *Wenwu* 1988.1, pp. 1–31; *Wenwu* 1989.12, pp. 48–52; *Orientations*, June 1989, pp. 37–43; *Wenwu* 1990.2, pp. 30–7; Beijing 1990a, nos 13, 14; Zhejiang 1990, no. 14; *Orientations*, June 1991, pp. 46–55; Hebei 1991–3, vol. 1, no. 138; Beijing 1992a, nos 23, 24; *Gugong wenwu yuekan* 1993.4, no. 124, pp. 126–37; Goepper 1995, no. 16.

16b

1 For a general discussion of the *cong* see Rawson 1995, section 3.

2 For the site at Jiangsu Wujin Sidun see *Kaogu* 1984.2, pp. 109–29.

3 A large number of theories about the functions and significance of the *cong* have been put forward, many, if not all of them, without much foundation. Numerous articles discuss the face motifs, their appearance on *cong* and the unusual beings they represent. For a discussion in English of the relationship between jade designs and later motifs on Shang ritual bronzes see Li Xueqin 1993a; for related discussions see Teng Shu-p'ing 1986, Hayashi Minao 1990a, Hayashi Minao 1991a, Mou Yongkang 1989, and references given in section II below. See also *Kaogu* 1988.3, pp. 236–45, 235; *Wenwu* 1989.5, pp. 64–8, 74; *Wenwu* 1989.12, pp. 48–52; *Wenbo* 1990.1, pp. 57–65, 42; *Wenwu* 1990.2, pp. 30–7; *Wenwu* 1990.12, pp. 32–6, 92; *Kaogu* 1992.10, pp. 915–23; *Kaogu* 1992.11, pp. 1039–44. Reduced forms of the face are especially typical of tall *cong* of the type seen in Rawson 1995, no. 3:6, and found in some numbers in Jiangsu, especially at Sidun and Caoxieshan. See also Sun Zhixin 1993.

    A possibility, which is difficult to explore on present evidence, is that a simple face pattern was introduced to the area from outside, from, say, the Hongshan culture (Rawson 1995, no. 1:4, fig. 1). It might then have been used by itself, as on such pieces as a bracelet from Jiangsu Wu xian.

17 Disc, *bi*

Neolithic period, Liangzhu culture, *c.* 3000–2000 BC
Yellowish jade with a multitude of grey veins
Diameter 18 cm; thickness 1.1 cm
Excavated in 1986 at Fanshan, Yuhang county, Zhejiang province
(M20:186)
Institute of Archaeology and Cultural Relics Bureau, Zhejiang province

The name given to large discs with central holes in modern Chinese is *bi*. Like the name *cong*, this is a term used in the ritual texts of *c.* 300 BC, which probably bears no relationship to the name given to the disc by its makers. This large disc is one of the most carefully worked of the many found in the tombs at Fanshan. It was found positioned near the centre of grave 20, and a further forty-two were spread over the area where the lower part of the body would have been. The same arrangement was found in grave 23.[1] Grave 20 was 3.95 m long and 1.75 m wide, and contained, in addition to the *bi*, two ceramic vessels, twenty-four stone axes, nine ivory objects, a shark's tooth and over five hundred individual jades, many of them the small parts of assemblages such as strings of beads. The wealth represented by the jades is remarkable, and suggests a concentration of resources in a few hands as extreme as anything known in much later periods.

The discs of the Liangzhu culture are generally large and thick. In this they contrast with the rather delicate ornaments of the Hongshan culture, which, although they bear some resemblance to discs in that they have large central holes, tend to take the form of axes, or rectangles, with rounded corners.[2] These Hongshan pieces generally have two tiny holes at the top, which were perhaps for attachment to clothing as some form of ornament.

The very thickness and size of Liangzhu discs, such as the

present piece, indicate that they belong to a different tradition altogether. They are much too large to have been worn and do not seem like a personal ornament. Discs that were assumed by later scholars to be of integral importance in all Chinese rituals seem to have been fully developed only by the Liangzhu peoples. Many discs were used during the Liangzhu period, but thereafter they were much less common. Simultaneously with the Liangzhu culture and indeed after its decline and demise, discs were used occasionally by other neolithic peoples, especially those in northern central and western China.[3] In reviewing the role of *bi* in Chinese culture overall, it is important to note how very rare such items were during the centuries of dominance of the main ancient dynasties of the Shang and early Zhou (*c.* 1500–850 BC). *Bi* seem only to have become significant again after the ritual revolution of *c.* 850 BC, when a new attitude to burial jades appeared. Among the jades buried in tombs, discs make a reappearance. But not until the Han period (206 BC–AD 220) were large numbers again used. Since many of the texts describing jades were compiled at this stage, it is likely that the later texts reflect only the notions of the Han, or at best the late Zhou, and bear no relation to the functions and significances of the jades of the neolithic and Shang periods (*c.* 3000–1000 BC). All manner of suggestions as to the significance of these discs are put forward today based upon later texts, but most are irrelevant. The discs were a specifically Liangzhu phenomenon whose meaning we cannot now guess. They are all the more remarkable for that, especially as in the following centuries discs were much less widely used and were presumably less important.

Published: *Wenwu* 1988.1, pp. 8–10; Beijing 1990a, no. 17; Zhejiang 1990, no. 76; Goepper 1995, no. 17.

1 For a description of the contents of the graves see *Wenwu* 1988.1, pp. 1–31.

2 Hebei 1991–3, vol. 1, no. 4; the Hongshan jades are considered in Rawson 1995, section 1; for a discussion of *bi* see Rawson 1995, section 4.

3 Yang Meili 1995, nos 9–21.

Fig. 17.1 *Signs found on a few* bi *discs. After Hiyashi Minao 1981, fig. 3.*

17

18 Jade plaque

Neolithic period, Liangzhu culture, *c*. 3000–2000 BC
Whitish grey jade with yellowish areas
Height 6 cm; width at widest point 9.15 cm
Excavated in 1986 at Fanshan, Yuhang county, Zhejiang province
(M17:8)
Institute of Archaeology and Cultural Relics Bureau, Zhejiang province

This small plaque is approximately trapezoidal in shape. Its two outer edges are slightly curved and the centre of the upper one has a double cusp forming the focus. A narrow flange along the bottom is pierced with holes and indicates that the plaque fitted into something. Just below an oblong slot, which is pierced right through the plaque, towards the top, is an exceptionally fine version of the monster design seen on the *cong* (fig. 16.1). Subtly worked low relief suggests the form of the monster, with its two large oval eyes, whose surface is slightly dished. The bridge between the eyes and the blunt nose are similarly in relief. Across the surfaces, fine incised lines refine the motif, indicating the pupils of the eyes and providing a dense surface of spirals and small dashes to emphasise the subject; they also describe a wide mouth with projecting fangs and indicate small folded arms and legs. As already mentioned in connection with no. 16, we have no idea what the monster signified.

A single jade plaque of this type was found in all the burials at Fanshan in Yuhang county, with the exception of tombs 19 and 21, which had been disturbed.[1] They seem to have

18

Fig. 18.1 *Drawings of plaques from Yaoshan, Yuhang county, Zhejiang province. Liangzhu period, c. 3000–2000 BC. After Rawson 1995, p. 137, fig. 1.*

been placed in the region of the shoulder, and the flange suggests that they fitted into some other object or item of dress. Zhang Minghua suggests that such jades were inserted into a wooden object of some form.[2] As these particular plaques are often found in association with beads, they have

sometimes been thought to be part of an item of jewellery, but at present this hypothesis seems unlikely.[3] We have no idea at present what their supports were like and thus we can only guess how these jades functioned.

However, two features are important. In the first place the fine workmanship, and especially the carving of the monster face, associates this plaque with others of set shapes, including the half-moon seen in the next entry (no. 19). Secondly, the use of set shapes and their careful distribution (one of these trapezoidal plaques to each one of a group of tombs) indicate that the plaques had some sort of role in the formal dress or ritual objects of the society. The Liangzhu plaques vary in shape (fig. 18.1), but all those that are decorated bear versions of the monster, or man and monster design, illustrated in relation to the *cong* (no. 16).

Repetition of set shapes suggests that each served a particular function. Thus the trapezoidal plaques may have been used in one way, and the half-moon ones in quite another. If this was so, it is very likely that such plaques indicated the role or status of those who wore or carried them. Further, it is likely that the plaques reinforced that status, for their presence would have indicated to the associates of the user or wearer the particular role that they signified.[4] In this way we can view the plaques as having the sort of social role that jewellery and insignia had and still have in Western societies.

Published: *Wenwu* 1988.1, pp. 19–21; *Wenwu* 1990.12, p. 33; Beijing 1990a, no. 15; Zhejiang 1990, no. 115; James 1991, p. 52; Hebei 1991–3, vol. 1, no. 268; Beijing 1992a, no. 10; *Kaogu* 1994.4, pp. 343–5, 354; *Wenwu* 1994.7, p. 58; Goepper 1995, no. 18.

1 For the tombs at Fanshan see *Wenwu* 1988.1, pp. 1–31.
2 *Orientations*, October 1985, p. 36; Zhang Minghua 1989.
3 Rawson 1995, p. 137, fig. 1.
4 Renfrew 1988.

19 Half-moon plaque and beads

Neolithic period, Liangzhu culture, *c.* 3000–2000 BC
Whitish jade with brown spots on the beads
Half-moon pendant, height 4.2 cm; width 6.3 cm
Beads, length 2.7 cm; diameter 1.1 cm
Excavated in 1986 at Fanshan, Yuhang county, Zhejiang province
(M22:8)
Institute of Archaeology and Cultural Relics Bureau, Zhejiang province

This plaque and its associated beads are typical of another category of plaque from the Liangzhu assemblages. Like the trapezoidal plaques, these ones also seem to have had a particular role and probably contributed to the social or ritual definition of an object or dress and its owner. This plaque and beads were found near a trapezoidal plaque in tomb M22 at Fanshan. They may have been on the same item of dress or object.

Like the plaque described at no. 18, this plaque and the tubular beads are very carefully made. The plaque is slightly bowed, and on the front is the full design of the human-like figure grasping a monster with large oval eyes. As with the previous example, the design is worked in relief and then enhanced with very fine incised lines. Extremely careful modulation of the surfaces of the design demonstrates the great refinement of the workmanship.

Two holes at the corners of the plaque were probably for attaching the beads or some other part of the object with which the plaque was associated. The beads consist of neat, straight tubes, without the slightly bowed profile that was more common for beads. This distinction suggests that they had a specific function.[1]

The plaque and beads were found in a tomb with other carefully worked plaques. As there were neither axes nor *cong* in the grave, the excavators assume that the burial was that of a woman of high rank. A number of authors have tried to identify the genders of the tomb occupants at Fanshan and Yaoshan on the basis of grave goods. The differences between the range of fine jade carvings in the tombs is intriguing, but as very little other evidence, such as bones, has been found, it is impossible to confirm the identifications.[2]

Published: *Wenwu* 1988.1, p. 28, fig. 58, and pls 3, 4; Beijing 1990a, no. 20; Zhejiang 1990, no. 164; Hebei 1991–3, vol. 1, no. 215; Beijing 1992a, no. 13; Goepper 1995, no. 19.

1 For illustrations of strings of beads see Zhejiang 1990, no. 133 ff.
2 *Kaogu xuebao* 1980.1, pp. 29–58; James 1991.

20 Jade plaques in the shapes of animals

Neolithic period, Liangzhu culture, *c.* 3000–2000 BC
Ivory-coloured jade with brown spots
Bird, length 5.5 cm; width 5.8 cm (M16: 2)
Bird, length 2.6 cm; width 4.7 cm (M17: 60)
Fish, length 4.9 cm (M22: 23)
Turtle, length 3.2 cm (M17: 39)
Excavated in 1986 at Fanshan, Yuhang county, Zhejiang province
Institute of Archaeology and Cultural Relics Bureau, Zhejiang province

These jade animals are extremely rare among the finds from Liangzhu tombs. Seven such pieces were found in five burials at Fanshan: four birds shown in flight came from tombs M14, M15, M16, and M17, a cicada-like creature came from tombs M14 and M17 with the present turtle, while the fish was found in tomb M22. With the exception of the fish, which has holes visible from the front, all the creatures have holes on the reverse by which they must have been attached to clothing or some such material.

These creatures occupy a position very different from the jade plaques just described. The fine plaques with the man

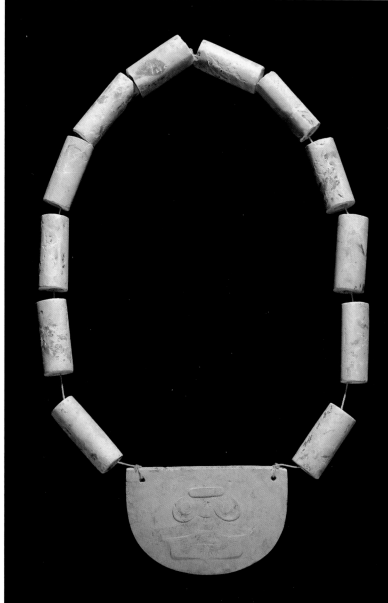

19

and monster motif are made in set shapes, and their distribution in a number of graves suggests that they were essential to the definition of particular roles or the status of high-ranking men and women of the Liangzhu culture. The animals are, by contrast, extremely rare. This may indeed mean that they were more precious and more unusual than the plaques. On the other hand they cannot have been as important as the plaques in the definition of status, unless of course the number of people entitled to them was very small. Not only are very few animal carvings known from excavations, but the collections formed over the last 150 years, which include chance finds and plaques, do not seem to contain any other such pieces.

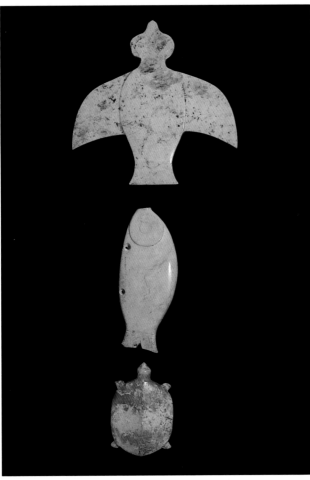

20

Jade animal figures played a larger role in the Hongshan culture, where both turtles and birds in flight were carved.[1] In later times, too, animal-shaped carvings were employed, especially at the time of Fu Hao during the Shang occupation of Anyang (no. 49). These Shang carvings may have been stimulated by the rediscovery of earlier animal carvings, especially those of the Hongshan or Shijiahe cultures.[2]

Published: *Wenwu* 1988.1, pp. 28–30; Zhejiang 1990, nos 198, 200; Hebei 1991–3, vol. 1, nos 202, 197, 196; Goepper 1995, no. 20.

1 Hebei 1991–3, vol. 1, nos 18–22.
2 Discussed in Rawson 1995, section 12.

21 Hair ornament

Neolithic period, Longshan culture, *c.* 2000 BC
Jade with turquoise inlay
Length 23 cm
Excavated in 1989 from tomb M202 at Zhufeng, Linqu county, Shandong province
Institute of Archaeology, Beijing

Although this jade hair ornament comes from a neolithic culture considerably further north than that of the Liangzhu, which produced the five previous examples (nos 16–20), it still belongs within the east-coast tradition of fine jade carving. In fact, pieces such as this Longshan culture hairpin lend support to the view that the eastern neolithic peoples attached great importance to jade carvings of exceptional quality.

The tomb in which this hair ornament was found was a large burial with an inner and outer coffin. In addition to this exceptionally fine jade, the burial yielded another hairpin and two jade axes, as well as some very fine black pottery typical of the Longshan culture in Shandong province.[1]

The hair ornament is in two parts. The pin itself consists of a slender shaft carefully turned to vary its width. Thus it has groups of ridges and curved surfaces that take their forms, it would seem, from plant stalks. The attention devoted to this shaft is quite remarkable, given that the whole of it is likely to have been hidden once the ornament was attached to the hair or headdress of the owner. The main plaque supported by the shaft is also highly unusual, being slightly arched and carved in openwork. The small slots that pierce the surface, together with the shallow incised lines around these openings, appear to indicate a composition of imaginary creatures. The projecting sections on the two sides bear a faint resemblance to dragon heads, for instance. But the design is in fact very difficult to read.

The symmetrical organisation of the ornament is reminiscent of other similar designs in jade, such as the man and monster motif on Liangzhu jades (fig. 16.1). Indeed, two hook-like slots on either side of the axis would appear to take the place of the eyes of the monster, while the central section of the plaque could be read as a simplification of the central human-like figure of the Liangzhu pieces. However, the jade is considerably removed from the earlier categories of ornament. It can also be compared with another neolithic tradition of jade carving, that of the Shijiahe culture in Hubei province. A fine face from this culture found in a much later tomb is illustrated at no. 54. The projecting edges of the present plaque resemble the fins that appear on some of the rare jade carvings attributed to the Shijiahe (fig. 54.1). An axe, also of the Longshan culture, carries two faces worked out in fine scrolls that may be related to the design of this piece.[2]

The finds from Zhufeng suggest that the peoples of the Longshan culture in Shandong had exceptionally fine jade carving, of a quality similar to the better known Liangzhu

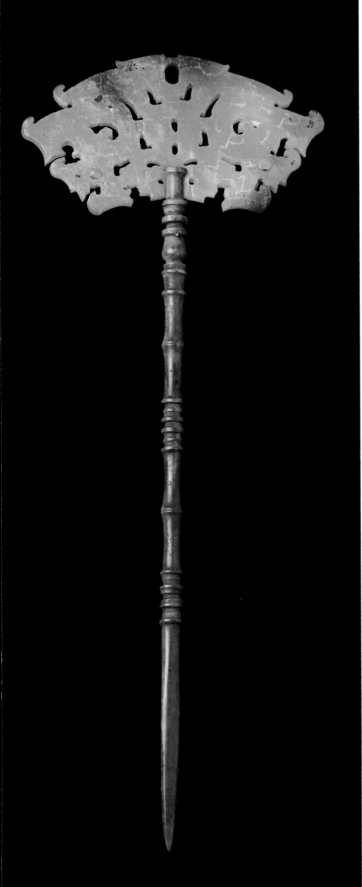

and Shijiahe jades. While a number of jade axes and other blades have been found, fine ornaments are rare, and indeed the quality of this hairpin is unprecedented. It is likely that such pieces were often too highly valued to be buried, suggesting that in the Longshan area jade may have been less abundant than further south in the regions dominated by the Liangzhu. A number of fine carvings in collections may be further examples of this Longshan tradition (Rawson, fig. 12a), but more scientifically excavated pieces are required for comparison in order to confirm the provenance of such pieces.

Published: *Kaogu* 1990.7, pp. 587–94, pl. 2: 1, 2; Beijing 1992b, no. 60.

1 For discussion of the Longshan culture see Chang Kwang-chih 1986a, pp. 245–67.
2 Chang Kwang-chih 1986a, p. 254, fig. 211.

The sacrificial pits at Sanxingdui

The discovery in 1986, in Guanghan county in Sichuan province, of two large pits containing bronzes in the shape of human heads, fragments of gold, many jades and a large number of elephant tusks was probably the most startling archaeological find of the decade.[1] The contents were unique: nothing like them had ever been found in China before. Moreover, some of the bronzes, especially the complete figure (no. 22), some of the human-like heads (nos 23, 24) and several extraordinary masks (no. 25) were of a quality which indicated that their makers had great technical skill and worked within a complex society. Yet nothing is known about the peoples who lived in this area during the latter part of the second millennium BC, and for this reason their artefacts are included under the heading 'Unknown China'. It is clear, however, from the artefacts that their makers were contemporaries of the great Shang dynasty centred at Anyang in Henan province (c. 1300–1050 BC), whose ritual bronzes and jades are illustrated in the next part of the catalogue. But we do not know what form their relationship with the Shang took – did these peoples develop bronze vessels and jades similar to those used in Henan through trade, war or via intermediaries in Hunan or Hubei?

While some sort of contact with the Shang cultures of Henan is indicated by the use of bronze and jade and by the shapes of a number of the artefacts, especially the ceramic and bronze vessels, the range and type of items found in the sacrificial pits belonged to a culture whose beliefs and practices must have been quite unlike anything known to date. Neither the neolithic peoples discussed above, nor the Shang who built up a state in Henan described below, made massive images of priests or deities in human-like form. A society that made human-like figures with large quantities of bronze must have visualised them set within their own religious and intellectual worlds. Moreover, so sophisticated are the figures from Sanxingdui that these cannot be the tentative beginnings of a culture using bronze and jade for the first time in the service of religious belief. These finds must have a long history behind them. But as yet we have no way of establishing what this history was.

For although these people lived at a time when the Shang peoples at the city of Anyang were already writing, and when states such as that of the Shang must have been conscious of other powers with the capacity to make bronze weapons, no direct mention of the peoples of Sanxingdui has come down to us. Nor are they known from later writings. So far the archaeological remains are our only source for studying what must have been an unusual, not to say remarkable, group of people.

The two main pits were found within the remains of a massive city wall at Sanxingdui, which enclosed an area of about 12 square km (Zhao, fig. 1). The wall itself implies the need for defence; jade versions of weapons found in the pit also suggest that warfare was a major preoccupation if it were thus incorporated into ceremonial life. The expenditure of bronze was truly remarkable; the largest complete figure (no. 22) found in pit 2 weighs over 180 kg. The forty heads similar to the head of the complete figure indicate that a large number of images, though not necessarily all of bronze, existed simultaneously.

Moreover, the heads were found together with a completely different kind of face in the form of a large mask with enormous ears and strange projecting eyes (no. 25). Such complex images suggest an equally complex system of beliefs. To this system belonged also the use of jade, gold and elephant tusks (Zhao, figs 2–4). Other mysterious objects in the pits are fragments of trees in bronze (Introduction, fig. 8). These consist of long hollow tubes supporting curved branches, with small sprigs of bronze suggesting leaves and fruits, on which perch small birds. Again these trees with their birds are unlike anything known in other parts of China at this early date. To compound the mystery, the pits were not packed with random debris but had been ceremonially filled with objects that were already deliberately broken and burned.

1 For further discussion of the find see the essay by Zhao Dianzeng and Bagley 1988, Bagley 1990.

22 Standing figure

c. 1200–1000 BC
Bronze
Overall height 262 cm; height of figure 172 cm; weight 180 kg
Excavated in 1986 from pit 2, Sanxingdui, Guanghan county, Sichuan province (K2,2: 149–50)
Institute of Archaeology and Cultural Relics Bureau, Sichuan province

This standing, life-size figure is the single most remarkable Chinese archaeological find made in the last decade. It demonstrates that the peoples of western China used bronze

Fig. 22.1 *Miniature bronze figures with large hands from Shaanxi Baoji Rujiazhuang. Middle Western Zhou period, c. 900 BC. After Lu Liancheng and Hu Zhisheng 1988, p. 315, fig. 221; p. 375, fig. 257.*

figural sculpture on a massive scale. The figure cannot have existed in isolation, and the fifty or so heads found in the two main sacrificial pits probably also belonged to large figures whose bodies may, however, have been made of less precious materials.[1] We have no means of ascertaining at present whom the figures represented. Were they deities, ancestors, priests or shamans – or other figures whose roles we cannot even imagine?

The force and austerity of the human-like figure are very striking. Strong features and simple forms contribute to this impression. The figure is extremely narrow in proportion to its height, with a relatively large head and massive arms and hands. A pair of huge slanting eyes dominates the face, with large brows above and a deep sunken groove below them. The nose is fairly broad, with strongly curved nostrils; a large mouth has thin, tightly drawn lips. A sharply defined chin is mirrored by the strong horizontal line of the hat or headdress. This headdress consists of a headband with incised oval motifs, crowned by a section that flares outwards and is also decorated with intaglio lines.

The most striking feature is the pair of immense hands, each one coiled to create a circle at the ends of the two long uplifted arms. These hands must have been made to hold something. As their circumference is greatly exaggerated, presumably they held something massive, and as they are not set in a straight line, they may have held a curved piece like an elephant's tusk (Introduction, fig. 6). Whatever was in these hands must have been central to the role of the figure, and once we know what the object was, we will have a better understanding of what the figure represented.[2] The only other comparable bronzes are miniature figures from Western Zhou tombs of *c.* 900 BC, at Shaanxi Baoji Rujiazhuang

Fig. 22.3 *Detail of the base.*

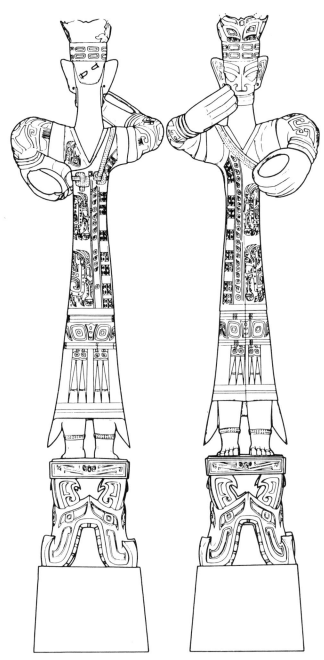

Fig. 22.2 *Drawings of the figure showing details of the dress.*

(fig. 22.1), which may imitate much larger pieces. The western part of Shaanxi was indeed in contact with Sichuan province by way of the passes over the Qinling mountains, but if there is some sort of link between the enormous figures of Sichuan and the miniature ones of Shaanxi, it is likely that both played very different roles and had different significances for their users.[3]

The dress of the present figure is remarkable for the suggestion of fine embroidered patterns on it (fig. 22.2). There seem to be three garments, whose layers can be seen at the neck and sleeves. The outer garment leaves the left shoulder

free and has a short sleeve on the right and thus reveals the ones below it. On one half of the outer garment are patterns of dragons, while on the other are heads in a transverse position; on the lower part is a design of eyes. The middle garment has a triangular neck opening and two short sleeves. The undergarment has long sleeves. It is shorter at the front than the back and ends in two swallow-like tails at the bottom. The figure also wears tight leg garments, terminating in a decorated band at the ankle, and he is barefoot, perhaps because he is represented as being in a temple or palace building where shoes were not worn.[4]

A square base supported by four elephants' heads raises the figure to a dramatic dominating position (fig. 22.3). Each elephant head faces a corner, with its trunk curled up at the bottom.[5] Their eyes slant and the creatures have very small ears. These faces are in openwork, but below them is a further section of base with solid sloping sides, which may have been dug into a platform or the ground.

The figure had been deliberately broken at the waist before burial in pit 2. The torso lay in the middle section of pit 2, while the lower part was in the north-west section. The base was put into the pit separately.

There is some debate as to how the figure was made. It seems, however, to have been made in sections. The arms were probably cast first and then inserted into the mould for the body. Thus the body was cast onto them. The main torso is said to consist of four sections.[6]

Published: *Wenwu* 1987.10, pp. 16–17; *Wenwu* 1989.5, pp. 1–20; Beijing 1990a, no. 30; Beijing 1992a, no. 131; Beijing 1994b, pls 1–4; Goepper 1995, no. 37.

1 Bagley 1988; Bagley 1990.

2 The question of what the figure held has been much discussed by Chinese scholars. The most traditional view is that the object was a jade *cong* (see no. 16). However, even a very large tall jade example would require the hands to be set in a straight line (*Wenwu* 1987.10, pp. 16–17). The suggestion that the object may have been an elephant tusk has been made by Noel Barnard (1990, p. 256). Qian Yuzhi has argued that the figure held a two-part tube-like container of wood or bamboo called a spirit tube (*shen tong*). This argument depends upon relating the figure and its attributes to the present-day minority Yi people who inhabit south-western China (Qian Yuzhi 1992). It seems very unwise to draw any firm conclusion from such tenuous evidence.

3 For a description of the tombs at Shaanxi Baoji Rujiazhuang, see Lu Liancheng and Hu Zhisheng 1988.

4 For a discussion of the dress, see *Wenwu* 1993.9, pp. 60–8. The complex and highly decorated dress obviously indicated the status and role of the figure.

5 Elephants were popular in the bronze cultures of southern China (Bagley 1987, introduction, pp. 35–6). They were also employed in early Western Zhou bronze design, as seen in a *fang ding* from Shandong Jiyang (*Wenwu* 1994.3, p. 75, inside cover).

6 Barnard 1990, pp. 255–7.

23 Human-like head

c. 1200–1000 BC
Bronze with applied gold leaf
Height 48.5 cm
Excavated in 1986 from pit 2, Sanxingdui, Guanghan county, Sichuan province (K2,2: 214)
Institute of Archaeology and Cultural Relics Bureau, Sichuan province

This bronze head is one of two with gold leaf from among the forty-one heads found in pit 2 at Sanxingdui.[1] The gold leaf has not been applied to the large slanting eyes and brows, thereby emphasising them, but it was obviously intended to cover the rest of the face.[2] The remaining gold now lies over the forehead below a curved line (which might suggest a cap, or some other sort of headgear), over the ears, the cheeks and lips, and it must originally also have reached the bottom of the chin. From the side view, it is evident that the gold is bounded by a double line drawn to a point above and behind the ears (fig. 23.1).

The features of this head are very like those of the large complete figure (no. 22) and include a short nose with coiled nostrils and a very broad, thin-lipped mouth. The ears stick out at right angles to the head and are pierced at the bottom,

Fig. 23.1 *Side view of head.*

Fig. 23.2 *Back view of head.*

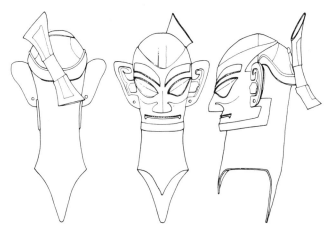

Fig. 23.3 *Drawing of a comparable head from pit 2. After* Wenwu *1989.5, p. 6, fig. 10.*

as if earrings were originally inserted in them. Within the ears are two relief cusps, a schematic rendering of the inner hollows. A sharp right-angled ridge bends back behind the ears, extending the line of the jaw. Around the lower part of the rear of the head is a slightly projecting flange that might represent some part of a close-fitting cap (fig. 23.2). There are two holes in the upper part of the back of the head, as though some further element of headgear was inserted here. Another figure from pit 2 seems to have a more elaborate form of this headgear, with an additional section attached at the back of the head (fig. 23.3).

Like many of the other heads, this one has a rather long neck, which is cut to points front and back. It is possible either that this head was part of a more complete figure in bronze, or that it and others were mounted on bodies of some different material. The archaeologists report traces of clay inside the heads that do not seem to have been part of the original casting core.

The fifty-four heads found in the two pits seem to belong to two quite distinctive categories. This present head and the one described in the next entry are typical of the heads found in pit 2. These generally have rather strongly slanting eyes and high cheekbones that give a somewhat surreal impression. In addition they wear distinctive headgear or have unusual hairstyles. The head illustrated in the next entry appears to wear a pleated textile in his headdress, some have a twisted coil of cloth or hair around their heads, and others wear flat-topped caps, which may have had a flared top like that worn by the complete figure (no. 22). The heads from pit 1, on the other hand, are much more realistic, with softer lines to their faces and less schematic and uniform features.

Published: Beijing 1994b, pls 23, 24; Goepper 1995, no. 39.

1 Thirteen heads were recovered from pit 1 (*Wenwu* 1987.10, pp. 1–15). For the second head with applied gold leaf see Beijing 1994b, pls 21, 22.

2 For a study of the application of gold leaf see Sichuan 1992, pp. 93–6.

24 Human-like head

c. 1200–1000 BC
Bronze
Height 36.7 cm
Excavated in 1986 from pit 2, Sanxingdui, Guanghan county, Sichuan province (K2,2: 34)
Institute of Archaeology and Cultural Relics Bureau, Sichuan province

This head, like the previous one, belongs to the category of human-like images with strong, rather schematic features. This is the predominant type among the forty-one heads found in pit 2 at Sanxingdui. Like the previous head and many of the other surviving examples, it has a long neck, drawn to points front and back, and may have been fitted to a body of some other material. It shares the principal features of this type of head, namely large slanting eyes, heavy rough brows, a broad nose with curled nostrils, and a wide horizontal mouth with thin lips. The ears project at right angles to the head and have large sunken scrolls indicating the hollows. As on the other pieces, the ears are pierced for earrings or other ornaments. Both the chin and the top of the head are very flat. Also, as on the previous example, the jaw line runs up behind the ear.

The headdress, on the other hand, is quite different from that of the previous head. Seen from the rear, the figure has some sort of flat cap, which is drawn into a horizontal band behind the head. Below that is a large plait (fig. 24.1). It is not clear whether this plait is of cloth or hair, or perhaps a

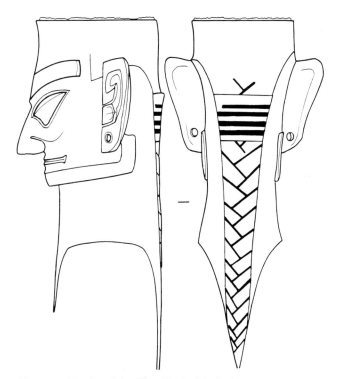

Fig. 24.1 *Drawing of the side and back of the head.*

24

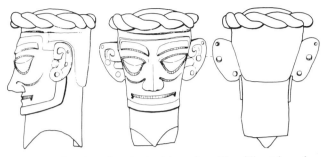

Fig. 24.2 *Drawings of another head from pit 2 with a different form of headgear. After* Wenwu *1989.5, p. 7, fig. 11.*

25 Mask with ornamented forehead and protruding pupils

c. 1200–1000 BC
Bronze
Overall height 82.6 cm; width 77 cm; weight 17 kg
Excavated in 1986 from pit 2, Sanxingdui, Guanghan county, Sichuan province (K2,2: 142)
Institute of Archaeology and Cultural Relics Bureau, Sichuan province

combination of both. There are several examples of this style of headdress. Other notable examples have a rolled turban around the head, or a cap like that on the large complete figure (fig. 24.2).

The bronze heads in pit 2 were almost all placed around the edge of the pit, and many had been deliberately damaged and burned before being interred. There are traces of paint on quite a number of them, including black on the hair and brows and a reddish colour on the lips. Cowrie shells were inserted into a number of the heads, further evidence that the pits contained some sort of ceremonial offering or sacrifice.

Published: *Wenwu* 1989.5, p. 5, fig. 8 and pl. 2: 1; Beijing 1994b, pl. 10; Goepper 1995, no. 40.

Three large masks were found in pit 2 at Sanxingdui. The term mask is used deliberately, as, unlike the heads just discussed, these faces were not complete in themselves. They lack a back and, with rectangular holes in their sides, must have been attached to part of a building or a clay body of some sort (fig. 25.1).

They are much more grotesque than the human-like faces, although they share some of their features, such as the broad, tight-lipped mouths. In other major respects they are quite different. In the first place they are on a much greater scale, the largest mask measuring 134 cm in width (Zhao, fig. 5).[1] They are also much wider than they are high, with a horizontal emphasis given by their large projecting ears. The ears of the present mask are drawn to sharp tips, and they enclose small bands of relief to suggest their hollows. As with the human faces and the elephants on the stand of the complete figure (no. 22), the slant of the eyes is pronounced and the

Fig. 25.1 *Side view of mask.*

Fig. 25.2 *Rear view of mask.*

Fig. 25.3 *Drawing of a mask with human-like features. After* Wenwu *1989.5, p. 9, fig. 14.*

deep sunken grooves below them seem to indicate cheek-bones. But the most startling features are the pupils of the eyes, which project on stalks and seem to have been cast first and then inserted into the mould for the whole face, thus being fixed into position by the second casting (fig. 25.2).[2]

A further remarkable feature is the long upstanding projection rising from the nose of the mask. This projection is scroll-shaped, with an upright section coiled at the top and with a double loop at the bottom. In between is a cusped, quill-shaped projection that resembles the cusps which ornament the dragons on the clothes of the large figure. The combination of the large ears, the protruding eyes and the tall quill makes this face completely fantastic. These features must have contributed to some specific representation, but we cannot, from the evidence available at present, reconstruct what that might have been.

Some masks from the pits combine the u-shaped structure of the present fantastic piece with the more human-like facial

features of the two faces described above (fig. 25.3). There thus seem to be not just two, but three or four slightly over-lapping categories of image or representation.[3]

Published: Beijing 1994b, pl. 30; Goepper 1995, no. 38.

1 Beijing 1994b, pls 27–35.
2 Chinese scholars have sought explanations for the protruding pupils in much later literary texts, citing passages in the Han period *Shan hai jing* and the *Huayang guozhi*, composed about AD 350. Mythical creatures are there referred to as having 'protruding eyes' (*zongmu* or *zhimu*), a feature attributed also to the legendary first ruler of the state of Shu in Sichuan. He had the name of Cancong, and it is said that his 'eyes protruded vertic-ally'. These later notions linking the mask to the legendary history of the state of Shu in Sichuan depend, of course, on the term *zongmu* being under-stood as 'protruding eyes', an interpretation which has been disputed (Barnard 1990, pp. 257–8).
3 Beijing 1994b, pls 31–5.

26 Animal mask

c. 1200–1000 BC
Bronze
Height 20 cm; width 23.5 cm
Excavated in 1986 from pit 2, Sanxingdui, Guanghan county, Sichuan province (K2,3: 227)
Institute of Archaeology and Cultural Relics Bureau, Sichuan province

Several small, bronze, animal-like faces measuring about 20 cm in height were found in pit 2 at Sanxingdui. These display small differences in detail and in proportion. They

◀ 25

26

appear to be a local variant on the animal face, known as a *taotie*, employed as decoration on ritual vessels in Henan province and copied on bronze vessels made elsewhere, including the vessels from Sanxingdui itself (nos 27, 28). As these plaques are plain or slightly hollow on the back and have small holes for attachment, they must have been fitted to some other object.

The present face has two slightly bulging eyes above a narrow but wide mouth filled with teeth. At the top are coiled horns which arise from the brows and have a central spine of relief. Below the jaw is a pair of what look like eyes, rising to sharp tips with the corners turned down at the centre. A sharp central ridge divides the face at the nose.

Although this face bears a general resemblance to the Shang *taotie*, it is quite different in general form and detail from the *taotie* on the ritual vessels from Sanxingdui. As seen at entry no. 27, a large *lei* bears a typical *taotie* of the type used on ritual vessels in the metropolitan Shang area. While this design, as discussed in the entry, shows some very clear deviations from the traditional forms, it is none the less directly recognisable as being a local version of the metropolitan motif, possibly transmitted by way of Hunan province. The present plaque presents a face with rather different proportions. Its principal features, eyes, horns, nose and jaw, are generally similar to those of the *taotie*, but the detailed form and the surface embellishment seem specific to Sanxingdui and are unlike anything seen at the main Shang sites in Henan province. The face is also unlike the design on the *lei* (no. 27). Even if the sources of the two motifs were the same, the two versions of the face design employed at Sanxingdui probably had different functions and meanings.

Published: Beijing 1994b, pl. 38; Goepper 1995, no. 41.

27 Vessel, *lei*

c. 1200–1000 BC
Bronze
Height 54.5 cm; diameter of opening 26 cm
Excavated in 1986 from pit 2, Sanxingdui, Guanghan county, Sichuan province (K2,2:158)
Institute of Archaeology and Cultural Relics Bureau, Sichuan province

This bronze container is further evidence of the impact of metropolitan Shang practices on the western province of Sichuan. The Shang made considerable use of food and wine containers of bronze for offering food to their ancestors (nos 39–45). Such bronze vessels were quite widely used during the Erligang period (*c.* 1500–1300 BC) in many parts of what is today China (Zheng, figs 6–9). After the Erligang period, little, if any, use was made of the full range of bronze containers in areas such as Sichuan, Hunan and further east in Jiangxi province. It appears that different groups of people

employed them selectively.[1] In Jiangxi province, for example, tripods, known as *ding*, were extremely popular. In Hunan and Sichuan, on the other hand, almost the only vessels in use were wine jars, such as this one, known as a *lei*, and a jar with a wide trumpet neck called a *zun* (no. 28).

The variation in vessel types indicates that the ceremonies performed with them differed from area to area. If many types of container were available, then a number of functions could be fulfilled. This would simply not have been possible with only one or two types of container. Indeed, we do not know whether the bronzes found in Sichuan province were employed for wine offerings at all, or whether offerings were even made to ancestors. It does not seem likely that the same religious rites were practised in Sichuan as in Henan. Cowrie shells in the containers in the pits at Sanxingdui suggest that the functions of the vessels were almost certainly different from those used in Henan. The practice of filling bronzes with precious materials, including jade beads and cowries, seems to have been developed in the south and to have been adopted by the peoples of Hunan and the later inhabitants of Yunnan.[2] Such bronzes were perhaps precious containers rather than sumptuous banqueting utensils. Or perhaps they fulfilled both functions.

Not only were the functions of such bronzes peculiar to southern China, but the shapes and decorative details also vary considerably from their Henan counterparts. The present shape is derived from a vessel type particularly common in the Erligang period in Henan and much less used at Anyang (Zheng, fig. 7).[3] This vessel type generally has, as here, a relatively short neck, a slightly rounded body and a tall foot. The body and the foot are divided vertically by four pairs of flanges. The hooked profile of the flanges on this *lei* were copied from early bronze vessels made at Erligang and were not typical of Shang casting at Anyang. A notable southern feature is the use of bold three-dimensional animal heads on the shoulders, alternating with small fin-like birds. Almost identical combinations are seen on *lei* from Yueyang in Hunan province (Zheng, fig. 8). It seems probable that the peoples from Sichuan and Hunan copied their bronze vessels from a common source.[4]

As mentioned in the previous entry, this vessel and the next one are decorated around the belly and the foot with animal faces of the type that later historians have called *taotie*. We have no idea what the motif was called or to what it referred in its own day. It is likely that if the motif had specific references or meanings in Henan, it had completely different ones in the south-west, where the peoples patently developed quite different societies and beliefs.[5] In all areas where such motifs were employed, the creatures have the standard features of a central, vertical nose, with symmetrically arranged horns, eyes, jaws and claws. On either side is a residual tail. The *taotie* on the footring has tall upstanding ear-shaped horns

of a type particularly common on southern bronzes. The designs are so set out that the features of the faces appear in a sea of small spirals or *leiwen*. Face motifs on a ground of spirals are typical of the mainstream of Shang casting in Henan province (Rawson, fig. 6). In this instance, a motif and its decorative style from another region have been copied reasonably accurately by the peoples of Guanghan Sanxingdui. Such care in reproducing an original design from elsewhere is quite unlike the independence shown by the bronze casting described in the other entries: the figures, masks and strange fittings (nos 22–26). With this vessel the peoples of Sichuan have borrowed an exotic item and reused it with little significant change to its form and decoration. In the case of the animal mask discussed at entry no. 26, a related exotic design has been borrowed and completely integrated by the borrowing society.

Published: Beijing 1994b, pls 68, 69; Goepper 1995, no. 42.

1 For a discussion of the uses of ritual vessels and the ways in which they were exploited in the separate regions of China see the essay by Rawson.
2 Jades have been found in bronze vessels discovered in southern China: see Bagley 1987, no. 64 and fig. 64.2, who illustrates a *you* from Hunan Ningxiang (*Kaogu* 1963.12, pp. 646–7, figs 1, 2). Many of the large drum-shaped bronzes of a much later date from Yunnan province were employed in burial for holding cowries (Rawson 1983b).
3 For a discussion of the *lei* form see Bagley 1987, no. 1.
4 For a discussion of fin-like birds see Rawson 1983a; Bagley 1987, pp. 30–2.
5 The *taotie* is described in the essay by Rawson, see fig. 6, and also in Whitfield 1993.

28 Vessel, *zun*

c. 1200–1000 BC
Bronze
Height 45.5 cm; diameter of opening 43.5 cm
Excavated in 1986 from pit 2, Sanxingdui, Guanghan county, Sichuan province (K2,2:129)
Institute of Archaeology and Cultural Relics Bureau, Sichuan province

This second container, known as a *zun*, belongs to the other major category of bronze vessel employed in southern China, especially in Hunan province. It has a large trumpet-shaped neck, a short rounded body and a tall sloping foot. On the shoulders are three rams' heads with coiled horns alternating with fin-like birds similar to those seen on the previous vessel. Three pairs of flanges divide the body and footring vertically and, like the flanges on the previous vessel, they have a hooked profile.[1]

Although there is some resemblance between the *taotie* on the body and foot of this bronze and those on the previous one, the faces seen here are somewhat more bizarre than those on no. 27. In the upper register, around the body, the focus of the motif is the pair of rounded pupils in the eyes either side of the central vertical nose. Above the eyes are

very heavy brows and vertical leaf-shaped horns. On either side horizontal bands, which are derived from the sections of design normally used to indicate a *taotie*'s body, run from the middle of the horns. In other words, the original design has been misunderstood and the body section is here used as some sort of filler motif. Additional bands of relief fill the edges of the field. Unlike the previous vessel, here the designs are shown as consisting of solid sections of relief against a spiral ground, rather than a series of discrete and separate elements. The vessel is very like large *zun* employed in Hunan province (fig. 28.1), and was probably copied from such southern provincial versions of mainstream Shang casting.

If the casters of Sichuan and Hunan had sufficient knowledge of Henan or Anyang casting to produce the types of vessel of which the present two examples are typical, they must have had considerable familiarity with the bronzes of peoples from adjacent areas. These two vessels show, for example, that the peoples of Sichuan were familiar with bronzes made in either Henan or Hunan over the period of the late Erligang and Anyang stages of Shang culture (*c.* 1500–1200 BC). In addition, they must have had more than one model, as the differences in the details of the *taotie* motifs suggest that at least several were available.

In this context it is noteworthy that the peoples of western and southern regions limited their interests to these two

Fig. 28.1 Zun *from Hunan Huarong. Shang period but made in southern China. Height 72.3 cm. After Li Xueqin 1985c, no. 108.*

29

vessel types, the *lei* and the *zun*. Their concentration on the two wine containers and their indifference to such vessels as tripods and smaller wine cups suggest that they had no use for these other types. They did not, it would seem, perform the rituals that would have justified the full range of ritual vessels. If we are to understand the cultural currents in China of the period before 1000 BC, it is necessary to consider what such distinctions suggest. Above all they indicate that the possessions and thus the roles of the élite in different areas of the landmass of China were quite distinct. Such distinctions imply not just different practices but also different beliefs. And different beliefs point in turn to very different societies.

The extraordinary figures and masks employed by the peoples of Sanxingdui certainly suggest that the practices and beliefs of the peoples of this region differed sharply from those of the peoples inhabiting the better known centres of Chinese culture in Henan province. Even shared items, such as these two bronze ritual vessels, indicate profound differences between the cultures of Henan and Sichuan. As discussed in the Introduction, these differences give us a very new picture of the diversity of ancient China.

Published: Beijing 1994b, pl. 90; Goepper 1995, no. 43.

1 For a discussion of provincial forms of *zun* see Bagley 1987, no. 43.

29 Bird's head

c. 1200–1000 BC
Bronze with traces of pigment
Height 43.3 cm
Excavated in 1986 from pit 2, Sanxingdui, Guanghan county, Sichuan province (K2,2: 141)
Institute of Archaeology and Cultural Relics Bureau, Sichuan province

This magnificent bronze portrays a bird's head. It is a large hollow casting in three dimensions. An enormous eye almost fills the head and, like the complete figure and the human heads (nos 22–24), it is typified by strongly moulded forms. A steeply sloping frame encircles the eye, and this continues into the neck, being divided from the beak by a small comma-shaped intaglio line. The hooked beak is marked again by a pronounced sunken line. A shallow crest runs over the top of the head, ending behind it in a hook. Small holes for attachment are sited at the base of the neck, suggesting that the head was fitted to something in wood or clay.

This large head resembles those of other birds found in pit 2 at Sanxingdui. Among these are a small bell in the shape of a bird (fig. 29.1) and the birds on the three bronze trees found in fragments in the pits (Zhao, fig. 6). These birds, all with their pronounced, hooked beaks, seem characteristic of the workmanship of this area, as they are not found among

Fig. 29.1 *Bell in the shape of a bird, from pit 2. After Beijing 1994b, pl. 61.*

peoples in Sichuan at that time shared a language and a set of beliefs with the peoples of Henan. It would indeed be dangerous to assume that they did. The bird is thus likely to belong to a miraculous world that so far we know only from the bronzes at Sanxingdui.

Published: Beijing 1994b, pl. 47; Goepper 1995, no. 45.

1 For a discussion of the possible origin of these myths in the Shang period see Allan 1991, chapter 2.

30 Imaginary being

c. 1200–1000 BC
Bronze
Height 12 cm
Excavated in 1986 from pit 2, Sanxingdui, Guanghan county, Sichuan province (K2,3: 154)
Institute of Archaeology and Cultural Relics Bureau, Sichuan province

This small bronze figure represents some sort of imaginary being with a crowned human-like head. Its eyes are heavily

the bronzes of the Shang peoples at Erligang or Anyang in Henan province. One of the major bird types represented there was the owl, with a broad, rather rounded beak. The present bird is paralleled in the handle of a piece from Anyang, namely a very precious ivory beaker from the tomb of Fu Hao (no. 47). Is it possible that the ivory cup was made with reference to such southern birds? At present we do not know, but the resemblance is tantalising.

We have no way of knowing what the bird signified to the peoples of Sanxingdui. However, from the existence of the large bronze trees decorated with birds, we can infer that such birds played an important role in the ceremonial and religious worlds of the peoples of the area. Perhaps the birds represented gods, or were spirits who protected particular groups of people, or were elements in the landscape of a spiritual realm. For the use of trees in a precious material, namely bronze, seems to imply a wish to depict some sort of non-material world outside the usual one of humans, for the trees of this world are made of wood not bronze. In the mythologies of later China, birds figure among the sun legends. However, there is little firm evidence to date that the early Chinese-speaking peoples of Henan shared these later beliefs.[1] We have even fewer grounds for thinking that the

rimmed, rather like the eyes of the large bird just described, and it has a slightly beaked nose. Its mouth, on the other hand, resembles those of the large heads and masks discussed above (nos 23–26). The crown consists of large upward-sloping hooked bands. The rest of the creature is bird-like. A rounded breast carries deep scrolls that are repeated at the wings, of which only one large double hook remains. Intaglio scrolls embellish claws that bend inwards and grasp a petal-like support, which terminates in a tube.

This small tube was inserted into the upper part of one of the three bronze sacred trees discovered in pit 2 (Introduction, fig. 8). As already mentioned, the making of large and highly complex trees, on which perch birds in bronze, suggests that such images were extremely important to their makers.[1] While it is possible that these images were the focus of worship, it is also likely that they were part of the depiction of an imaginary or spiritual landscape. This small imaginary being reinforces the impression that we are here dealing not with the real world, but with an invisible spiritual realm.

Although some Chinese scholars have interpreted the trees and their birds with reference to texts of nearly a thousand years later, this seems an unfounded approach. It is more likely that we shall gain understanding of the trees and birds and their meanings from discovering other objects that provide a fuller context of the surroundings in which they were placed, and hence of the type of religious or royal context in which they were used.

Published: Beijing 1994b, pl. 45; Goepper 1995, no. 46.

1 The large sacred tree *(shenshu)*, recently reconstructed from its individual parts by the Institute of Archaeology in Sichuan, is about 4 m high. It has nine curving branches, as if swinging in the wind, on each of which sits a bird. If the bird on the top of the tree is included, this makes a total of ten birds. Fruit, figures of immortals *(xianren)*, a dragon and possibly small bells were also fixed to it. All interpretations by Chinese scholars of these trees are based upon much later texts. For such discussions see Sichuan 1989, pp. 65–8.

31 Mounting in the form of a wheel

c. 1200–1000 BC
Bronze
Diameter 85 cm
Excavated in 1986 from pit 2, Sanxingdui, Guanghan county, Sichuan province (K2,3: 1)
Institute of Archaeology and Cultural Relics Bureau, Sichuan province

The present bronze and the three pieces in the next catalogue entry are among the most enigmatic objects found in the pits at Sanxingdui. Four of the present wheel-shaped objects came to light in pit 2. They are all hollow on the rear and relatively thin, indicating that they must have been mounted on a building or an object such as a shield. Five spokes emerge from a rounded, almost bulbous centre, which has been identified both as the pupil of an eye and the centre of the sun. Each spoke is raised to a centre rib and indented slightly before it meets the centre disc. If this disc was intended to be the sun, the spokes would be the sun's rays. However, none of the present interpretations is convincing.

Our lack of understanding of what the piece was used for is a major barrier to our understanding of what the bronze is. Understanding the meaning of an object is in very large part dependent on understanding its function. One possibility is that the bronze was part of the ornament of a ceremonial building. If this were the case it is probable that it had some symbolic purpose, referring to a major force such as the sun, or it may have been one element in a system of decor that gave the piece status and mystery, without having a single meaning but carrying a range of associations. In a similar way the gargoyles on the roofs of European medieval buildings do not have single meanings, but carry several associations including those of the buildings they are on. If, on the other hand, the bronze was attached to a shield or some other object it would have had a different range of references and meanings. If the shield were ceremonial rather than functional, then the references would again have been different.

While the animal masks (no. 26) and the two vessels (nos 27, 28) indicate some contact with Henan, the large figure and heads (nos 22–24) and the present fitting, with those that follow (no. 32), demonstrate that here was a people with a material and intellectual culture quite unlike anything hitherto discovered in China.

Published: Beijing 1994b, pl. 56; Goepper 1995, no. 44.

31

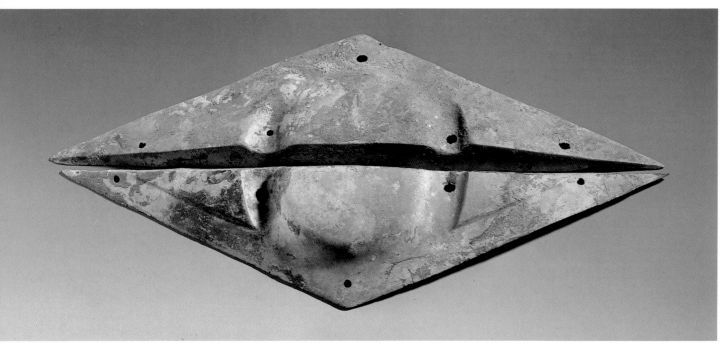

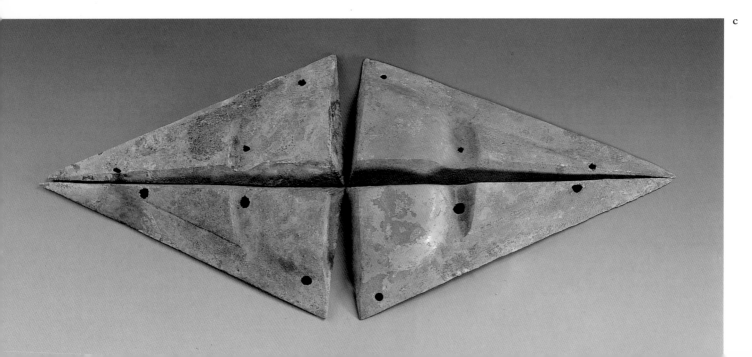

32 Three diamond-shaped fittings

c. 1200–1000 BC
Bronze

a Single-part form
Length 76.3 cm; height 23.7 cm (K2,3: 158)

b Two-part form
Length 54.5 and 55 cm; height 12.7 and 13.2 cm (K2,2: 8 and 158)

c Four-part form
Length 27.5 to 29.3 cm; height 12.2 to 13 cm (K2,3.8, 98, 101 and 106)

Excavated in 1986 from pit 2, Sanxingdui, Guanghan county, Sichuan province
Institute of Archaeology and Cultural Relics Bureau, Sichuan province

Like the wheel-shaped bronze, these three fittings are thinly cast and hollow on the rear. Perhaps they too were for display on a ceremonial building or on a wooden shield or implement. About thirty examples of this type of casting have come from pit 2.

The archaeologists involved in the excavations have suggested that these fittings may depict eyes. They are all diamond-shaped, with raised circular centres, and triangular ends filled with relief. A most perplexing feature is the way in which these diamond-shaped fittings are divided into sections. Thus, of the three displayed here, the first is a complete diamond, the second is cast as two separate portions and the third as four. All of the pieces have small holes for attachment to another surface or part of a building.

In addition to the present pieces, there are about twenty examples of a smaller type of eye with large pupils and narrower surrounds ending in a hook. It is noteworthy that if these fittings are indeed eyes, then they are quite unlike the eyes of the main human-like figures discussed above.

Published: Beijing 1994b, pl. 57; Goepper 1995, no. 47.

33 Ceremonial dagger axe, *ge*

c. 1200–1000 BC
Jade
Length 59.5 cm; width 8.4 cm; thickness 0.7 cm
Excavated in 1986 from pit 2, Sanxingdui, Guanghan county, Sichuan province (K2,3: 157)
Institute of Archaeology and Cultural Relics Bureau, Sichuan province

A very large number of jade items was found in the two main sacrificial pits at Sanxingdui. Many of them were fine blades carved from thin slabs of the stone. Among such blades, *ge* formed a significant group. The present piece has a long pointed blade with an extended tip that turns slightly at an angle to the main blade. It has a ridge at one end produced by the

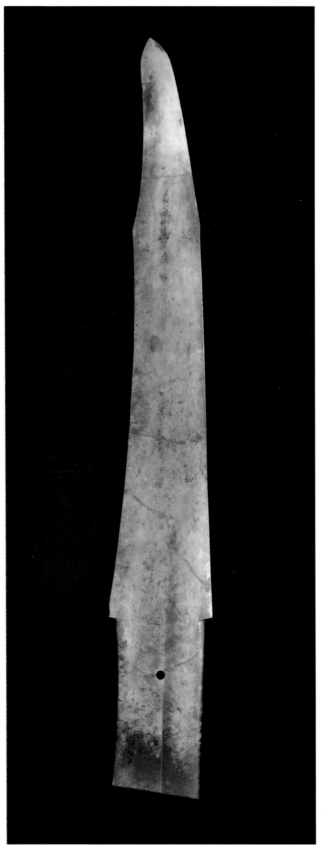

33

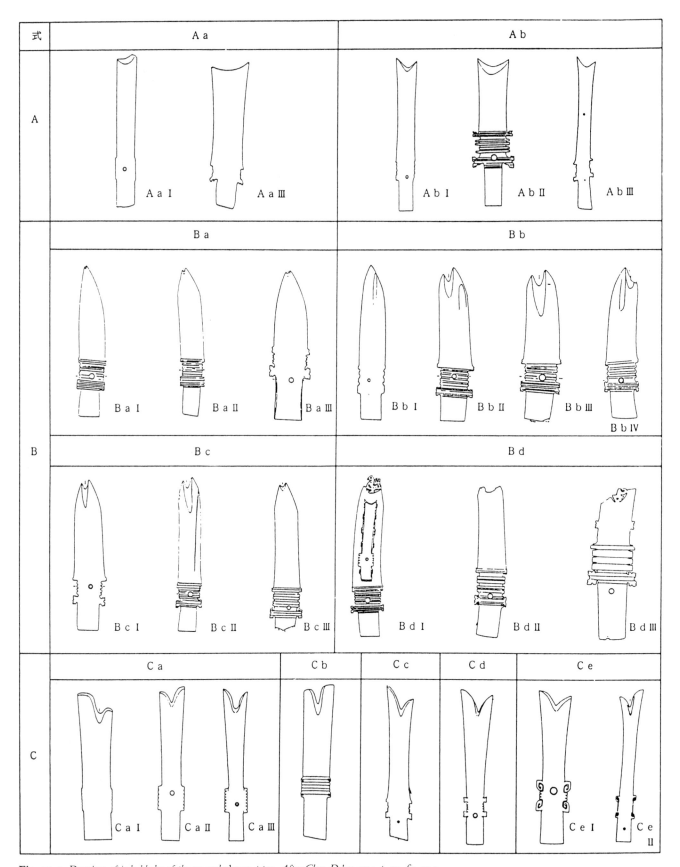

Fig. 33.1 *Drawings of jade blades of the* ge *and* zhang *types. After Chen De'an 1994, p. 92, fig. 13-1.*

methods used to cut the original block and there is a single hole in the tang. The stone is a mottled grey white colour.

Jade blades have a long history, beginning with the axes and reaping knives of the neolithic period. These originally utilitarian tools were worked in ever more ceremonial versions. Their non-functional character was highlighted by the use of a fine material, that is jade, rather than ordinary stone. This was then worked so thinly that the tool would have snapped if used, and the holes in the blade for attaching it to a handle were insufficient for practical use.[1]

The present dagger axe belongs to a later tradition. In the early bronze-using stage of the Erlitou culture in Henan province (c. 1700 BC), dagger-like weapons were made in bronze. As the Erlitou peoples already used other types of jade blade, a practice they had borrowed from their neolithic predecessors, they seem to have been inspired to copy this bronze weapon type in jade. In actual combat, a jade blade was obviously far less useful than a bronze one. Its value must have lain in other properties, such as the display of power through command of the resources needed to make such weapons – material and manpower. This jade weapon probably also referred to both real and symbolic weapons, to military power and to the authority of those who could own jade in place of bronze. It is also possible that jade was seen as spiritually or materially more enduring, as the pits at Sanxingdui, clearly filled with precious items, contain jade but not bronze weapons.

The jade *ge* shape was taken over by the inhabitants of Sanxingdui from the Erlitou or early Shang peoples. However, the range of blades found in the pits is unorthodox, if the shapes of *ge* current in Henan are taken as the norm. Some *ge* were hybrids. The original shape, copied from a bronze weapon, was modified by reference to other jade types, including the blades described in the next entry. Some of the *ge* have notched sides similar to those found generally on the blades with curved ends. One or two pieces are yet

more unusual: a small bird sits in the curved mouth of a fish, whose outline is suggested by the shape of one of the blades (fig. 33.1).

The range and number of blades found at Sanxingdui and at other sites in the area indicate the importance of this type of implement for the peoples of the area. Further, the jade blades from Sanxingdui seem to have had more in common with those found in other southern sites than with the blades used by the peoples of Henan, with whom the inhabitants of Sanxingdui were presumably contemporary.

Published: Sichuan 1989, pl. 1.3; *Wenwu* 1989.5, p. 16, fig. 34.3; Hebei 1991–3, vol. 2, pl. 154; Goepper 1995, no. 48.

1 This subject is discussed in Rawson 1995, section 10.

34 Two ceremonial blades, *zhang*

c. 1200–1000 BC

a Dark green jade
Length 68 cm; width 10.7 cm (K2,3: 314–2)

b Greyish yellow jade
Length 41 cm; width 8 cm (K1: 231)

Excavated in 1986 at Sanxingdui, Guanghan county, Sichuan province
Institute of Archaeology and Cultural Relics Bureau, Sichuan province

Blades of the present type are often called *zhang* in later Chinese terminology. The pieces shown here belong, however, to two rather separate categories. The first (a) is a local version of a widely known category of blade with a splayed end. The second piece (b) is a hybrid of the type already mentioned in the previous entry.

The blade with the splayed or v-shaped end (a) has two outstanding features: the v-shaped end and the hooks and small spikes on each side further down. Both features are

Fig. 34.1 *Jade blade from Erlitou, c. 1700 BC. Length 54 cm. After Osaka 1993, no. 20.*

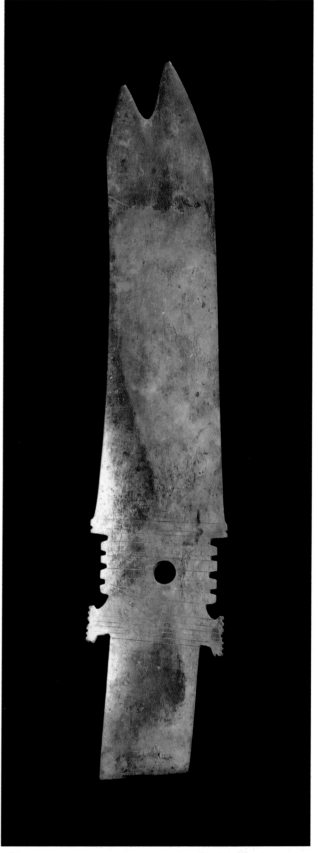

34a

34b

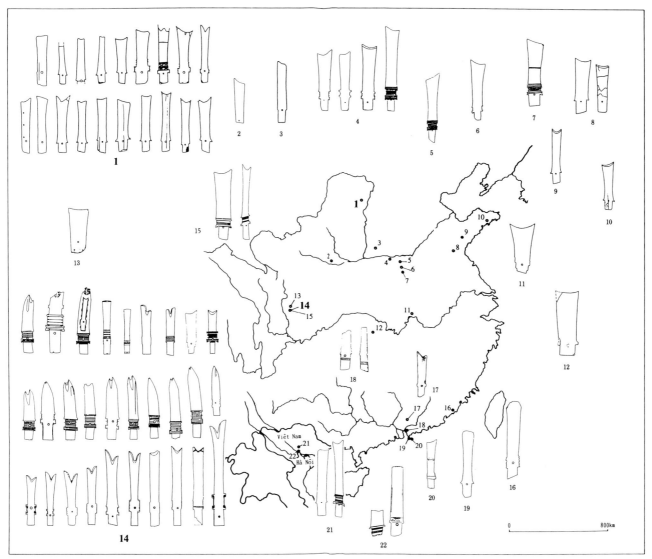

Fig. 34.2 *Map showing distribution of blades with splayed ends. After Hong Kong 1994b, endpapers. Blades at no. 1 are from Shenmu xian in Shaanxi province, and those at no. 14 from Guanghan Sanxingdui.*

provincial variations of a fine type of blade typical of eastern and central China and seen at its most elaborate in blades from Erlitou. The origin of these blades is uncertain, although it may well have been in the neolithic cultures of the east coast. They certainly appear in full and carefully worked forms at Erlitou (fig. 34.1). The Erlitou blade is much broader in proportion to its length than the present piece, but it has the notched sides and straight incised lines typical of the type.

As shown by a map reproduced from a volume on jade sceptres (fig. 34.2), the distribution of the form is widely dispersed and the finds from Guanghan Sanxingdui are among the important concentrations. Other examples were found in the same area before 1949. In addition, a number have come from a deposit in northern Shaanxi at Shenmu xian. These later pieces are rather different from the blades from Sichuan

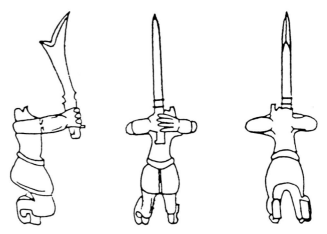

Fig. 34.3 *Drawing of a bronze figure from pit 2. The figure holds a sceptre. After Chen De'an 1994, p. 98, fig. 13-7.1.*

and other areas, in that many of them are very thin, as though they had been made simply for burial or as offerings.

The second blade (b) is highly idiosyncratic. It has a pointed rather than splayed tip, divided as though it were the mouth of a fish, although the division may have in fact been an attempt to imitate the other blade category, seen above. The blade also has a notched handle with the incised horizontal lines typical of the so-called *zhang* type. The notches are less refined than those seen on the Erlitou blade (fig. 34.1).

We can imagine how these blades were carried by looking at a small headless bronze figure found in pit 2 (fig. 34.3). The kneeling figure holds such a blade in his outstretched hands. This probably is the most vivid depiction of the use of any jade blade in ancient China. In no other context do we have such an illustration.

Published: Goepper 1995, no. 49.

35 Disc or ring

c. 1200–1000 BC
Jade
Diameter 18 cm; diameter of hole 6.5 cm
Excavated in 1986 from pit 2, Sanxingdui, Guanghan county, Sichuan province (K2,3: 57-2)
Institute of Archaeology and Cultural Relics Bureau, Sichuan province

Jade rings or discs with holes have a long history in China and have been described and discussed in many texts of great authority. For us the irony of such commentaries is that most of them were composed long after the discs or rings were

35

made, and it is likely that the writers had no idea what the discs or rings functioned as or signified for their original owners.

Some early jade rings are found in the graves of the Hongshan peoples in north-east China, *c.* 3500 BC, but these were relatively small, slightly rectangular rather than completely round, and were pierced to wear as ornaments.[1] Large jade discs used independently (that is, not as a personal ornament), sometimes called *bi*, were popular in the neolithic cultures of the east coast, especially the Liangzhu (*c.* 2500 BC) (no. 17); they were much less widely employed in other cultures. The quantities found in Liangzhu tombs were not matched again until the Han period (206 BC–AD 220).[2] In particular, discs were not especially common among the Shang peoples of Henan (*c.* 1500–1050 BC), although rings were popular in southern China at a time contemporary with the Shang. The most widely distributed ring type is the present one: a ring with a vertical flange around the centre.

It is possible that we should not see such rings as versions of the *bi*, or neolithic disc, but as modified forms of bracelets. Certain tall bracelets with narrow central flanges, such as one found in the tomb of Fu Hao and another more spectacular one in the British Museum, may be the ancestors of the present type of ring. In jade the tube was hard to execute, the ring much less challenging. Thus the flange on such bracelets may have been enlarged in order to reduce the height of the ring and the tube. In some parts of southern China and northern Vietnam, rings with flanges around the inner hole have been found on the wrists of the dead, indicating that they were indeed used as bracelets.[3]

Quite a range of rings with flanges has been found, many of them quite thinly worked and therefore like the fine jade bracelets mentioned. Such pieces come predominantly from sites in Sichuan, such as Sanxingdui. Some of these jades survived for many centuries, such as a remarkable flanged ring found in the Huang state tombs of the seventh century BC, at Xinyang in Henan province. This jade is very likely to have come from Sichuan. Others are somewhat thicker and broader, as is the present piece. Versions of such jades were also made at Anyang, where they should probably be understood as copies of an exotic, non-Shang type of jade.[4] While all these jades may have had a ceremonial or ritual significance, they were probably also valued for other associations, such as their fine stones and workmanship, and their references to exotic places whose products were difficult to acquire.

Published: Sichuan 1989, pl. 1: 5; Goepper 1995, no. 50.

1 Hebei 1991–3, vol. 1, pl. 4.
2 For a discussion of *bi* discs see Rawson 1995, sections 4, 15.
3 For a discussion of the distribution of these rings see Yoshikai Masato 1994.
4 Rawson 1995, no. 9: 3, fig. 1.

PART II

THE GREAT DYNASTIES

This second part of the catalogue covers the period when northern central China was ruled by the great ancient dynasties of the Shang (c. 1500–1050 BC) and the Zhou (c. 1050–221 BC), hence the title 'The Great Dynasties'.

The rulers of these early states were renowned among all later generations of Chinese from accounts in some of the earliest historical texts, especially the history written by Sima Qian in the second century BC, the *Shi ji (The Records of the Historian)*. As with earlier texts such as the *Shu Jing (The Book of Records)* and the *Shi Jing (The Book of Poetry)*, which appear to transmit speeches and poems relating to events of around 1000 BC, the earliest parts of this history were compiled many centuries after the events described. Although such texts give the period a sense of unity, even of progression, this is almost certainly a unity accorded by hindsight; indeed, the Zhou court historians are responsible for creating in their narratives an artificial framework from which it is now difficult to escape. The actual history of the period must surely have been much less coherent than the later texts would have us believe.

The texts set out a sequence of three dynasties, starting with the Xia, followed by the Shang and then by the Zhou themselves. The Xia are thought, by present-day Chinese archaeologists, to have encompassed the culture known as the Erlitou, but this is by no means certain. The Shang, who came to power in about 1500 BC, created one of several strong states; equally impressive contemporaries, unrecorded in the texts, include the peoples who made the bronzes found at Guanghan Sanxingdui, described in Part I (nos 22–35). Only with the Zhou, who overthrew the Shang in about 1050 BC, did one particular ruling power become the dominant force. And even then, Zhou power probably only controlled parts of the territories they appeared to claim. Centralised Zhou rule survived for several centuries, but in the mid-eighth century it too broke down, and the Chinese landmass was divided into competing states. The following six centuries of divided rule are often known as the Spring and Autumn period, and the period of the Warring States. This part of the catalogue briefly describes the Erlitou period as a prelude to the Shang dynasty, a dynasty primarily represented by the fine bronzes and jades found in the tomb of Fu Hao, consort of the great king Wu Ding who ruled about 1200 BC. A short section on the establishment of the Zhou dynasty considers the proclamations in texts and on objects of the first fully articulated aspirations to a unified Chinese state. The third principal section of Part II illustrates the magnificent bronzes and jades made for the rulers of the many states of the later Zhou period as they sought to outshine one another.

In place of the supposed political unity of the territory claimed by the Shang and the Zhou, which may be illusory, the long period of over a thousand years is unified by language, by material culture, and to some extent by religious practice. We do not know what language the peoples of the Erlitou culture spoke, but from the Shang period remains of writing, especially the oracle bone texts (no. 37), show that the Shang wrote and therefore spoke Chinese. In their material culture bronze, above all, but also jade, ivory, lacquer and silk were exploited by the rulers, and these élite materials were deployed in temples, palaces and tombs. Although the Shang and the Zhou no doubt revered many spirits and deities, the predominant element of their religious practices (from which we deduce their beliefs) was reverence or respect for the ancestors. Offerings of food and wine were presented to the ancestors in exceptionally fine cast bronze vessels on a regular ritual cycle. Because the ancient Chinese appear to have believed that the dead would continue to make offerings, such bronze vessels were also buried in tombs. They were made in sets, which implies that the ceremony comprised an elaborate formal banquet with different foods and wines offered in different types of vessel. Bronze vessels, notable examples of which are illustrated here, were first made in the Erlitou period and continued in use to the end of the Zhou and beyond.

The Erlitou period, c. 1700–1500 BC

The early cities, temples and tombs that have been unearthed in Henan province are the foundation upon which the later Shang state developed. Remains of a city excavated at Erlitou, near present-day Yanshi, were sufficiently elaborate to have been those of some sort of political or religious centre. A large building within a courtyard excavated there probably had some ceremonial function. Tombs discovered in this area have revealed some of the earliest cast bronze vessels that survive, but such bronzes are rare and they are found with other vessels made of ceramic. At this time neolithic practices were being transformed by a new technology, that of bronze casting. Bronze casting and the organisation of cities are the most significant features that the Erlitou culture contributed to their successors in Henan, the Shang. The Erlitou peoples also worked fine jade, a practice they had probably borrowed from the élites of eastern China, some of whose fine jades are described at nos 16–21. This craft, too, the Erlitou culture transmitted to the Shang.

36 Ornamental plaque

Erlitou culture, c. 1700–1500 BC
Bronze with turquoise inlay
Height 14.2 cm; width 9.8 cm
Excavated in 1981 at Erlitou, Yanshi, Henan province
(81YL V M4: 5)
Institute of Archaeology, Beijing

Earlier entries in the catalogue illustrate the fine jade plaques used as personal ornaments in the neolithic period culture of Liangzhu (nos 18–20). The present plaque, which has a flat back and four small loops for attaching it to something else, is made of bronze and inlaid on the front with turquoise.

The shape of the plaque and its inlay suggest a monster face. Two bulbous pupils draw our attention to circular eyes above a small nose, sunken lines indicate a jaw, and large scrolls above the eyes suggest ears or elaborate horns. We have no idea what this face is supposed to represent or refer to.[1] It seems to be related to the later animal faces decorating Shang dynasty bronze ritual vessels (no. 43; Rawson, fig. 6), although in the later Shang period such plaques were not made or used. It is rather surprising to find such a full and detailed form at this early date.

The plaque was found on the centre of the body in tomb M4 excavated in 1981 at Erlitou.[2] The tomb evidently belonged to an important individual, as in place of the more usual ceramic containers were numerous fragments of lacquer, indicating that the owner had vessels made of this fine material. He had a bronze bell at his chest, and a jade tube (originally wrapped in cloth) and two turquoise beads at his neck. Plaques similar to this one have been found in other richly equipped tombs at Erlitou, in one of which the plaque was again placed on or near the chest. Such plaques obviously belonged with jades, turquoise beads and shells as ornaments of high status.

Turquoise combined with bronze is a characteristic of the Erlitou period, and especially of plaques of this type. At some

36

periods in the subsequent Shang dynasty, turquoise was set into the tangs of bronze weapons. Perhaps the interest in turquoise was the result of the import of the material from other parts of the Chinese landmass, where it had been more extensively used at an early stage. Turquoise was employed both in the Hongshan neolithic culture of the north-east and among some other neolithic peoples, including the Majiayao of the north-west.

Published: *Kaogu* 1984.1, pp. 37–8; Chang Kwang-chih 1986a, fig. 268; Yang Xiaoneng 1988b, fig. 64; Osaka 1993, no. 17; Beijing 1993a, p. 121, fig. 1; Goepper 1995, no. 21.

1 For a discussion of the origins of the *taotie* see Bagley 1987, introduction. A range of views on the ways in which such faces might be interpreted is set out in Whitfield 1993. To date no overall satisfactory explanation of the meanings and references of the face has been proposed.
2 *Kaogu* 1984.1, pp. 37–40; see also *Kaogu* 1986.4, pp. 318–23, fig. 6; *Kaogu* 1992.4, pp. 294–303, fig. 2.

The Shang dynasty, c. *1500–1050 BC*

We know about the Shang dynasty from later historical texts, from divinations incised on oracle bones and from the large tombs and foundations of buildings that have been unearthed at several major sites in Henan province. Cities have been excavated at Erligang, near modern Zhengzhou, and at Anyang, north of the Yellow River. Erligang would appear to belong to a stage before the occupation and development of Anyang, but there were other cities of the same periods, as far north as Hebei province and as far south as the Yangzi. We do not know if we are looking at the cities of a single state, or whether, as is more likely, these cities were strongholds of related centres of power with a common culture, including a common set of beliefs.

The surviving remains demonstrate the strong religious framework within which Shang political and court life was organised. Ancestors were the key figures. Indeed, Shang society was viewed as incorporating them. Before any major activity, such as war, hunting or agriculture, was undertaken, the ancestors were consulted and the questions posed were written on turtle plastrons and oracle bones (no. 37).

As the ancestors played such an essential part in society, they had to be shown honour and respect in accordance with their roles and ranks. We do not know what form the ceremonies for the ancestors took, but extraordinarily fine cast bronze containers for food and wine are evidence of the wealth and attention expended on these rites. The large number of different but set shapes suggests a formal meal, with prescribed foods and wines offered in a prescribed sequence. Included here are the bronzes found in the tomb of Lady Fu Hao, who was consort of the Shang king Wu Ding, and who died about 1200 BC.

The high-quality bronze casting and jade carving of the period and the large numbers of surviving items suggest that the Shang had highly developed methods of production. Workshops were probably large, with many artisans, each no doubt with a specific task such as smelting the metal, producing the ceramic moulds, or forming and finishing the bronzes. The organisation of a workshop was probably simply one aspect of a highly organised society. Massed, organised labour would also have been needed to dig the tombs and to construct the walls that survive to this day. Moreover, the roles and practices of the élite in court life and religious ceremonies were probably developed to an equally high level of complexity, one that was expressed by the complicated objects illustrated here.

37 Turtle plastron and oracle bone

Late Shang period, Anyang phase, *c.* early 13th century BC

a Turtle plastron
Height 19.5 cm; width 12 cm
Excavated in 1992 at Anyang, eastern area of Huayuanzhuang, Henan province (H3: 52)

b Shoulder blade of an ox
Height 40 cm; width 21 cm
Excavated in 1971 at Anyang, western area of Xiaotun, Henan province (no. 6)

Institute of Archaeology, Beijing

The earliest surviving texts in China are those inscribed on ox scapulae and turtle plastrons used for divination. These texts, which are written in an early form of Chinese characters, record communications with the ancestors and spirits (fig. 37.1). The divinations were made by first applying hot brands to depressions in the bones or plastrons and then observing and interpreting the resulting cracks.[1]

Divination was one of the primary functions of the Shang ruling house and its nobles, officials and servants. The questions addressed to the ancestors and spirits are often of a

37a

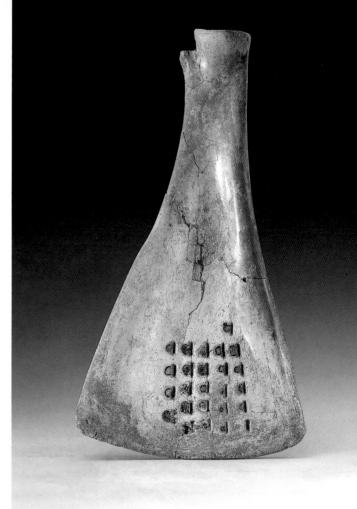

37b

practical nature, and concern all aspects of daily life and political and social control, as well as many ritual matters. Frequent topics include illness and childbirth, the weather and the harvest, and the king's military expeditions, campaigns and hunting exploits. The animal and human sacrifices required for favourable outcomes were precisely registered.

From the latter part of the Shang period, that is to say from the period when the site of Anyang became an important centre (c. 1300–1050 BC), bones and plastrons were inscribed with both questions and answers. What we do not know is quite how these questions were intended to be put to the ancestors or spirits.[2]

When the bones and plastrons had been used, often many times, they were carefully stored away in special pits as archives. In 1991 two such pits were discovered near remains of Shang buildings. In one were no less than 1558 fragments of turtle plastrons, with as many as 579 characters incised on one of them. The number of characters on a piece varies from one or two to about two hundred, and some were filled in with black or red ink.

a Turtle plastron

On the plastron of a turtle illustrated here there are altogether eight inscriptions, arranged to the left and right of the centre line in such a way that, in each case, the rows of characters start at the centre line. They refer to hunting expeditions and read:

1 Divination *(bu)* on the *yiyou* day [the day with the cyclic symbol *yiyou*], the 22nd day of the sixty-day cycle: The Prince *(zi)* goes into the small hills of XX [place name not identified], to catch wild boar with the net. He will catch some.

2 Divination on the *yiyou* day: He will probably not catch any.

3 Divination on the *yiyou* day: The Prince will hunt wild boar in the southern hills of XX (?) on the following day [with the symbol] *bing*. He will catch some. One, two, three, four.

4 Wild boar will be caught, one, two.

5 Divination on the *yiyou* day: After Bi has gone to Hu (?), he will catch wild boar. One, two.

6 Stags will be caught in XX (?). The Prince asked the oracle *(zhan)*, which said: Stags will be caught. One, two.

7 One, two.

8 One, two.

Published: *Kaogu* 1993.6, pp. 488–99, fig. 11; Goepper 1995, no. 23.

b Shoulder blade of an ox

This oracle bone has drilled holes for the application of brands on both sides. The inscriptions refer to various sacrifices to the ancestors and date to the period of the king Wu Ding, *c.* 1200 BC. The deceased ancestors to whom the sacrifices are dedicated are named by a system formed from sets of characters known as the *tiangan*. The inscription is not so much a question to an oracle as a note on the costs incurred in particular rituals. It reads:

> For the honourable elder brother of Ri Bing, a pig is brought as a sacrifice. For the deceased mother *(bi)* by the name of Ding, a pig is also slaughtered. Also for the deceased mother Mou a pig. Also a pig for Father Yi.

Published: *Kaogu* 1972.2, pp. 2–11; Osaka 1993, nos 62–4; Goepper 1995, no. 23.

1 For a general discussion see Keightley 1978.

2 For a discussion as to whether the inscriptions on oracle bones are true questions see *Early China,* vol. 14, 1989, pp. 77–172.

38 Potter's tool, *dishou*

Possibly Shang period
Clay ware mixed with sand
Height 5.9 cm; diameter 9.2 cm
Excavated in the 1960s at Shamaoshan, Hanyang district, Hubei province
Hubei Provincial Museum, Wuhan

This small pottery-making implement has been included in the exhibition because it has a most unusual incised motif on it (fig. 38.1).[1] The implement is almost mushroom-shaped and consists of a pottery disc with a loop behind it. The potters, with their fingers through the loop, could press the slightly convex disc against the sides of the pots on which they were

Fig. 38.1 *Drawing of the motif incised on the tool. After* Jianghan kaogu *1984.3, pp. 108–9.*

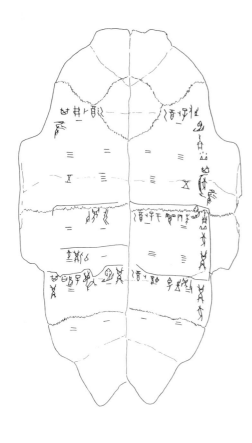

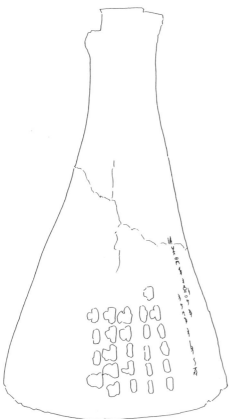

Fig. 37.1 *Drawings showing the inscriptions.*

38

working to smooth them or to give them a texture. A number of similar pieces have been found at various Shang sites.[2]

The unusual design is incised across the handle of the piece. It comprises a roughly drawn figure of a man, with deeply scored lines suggesting a thin match-like body, arms and legs, from which project fingers and toes. A pair of bold angular spirals trails a slight zigzag line. Most remarkable of all, an arrow descends threateningly from the pair of angular spirals on to the head of the man. As such angular spirals are often thought to represent thunder, it seems probable that the arrow was intended to indicate lightning. Chinese archaeologists view this incised drawing as illustrating a man struck by lightning, but quite why such an improbable design should appear on a small utilitarian item is difficult, if not impossible, to explain.

Published: *Jianghan kaogu* 1984.3, pp. 108–9; Goepper 1995, no. 22.

1 The implement is dated to the Shang period on the evidence of the incised design; see Wu Shan 1988, p. 279, and *Jianghan kaogu* 1984.3, p. 108.
2 For comparable items from other sites see *Kaogu xuebao* 1957.1, p. 60; *Wenwu* 1975.7, p. 54; *Kaogu xuebao* 1989.2, pp. 25–7; *Kaogu* 1953.2, pp. 196–7; Yang Xiaoneng 1988b, fig. 53.

The tomb of Lady Fu Hao at Anyang Xiaotun

The discovery of the tomb of Lady Fu Hao in 1976 was of immeasurable importance for our understanding of the great wealth and authority of Shang rule and the aspirations of the Shang royal household. It is the only royal Shang tomb to have been found intact and to have been scientifically excavated. Fu Hao was buried within an inner coffin inside a tomb chamber, constructed over a small pit. The grave goods were placed inside the inner coffin and in the tomb chamber. Over the coffin was a layer of earth in which were found two jade vessels, of which one is included here (no. 48), and a stone buffalo.

The most spectacular finds were bronze ritual vessels that were probably intended for offering banquets to Fu Hao's ancestors. Among these several hundred ritual bronzes were both massive and tiny pieces, some rare and exotic items and a large range of impressive, high-quality vessels. The different inscriptions on the vessels indicate that Fu Hao owned some that had originally been made for other people. She may have acquired them as gifts or booty, and when using them she must have been aware of the associations they embodied. The great wealth expended on these vessels, in terms both of raw materials and craftsmanship, demonstrates the importance of ritual offerings for the well-being of the Shang royal family and indeed the Shang state.

In addition, Fu Hao had some extraordinary jades.

Like the bronzes, the jades are often highly exotic and show that Fu Hao had collected not only pieces of great antiquity, which came from a considerable distance, but also Shang period versions of these foreign or exotic pieces. Some of the best of the bronzes and jades are shown here.

Although the offering vessel from Hunan province (no. 51) belongs to the same category as Fu Hao's rectangular food vessels (nos 39, 40), it is evidence of the diversity of the period. With hindsight, later Chinese historians viewed Shang rule at Anyang as providing a centre for an extensive state, but the decoration of faces on this bronze (no. 51) tells a different story. These faces are not products of the intellectual or religious world view of Fu Hao and her compatriots. They are quite unlike, and distinct from, the animal-like faces known as *taotie* which can be seen on Fu Hao's bronzes. The bronze belongs to a different artistic tradition and it must have been cast for a people with a different outlook. While the technology of bronze casting was shared between Anyang and the more southerly province of Hunan (where no. 51 was found), the intellectual culture differed. Such differences give the lie to later claims of Shang universal power at the time when the Shang centre was at Anyang.

39 Rectangular vessel for offering food, *fang ding*

Late Shang period, Anyang phase, *c.* 1200 BC
Bronze
Height 80.0 cm; weight 117.5 kg
Excavated in 1976 from tomb M5, Xiaotun, near Anyang, Henan province (M5:809)
Institute of Archaeology, Beijing

Among the most imposing of all ritual vessels were large rectangular (*fang*), high-legged sacrificial cauldrons (*ding*). They were probably used for cooking and reheating meat and other food. This one is impressive for its size, simple form and careful decoration of a narrow border of animal faces, known as *taotie*, below the lip and of borders of projecting bosses around the sides. The earliest forms of *taotie* were cast in narrow thread-like lines. But during the Erligang period (*c.* 1500–1300 BC), such decoration was replaced by relief forms of the same creature (Rawson, fig. 6). Bronzes from Fu Hao's tomb in the following entries illustrate some of the variations evident during the Anyang period. The present narrow borders appear to have become traditional for large rectangular cauldrons from the time when they were first made in the Erligang period (Rawson, fig. 5).[1] Thus this is an old-fashioned form of the *taotie*. Complex forms typical of

the more advanced designs popular in the Anyang period are seen on nos 40 and 43.

So valuable were large rectangular cauldrons such as this one that they are rarely found in tombs. Indeed, the surviving Erligang period pieces, the ancestors of the present bronze, have all come from hoards, buried either as some sort of offering to spirits or to keep the precious bronzes from harm during times of political upheaval or war. The expenditure of bronze on large cauldrons was so great that a family, however distinguished, probably owned but a single pair and could not afford to bury them with particular individuals. Because Fu Hao was a royal consort she probably merited her own pair of rectangular cauldrons (this one is one of a pair), and because she was a queen it was perhaps thought appropriate to bury them with her. The other surviving large late Shang *ding* may also have come from an important, indeed royal, tomb (fig. 39.2).[2] In the subsequent Western Zhou period (*c.* 1050–771 BC) large cauldrons were usually circular (Fu Hao also had large circular ones) and the rectangular vessels were generally small.

The present *fang ding* was recovered with its pair to the north of the inner coffin (*neiguan*), but within the outer chamber (*guo*). On the inside of the cauldron is the inscription 'Si Mu Xin', or Queen Mother Xin (fig. 39.1). Inscriptions in bronzes generally name either the owner or the patron of the bronze and on later pieces may give details of why and when the bronze was cast. Here the inscription is probably Fu Hao's posthumous title. 'Mu' not only means mother or matriarch, but is the highest honorary title, in the sense of Ancestress, that could be given to a woman. 'Xin' is one of the

Fig. 39.1 *Inscription in the vessel.*

Fig. 39.2 *Bronze* fang ding *inscribed 'Si Mu fang ding'. Late Shang dynasty, 12th–11th century* BC.

characters used as a posthumous title for Shang and early Zhou ancestors. The title 'Bi Xin' is mentioned in oracle bone texts and is thought to refer to a consort of Wu Ding, namely to Fu Hao. The character 'Si' can be interpreted in different ways, one of which is as an equivalent to 'Hou' or queen.[3] It is likely then that these bronzes were cast after Fu Hao's death to complete a ritual vessel set. Most, but not all, of the vessels in Fu Hao's tomb were inscribed with the name Fu Hao, and these may have been used by her when she was alive. We may be witnessing a special honour accorded to Fu Hao, providing her in the afterlife with large cauldrons of her own, whereas in life she had probably used vessels in the communal ownership of the royal family.[4]

The other vessels in the tomb that are inscribed with the same title include a pair of animal-shaped wine vessels and a rectangular pedestal. The stone buffalo already mentioned was also so inscribed. From such inscriptions we can perhaps assess what belonged to Fu Hao in her lifetime and what was prepared specifically for her burial.

Published: *Kaogu xuebao* 1977.2, pp. 1–22; Beijing 1980a, pl. 3; New York 1980, no. 28; *Gugong wenwu yuekan* 1983–4 (1), pp. 30–64; Beijing 1985a, pl. 3; *Kaogu* 1991.6, pp. 533–45; Osaka 1993, no. 24; Goepper 1995, no. 25.

1 Large *fang ding* with this type of design but of rather different proportions have come from sites at Zhengzhou in Henan province (Rawson, fig. 5; New York 1980, no.11; *Wenwu* 1975.6, pp. 64–8; *Wenwu* 1983.3, pp. 49–59). This vessel type was not only perpetuated at Anyang, but was, before the Anyang period, used and buried in southern China. Southern versions of the vessel type, much more faithful to the Zhengzhou versions than

are the Anyang ones, have come from the large tomb deposits at Jiangxi Xin'gan Dayangzhou (Bagley 1993a, fig. 6; see also Rawson 1994).

2 For handle design on the Si Mu Wu *fang ding* see fig. 46.4c. The inscription on this *ding* is in the same form as that on the present bronze and almost certainly names another royal consort, possibly another wife of the king Wu Ding.

3 For a discussion of the inscriptions in the vessels from Fu Hao's tomb see Chang Cheng-lang 1986 and Cheng Chen-hsiang 1986.

4 See Rawson 1994 for a discussion on the use and burial of large circular and rectangular cauldrons.

40 Rectangular vessel with flattened legs for offering food, *fang ding*

Late Shang period, Anyang phase, *c.* 1200 BC
Bronze
Height 42.3 cm; weight 18 kg
Excavated in 1976 from tomb M5, Xiaotun, near Anyang, Henan province (M5:812)
Institute of Archaeology, Beijing

This much smaller rectangular cauldron is also one of a pair, but its shape and lineage are very different from those of the previous vessel. Its flat sides are completely decorated with fine relief *taotie* faces and small vertical dragons. This decoration alone indicates that the vessel belongs to a completely different tradition and therefore to a different sacrificial use from the previous one. The difference in decoration indicates that the vessel does not descend directly from the Erligang bronzes which were the predecessors of no. 39.

The key to understanding the history of this very rare vessel type lies in the shape of its legs. These are formed as small dragons with long s-shaped tails. Their heads support the bottom of the vessel. The centres of their bodies are rounded, and rows of fine scales are cast along them. These scales suggest that the casters had borrowed the leg form from the south and not from the Anyang casting tradition. For, although round vessels on flat legs had been developed in Henan province as early as the Erligang period, rectangular ones were not made there. The fashion for flat legs, especially legs decorated with small scales, was propagated in the south.

Ding with strange dragon- or tiger-like legs decorated with stripes or scales have been found in large numbers at the site of Dayangzhou in Xin'gan county, Jiangxi province (fig. 40.1).[1] In fact, here such vessels far outnumber other types. Several of Fu Hao's vessels seem to be based on vessel types from Xin'gan, perhaps because there was an interest in such exotic pieces (as indeed in exotica in other materials) at this time.[2] Very few rectangular *ding* were made with these dragon- or tiger-like legs. It may be that in the Shang period only the very highest ranking individuals, such as Fu Hao, could or would wish to own unusual objects that referred to distant and unusual places. Some rectangular *ding* were made in the Western Zhou period, but these too may refer to southern

40

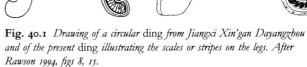

Fig. 40.1 *Drawing of a circular* ding *from Jiangxi Xin'gan Dayangzhou and of the present* ding *illustrating the scales or stripes on the legs. After Rawson 1994, figs 8, 15.*

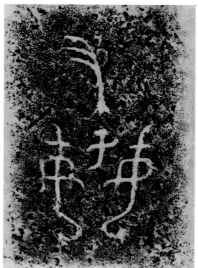

Fig. 40.2 *Inscription in the vessel.*

prototypes, for the early Western Zhou were in contact with remote areas and borrowed objects from wherever they thought appropriate.

The pair to the present piece carries an inscription naming Fu Hao (fig. 40.2). Only part of one of these characters remains on the present vessel. The two bronzes thus contrast with the previous piece, which carries her posthumous title, and it is possible that the present *fang ding* and its pair were used in Fu Hao's lifetime. As they are much smaller than the previous vessel, they probably served a different function at a different stage in the ritual.

Published: *Kaogu xuebao* 1977.2, pp. 1–22; *Kaogu* 1979.2, pp. 165–70; Lienert 1979; Beijing 1980a, pl. 4: 1; New York 1980, no. 32; Beijing 1992a, no. 114; Osaka 1993, no. 28; Beijing 1993a, p. 150, no. 2; Goepper 1995, no. 26.

1 For illustrations and discussions of the site see Bagley 1993a and *Wenwu* 1991.10, pp. 1–26.
2 Rawson 1994.

41 Vessel for offering wine, *jue*

Late Shang period, Anyang phase, *c.* 1200 BC
Bronze
Height 37.3 cm; weight 4.4 kg
Excavated in 1976 from tomb M5, Xiaotun, near Anyang, Henan province (M5: 1579)
Institute of Archaeology, Beijing

Three-legged vessels with a long spout, a pointed lip and posts with knobs on the rim are described as *jue*. This piece and its pair, both over 37 cm in height, are the largest *jue* known to date. Both are inscribed with the name Fu Hao (fig. 41.1). These vessels were used for the heating and ritual pouring of wine, or for drinking out of, at the banquets offered to ancestors and in other rituals. *Jue* were among the most common of all ritual vessels. They appear regularly in tombs of both high-ranking and low-ranking members of the élite. This vessel type was obviously essential to all Shang

Fig. 41.1 *Inscription in the vessel.*

Fig. 41.2 *Drawing of the forty* jue *in Fu Hao's tomb. After Beijing 1980a.*

41

rituals and demonstrates the importance of wine offerings in the religious practice of the time.

The name *jue* goes back to Shang period oracle texts, which also provide evidence of the use of the vessel during the cult of the ancestors. A text on an oracle bone reads: 'On the *ji mao* day, the oracle was asked whether the deceased brother of Geng should be offered a drink by pouring out on the earth from a *jue* vessel and a sheep should be killed with the ritual axe (on the next day, *geng chen*)'.[1]

On present evidence *jue* are the oldest vessel types made in bronze, being found in the Erlitou culture.[2] These early *jue* were less well developed than the present examples, but their principal features were essentially the same. Indeed, the *jue*

form changed little over the two thousand years of its use before its disappearance in the ritual revolution of the Western Zhou period, *c.* 900–850 BC.

The very standard form of the *jue* can be seen in the similarity of the forty possessed by Fu Hao (fig. 41.2). The only type to exceed the *jue* in number is the *gu*, of which she had fifty-three. Among the *jue* and *gu* were three sets inscribed with names other than those of Fu Hao. The *jue* and *gu* indeed seem matched for there are nine *jue* and ten (or eleven) *gu*, each dedicated in the names of Si Tu Mu, Ya Qi and Su Quan. These clear groups indicate that Fu Hao had been given sets of vessels from several sources. Rather surprisingly, all forty *jue* were found outside the main coffin chamber.

Published: *Kaogu xuebao* 1977.2, pp. 1–22; *Wenwu* 1977.11, pp. 32–7; *Kaogu* 1978.4, p. 270; Beijing 1980a, pl. 54: 1; Beijing 1985a, colour pl. 38; Osaka 1993, no. 35; Goepper 1995, no. 31.

1 After Brinker and Goepper 1980, p. 47.
2 The use of *jue* is discussed in Childs-Johnson 1987.

42 Square-sectioned vessel for offering wine, *fang jia*

Late Shang period, Anyang phase, *c.* 1200 BC
Bronze
Height 66.8 cm; width at lip 23.4 cm; length at lip 25 cm; weight 19.05 kg
Excavated in 1976 from tomb M5, Xiaotun, near Anyang, Henan province (M5:752)
Institute of Archaeology, Beijing

This imposing angular vessel is a rare form of a standard ritual vessel type, the *jia*, better known with a circular cross-section. The *jia*, as a circular vessel on three legs with a handle, was in use from early Shang times.[1] Versions such as this one, with a square cross-section, are exceptionally rare and were perhaps highly valued. The square shape would have been almost impossible to achieve in ceramic, but was perhaps relatively easily produced in cast bronze and would of course have indicated to the viewer that the vessel was indeed of bronze and not ceramic. It would thus display the wealth of the owner. The sumptuousness of this bronze is also evident in its very large size and fine decoration.

Fu Hao had three almost identical *fang jia* which would have made a very imposing group. They are inscribed with her name, and one shows traces of textile impression, which suggests that they were once wrapped up (fig. 42.1). Fu Hao's tomb also contained several *jia* of circular cross-section, some of which carry inscriptions that show they had originally been made for someone else (fig. 42.2). Fu Hao or her family had obviously assembled these *jia* from a number of different sources. When using these vessels, the priests, Fu Hao and presumably, it was thought, her ancestors would have been aware of these different sources.

Fig. 42.1 *Inscription in the vessel.*

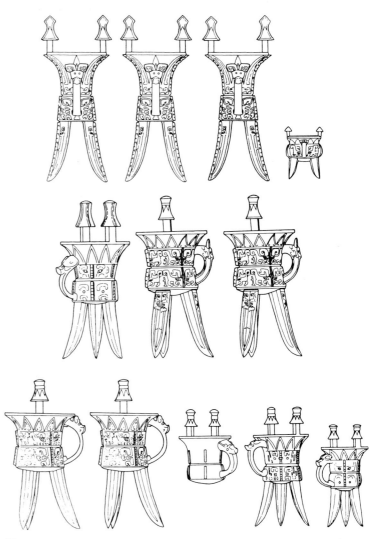

Fig. 42.2 *Drawing of twelve* jia *from the tomb of Fu Hao. After Beijing 1980a.*

43

The twelve *jia* in Fu Hao's tomb perhaps had a number of functions and were either used at different stages in a single ritual procedure or on different occasions (fig. 42.2). The variety of forms of vessel and the large numbers of certain types of vessel in Fu Hao's tomb point to the inadequacy of our knowledge of the different combinations in which the ritual vessels may have been used for the offerings to the ancestors.

Published: *Kaogu xuebao* 1977.2, pp. 1–22; *Wenwu* 1977.11, pp. 32–7; New York 1980, no. 33; Beijing 1980a, pl. 33: 2; Beijing 1985a, colour pl. 33; Beijing 1993a, p. 151, no. 1; Osaka 1993, no. 32; Goepper 1995, no. 30.

1 Osaka 1993, no. 15; Rawson 1987a, fig. 1.

43 Vessel for holding wine, *pou*

Late Shang period, Anyang phase, *c.* 1200 BC
Bronze
Height 33 cm; weight 13 kg
Excavated in 1976 from tomb M5, Xiaotun, near Anyang, Henan province (M5: 830)
Institute of Archaeology, Beijing

While the two previous vessels were for pouring or for heating wine, this much more substantial covered jar was obviously for holding large quantities of liquid. Bronze *pou*, as this vessel type is known, had been in use for some centuries by the time of Fu Hao, but earlier forms tended to be wider and did not have lids.[1] They were probably much closer in general form to the pottery jars or basins that provided the prototypes for the shape.

This magnificent example is far removed both from the ceramic originals and the earlier bronze forms. While early bronze *pou* have no flanges, the lid and body of this example are divided into three main segments by straight flanges. Each of these three main segments is further divided by flanges which separate each relief *taotie* face vertically into two sections. Such *taotie* are typical of the full and florid designs of the period (Rawson, fig. 6). Minor variations in the shapes of the horns, eyes, bodies and claws distinguish the creatures in the four main registers: the lid, the shoulders, the belly and the foot. In the first place such variation was functional, making it possible to enlarge or compress the motif to fit the space. Thus the creatures in the panels of the lid have wider horns than those on the body in order to fill the wide rim area. Those on the belly, by contrast, are more compact, making the face rectangular rather than triangular. To fill the greater space of the body, small dragons have been placed vertically to either side of the faces. The narrow borders of the shoulder and the foot also contain dragons, those on the shoulder being subdivided front and back by a bovine head. However, as well as being functional, such variation was probably a source of visual interest to the craftsmen and their patrons. If all the *taotie* and dragons had been the same, the

Fig. 43.1 *Inscription on the* pou.

visual effect could have been one of monotony rather than one of mystery and intrigue. The vessel is inscribed 'Fu Hao' (fig. 43.1).

Published: *Kaogu xuebao* 1977.2, pp. 57–98, pl. 9: 1; Beijing 1980a, pl. 29: 2; Beijing 1985a, pl. 30; Osaka 1993, no. 41; Goepper 1995, no. 27.

1 For discussion of the history of the *pou* see Bagley 1987, nos 51–7.

44 Rectangular vessel for offering wine, *fang hu*

Late Shang period, Anyang phase, *c.* 1200 BC
Bronze
Height 64 cm; weight 31 kg
Excavated in 1976 from tomb M5, Xiaotun, near Anyang, Henan province (M5: 807)
Institute of Archaeology, Beijing

This vessel is a rectangular variant of a flask, known as a *hu*, which was usually of circular cross-section, and was used for holding wine. The original flask shape derived from a pottery container. As explained in connection with the *jia* (no. 42), rectangular forms of standard vessels are found only in tombs of the very highest ranking. As they are so clearly differentiated from the pottery originals, these rectangular or square-sectioned vessels display better than those of oval or circular cross-section that they are of metal, thus suggesting the wealth and status of their owners. This rectangular *hu* is a much more unusual bronze than the preceding *pou* of circular cross-section.

Not only are this vessel and its pair remarkable for their square cross-sections and their size, but they also have unusual and dramatic decoration. On the main sides are rams' heads, divided at the corners of the vessel by a vertical flange. Above them are bottle-horned dragons with long s-shaped bodies shown twice, that is either side of the head.[1] Such double-bodied creatures arise from the symmetrical treatment of animal forms. On the shoulders are birds. The rams' heads are repeated on the lid, while the foot is decorated with a *taotie* face.

Fig. 44.1 *Inscription in the vessel.*

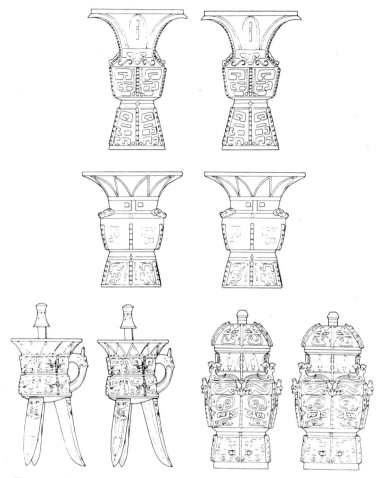

Fig. 44.2 *Drawing of some of the vessels inscribed 'Si Tu Mu' from the tomb of Fu Hao. After Beijing 1980a.*

This combination of motifs, the rams, the dragons and the birds, is found on a famous vessel from southern China, a four-ram *zun* from Ningxiang in Hunan province.[2] As rams appear on southern bronzes at this time, it seems likely that the present vessel is another example of a metropolitan Shang bronze, made at Anyang, based upon a vessel form and design current in the south. In both areas the motifs probably had important, but different, meanings. At Anyang the present vessel may well have been especially prized for its exotic associations.

This *hu* and its pair are inscribed 'Si Tu Mu' or Queen Mother Tu (fig. 44.1). As Fu Hao was addressed after her death as Si Mu Xin or Queen Mother Xin, the vessels may have been made for someone other than Fu Hao, although this is by no means certain.[3] The same inscription appears on the pair to the *hu* and on twenty-six other wine vessels from the tomb (fig. 44.2). From the writing of the graphs it would appear that the inscriptions on the twenty-eight vessels were made by four or five different scribes. A few other vessels with the same name are recorded in compendia of inscriptions and were obviously found by chance over the centuries

since the Song period, when such records started with the *Kaogu tu,* compiled by Lu Dalin in the late eleventh century AD.

The identity of Si Tu Mu is a perplexing problem. Some scholars have suggested that this is just another name for Fu Hao herself, but this seems unlikely. As one of the inscriptions recorded in reference works is to 'Si Tu Mu Gui', one possibility is that these bronzes belonged to another consort of the Shang king Wu Ding, who is known from oracle bone inscriptions as Bi Gui. The question remains, however, as to why Fu Hao should have been buried with such obviously fine bronzes belonging to another queen. Yet it is clear that quite a number of the bronzes in Fu Hao's tomb belonged to other people, as for instance some of the *jue* shown in figure 41.2. Unlike the *jue,* the Si Tu Mu bronzes are particularly magnificent and may have been included in the tomb to add to the majesty of Fu Hao. The burial of bronzes belonging to one person with another must almost certainly have been connected with aspects of Shang social relationships with which we are not familiar.

Published: *Kaogu xuebao* 1977.2, pp. 1–22; *Wenwu* 1977.11, pp. 32–7; Beijing 1980a, fig. 23: 2; Du Naisong 1980; *Kaogu* 1983.7, pp. 716–25; Beijing 1985a; *Kaogu* 1985.10, pp. 940–7, 939; Chang Ping-ch'üan 1986; *Gugong*

wenwu yuekan 1988.12 (60), pp. 18–41; Osaka 1993, no. 33; Beijing 1993a, p. 151, no. 2; Goepper 1995, no. 29.

1 For a discussion of the role of dragons with a snake-like body see no. 7, where a ceramic basin from the late neolithic site of Taosi is described. A creature, also with a snake-like body, is incised in a sherd from Erlitou (*Kaogu* 1965.5, pp. 215–24, pl. 3: 10). The graph for dragon, *long,* is also drawn with a snake-like body and has a bottle horn as here (Rawson 1990, p. 601, fig. 93.7).
2 Bagley 1987, pp. 30–6. See also vessels in the shape of addorsed rams (Bagley 1990, figs 173, 175).
3 For a discussion of the vessels with the Si Tu Mu inscription see Cheng Chen-hsiang 1986.

45 Vessel for offering wine, *gong*, in animal form

Late Shang period, Anyang phase, *c.* 1200 BC
Bronze
Height 22 cm; length 28.4 cm
Excavated in 1976 from tomb M5, Xiaotun, near Anyang, Henan province (M5: 802)
Institute of Archaeology, Beijing

This animal-shaped vessel is known as a *gong*, the type being defined as a jug with a lid. This lid is almost always in the

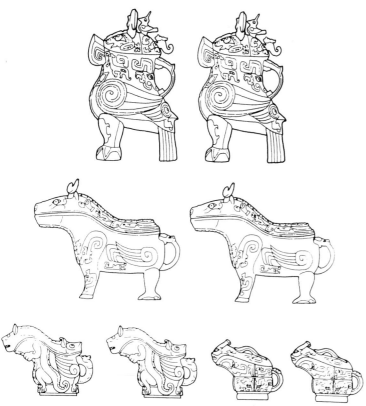

Fig. 45.1 *Drawing of animal-shaped vessels from Fu Hao's tomb. After Beijing 1980a.*

Fig. 45.2 *Inscription in the vessel.*

shape of an imaginary animal. Sometimes the body of the *gong*, as here, is also made in the shape of a creature. The *gong* is thought to have been used for holding wine.

Gong appear at Anyang for the first time in Fu Hao's tomb, that is about 1200 BC, and they are therefore relative latecomers to the repertory of bronze vessels employed for offerings to ancestors. The earliest known examples are in the present very elaborate form, with a tiger at the front and a bird, possibly an owl, at the rear. The heads of the two creatures are shown on the vessel lid, while their bodies

appear back to back on the lower part of the container.

As these first examples are elaborate and have decoration completely unlike that developed over several hundred years in the Henan area for ritual vessel ornament, it seems likely that the vessel shape and its decoration were suggested by objects made elsewhere.[1] Tigers and birds were motifs widely used on bronzes at the southern site of Dayangzhou at Xin'gan in Jiangxi province. It seems a possibility that *gong* were made at Anyang in response to the animal-shaped bronzes of the south. In other words, the Shang borrowed forms they thought were intriguing, and perhaps powerful, and adapted them to their own uses, drawing them into their own religious rituals: the offerings of sacrifices to their ancestors. Indeed several types of animal-shaped vessels appear in Fu Hao's tomb (fig. 45.1). At the same time marble sculptures in the shapes of tigers and owls found at Anyang indicate that these creatures had become integrated into the religious beliefs or customs of the Shang.[2]

However, this interest in images of real creatures did not last at Anyang. *Gong* in the shapes of tigers and birds seem to have been made for only a relatively short time. The tomb of Fu Hao also had *gong* decorated, not with tigers and birds, but with the animal face known as a *taotie*, seen already on the *fang ding* (no. 40) and the *pou* (no. 43). These *gong* are more upright and less animal-like than the present example. Their bodies are also divided vertically by flanges, obscuring yet further the realistic character of the original *gong* form. This *taotie*-decorated *gong* type continued into the Western Zhou, when it disappeared. The very short life of the *gong* decorated with tigers and birds reinforces the suggestion that these motifs were taken from an alien culture and adapted for a short time to metropolitan Shang use, but soon modified and obliterated.

The features of this *gong* draw to our attention two important aspects of the use of alien designs within a society in which they are unfamiliar. When motifs such as the tiger and the bird were introduced from one context, the cultures of central southern China, to another, the metropolitan Shang culture of Anyang, they are likely to have had different meanings and significances in the two different contexts. Secondly, alien objects can only be introduced to a society when it is in a receptive mood. It is likely that the Shang at the time of Fu Hao were in a buoyant social and military position, willing to exploit the goods and ideas of their neighbours. Once the strength of the Shang declined, as it did towards the end of the dynasty, they turned in on themselves and abandoned many of the exciting exotic objects and decorative motifs they had adopted earlier.

The present *gong* has a pair and both are inscribed with the name Fu Hao (fig. 45.2). On both are traces of textile impression, as these bronzes, like many others, were obviously wrapped in fine textiles in burial.

Published: *Kaogu xuebao* 1977.2, pp. 1–22, pl. 7: 2; *Wenwu* 1977.11, pp. 32–7; Beijing 1980a, pl. 26: 1; *Kaogu* 1981.6, pp. 511–18; *Kaogu* 1983.7, pp. 716–25; Osaka 1993, no. 31; Beijing 1993a, p. 150, no. 1; Goepper 1995, no. 28.

1 The possible alien origins of the *gong* are discussed in Rawson 1994. For the development of the vessel type see Bagley 1987, no. 73.
2 Varying interpretations of the tiger and the owl have been made, but as most of these are based on later texts they remain open to question. The owl, a nocturnal predator, has been considered both as a symbol of misfortune and death, and as a bird of night with a protective spirit. The tiger is generally thought to represent power, but the strange squatting position of this so-called tiger has caused a number of authors to refute its interpretation as such in the first place.

Fig. 46.1 *Inscription on the axe.*

46 Ceremonial axe, *yue*

Late Shang period, Anyang phase, *c.* 1200 BC
Bronze
Length 39.3 cm; width 38.5 cm; weight 9.0 kg
Excavated in 1976 from tomb M5, Xiaotun, near Anyang, Henan province (M5: 799)
Institute of Archaeology, Beijing

This large axe, of a type known in Chinese as *yue*, was found with three others in Fu Hao's tomb. This is the largest group of ceremonial axes to be found in a single burial. The *yue* is inscribed with Fu Hao's name (fig. 46.1). It is thought that such axes were employed for the ceremonial execution of humans or animals. A pictogram that is often seen in bronze inscriptions (fig. 46.2) provides information on the function of the axe. The graphs show a human body above which is an axe in lieu of a head, perhaps indicating that the axe was used to decapitate men.[1] Large numbers of decapitated people buried in the tombs of the Shang kings suggest that human sacrifices were required for funeral rites and possibly other rituals.[2] The decapitated victims may have been captives. Skeletons discovered in some of the Shang royal tombs show that

Fig. 46.2 *Examples of the pictograph* yue. *After Yang Xizhang and Yang Baocheng 1986, fig. 3.*

intact bodies, probably wives and relatives of the king, were also buried. The remains of skeletons of sixteen people were found in Fu Hao's grave.

The *yue* axes were descended from the large stone neolithic axes that were interred in the tombs of the powerful. The

Fig. 46.3 *Rubbing of the decoration on the* yue.

earliest bronze versions, such as that found in a Shang tomb at Huangpi Panlongcheng in Hubei province, have large central holes, imitating those of stone axes.[3] Subsequently this hole was turned into the fanged jaw of a *taotie*-like monster. Later axes were decorated with other sorts of almost human-like faces.[4]

The present axe, however, lies outside this tradition because it is decorated with a human head flanked by two tigers in profile (fig. 46.3).[5] This design is undoubtedly southern in origin, appearing first on a *zun* in Erligang style, but probably of somewhat later date, from Anhui Funan (fig. 46.4a). Exactly the same design was found on a fragment of a vessel excavated with the human-like heads discussed above, at Sanxingdui in Guanghan county, Sichuan province (fig. 46.4b). Thus the design had travelled up most of the length of the Yangzi River. It also seems to have travelled to Anyang, where it appears on a pair of axes and on the handles of a very large cauldron (fig. 46.4c), made perhaps for one of the other consorts of the king Wu Ding (fig. 39.2). But at Anyang, unlike the southern sites, the design never seems to have been used on the main body of ritual vessels. This restriction of the design in the Anyang casting practices suggests that it was of interest to the Shang, but not central to their beliefs.

We do not know what the design signified either to the original users of it in the south or to the craftsmen and their patrons when it appeared at Anyang. It is likely that the addition of an obviously alien design was thought to add power and authority to the axe and its owner. The owner of the axe is signified by the name Fu Hao, which is cast on it.

Published: *Kaogu xuebao* 1972.2, pp. 1–22; *Wenwu* 1977.11, pp 32–7; *Wenwu* 1978.4, p. 90; Beijing 1980a, pl. 13: 1; Beijing 1985a, pl. 142; Yang Xizhang and Yang Baocheng 1986; *Kaogu* 1991.5, pp. 442–7; Osaka 1993, no. 42; Beijing 1993a, p. 153, no. 2; Goepper 1995, no. 32.

1 Yang Xizhang and Yao Baocheng 1986.
2 *Wenwu* 1987.11, pp. 48–56; *Kaogu* 1987.2, pp. 159–62; *Wenwu* 1982.2, pp. 69–72.
3 New York 1980, no. 7.
4 New York 1980, no. 23. This change is discussed in Rawson 1993b.
5 There have been conflicting accounts of the role of this design in the art and religion of ancient China. Those who concentrate primarily on myth and religion, namely Sarah Allan and Chang Kwang-chih, have assumed that the motif was common to a large area of Shang period China and that it was an essential element of Shang religious life (Allan 1991 and Chang Kwang-chih 1983). Both writers fail to distinguish between the use of the motif at southern centres and in the metropolitan Shang area of Anyang. Further, neither author considers the possibility that in the different areas of China the design is likely to have had different significances. Indeed, it is possible that the southerners spoke languages different from those used in Henan and thus expressed themselves in different ways. Distinctions between languages probably reinforced differences in social and religious practices and beliefs. For further comment see Rawson 1993a and b.

Fig. 46.4 *Designs of tigers with the figure of a man:*
a *Zun from Anhui Funan. After Anhui 1987, no. 1.*
b *Fragment from Sichuan Guanghan Sanxingdui. After* Wenwu *1987.10, p. 7, fig. 11:3.*
c *Handle on the Si Mu Wu fang ding (fig. 39.2). After Beijing 1984a, no. 589.*

◀ 46

47 Ivory vessel, *bei*, with turquoise inlay

Late Shang period, Anyang phase, *c.* 1200 BC
Ivory with turquoise inlay
Height 30.3 cm; diameter of rim 11.2–12.5 cm; wall thickness 0.9 cm
Excavated in 1976 from tomb M5, Xiaotun, near Anyang, Henan province (M5: 100)
Institute of Archaeology, Beijing

A hollow elephant tusk has been worked into a beaker that resembles the bronze ritual vessel form, *gu*. Here, however, a handle in the shape of a bird has been added, a bird that incidentally resembles the vigorously cast bird's head from Guanghan Sanxingdui (no. 29). The handle is fixed to the beaker by pegs at the top and bottom. The bird and decoration of *taotie* faces in four zones around the body are inlaid with turquoise, and the inlay is surrounded by a dense network of incised lines that resemble the angular spirals known as *leiwen*, used on bronzes.

Ivory of such an early date is rare, in part because the material decays readily. The present beaker was found in several pieces and has been extensively repaired, and some of the turquoise inlay has been replaced with modern materials.[1]

It seems likely that the Shang had some supplies of ivory, as elephants were still being hunted in the Yellow River region. An oracle bone inscription reads: 'This evening it is raining and we have killed an elephant'.[2] Elephant bones have also been found in Shang tombs.[3] Although elephant motifs occur occasionally on Shang period bronzes, again, as with so many representational motifs, vessels in the shape of elephants belong to the southern bronze tradition.[4] Carvings of elephants in jade (no. 49e) may thus be based upon a southern tradition.

The present ivory beaker and its pair were found with about eighty other items in ivory, jade, malachite and cowries in the earth fill above the main coffin chamber of the tomb. The objects were mainly hairpins, mirrors and small carvings in jade and other stones. Fragments of red lacquer were found in the same area, and the archaeologists report that the objects were all placed together very neatly. It is thought that these items were originally buried together in a box and may have been Fu Hao's personal possessions.[5]

Published: *Kaogu* 1977.5, pp. 341–50; Beijing 1980a, colour pl. 39; *Gugong wenwu yuekan* 1983.9 (1), pp. 68–9; Liu Daofan 1984, pp. 59–60; Yang Xiaoneng 1988b, pp. 37–9; *Gugong wenwu yuekan* 1988.10 (67), p. 85; *Kaogu* 1989.3, pp. 274–5; Osaka 1993, no. 43; Beijing 1993a, p. 154; Goepper 1995, no. 33.

1 For a discussion of the use of ivory see London 1984 and Hong Kong 1990. For a similar-shaped cup in marble see Umehara 1964, pp. 102: 1.
2 Liu Daofan 1984, p. 59.
3 Chang Kwang-chih 1980, p. 119.
4 Bagley 1987, figs 159, 184.
5 Beijing 1980a, p. 12, fig. 5, pl. 2: 2.

48a

48 Jade bowl, *gui*, with three spoons

Late Shang period, Anyang phase, *c.* 1200 BC

a Bowl, white jade with brownish yellow spots
Height 10.8 cm; diameter at rim 16.8 cm (M5: 321)

b Bone spoon (*shao*) with animal decor
Length 14.4 cm (M5: 323)

c Bone spoon (*shao*) with heart decor
Length 13.2 cm (M5: 324)

d Shell-shaped bronze spoon (*bi*)
Length 10 cm (M5: 329)

Excavated in 1976 from tomb M5, Xiaotun, near Anyang, Henan province
Institute of Archaeology, Beijing

This extremely rare jade bowl is shaped like the bronze ritual vessel type known as a *gui*. It is very unlikely to have been a standard ritual vessel, as the basin was not found with the

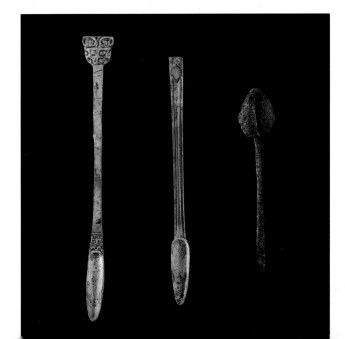

49a

main bronze ritual vessels within the burial chamber. Instead the basin and the three spoons inside it were found with a further jade basin and a stone carving of a buffalo in the midst of a layer of earth above the main chamber of Fu Hao's tomb. There were numerous skeletons of humans and dogs in the same area.

Vessel in jade are exceptional. Perhaps because a vessel in jade required first of all a large block, much of which was probably wasted in the process of working, very few attempts were made to create vessels in jade. If only a few were made, each would have been much prized, but they could never have become essential elements of ritual paraphernalia. Supplies of material were simply insufficient to make it possible for an appropriate number of the élite to own them. Indeed, the pieces belonging to Fu Hao are the only early jade vessels known. A few marble vessels exist, perhaps retrieved from other royal Shang tombs. Probably marble was viewed as a coarser and more abundant form of precious stone, less valuable than the material known today as nephrite or jade.

As with the ivory beaker described above, the jades and the marble vessels are decorated with designs also seen on the ritual bronzes. The present basin has an upper border of triangles, a central band of *taotie* pattern and a lower border of lozenges. Around the footring is a border of scrolls, also seen on many bronze vessels.

The spoons are all very slight, especially the two in bone. One of the bone spoons is ornamented with *taotie* heads in the manner of bronzes.

Published: *Kaogu* 1976.4, pp. 229–33; *Kaogu* 1977.5, pp. 341–50; Beijing 1980a, colour pl. 14: 2; *Wenwu* 1991.3, pp. 61–7; Osaka 1993, no. 44; Goepper 1995, no. 34.

49a,b **Two kneeling figures**

Late Shang period, Anyang phase, *c.* 1200 BC

a **Brownish jade with green and yellow spots**
Height 8.5 cm (M5: 372)

b **Stone**
Height 9.5 cm (M5: 376)

Excavated in 1976 from tomb M5, Xiaotun, near Anyang, Henan province
Institute of Archaeology, Beijing

The two kneeling figures are of two different materials: stone and jade. They formed part of a small group of five such kneeling human figures, three in jade and two in stone. It is interesting to note that most of the surviving Shang period carvings of humans are shown in this posture of subservience.

The jade carvings are generally more elaborate than those in stone. In the present case, the incised designs on the garments of the jade figure show snakes and a *taotie* face. The hair and features are also carefully rendered. The stone figure, on the other hand, is shown wearing an apron at the front between the knees, but any other garments are indistinguishable. The hairstyle is quite different from that of the jade figure, and the individual wears a headband.[1]

The function and significance of these figures are completely unknown. It is not clear whether they represent servants, ritual or priestly figures, or foreign tributaries. As they are great rarities, among the only examples of small Shang period human carvings to survive, they are likely to have been extremely valuable and to have offered Fu Hao some sort of power or access to power. All items made of jade were probably highly valued and considered to have special qualities as a result of the permanence and translucence of the stone.

Published: *Kaogu* 1976.4, pp. 229–33; *Kaogu* 1977.5, pp. 341–50; Beijing 1980a, colour pls 23: 2, 24: 2; *Wenwu* 1982.12, pp. 84–6; *Kaogu* 1984.10, pp. 945–8; Zhou Xibao 1984; Zhou Xun and Gao Chunming 1988 and 1991; Shen Congwen 1992; Osaka 1993, no. 47; *Wenwu* 1993.9, pp. 60–8; Beijing 1993a, p. 156, no. 2; Goepper 1995, no. 35a–b.

1 For other figures see Beijing 1980a, pp. 150–6; Umehara 1964, pls 134–7; New York 1980, no. 39.

49c

49c–f Animals

Late Shang period, Anyang phase, *c.* 1200 BC

c Bird, jade
Length 6 cm (M5: 403)

d Tiger, jade
Length 11.7 cm (M5: 409)

e Elephant, jade
Length 6 cm (M5: 510)

f Monkey, rock crystal
Height 4.6 cm (M5: 407)

Excavated in 1976 from tomb M5, Xiaotun, near Anyang, Henan province
Institute of Archaeology, Beijing

49d

The three carvings in jade represent an imaginary bird, a tiger and an elephant, and the fourth, in rock crystal, portrays a monkey-like man. The three jades are typical of the exceptionally large and fine jade carvings found in Fu Hao's tomb, which far surpass in quality and quantity those known from other Shang burials. This may be because such tombs as have been excavated belong to individuals lower down the social scale, while most of the royal Shang tombs may have been looted by the Zhou at the conquest *c.* 1050 BC. We have evidence of this destruction from later Zhou period tombs in Shanxi province at Tianma Qucun, where tombs of the ninth and eighth centuries BC have been found to contain jades of the Shang period, probably seized during the conquest.[1]

At the time of Fu Hao, animal-shaped jades were a relatively recent introduction to the Shang repertoire.[2] Many were copied from much more ancient jades of neolithic times, which had been passed down over long periods or recently amassed during Shang military campaigns outside Henan. For example, jades in the form of coiled dragons, of which there are many in Fu Hao's tomb, seem to have been copied from much earlier dragons of the Hongshan neolithic period in Liaoning province (Introduction, fig. 2).[3]

The animals shown here were developed at the time of Fu Hao and possibly by analogy with Shang copies of much earlier dragon sculptures. Here the tiger and the elephant

49e

49f ▶

resemble forms, developed in the southern cultures of Jiangxi and Henan provinces.[4] This interest in animal carvings probably accompanied the Shang concern with exotic bronze designs and forms, which also depicted animals. The Shang may have adopted animal designs from elsewhere, not only because of their interest in the alien and the curious, but also because they thought the animal designs would give them additional power and good fortune.

The fine, three-dimensional jade carvings did not, however, endure. Later Shang animal-shaped jades are much flatter, and during the early Western Zhou the skill and interest in carving such jades disappeared,[5] and their supposed meanings and significances must have been forgotten. When ancient animal-shaped jades were buried at Tianma Qucun in the Western Zhou period, as mentioned above, presumably their significance and value lay not in their ancient meaning, but in the simple fact that they were ancient.

The carvings are all pierced and would have been worn.

Published: *Kaogu* 1976.4, pp. 229–33; *Kaogu* 1977.5, pp. 341–50; Beijing 1980a, pls 134: 1, 135: 2, colour pl. 29: 1, pl. 136: 4; *Wenwu* 1982.12, pp. 84–6; *Kaogu* 1984.10, pp. 945–8; Zhou Xibao 1984; Osaka 1993, nos 51: 1, 48: 1, 48: 2, 48: 4; Beijing 1993a, p. 157; Goepper 1995, no. 35c–f.

1 *Wenwu* 1994.8, pp. 1–21, figs 26, 28.
2 Rawson 1992a.
3 Rawson 1995, section 12.
4 See also animals in marble, Umehara 1964, pls CXXXIV–CXXXVII.
5 See, for example, jade fish and bird amulets from Western Zhou tombs at Shaanxi Chang'an Huayuancun (*Wenwu* 1986.1, pp. 1–31, figs 50: 10–13; 51).

50 Comb and three hairpins

Late Shang period, Anyang phase, *c.* 1200 BC

a Jade comb with bird decoration

Height 10.4 cm; width 5.1 cm; thickness 0.3 cm (M5: 512)

b Bone hairpin with dragon decoration

Length 19.3 cm (M5: 103)

c Bone hairpin with lozenge decoration

Length 14 cm (M5: 116)

d Bone hairpin with bird decoration

Length 13.2 cm (M5: 153)

Excavated in 1976 from tomb M5, Xiaotun, near Anyang, Henan province
Institute of Archaeology, Beijing

Three combs and 527 hairpins of jade or bone have been found in Fu Hao's tomb, indicating her wealth and high status. The comb illustrated here is of jade and the pins are of bone. Three of the tines of the comb are missing; it is ornamented with two confronted birds. Each of the three hairpins has a different decoration at the end: one has a dragon's head with a v-shaped notched body, the second has a trapezoidal end and the third has a tufted bird.

Of the 527 hairpins, the 499 made of bone were found arranged in neat rows with the ivory beaker (no. 47). It is likely, as mentioned in that entry, that these items were placed together in a box. The jade hairpins were found inside the inner coffin in the grave chamber.

50a

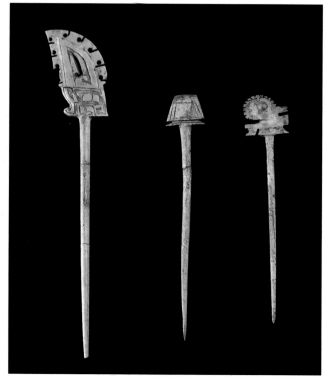

50b,c,d

Combs and hairpins had been used by women and probably also by men from the neolithic period. For example, a stone hairpin was found at the neolithic site of Taosi, the source of the dragon-painted bowl (no. 7).[1]

Published: Beijing 1980a, pls 149, 209–13; Goepper 1995, no. 36.

1 *Kaogu* 1980.1, pp. 18–31, pl. 6: 1.

51 Rectangular vessel for offering food, *He Da fang ding*

c. 1200–1000 BC
Height 38.5 cm; length at lip 29.8 cm; width at lip 23.7 cm
Excavated in 1959 in Ningxiang county, Hunan province
Hunan Provincial Museum, Changsha

The four large human faces decorating this rectangular cauldron render it quite exceptional. The vessel's shape is similar to that of nos 39 and 40, but no other rectangular cauldron is known with such decoration. Indeed, there are very few bronze ritual vessels decorated with anything remotely resembling a human face. As illustrated by the ritual bronzes from Fu Hao's tomb, the majority of Shang period wine and food vessels carry monster face designs of the genre generally known as *taotie*. Some exceptional pieces display real creatures among the designs. But, as mentioned above, it seems likely that these realistic creatures were borrowed from southern bronze casting.

The present vessel was found in several pieces on a scrap heap in Hunan province and is thought to have come from a site in Ningxiang, an area that has produced a number of very fine bronzes with what are, by the standards of Anyang, very unconventional forms and ornament. Among these is the four-headed ram *zun* mentioned above. Indeed, the human heads seen on this *fang ding* share with the rams' heads on the *zun* an exceptional realism and a very fine degree of casting. We do not know why the southern areas of China produced these fine bronzes with realistic designs which, it seems, were shunned at Anyang. We can simply observe the difference.

Moreover, we can see the impact made by such southern designs on the metropolitan Shang and later Western Zhou areas. For example, there are two surviving large *fang ding* from Anyang that carry, in place of the human heads, deer and buffalo heads respectively. These motifs do not, however, fill the spaces provided and are densely covered in intaglio lines.[1] They do not seem fully accommodated to their positions in the vessel's ornament and lack the boldness of the present heads. Indeed, they highlight the contrast between the emphatic and realistic bronze motifs of the southern casting tradition, exemplified by the present *ding*, and the much more intricate and less representational motifs characteristic of

Fig. 51.1 *Inscription inside the vessel.*

Anyang ritual vessel casting.

In areas dominated by the Shang, human heads were more frequent on chariot fittings and weapons. This use continued into the Western Zhou (no. 52). Interest in human heads on weapons and chariot fittings reinforces the observation that at Anyang such motifs were rare if not entirely absent from ritual vessels.

As the present bronze belongs to a quite different culture from that of the Anyang ancestral cult illustrated by the Fu Hao bronzes, it is impossible to fathom the significance of the human head. On each side of the head are small horns and claws, but these may be no more than vestiges of the *taotie* motifs generally employed on the vessels that the southern casters must have known from the Anyang tradition. We have little enough understanding of what bronzes made at Anyang may have been for; we have almost none for exotic pieces such as this one.

Inside the long side of the container is an inscription showing a blade of cereal and the figure of a man. The two graphs may be a clan sign reading, in modern Chinese, *He Da* (fig. 51.1). The use of Chinese graphs in this area indicates that a language similar to that employed at Anyang was known in the south. However, the use of Chinese graphs was probably fairly restricted in the south. The inscription perhaps indicates a relatively late date in the Shang period.

Published: *Wenwu* 1960.10, pp. 57–8; Watson 1973, no 79; Li Xueqin 1985c, no. 112; Yang Xiaoneng 1988b, no. 128; Beijing 1990a, no. 38; Beijing 1992a, no. 118; Goepper 1995, no. 24.

1 Li Xueqin 1985c, no. 25.

51

Zhou unified: The Western Zhou period, c. 1050–771 BC

In about 1050 BC a group of peoples, known to both themselves and the Shang as the Zhou, attacked and overthrew the Shang state and became the dominant power in northern central China. The Zhou conquest and their subsequent ordering of the state are the subjects of the earliest surviving long transmitted text, the *Shu jing (Book of Documents)*. This text gives a dramatic account of some of the principal events in early Zhou history. In addition, the Zhou cast long inscriptions in their ritual vessels. Thus, in contrast to the preceding period – the dynasty of Shang and the era of their contemporaries in such places as Sanxingdui in Sichuan province – we have both considerable archaeological evidence and long texts for the Zhou. These two kinds of evidence provide two rather different views of the Zhou and the ways in which they advanced their control over the inhabitants of the present-day provinces of Shaanxi, Shanxi, Henan, Hebei, Shandong and some regions further south.

We do not know where the Zhou came from, but they seem to have had strong links with areas to the west of the principal Shang strongholds in Henan and Shandong. They are thought to have originated either in Shanxi or much further west in eastern Gansu or western Shaanxi. With the fall of the Shang, the Zhou established their capital near the present-day city of Xi'an and set up a centre, where ancestor temples were housed, in the area of Qishan and Fufeng counties, known as the Zhouyuan. A secondary centre was founded at Chengzhou (present-day Luoyang). Relatives of the Zhou kings helped to control the new territories as rulers of small city states, including the state of Jin near Houma in Shanxi, the state of Yan near Beijing, and the states of Qi and Lu in Shandong. During the first two centuries of Zhou rule, a fairly homogeneous élite culture was established in all these areas.

The material remains left behind by the Zhou, as by the Shang, comprise large numbers of richly equipped tombs and traces of substantial cities. The inscribed bronze ritual vessels which the Zhou bequeathed to later generations have, by and large, been found in hoards rather than in tombs. The hoards were hastily buried in 771 BC, when the Zhou had to flee in the face of invaders from the west, deserting for ever their ritual centre in the Zhouyuan and the capital near Xi'an.

Zhou tombs and their contents reproduce many features of Shang burial practices. They comprise stepped pit graves in which the deceased was placed within two wooden coffins (or one if of lower rank), and the burial goods included ritual vessels. Pits with chariots and their horses, or just horses, might be located next to the tombs of higher-ranking members of Zhou nobility. As the Zhou do not seem to have used Shang practices quite so faithfully before their conquest, it seems likely that they deliberately copied them later. Indeed, close verisimilitude with their predecessors may have given the Zhou a sense of having replaced them satisfactorily, a feeling of legitimacy.

We know from their documents that the Zhou were preoccupied with creating and asserting a sense of their legitimacy. They claimed to have inherited the mandate of Heaven, granted them through success in battle, because the Shang had finally proved themselves unworthy of trust by treating the peoples of their territories harshly and disregarding the decorum proper to the ruler. Claims to legitimate power, supported by the will of Heaven, which was manifested by success in war and prosperity in peacetime, and recorded for posterity in writing, established a theory of rulership that was not superseded until the twentieth century. Moreover, their well articulated claims, read by all later generations as evidence of Zhou control of a unified China, provided a model to which all later rulers aspired.

From textual sources it would appear that the Zhou believed themselves and wished to be seen as rulers of a single unified state. Indeed, the scope of their power was impressive. The present-day province of Shaanxi was densely inhabited along the Wei River and its tributaries, establishing a large if somewhat diffuse power base. In addition, the Zhou controlled much of the central area of northern China, as far north as Beijing and as far east as Shandong. But, over the following century or so, the Zhou were threatened by attacks, first from the south and east and later from the west, to which they finally succumbed. As central control fluctuated, we can see traces of the political and military upheavals in both the distribution of bronzes and high-ranking tombs, which after all represented economic power, and the contents of inscriptions. These speak of campaigns in the south, honours given to lords who helped the kings, and even of such social and economic issues as land transactions and court cases. Thus, although the picture the Zhou obviously hoped to create was of a strong and centralised state with a single powerful ruler, in practice the Zhou house was threatened from without and perhaps even from within.

The traditional and best known Zhou artefacts, not included in the catalogue, are their bronze ritual vessels, and several examples are illustrated in the essay on bronze vessels (Rawson, figs 9, 11, 14). The diverse figures and faces displayed here show that, although the Zhou seem to have wished to emphasise their inheritance of the Shang right to rule through a continuity with Shang ways of life and religion, they incorporated in their material possessions features of non-Shang culture.

As illustrated at no. 43 above, the principal decorative motif on the major Shang ritual bronzes was an animal-like creature with two large eyes, florid horns and a large jaw. This creature was given the name of *taotie* in the fifth century BC or thereabouts, long after the Shang had disappeared. The Zhou likewise took over the *taotie* to decorate their ritual vessels (Rawson, fig. 9). Indeed, in the arena of sacrificial rites to the ancestors they followed Shang practices fairly closely in casting and decorating bronzes. Human faces and figures did not appear on bronze vessels in either the Shang or Zhou periods, with the exception of very occasional decoration on vessel handles (fig. 46.4c).

However, as we know, bronzes were cast with decoration of human faces in southern China, as illustrated by the *fang ding* (no. 51). Moreover, in parts of China well beyond the control of the Shang, at Sanxingdui (nos 22–35) and in central eastern China at Dayangzhou in Xin'gan county, Jiangxi province, human-like figures and faces appear in bronze to depict spirits, priests and other mysterious beings (fig. 52.4). Features of the bronzes made by the Zhou indicate that they were aware of or had in their possession some of these strange southern human-like faces. They made copies of the great figures from Sanxingdui in miniature (fig. 22.1), and they reproduced faces from Jiangxi in their chariot fittings (figs 52.3, 52.4). We do not know how the Zhou became aware of these alien exotic pieces or came to quote features of them in their own fittings.

On the other hand, a jade in the catalogue (no. 54) does help to illustrate the links between north and south, past and present. This jade plaque in the shape of a strange imaginary being with enormous tusk-like teeth was carved in the late neolithic period, *c.* 2000 BC, either in central southern China or on the east coast. It was found, however, in a tomb of the Western Zhou period close to the Zhou capital near Xi'an. No other jades of a comparably early date have turned up in these tombs. Thus it would seem that this stray was rediscovered at some point after the neolithic period and then transmitted or traded at least 500 km to the site in which it was found.

52 Two human-like masks

Early Western Zhou, 11th–10th century BC
Bronze

a Naturalistic mask (M1193:175)
Height 18.5 cm; width 17.6 cm

b Stylised mask (M1193:42)
Height 21 cm; width 22.3 cm

Excavated in 1986 from tomb M1193 at Liulihe, Fangshan county, near Beijing
Bureau of Cultural Relics, Beijing City

Remains of a substantial city have been found at Liulihe in Fangshan county to the south of the present-day city of Beijing. This city was the centre of the state of Yan, founded by the descendants of the Duke of Shao, brother of King Wu, the first king of the Zhou. Small powers such as the state of Yan, which were governed by associates of the king, were essential components of Zhou rule outside their main power base in Shaanxi province. From these strong centres the Zhou lords seem to have been able to dominate the surrounding areas for about 150 years. Thereafter, as central power declined, so too did some of these regional states.[1]

A large cemetery has been discovered and partially excavated near the city remains. The tombs vary in size, presumably depending on the status of their occupants. A significant number of chariot burials have also been discovered. Among the tomb contents are inscribed bronzes that name Zhou nobles, including the Tai Bao (the title given to the Duke of Shao) and the Yan Hou (the Marquis of Yan), or the ruler of the state. These ritual bronzes follow the shapes and the decoration of pieces cast at the capital. Indeed, their inscriptions are also in the formal Chinese script used for inscriptions cast on the bronzes found in Shaanxi.[2] Communication between Yan near Beijing and the centre of metropolitan

Fig. 52.1 *South wall of tomb* M1193 *at Liulihe, Fangshan county, near Beijing.*

52a

52b

Fig. 52.2 *Human-like face on a chariot fitting from a tomb at Xibeigang in Anyang, Henan province. Shang dynasty,* c. *1200 BC. After Bagley 1987, fig. 134.*

Zhou power, 1000 km away, must have been very good.

The two bronze faces exhibited here came from one of the major tombs excavated at the Yan state cemetery. Tomb M1193 was over 10 m below ground level, the depth alone

indicating the importance of the burial. It had four access ramps located at the corners of the tomb, a highly unusual arrangement. In addition, although the tomb had been partially robbed, among the ritual vessels recovered were two whose long inscriptions contained references to the Tai Bao, indicating that the tomb occupant was probably a member of the ruling family of Yan.[3]

The bronze faces were found against the walls of the burial (fig. 52.1). Traces of red, black and yellow lacquered fragments near them may indicate that shields were laid against the walls, and that bronze faces or ornaments probably decorated the shields. The bronze ornaments are sometimes simply circular and undecorated. Four were cast in the shape of relatively naturalistic faces and five as stylised faces. All had four double holes at the edges for attachment to the shields.

The naturalistic face is oval in form with a rounded surface, modelled to show the prominent nose and cheekbones. It also has relief eyebrows and projecting ears. The eyes are almond-shaped with sunken pupils, while the mouth is crescent-shaped and has small openwork teeth. The stylised face is completely different in shape and execution. It is considerably wider in proportion to its length, with relatively small ears. The eyes and mouth are enormous, and the pupils and teeth are in bold openwork, as are the nostrils of the nose and the slits for eyebrows.[4]

The sources of these two faces are also completely different. As already mentioned, faces are almost unknown on Shang and Zhou ritual bronzes. However, both states employed human figures as decoration for chariot and harness fittings. The nearest ancestor to the human face is a

Fig. 52.3 *Drawing of a face on a drum. Shang period, but from southern China. Sumitomo Collection. For whole drum see Bagley 1987, fig. 183.*

Fig. 52.4 *Drawing of a standard in the form of a face with two large horn-like extensions on the head. From a large tomb mound at Dayangzhou, Xin'gan county, Jiangxi province. Shang period, but made in southern China. After Beijing 1992a, no. 129.*

Fig. 52.5 *Drawing of a fitting in the form of a face from Chenggu county, southern Shaanxi province. Shang period, but made in southern China. After* Kaogu *1992.12, p. 1112, fig. 1.*

relatively realistic face on a harness fitting found at Anyang (fig. 52.2). The present human-like face seems a simple and direct continuation of this tradition.

The rather grim stylised face has a quite different history. It seems to belong to the southern, non-Shang bronze casting tradition of around 1200 BC. A possible ancestor is found in the decoration of a drum in the Sumitomo Collection that probably came from Hunan province (fig. 52.3). It has eyes with sunken circular pupils and a grimacing open mouth displaying teeth comparable to those that are among the defining features of the present face.[5] Similar features in a more exaggerated form can be seen in two other southern bronzes: a large standard in the shape of a strange head with two projecting horns (fig. 52.4), similar to those on the head of the Sumitomo drum, and a chariot fitting from Chenggu county near the Han River (fig. 52.5). Both these areas used bronzes around 1200 BC and belonged to southern non-Shang cultural areas.[6] In the Shang area, related faces appear on two axes from Sufutun in Shandong province.[7]

It seems that, during the early Zhou period, contact between the metropolitan Zhou and such non-metropolitan areas brought strange bronze faces to their attention, and the Zhou then adapted these to their own uses. These southern features are particularly evident in western and central Shaanxi, near the principal Zhou centres of power, and in the extreme north in the Yan state. This sharing of exotic motifs is perhaps another indication of the close contacts between Yan and the metropolis.

Published: *Kaogu* 1990.1, p. 30, fig. 9; *Kaogu* 1992.12, p. 1112, figs 1, 2; Goepper 1995, no. 52.

1 The early Yan state, although remote from the metropolitan centres of power, seems from its physical remains to have been an important force with close links to the capital.
2 For reports of excavations at Fangshan see Beijing 1995; *Kaogu* 1984.5, pp. 405–16, 404.
3 *Kaogu* 1992.12, pp. 1111–21.
4 For discussion of human faces in Shang and Western Zhou bronze design see Rawson 1993b.
5 It has been suggested that Liangzhu period jade faces (no. 16) are the distant sources of designs such as those on the Sumitomo drum (fig. 52.3). If this comparison is correct, the resemblance is likely to have arisen because jades of great antiquity were rediscovered in the Hunan area and may have provided models for the bronze industry, rather than because a continuous series of faces was developed from the jade, remaining in use down to the time of the Sumitomo drum.
6 Bagley 1987, pp. 32–6.
7 For hybrids see fittings from Qishan (*Kaogu* 1980.3, p. 215) and from Xi'an (*Wenwu* 1988.6, p. 14, fig. 22).

53 Axle pin decorated with a human figure

Middle Western Zhou period, 10th–9th century BC
Bronze
Length 19 cm; width 10 cm; height of human figure 18.3 cm
Excavated in 1966 from tomb M451 at Beiyao Pangjiagou, near
Luoyang, Henan province
Luoyang City Museum, Henan province

This highly decorated fitting was the pin that attached a
bronze cap to a wooden chariot axle. The drawings in figure
53.1 illustrate how this was done. Although axle pins were
often decorated with animals or figures, the present example
is more elaborate than usual. The ornament consists of a fully
modelled figure of a kneeling man, his facial features shown
in detail. He wears an elaborate topknot. His dress has a conspicuous collar and behind his back is a flat plate on which
is cast an abstract motif in relief.

Chariots were first used in China in the Anyang phase of
the Shang dynasty, c. 1300–1050 BC.[1] The basic structure of
the chariot is likely to have been brought to China from areas
to the west – the Shang chariot shares features such as the
bent circles of wood, or felloes, forming the wheel, with
chariots buried in the Caucasus. Chariot burials, in which
complete chariots were interred with their horses and drivers,
appear at Anyang for the first time. The bronze sections of
such chariots, including the axle caps and linchpins, and harness ornaments for the horses, were buried along with the
wooden frame. Presumably such chariots were intended for
use by the tomb occupants in the afterlife.

It would appear that the Zhou had adopted from the Shang
the practice of using chariots for military purposes and then
burying them in pits. Zhou burials in Shaanxi, the centre of
Zhou rule after the conquest, are equipped both with ritual
vessels in the Shang manner and, if the burial was a major
one, with subordinate pits containing chariots and horses.
Such chariot burials were not confined to the Zhou capital
near Xi'an, but are found at the tombs of smaller Zhou states
such as Yan and Yu. Thus chariots were deployed both as
instruments of war and as statements of status by the Zhou
nobles and rulers in all the principal Zhou domains. They do
not seem to have been buried, and therefore may not have
been used, in non-Zhou areas.[2]

Nevertheless, the drivers of the chariots may have come
from other regions and then been employed by the Zhou.
Thus a chariot fitting from the Yu state tombs at Baoji in
western Shaanxi province depicts a driver with patterns of
deer on his dress.[3] This individual may have come from the
extreme west. Other figures, as here, show different regional
features. In the present case the topknot of hair is especially
distinctive. Human figures on chariot fittings, and especially
linchpins, seem to have been part of a decorative tradition

53

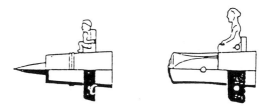

Fig. 53.1 *Drawings illustrating linchpins combined with axle caps. After
Wenwu 1985.8, p. 31, fig. 10.*

quite separate from that of the bronze ritual vessels of the
time, indicating a different intellectual outlook on objects
which had a more practical and often military function.

Published: Beijing 1972b, no. 88; Jin Weinuo 1986, no. 92; Luoyang 1990,
no. 14; Ledderose and Schlombs 1990, p. 50, fig. 21; Goepper 1995,
no. 51.

1 For the sources of Chinese chariots see Shaughnessy 1988.
2 For a survey of Zhou chariot burials see Lu Liancheng 1993.
3 See for example Lu Liancheng and Hu Zhisheng 1988, vol. 2, pl. 213.

54 Ornament in the shape of a monstrous human-like face

Neolithic period, probably Shijiahe culture, *c.* 2500–2000 BC
White translucent jade
Height 5.2 cm; width 4.1 cm; thickness 0.6 cm
Excavated in 1985 from tomb M17 at Zhangjiapo, Chang'an
county, near Xi'an, Shaanxi province (M17:01)
Institute of Archaeology, Beijing

Although it was found in a Western Zhou tomb of the tenth
to ninth century BC, this exceptionally fine carving of a jade
monster-like face dates to a much earlier stage and probably
comes from a neolithic culture based some 500 km away. It
may have been passed down through generations or raided
from an earlier tomb and then buried at this much later date.
Both the shapes and features of the face and its manner of
execution are typical of the very fine jade working of the
neolithic Shijiahe culture of Hubei province (*c.* 2500–2000 BC).
A bird coiled in a circle with wings and tail feathers in fine
thread relief, excavated at Shijiahe (fig. 54.1), demonstrates
that jades with fine thread relief are of this early date. A very
similar bird has come from the tomb of Fu Hao at Anyang.[1]
A number of faces with related thread relief indicating eyes
and other features are also known (fig. 54.2). They all seem
to be of the same period, namely of neolithic date.[2] Many of
these faces have open mouths with pairs of large tusk-like
teeth at the corners, as here. Most of these neolithic jades
have not been scientifically excavated. One such jade that has
been (fig. 54.3) is from the large tomb at Dayangzhou, already
mentioned in connection with the face-like fittings in no. 52
(fig. 52.4).[3] It is possible that the jade from Dayangzhou is
another example of the survival of a much earlier piece in a
later context.

We do not know what the original faces signified for the
peoples who made them, nor indeed have we any idea what
the Western Zhou, or for that matter the earlier inhabitants
of Dayangzhou in Jiangxi province, might have made of these
strange faces they inherited or rediscovered. It is likely that
these faces had completely different meanings and significances for the different peoples who owned them. However,
both the very fine carving and the strange features must
always have attracted attention.

The Zhou certainly possessed a number of southern jades,
including jades in which birds were combined with human
heads or faces. These combinations were copied in middle
Western Zhou jades, making for one of the most innovative

54

Fig. 54.2 *Drawings of human-like faces with large tusk-shaped teeth. Mainly neolithic period,* C. *2000* BC. *After Zhang Changshou 1987, p. 471, fig. 3.*

Fig. 54.1 *Drawing of a coiled bird with feathers in thread relief. From Shijiahe, Hubei province. Neolithic period, Shijiahe culture,* C. *2500* BC. *After Kaogu xuebao 1994.2, p. 226, fig. 23.*

Fig. 54.3 *Drawing of a monstrous human-like face in jade. From a large tomb mound at Dayangzhou, Xin'gan county, Jiangxi province, c. 1200 BC. After Rawson 1995, p. 37, fig. 22.*

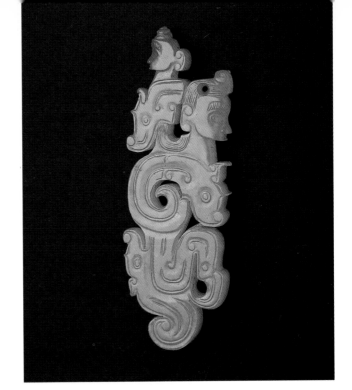

55

decorative styles of the ancient jade carving tradition. Neolithic jades with birds clutching heads in their talons are found in several forms, including a very fine piece in the Palace Museum in Beijing (Rawson, fig. 12a). This motif is reworked in complex designs on a large jade handle of the middle Western Zhou in the Metropolitan Museum, New York (Rawson, fig. 12c). Indeed, the durability that was one of the main attractions of Chinese jade made possible its long survival and gave rise to the copies of ancient pieces at later periods.

Published: Osaka 1993, no. 74; Goepper 1995, no. 55.

1 Beijing 1980a, fig. 85.8.
2 These faces have been much discussed. For a summary of references see Rawson 1995, section 11.
3 For a description of the finds at Dayangzhou in Xin'gan county, Jiangxi province, see Bagley 1993a.

55 Pendant of complex creatures with human heads and dragons

Middle Western Zhou, 10th–9th century BC
Green jade
Height 6.8 cm; width 2.4 cm; thickness 0.5 cm
Excavated in 1984 from tomb M157 at Zhangjiapo, Chang'an county, Shaanxi province
Institute of Archaeology, Beijing

The pendant comprises two small human-like heads in openwork combined with three dragon heads and parts of their coiled bodies. The detail and quality of the carving are exceptionally fine. Such complex combinations of creatures were new to the jade carvers of the middle Western Zhou. As mentioned in the previous entry, some time around 950 BC the Zhou seem to have acquired jades from southern or south-eastern China on which human heads were the principal motifs, or which combined human heads with birds. One example of such an ancient neolithic jade acquired by the Zhou is the previous ornament (no. 54). We have no certain evidence that the Zhou knew of the other type with birds and humans carved in the same piece. However, Zhou carvings indicate that some such combinations of motifs had become known to them.

Fig. 55.1 *Rubbings of two Western Zhou period jades. After Yang Jianfang 1987, p. 343, fig. 78: 2–3.*

Complex jades appear first in middle Western Zhou tombs. However, they were developed more fully at the beginning of the late Western Zhou, as jades came to be used in much greater quantities than they had been in earlier centuries. A change in bronze ritual vessels, amounting to a ritual revolution, was accompanied by a great increase in the numbers of jades buried and a change in the motifs with which they were decorated (fig. 57.1).[1]

Indeed, in the early Western Zhou, jade carving had been very scarce; only rather stereotyped jades were buried. But from the time of the ritual changes many more jades were interred, often combined with long strings of beads, such as the following two examples (nos 56, 57). The complex incised motifs of birds and human heads were in the main exchanged for designs comprising either human heads and dragons, or dragons alone. Many of these complex motifs were intertwined on single, relatively small pieces of jade, and interlaced motifs stemmed from this source.[2]

Tomb M157, in which the present jade was found, is one of a group of tombs in the cemetery at Zhangjiapo belonging to the Jing Shu family. The tomb had been partially robbed, but the excavation revealed a magnificent burial with long access ramps, on which were interred numerous chariot wheels. Several jades were recovered, including sections that would have covered the features of the face. Such jades as coverings for the features of the face are another aspect of the ritual changes. For the burial of jades deliberately placed on the body, as if to protect, or even to preserve it, is a development new in this period. In the first part of the Western Zhou such jades were not known. They were developed to an even greater level as the dynasty wore to a close (fig. 55.1). Some of the most elaborate examples have been recovered from the tombs of the Jin state in Shanxi province, near Houma at Tianma Qucun (fig. 57.1).[3] The Jin state was contemporaneous with the Western Zhou.

These Jin state tombs have produced jades of a more advanced form of the present example combining human heads and dragons. Similar pieces have also come from the Zhouyuan, from a tomb at Qiangjia in Shaanxi province. This wide distribution of a similar jade type, following a period when there had been a scarcity of jades, indicates the wide-reaching changes that had been wrought in burial patterns and the conformity that had been achieved.[4]

Published: Osaka 1993, no. 77; Goepper 1995, no. 56.

1 The ritual revolution is discussed in the essay by Rawson.
2 For a discussion of the origins of interlace see Rawson 1990, vol. 1, pp. 113–25.
3 Such jades are discussed and illustrated in Rawson 1995, section 24, figs 1–3.
4 The site at Qiangjia is reported in *Wenbo* 1987.4, pp. 5–20.

56 Necklace in 179 sections

Early Western Zhou, *c.* 950–900 BC
Jade, agate and turquoise
Excavated in 1984 from tomb M251 at Liulihe, Fangshan county, near Beijing
Bureau of Cultural Relics, Beijing City

The present necklace belongs to the complex jade ornaments of the type mentioned in the previous entry. It was found in one of the major tombs at the Yan state burial ground, at Liulihe in Fangshan county to the south of Beijing. Two face-like bronzes from the same cemetery have been discussed (no. 52).

The necklace came from a tomb containing exceptionally fine cast bronzes, still in place as they were buried (fig. 56.1). Among these bronzes a vessel cast for one Bo Ju is famous for its fine ornament of *taotie* face with projecting buffalo horns (fig. 56.2). On the grounds of the shapes, decoration and inscriptions in such bronzes, the tomb can be dated to the early Western Zhou. Because the grave was undisturbed, the necklace can be reconstructed with some confidence. The

drawing shows how it was found (fig. 56.3). The strings of beads were joined together in the front by a ring, a small bead or tube and a frog. Intermingled with the beads are a number of small flat decorated plaques, some of which may originally have been intended for quite different purposes but had here been reused.

Ornaments comprising strings of beads combined with plaques seem to have originated in the extreme west of the Zhou domain at Baoji in Shaanxi province. Among the earliest examples of such strings are the beads found in tomb M13 at Baoji Zhuyuangou.[1] As already mentioned, the Yan state seems to have had quite strong links with this very western area of the Zhou domain. Indeed the tripod (*li*) from the same tomb (fig. 56.2) carries decoration that probably also derived from this western area. It may be that the wearing of beads combined with jades was introduced to the northeast from the west. In due course such beads were adopted in the whole of the metropolitan Zhou area, especially after the ritual changes at the end of the middle Western Zhou (fig. 57.1). Thus the peripheral areas anticipated by a few decades a practice that was to become uniform. Following the Western Zhou invention of these long jade necklaces and other jade

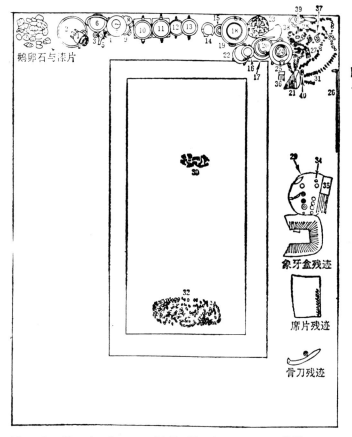

Fig. 56.1 *Plan of tomb M251 at Liulihe, Fangshan county, near Beijing. After Beijing 1995a, p. 34.*

Fig. 56.2 *The Bo Ju li from tomb M251 at Liulihe, Fangshan county, near Beijing. Early Western Zhou period, c. 950–900 BC. Height 33 cm. After New York 1980, no. 56.*

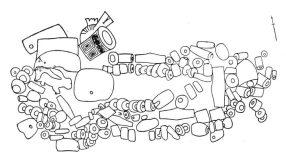

Fig. 56.3 *Drawing of the beads as found in tomb M251 at Liulihe, Fangshan county, near Beijing. After Beijing 1995a, p. 35.*

57 Ornament

Late Western Zhou period, 9th-8th century BC
Jade, agate and turquoise
Jade plaque, height 8 cm; width 5.5 cm. Strings contain 223 beads
Excavated in 1990 at Pingdingshan, Henan province
Institute of Archaeology and Cultural Relics Bureau, Henan province

56

ornaments, the use of pendants developed in the Eastern Zhou. As some of these bead strings include beads of faience introduced from Western or Central Asia, the use of bead strings may originally have come from beyond the boundaries of the metropolitan Zhou area.

Published: Beijing 1995, pl. 48:2; Goepper 1995, no. 53.

1 Lu Liancheng and Hu Zhisheng 1988, vol. 2, pl. 38.

The ornament is arranged about a substantial jade plaque, pierced along one side, from which hang strings of beads. The plaque is trapezoidal in shape and decorated on one face with confronted dragons that have small human-like heads at the ends of their tails. These creatures are a later form of the human head and dragon motif seen on no. 55. Indeed, the present jade and agate ornament developed out of the interest in elaborate jade and bead concoctions that flourished following the ritual revolution in the middle Western Zhou.

The present type seems to have come into existence at the end of the Western Zhou. A fine example has come from

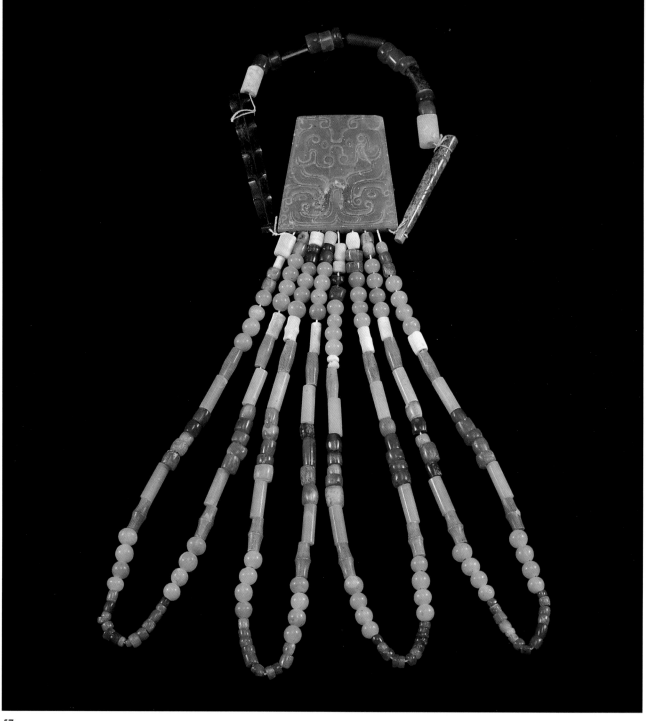

57

the late Western Zhou tomb, M31, of a Jin noble or lord in the Jin state cemetery at Tianma Qucun, near Houma in Shanxi province (fig. 57.1).[1] The shape seems to have continued in use into the early Eastern Zhou, and an example of this slightly later date has been excavated from tomb M102 in the same cemetery.[2]

The present jade and its agate beads come from another local state, the state of Ying, whose capital was at present-day Pingdingshan in central Henan province. Although it is some-times suggested that the tombs at Pingdingshan are of the late Western Zhou, it seems very likely that the majority of

tombs so identified could equally well belong to the early Eastern Zhou. For it was in the Eastern Zhou, when the capital at Xi'an had been destroyed, that wealth and activity shifted east.

The state of Ying had indeed had an existence well before the fall of the Zhou.[3] Political and economic instability during the middle and late Western Zhou may have led to a retreat of resources to Shaanxi, which were only liberated for use in Henan or Shandong once the Zhou strongholds further west had fallen. Certainly jades are abundant in the early Eastern Zhou tombs in the states of Jin, Guo and Ying.[4]

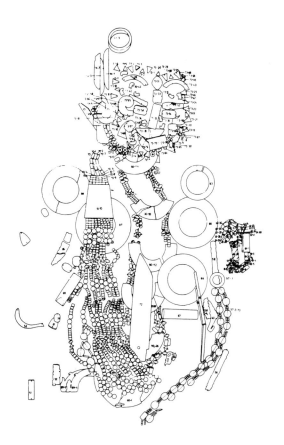

Fig. 57.1 *Drawing of jades for the upper part of the body (left) as recovered from tomb M31 at Shanxi Tianma Qucun and (above) a reconstruction of jades to cover the face. Western Zhou period, 9th–8th century BC. After* Wenwu *1994.8, pp. 22–33, figs 3, 7.*

Published: Beijing 1990a, no. 56; Hebei 1991–3, vol. 2, no. 276; Beijing 1992a, no. 22; Goepper 1995, no. 54.

1 *Wenwu* 1994.8, pp. 22–33, 68, fig. 3.
2 *Wenwu* 1995.7, pp. 4–39.
3 For vessels inscribed with the title of the Ying Hou, or Marquis of Ying, see Rawson 1990, no. 4.
4 *Huaxia kaogu* 1988.1, pp. 30–44, pl. 6.

Zhou divided: The Eastern Zhou period, 770–221 BC

When the Zhou strongholds in Shaanxi fell before the invading Quan Rong in 771 BC, the Zhou rulers and some of the nobility fled eastwards. As described above, they first buried many of their bronze vessels at the ritual centre of Zhouyuan in present-day Qishan and Fufeng counties. Once they arrived further east, they had to create new sets of vessels and to re-establish themselves in these new areas.

Never again were the Zhou to rule a unified state. The central area of northern China split into a number of states centred on the cities established early in the dynasty by relations of the Zhou king. Not far from the Yellow River, the Zhou ruled from their secondary capital at present-day Luoyang, known in the Western Zhou period as Chengzhou. The Jin dominated Shanxi from their capital near Houma. In the extreme north the Yan state established another capital west of Beijing, and the Qi occupied Shandong, with lesser states at Lu and Ji.

But it was central China that benefited most from the decline of the Zhou. Powerful lords set themselves up in southern Henan and northern Hubei, and it is

here that resources were concentrated, as we can deduce from the many splendid items from this area in the catalogue. The region was dominated first by a number of smaller states by the names of Zheng, Huang and Zeng. But in due course they all came under the sway of the state of Chu, and for this reason many of the objects in this section are described as products of Chu culture. Chu also swept up the states along the east coast, which had, by and large, preserved a culture distinct from that of the main Zhou area.

The history of Chu before the fall of the Zhou is not clear, but from the moment of its demise, Chu became a growing force. It is often described as being outside the normal range of Zhou culture, but there is every evidence that it followed Zhou ritual practices.

The most obvious outsider on the map of this period was the state of Qin. The Qin moved from the west into the vacuum left by the Zhou. Initially their activities were restricted, but they soon emulated Zhou practices, including ritual vessel casting. As the centuries of their rule in Shaanxi developed, they built ever greater tombs and palaces. It would seem that their grandiose construction projects developed well in advance of their conquest of the whole of China, which will be reviewed in the third part of the catalogue, under the heading 'Imperial China'.

The period of the Eastern Zhou is customarily divided into two timespans, known as the Spring and Autumn period (770–475 BC) and the period of the Warring States (475–221 BC). These names are taken from two texts which describe in slightly different forms the interstate conflicts and competition that were the staple of the politics of the period. This too was the time of the great philosophers, including Confucius. Such thinkers expounded their ideas as they sought employment at one of the competing courts.

While combat and alliance are the subjects of the texts, the material culture gives a different slant on events. The catalogue shows items from several of the different states. At first rulers of the states followed Zhou example in the types and styles of bronze and jade they made and employed in ritual display. After a century or more, however, the castings of the different courts began to diverge. Indeed, the contrasts within the Eastern Zhou period are very striking. The Western Zhou was remarkable for the relative uniformity of its castings across a vast area – some of the bronzes used in areas a thousand kilometres apart are almost identical. The Eastern Zhou, on the other hand, is renowned for variety. The majority of the basic vessel types were similar, but details of ornament differed from place to place. An attempt to excel through virtuosity of display was one of the principal motivating forces for the craftsmen and their patrons.

Within this section most of the objects are grouped by sites. However, a number of pieces (nos 68–73) come from diverse finds in several parts of central China and cannot easily be discussed as a group.

Chu state finds at Xichuan, southern Henan province

The state of Chu was one of the dominant powers throughout the Eastern Zhou period. Yet very few major tombs of members of the royal family or of its ministers have been found. Thus the discovery in 1976 of a major tomb and many lesser ones at Xichuan, near the Danjiang reservoir in southern Henan, was very important.[1] A large tomb, M2, was found to contain bronzes with sixth-century BC inscriptions indicating that they were made for a certain Prince Wu (died 552 BC), the son of King Zhuang of Chu. He served as marshal of cavalry under his brother, King Gong, and

seems to have been succeeded in office by one Peng whose name, in the form Chu Shuzhi Sun Peng, also appears on the tripods. The tomb M2 has variously been ascribed both to Prince Wu and to Peng. It is likely that it was the tomb of Peng, who was probably the same man as one Yuan Zifeng, who had served as the chief minister of Chu from 551 BC until his death in 548. The cemetery is evidently that of important members of the Chu state. The principal tomb, M2, which had been partially disturbed, was associated with three large unlooted tombs, which probably held the consorts of the main tomb occupant. Of these, tomb M1 was larger than tomb M2, but the lower quality of its grave goods indicates that it belonged to an individual of lesser standing – probably, therefore, a woman. There were also fifteen tombs of human victims, possibly the high officials or servants of the main tomb occupant. In addition to these human burials, the complex included a chariot pit. Although damaged by water, the pit was found to contain nineteen horses and the remains of six chariots.

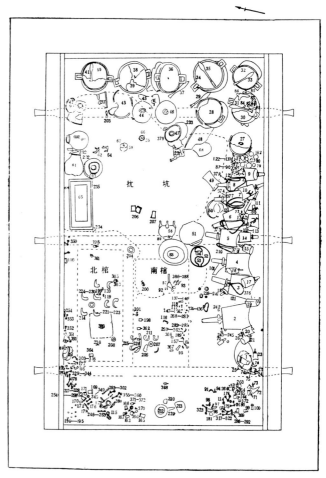

Fig. 1 *Plan of tomb* M2 *at Xiasi in Xichuan county, Henan province. After Beijing 1991c, fig. 84.*

The main tomb, M2, held two coffins: the principal one, and one perhaps belonging to an attendant (fig. 1). Although tomb M2 had been partially looted, the burial goods were particularly sumptuous. There were over five hundred bronze items, including a set of twenty-six bells, the largest single set of bell chimes surviving from ancient China.[2] Two hundred fragments of gold leaf, a substantial number of bronze ritual vessels such as the *ding* (no. 58), and a magnificent rectangular stand or altar, embellished with intricate decoration in lost wax casting, were also recovered. This exceptional piece is one of the two most famous examples of the use of this casting technique in Eastern Zhou China. The other is illustrated in the essay by Rawson (fig. 17). As explained there, the ancient Chinese had not taken up lost wax casting when they began to make weapons and vessels. Even in these sixth- and fifth-century BC examples, the technique was deployed for decorative purposes. Once this intricate filigree effect was no longer sought, lost wax casting was abandoned.[3] The tombs also contained many bronze weapons. The quality of the casting and the use of bells and gold hint at the courtly display to which so much endeavour was directed at this date.

1 For the archaeological report on the finds see Beijing 1991c. The inscription is discussed in *Zhongyuan wenwu* 1981.4, pp. 36–7.
2 Falkenhausen (1991) explains that the larger bell sets from Sui county comprise several chimes in a single complex (see no. 62).
3 Thorp 1988a, no. 10.

Fig 59.1 *Detail of a dragon-like flange on the* sheng ding.

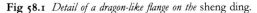

Fig 58.1 *Detail of a dragon-like flange on the* sheng ding.

58–59 Two vessels for offering food, *sheng ding*

Eastern Zhou, Spring and Autumn period, Chu state, 6th century BC
Bronze

58 *Ding* with ladle
Height 62 cm; diameter at lip 62 cm; weight 111.7 kg; ladle length 63 cm
Excavated in 1978 from tomb M2 at Xiasi, Xichuan district, southern Henan province (M2: 40)
Henan Provincial Museum, Zhenghou

59 *Ding* without ladle
Height 63 cm; diameter at lip 62.3 cm; weight 76 kg
Excavated in 1978 from tomb M1 at Xiasi, Xichuan district, southern Henan province (M1: 55)
Institute of Archaeology and Cultural Relics Bureau, Henan province

The term *sheng ding* is given to the type of tripod seen here, with a flat bottom and pronounced waist. The word *sheng*

58

refers to the meat sacrifices that were offered in them. Indeed, the seven *sheng ding* from the tomb of Peng contained bones of oxen and the two vessels of the woman in tomb M1 held the bones of pigs. The seven in the major tomb had lids and ladles, as shown here. This type of tripod was a peculiarity of the southern states, especially Chu.

The decoration of the two vessels is also typically southern.

The profiles of the two *ding* are accentuated by ridges at the lip and around their waists. On the *ding* from tomb M2, tightly interlaced dragons are outlined in fine relief ridges. The ornament on the second *ding* is different and rather more smoothly executed. It comprises dragon interlace in two borders, below the lip and above the waist. Below the waist is an area of scales or overlapping feather-like motifs. The most

59

striking features of both pieces are six creeping dragon-like creatures in relief attached to the waist and seeming to peer over the lips of the vessels. These so-called dragons are composed of a fantasy of relief interlace and openwork filigree coils on substantial flat sections of bronze (figs 58.1, 59.1). Such almost extravagant embellishments were cast by the lost wax process, which was, to the ancient Chinese, an unusual technique. Elaborate flanges, drawing attention to and emphasising the shapes of bronze vessels, were used throughout the centuries, but here the technique is a rarity. These dragon-like flanges are arched rather like the bowed handles, and their corrugated surfaces are echoed in the flanges of the legs.

The *ding* from tomb M2 has a long inscription inside the

Fig. 58.2 *Rubbing of the inscription inside the* sheng ding *(no. 58). After Beijing 1991c, p. 124, fig. 101.*

inner wall of the body. It tells that the Prince of Wu had precious bronze selected for the production of the *sheng ding*, and that the vessels were intended for the offering of sacrifices to the spirits of the ancestors to ask them for a long life. It describes the virtues and faithfulness of the prince, which he hopes will be recorded for all eternity and taken as an example for his descendants (fig. 58.2). A further four-line inscription inside the lid of the vessel mentions Peng, and for this reason it is thought that the *ding* came into his possession and that the tomb is his. The inscription inside the second *ding* is quite worn and very difficult to read.

Sets of tripods, or *ding*, were regularly buried in high-ranking tombs from at least the ninth century BC, if not earlier. In later texts they are described as being indicative of rank: 'In ritual offerings the Son of Heaven uses nine *ding* tripods, the feudal lords use seven, the senior officials five, and the lower ranks, *shi*, three.' This text was written several centuries after the date in question, and other texts assign twelve *ding* to the Son of Heaven.[1] Indeed, tombs of major lords of states have often been found to contain nine *ding*; there may have been a certain latitude in assigning the numbers in sets to particular levels or ranks. In fact, as there was no central power or ruler who could command such matters, individual rulers probably made their own choices. However, the use of sets of *ding*, with some form of ranking in mind, seems to have been universal in much of central China at this time. The imposing forms of these two vessels and their elaborate decoration were obviously intended to contribute to the awesome impression that a long series of such tripods would convey to the court and the owner's family.

Published: *Wenwu* 1980.10, pp. 13–20, 21–6, 27–30; *Gugong wenwu yuekan* 1983.4, no. 1, pp. 55–6; *Jianghan kaogu* 1984.3, p. 69; *Wenwu* 1985.4, pp. 54–8; Li Xueqin 1985a, p. 158, fig. 69; Zhang Zhengming 1987, pp. 85–7; *Wenwu* 1989.12, pp. 57–62; *Kaogu* 1991.12, pp. 1121–4; Beijing 1991c; Beijing 1992a, no. 152; Goepper 1995, nos 59, 60.

1 Li Xueqin 1985a, p. 461.

60 Square-sectioned vessel for offering wine, *fang hu*

Eastern Zhou, Spring and Autumn period, Chu state, 6th century BC
Bronze
Height 79 cm; width at lip 18 cm
Excavated in 1978 from tomb M1 at Xiasi, Xichuan district,
southern Henan province (M1: 50)
Henan Provincial Museum, Zhengzhou

This large wine flask was found with its pair in what was probably the tomb of the senior wife of Peng, the occupant of tomb M2. She is named in inscriptions on objects in the tomb as Meng Tengxi and she was probably buried in the mid-sixth century BC at the time of her husband's death. Indeed, it is likely that all the subsidiary burials were put in place at the time of Peng's funeral in 548 BC. The woman was, it seems, of high status in her own right and had a particularly large grave, exceeding that of Peng in size. The tomb also held more grave goods than those of the other women buried nearby. Ritual vessels, including the *fang hu* illustrated here and the tripod, or *ding*, in the previous entry, were a major element in the tomb. In addition, a set of small bells and exceptionally fine jade carvings indicate the high-ranking position of their owner.

Large *hu*, or wine vessels, were developed in the ninth century BC and became an important component of ritual vessel sets. Early pieces were simple by comparison with the present one, the body of which is divided into quadrants by ridges that suggest straps. Four large dragon-like creatures, two as handles and two as feet, turn what is a quite straightforward container into an extravagant display of the bronze caster's art. Large openwork crests on the heads of the dragons are echoed in the fine filigree of the lid. The bodies of the creatures are covered in interlace raised in slight relief, while the vessel itself carries patterns based upon dragon interlace, executed, as on the *ding* (no. 58), in fine ridges.

Highly articulated vessels of this type, with elaborate appendages in the form of lids, handles and feet, seem to have been typical of central southern China, the sphere of influence of the Chu state. The earliest examples of the form do not come from a Chu state site but from Xinzheng, further north in Henan province (fig. 60.1), in what was in the sixth century BC part of the state of Zheng. Others have come from the south-eastern state of Cai.[1] It seems that, although divided into several independent states, a large part of the centre of what is today China shared ritual vessel types and probably practised similar rituals for offering sacrifices to ancestors. In addition, certain regional styles were shared by some (but not all) states. Thus pairs of tall wine flasks or *hu* were common to several areas, but the large examples such as this one, with substantial handles and dragon feet, were in the main typical of the south.

Fig. 60.1 *Wine vessel,* fang hu, *from Xinzheng, Henan province. Zheng state, 6th century BC. Height 118 cm. Palace Museum, Beijing.*

Published: *Wenwu* 1980.10, pp. 13–20, 21–6, 27–30; *Gugong wenwu yuekan* 1983.4, no. 1, pp. 55–6; *Wenwu* 1985.4, pp. 54–8; Zhang Zhengming 1987, pp. 85–7; *Wenwu* 1989.12, pp. 57–62; *Kaogu* 1991.12, pp. 1121–4; Beijing 1991c; Goepper 1995, no. 58.

1 Discussed by Jenny So in New York 1980, p. 266. For a northern version see So 1995, p. 41, fig. 57.

61 Imaginary creature

Eastern Zhou period, Spring and Autumn period, Chu state,
6th–5th century BC
Bronze with hardstone inlay
Height 48 cm
Excavated in 1990 from tomb M9 at Xujialing, Xichuan district,
southern Henan province
Institute of Archaeology and Cultural Relics Bureau, Henan
province

This fantastic creature is one of a pair that came from tombs at Xujialing, a few kilometres from the site at Xiasi near the Danjiang reservoir, which produced the previous three bronzes. When discovered by the archaeologists, the area had

been plundered by tomb robbers. Much had been looted in recent years, but tomb M9, which yielded the present piece and its pair, had been robbed in antiquity, perhaps over two thousand years ago. It is suggested that the two creatures together formed part of a drum stand or something equivalent. Both animals carry loops among the writhing serpents that crown their heads; cords to support a drum may have been pulled through them. It is not clear, however, what purpose could have been served by the small rectangular fitting on the back of the present creature, and at present it is impossible to reconstruct the stand to which these creatures may have belonged.

Both are lively, almost prancing creatures, but with their four legs planted firmly on the ground; their tails rise in an s-shape. Their heads are turned towards the viewer, with long tongues protruding from open mouths. Strong curvaceous outlines resemble those of creatures painted on lacquerware of the same period. A lacquered box from the tomb of the Marquis Yi of Zeng, who owned the box illustrated at no. 64, carries similar painted creatures.[1] Lacquer painting also shows examples of the imaginary beasts, devised to support musical instruments such as bells (fig. 65.2). The same flowing lines are employed for the designs of imaginary birds, which appear among abstract scrolls forming inlay patterns on the bodies of the creatures. The inlay is in small fragments of hardstone, which show up quite clearly against the present grey surface of the bronze. Inlay in both copper and semi-precious stones seems to have been stimulated by the growing use of colour in silk and lacquer for court display.[2]

A small secondary creature turns in an exaggerated s-shape on the back of the main beast. This second beast has a long tongue from which sprouts a further imaginary horned head. An s-shaped extension supports the creature. The complex is suggestive of acrobatics. Both the two main creatures and the head on the tongue of the second carry very spiky openwork horns in the manner of the filigree and projections seen on the bronzes of the previous entries. On the principal creature the horns are in the shape of further dragons. As mentioned above, this openwork was made possible by the discovery of the lost wax technique, which gave casters the chance to display lively organic movement as well as the spiky tension of the vessels above. Both the subject matter and the methods of execution are more varied than those of the bronzes of the earlier periods (nos 39–44). Musical entertainments and ceremonies were thus matched by fine instruments with exceptional stands and ornaments, which must have attracted the attention of spectators.

Published: *Wenwu tiandi* 1992.6, pp. 10–12; Beijing 1993b, no. 83; Goepper 1995, no. 57.

1 Compare Beijing 1989c, vol. 2, pl. 121.
2 Discussed in Mackenzie 1991.

The state of Zeng

In 1978 a large tomb was discovered at Leigudun in Sui county, Hubei province. This was the burial of the Marquis Yi of Zeng, who was interred in about 433 BC. The state of Zeng was one of the smaller northern states that succumbed to the rule of the state of Chu. The size of the burial, about 220 square metres in area and

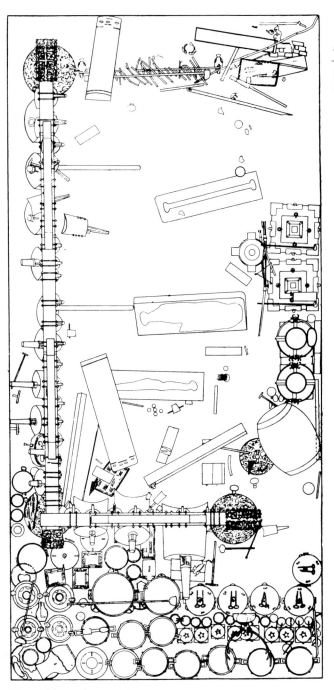

Fig. 1 *Plan of the central chamber of the tomb of the Marquis Yi of Zeng, containing bells. After Beijing 1989c, fig. 35.*

Fig. 2 *Bell set from the tomb of the Marquis Yi of Zeng.*

13 m in depth, announced a tomb of great wealth and complexity. When unearthed the tomb itself, M1, was found to be a massive timber construction with four distinct and separate chambers: a large central room (fig. 1); a room for the coffin accompanied by eight separate coffins holding attendants – essentially the private quarters of the marquis; a long chamber in which were thirteen further coffins; and a small rear room holding chariot parts and weaponry.[1]

The inscriptions on many of the bronze pieces identified the tomb occupant as the Marquis Yi of Zeng. Most magnificent of all was a large assemblage of bells, still suspended on a substantial lacquered wooden frame (fig. 2). Among the bells was one donated for the funeral ceremonies by the King of Chu, and the find has been dated from the inscription on this piece.[2] The mass of bells and the magnificent series of ritual vessels (Rawson, fig. 18) offer an extraordinary display of casting skills. In addition the tomb was filled with very fine lacquered wood, ranging from the main coffin itself (Introduction, fig. 10) to small boxes (no. 65), cups and dishes. Indeed, the contents are a remarkable example of the all-round provision made for the afterlife. Not only was the main central room filled with all that was needed for court ritual and ceremony, but the private chamber was separately equipped with further ritual vessels and musical instruments. There were even small hatch-like doors between the different rooms to allow the marquis to move from room to room during the afterlife, as need and inclination arose.

Tomb M2 was less well preserved than tomb M1. Unlike tomb M1 it had been disturbed, but the majority of the tomb contents were still in place, the most important of these being the bell chime illustrated here

(fig. 2, no. 62). Nearly seventy ritual bronzes also survived. But compared with the elaborately decorated pieces from tomb M1, the majority of these vessels are undecorated or have rather unassuming ornament. As the tomb occupant had a set of nine *sheng ding* and eight *gui*, it would appear that he or she was of a relatively high rank. It has been suggested that the tomb occupant was a female consort of the marquis of tomb M1, or a consort of a later ruler of Zeng.[3]

1 For description of the excavation see Beijing 1989c.
2 The bell set and the history of bells in China generally are discussed in Falkenhausen 1993.
3 For an outline discussion of the two tombs in English see So 1995, pp. 427–8.

62 Set of bell chimes, *bian zhong*

Eastern Zhou, Warring States period, Zeng state, 5th century BC

a Thirty-six bronze bells
Largest height 96.3 cm; weight 79.5 kg
Smallest height 36.8 cm; weight 6.75 kg

b Stand in bronze, wood and lacquer
Length 580 cm; width 180 cm

Excavated in 1981 from tomb M2 at Leigudun, Sui county, Hubei province (M2: 80–114, 116)
Suizhou City Museum, Hubei province

The thirty-six bells presented here were divided into two groups within the tomb: seven were lined along the western edge of the tomb and twenty-nine along the southern edge (fig. 62.1). In addition, twenty-two hooks of different sizes were found in the tomb: these would have been used for hanging the bells. On the evidence of the positions of the

Fig. 62.1 *Excavation of tomb* M2 *at Leigudun, Sui county, Hubei province.*

bells in the tomb, and by comparison with the structure of the bell set from tomb M1, whose wooden frame had survived intact, a reconstruction of the stand was made. Twenty-eight smaller bells were aligned along the top, while the eight larger ones were placed in the lower row. Supports in the form of human figures (Introduction, fig. 5) were devised by the restorers to correspond to those employed on the bell set from tomb M1. The basis of their forms – male figures holding snakes in their hands – is the motif on the four larger bells.

Ancient Chinese bells had, by the fifth century BC, been developed over more than eight hundred years and were sophisticated musical instruments. Their elliptical cross-section is crucial to the musical quality and determines the two notes that can be achieved: one by striking the bell on the outside at the central point of the lip, and the other by striking the corner. Early versions of the bells were mounted mouth upwards. Later the bells were turned the other way up and the handle lengthened and given a loop from which the bells could be suspended, as here. Lines of bosses, in three rows, became customary. The Chinese names given to the different parts of the bell type, known as a *yong zhong*, are shown in figure 62.2. These bells could be combined into graded sets and then the sets, either in whole or in part, grouped together to make complex musical instruments, as here and in the set of the Marquis Yi of Zeng (fig. 2 above).

Like many of the bronzes from the Chu state area, the bells carry very detailed and finely cast designs. On the handles and the smaller borders are fine interlace patterns. In the broader panel above the lip of most of the bells is a monster face design. However, four of the bells carry the figure of a man holding snakes embedded in the complex surface, replacing the central part of the more usual face pattern. Snakes and

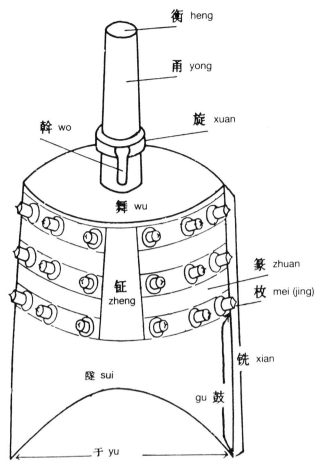

衡 heng

甬 yong

斡 wo

旋 xuan

舞 wu

篆 zhuan

钲 zheng

枚 mei (jing)

銑 xian

隧 sui

鼓 gu

于 yu

Fig. 62.2 *Drawing of a typical bell, with the Chinese names for the different parts.*

various serpent-like creatures were a continuing preoccupation in the arts of the south, especially in the state of Chu. They appear in three dimensions and on painted surface ornament, as on the coffin of the Marquis Yi of Zeng (Introduction, fig. 10). Indeed, the tombs at Leigudun, in Sui county, are representative of Chu culture, even though they lie on the northern periphery of the state. The contents of the tombs show the combination of standard ritual vessels and bells, known in ancient China from the Western Zhou period and before, with local interests and decorative practices.

Published: *Wenwu* 1985.1, pp. 16–39; Goepper 1995, no. 61.

63 Imaginary bird

Eastern Zhou, Warring States period, Zeng state, 5th century BC
Bronze
Height 143.5 cm; width 41.4 cm; weight 38.4 kg
Excavated in 1978 from tomb M1 at Leigudun, Sui county, Hubei province (E37)
Hubei Provincial Museum, Wuhan

This extraordinary bird was placed next to the coffin of the Marquis Yi of Zeng in the eastern chamber of the tomb. From its position and enormous size, we can infer that it was an exceptionally valued piece. It consists of a very tall, upright bird, with a long straight neck like that of a crane. It also has very straight legs, almost braced against the square bronze base on which it stands. Its head has a long curved beak and two enormous antler-like appendages sweeping upwards. Its wings are outstretched, as if about to fly. The antlers, head, neck, legs and talons were originally inlaid with fine gold lines, now mainly lost. Turquoise, also now mainly lost, was used

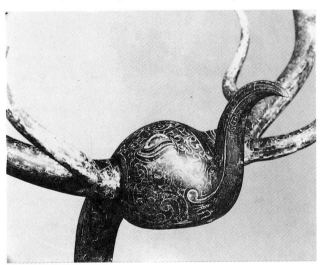

Fig. 63.1 *Two details of the bird.*

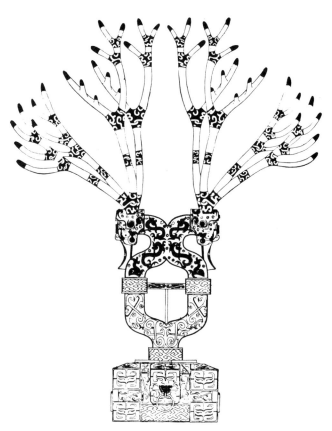

Fig. 63.2 *Carved wooden monster with antlers from tomb* M1 *at Jiangling Tianxingguan, Hubei province. Eastern Zhou period, 4th century* BC. *After* Kaogu xuebao *1982.1, p. 104, fig. 28.*

Fig. 63.3 *Carved bird with antlers as a tail from tomb* M1 *at Jiangling Tianxingguan, Hubei province. Eastern Zhou period, 4th century* BC. *After* Kaogu xuebao *1982.1, p. 103, fig. 27.*

birds probably had associations of good fortune and protection.

It is difficult to know, however, how far we should take a suggestion that the bird had a wider and more important function, namely to carry the spirit of the marquis on his flights through the universe.[2] At a later date, figures of spirits and men are shown riding on dragons, and it is possible that at this somewhat earlier stage similar ideas were beginning to form. A Han period sketch in ink on silk from a tomb at Changsha shows the way in which men were thought to ride on strange creatures (fig. 63.4). Descriptions of various paradises and other worlds appear in texts dating from the third century BC. But even at that date, the dead were not thought to reside in these paradises, which were the realms of gods and spirits. The poetry of the state of Chu, recorded in the *Chu ci (The Elegies of Chu)*, describes some of these later heavenly journeys.[3] It remains a tantalising matter of speculation to relate this bird to these later conceptions.

Published: *Wenwu* 1979.7, pp. 1–24; Thorp 1981–2, pp. 67–92; Beijing 1989c, pl. 83; Goepper 1995, no. 62.

1 *Kaogu xuebao* 1982.1, pp. 71–116; Beijing 1984c, pp. 110–11.
2 Discussed in Goepper 1995, no. 62.
3 Hawkes 1985, pp. 67–94; Birrell 1993, pp. 185–8.

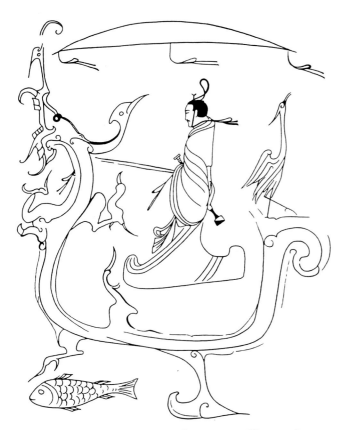

Fig. 63.4 *Drawing of a silk banner showing a man riding on a dragon. From Changsha, Hunan province. Han period, 2nd–1st century BC. After Shen Congwen 1992, p. 50, fig. 14.*

as inlay on the wings and back. The stand is carefully cast with fine patterns of clouds, serpents and birds (fig. 63.1). Four rings on the stand imply that it was either attached to something or that the creature was carried by means of them. The antlers, body, legs and wings of the bird were cast separately and assembled later. On the right side of the beak is an inscription of seven characters that can be translated as 'Made for the eternal use of the marquis'.

This bird bears some resemblance to a crane, but the antlers give it a fantastic appearance. Creatures carrying antlers, usually in monster form, are found in carved wood in quite a number of Chu tombs, both at Jiangling in Hubei (fig. 63.2) and at Changsha in Hunan.[1] It has usually been argued that such creatures were intended to protect the tomb from evil spirits. This bird, standing as it did next to the coffin, may indeed have had a protective function.

Later Chu tombs also contain wood carvings of birds, some very similar to the present bronze piece, with the same features of a long neck, compact body and outstretched wings. At Jiangling Tianxingguan tomb M1, a pair functions as a drum stand. Another piece, with antlers in place of a tail, stands on a tiger (fig. 63.3). Both bronze and wooden

64 Clothes chest

Eastern Zhou, Warring States period, Zeng state, 5th century BC
Wood painted with lacquer
Height 37 cm; length 69 cm
Excavated in 1978 from tomb M1 at Leigudun, Sui county, Hubei province (E61)
Hubei Provincial Museum, Wuhan

This substantial box with a curved lid was one of five clothes chests found in the eastern chamber of the tomb of the Marquis Yi of Zeng.[1] When discovered, the box was open and floating in groundwater that had penetrated the tomb. The function of the box is confirmed by the characters scratched on the side of the lid, *zhiyi*, meaning 'purple clothes'. Six items of purple cloth were listed on the inventory that was found in the tomb, but there were no traces of textile either in the chest or anywhere else in the tomb. These must have decayed completely or have been looted in antiquity.

The box is painted red inside and black outside with red motifs, most of which give rise to varying interpretations. In one corner of the lid is an inscription stating that the position of the stars represents a good omen and that the country is being ruled with great virtue.[2] The predominant decoration on the lid consists of large motifs with curved tops and narrow stems, which may represent mushrooms with magical powers. On one half of the lid are two almost identical hunting scenes, placed opposite each other and divided by a double row of the mushroom motifs. Each hunting scene

Fig. 64.1 *Drawings of hunting scenes from inlaid bronze vessels. Eastern Zhou, Warring States period, 4th–3rd century BC. After* Wenwu 1981.6, *pp. 75–6, figs 2, 4.*

consists of a pair of delicately painted trees topped with birds and animals, and a hunter shooting at a large falling bird. In each pair of trees, one tree has eight horizontally projecting branches, the other ten. Each of these branches terminates in a circular motif. On the two eight-branched trees perch two birds, and on the two ten-branch trees stand two animals whose heads are similar to the motifs at the ends of the branches. In each scene the hunter appears to have struck a bird mid-flight. A long cord hangs from the arrow, and is attached to a construction of short horizontal sticks, probably a hunting spindle. In one of the two scenes this hangs freely in the air, as if the man has only just shot the arrow. In the second picture the hunter raises his arms as if to catch the loosely dangling ribbons, which hang down from the transverse rods of the hunting spindle, and thus prevent the bird from escaping.

In Chinese literature, hunting scenes such as these are, as a rule, interpreted as illustrating the legends of the immortal archer Houyi and the ten suns, and Houyi killing the wild animal in the moon.[3] If the circular motifs on the trees are interpreted as suns then the scenes might represent the legend of the ten suns. The problem is, of course, that the trees topped with birds each have eleven suns, and the trees with animals each have either nine or eleven suns, depending on whether the animals' heads are taken to be suns. In the legend the simultaneous shining of ten suns was causing a drought and so Houyi was instructed to shoot down nine of them. The large falling bird may represent the sun that Houyi was in the process of shooting.

On the other hand, the scenes may illustrate the legend of Houyi killing the wild animal in the moon, in which Houyi kills a dangerous tiger who wanted to swallow the moon. Animals with manes, such as those atop the two eight-branch trees, are generally assumed to indicate this legend.

Yet another interpretation of the scenes is that they show Houyi shooting a gigantic bird of prey, which was doing foul deeds. It is reported that Houyi thought of a special technique to kill and catch the bird. He prevented it from escaping by

means of a long cord fixed to the arrow. The cord shown on the clothes chest, with the hunting spindle at its lower end, perhaps supports this interpretation.

The technique by which Houyi shot the bird, and which, according to legend, he himself had invented, was frequently employed in ancient China, particularly when hunting large wild birds (fig. 64.1).[4] The hunting spindle was fixed to the end of the cord attached to the arrow. The interpretation of the so-called ribbons that hang from the spindle in one of the hunting scenes is relatively new, and is based on a finding in the eastern room of the tomb of the Marquis Yi of Zeng. Beside a bow and arrow were found strange implements composed of a wide pedestal and a narrow pillar. Cords were wound round the leather-covered and lacquered pedestal element, to which small metal parts were fixed. These implements were originally thought to be weaving bobbins, but recent research suggests that they are the frequently portrayed hunting spindles.

Beside the hunting scenes, along one of the narrow edges of the lid, are two intertwined serpents, each with two angular heads and a tail from which radiate five arms or legs with hands or claws. These two serpents are generally regarded as the mythological figures Nüwa and Fuxi who, despite being brother and sister, married each other, but always hid their faces behind a fan when making love.

Published: *Wenwu* 1981.6, pp. 75–7; Beijing 1989c, vol. 2, pl. 123; *Kaogu* 1992.10, pp. 937–41; *Wenwu* 1993.6, pp. 83–8; Goepper 1995, no. 73.

1 The other four clothes chests are described in *Kaogu* 1992.10, pp. 937–41 and Beijing 1989c, vol. 1, pp. 353–9.
2 Beijing 1989c, vol. 1, p. 357.
3 Beijing 1985e, no. 334; Allan 1991, chapter 2.
4 *Wenwu* 1993.6, pp. 83–8.

65 Box in the shape of a duck

Eastern Zhou, Warring States period, Zeng state, 5th century BC
Wood painted with lacquer
Height 16.5 cm; length 20.1 cm
Excavated in 1978 from tomb M1 at Leigudun, Sui county, Hubei province (WC2: 1)
Hubei Provincial Museum, Wuhan

A neatly carved duck's head rotates on a wooden box made from its hollowed body (fig. 65.1). It has a small rectangular cover. The box is supported by the stylised duck's legs drawn in under the body. The head of the animal was discovered by itself in the coffin of a woman who was buried in the western area of the tomb of the Marquis Yi of Zeng. The duck's body lay in the same room, on the wooden floor, the two parts perhaps having been separated when the grave was robbed.[1] Presumably the duck's body had served as a luxurious container for cosmetics and had belonged to one of the many ladies buried in the tomb.

65

On one side of the duck's body is a painted panel displaying a music scene, filled almost completely by an immense instrument composed of bells and sounding stones. Two long-necked, narrow, fabulous animals hold a thick rod in their mouths, from which two massive bells of the *yong zhong* type, of different sizes, are suspended (see fig. 62.3).[2] Between the forelegs of the animals there is a thin rod, from which dangle two sounding stones (*qing*) of different shapes, fixed by cords. To the right of the instrument stands a man clothed in red with a bird's head, which is presumably a head covering. He strikes the bells with a long, slightly curved rod (fig. 65.2).

The panel on the other side of the duck's body shows a tall dancer who moves to the rhythmic sound of a drum

(fig. 65.3). The ring-shaped instrument is fixed to what is perhaps a tall branch growing vertically, or a rod decorated with feathers, which stands on an animal pedestal.[3] To the right of this, the drummer swings the drumsticks. He wears a bird mask, which is crowned by a triangular headdress standing on its apex. At the top right of this headdress are two attachments, presumably feathers. The much larger figure, who is dancing to the left of the drum, wears a similar headdress, shown frontally. He also wears a bird mask and has a long sword belted about his body. His movements appear graceful, the sinuous curves of his arms accentuated by the over-long sleeves of his garment, which come to a point.[4]

The two persons represented are thought to be *wu*, intermediaries with the spirits, who are perhaps performing in the

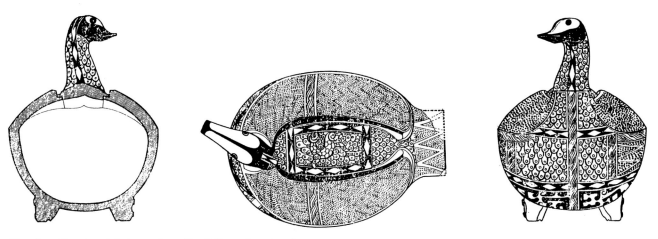

Fig. 65.1 *Drawings of the lacquer box. After Beijing 1989c, vol. 1, figs 222, 223.*

Fig. 65.2 *Drawing of the music scene on one side of the duck's body. After Beijing 1989c, vol. 1, fig. 224: 2.*

Fig. 65.3 *Drawing of the dance scene on one side of the duck's body.*

type of ritual ceremony thought to be performed by the Chu people of central southern China. A commentary, written in the second century AD by Wang Yi on the *Chu ci (The Elegies of Chu)*, indicates the great part played by music and dance in these ritual ceremonies: 'In the area of the southern capital city Ying of the former state of Chu, between the rivers Yuan and Xiang, the people believed in spirits and sacrifices. During the sacrifice they had to sing and to dance ecstatically, in order to please the different gods.'[5]

The duck-shaped lacquer box is unlikely itself to have been used in a ritual. However, the decoration of a utilitarian object, even though luxurious, with ceremonial scenes of music and dance illustrates how closely ritual events were interwoven with the everyday life of the upper echelons of Chu society.

Published: Beijing 1989c, vol. 2, pl. 130; Falkenhausen 1993, p. 64, fig. 22; Goepper 1995, no. 72.

1 Beijing 1989c, vol. 1, pp. 7–12.
2 Falkenhausen 1993, p. 355
3 Xiao Kangda 1992, pp. 73–5.
4 For dancers with long sleeves see no. 108. It is also possible that the present dancer is holding banners.
5 Cited in Li Zehou 1992, p. 121.

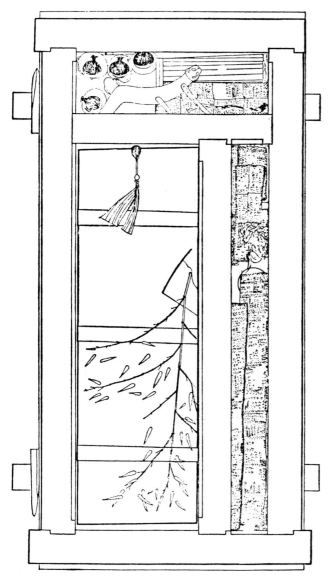

Fig. 2 *Wooden figure dressed in silk clothes from tomb MI at Mashan. The missing arms would probably have been made in cloth. After Beijing 1985f, p. 81, fig. 66.*

Fig. 3 *Painted lacquers from tomb MI at Mashan. After Beijing 1985f, p. 78, fig. 64.*

Fig. 1 *Drawing of the burial chamber of tomb MI at Mashan, Jiangling county, Hubei province. After Beijing 1985f, p. 10, fig. 12.*

Tomb MI at Mashan, Jiangling county, Hubei province

The tomb at Mashan belongs to a later stage in Chu culture than that of the finds from Xichuan (nos 58–61) and Leigudun (nos 62–65). Tomb MI was discovered in January 1982 some 8 km south of Ji'nan, the capital of the state of Chu in the fourth century BC, and the burial is thought to date from about this time. The tomb was exceptionally well preserved, with wood (no. 66), lacquer and silks still intact (no. 67).

A single chamber was constructed in wood, with three compartments (fig. 1). A woman clad in very fine silken clothes was buried within the main section (no.

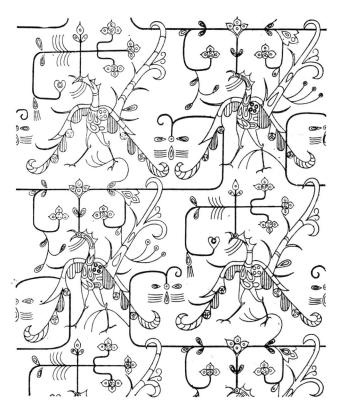

Fig. 4 *Embroidered textile design with flowing lines (above) and woven textile design organised in an angular and symmetrical form (below), both from tomb MI at Mashan. After Beijing 1985f, p. 66, fig. 54, p. 48, fig. 39.*

67). The long side compartment held vessels in ceramic, covered with matting, and on top of this, curled up, lay the skeleton of a small dog. The third compartment of the burial was at the head of the woman. In it were figures of attendants, carved in wood and dressed in silk (fig. 2), an extraordinary imaginary animal (no. 66), a number of inscribed bamboo slips, a neck rest or pillow in woven bamboo, and some fine woven bamboo boxes, two of which contained vessels in bronze and lacquer. The care with which these objects were stored away is fascinating and may indicate how they were stored during the life of their owner.

Textiles (described below) were in an extraordinary state of preservation (no. 67); the lacquers and baskets

were also still in much the same condition as when buried. The painting of these lacquers can be compared with the textile designs, as both materials incorporate geometric patterns and free-flowing designs of birds (fig. 3). Indeed, the decorative styles of the period appear to have developed out of an interchange of motifs between such different materials. Thus designs developed through the painting of lacquer – when a soft brush would have moved with flowing paint – were copied on textiles, while the more formal and symmetrical woven textile patterns (fig. 4) were borrowed by the lacquer painters. The possibility of using colour in both textiles and lacquers also stimulated the use of coloured inlays as well as the practice of painting on bronze. It is possible that the gradual decline in bronzework and the developing interest in textiles and lacquers were in part consequences of the limited range of colours available in bronzework.

66 **Imaginary beast**

Eastern Zhou, Warring States period, Chu state, 4th–3rd century BC
Tree root, bamboo and lacquer
Height 32 cm; length 69.5 cm
Excavated from tomb MI at Mashan, Jiangling county, Hubei province (MI: 1)
Jingzhou Regional Museum, Hubei province

This creature from tomb MI at Mashan, described above, is carved mainly from a root and is indeed the oldest surviving root carving in China. Its long slender body is completely smooth, showing that the original surface must have been rubbed down. In contrast, the four legs, which are made of bamboo, display the sections of the original. These legs stand out at a variety of angles. A tiger-like head with large pointed red and orange eyes and smaller ears, has been carved out of the body. Small teeth are shown through bared lips. A tiny coiled tail is carved at the rear. Four additional small creatures are carved at the tops of the bamboo legs, where they join the body. A thin snake with a tiny head wriggles along the length of the right front leg; on the right hind leg is a much shorter snake that bites a tailless lizard; on the left front leg is another lizard, which grabs the head of a bird with elegant plumage; at the top of the left hind leg is a tiny cicada. It is likely that this combination of creatures had some significance within the beliefs and practices of Chu culture, but without relevant texts scholars are unable to decipher their meaning.

The function of the whole beast itself is also elusive. From its position in the tomb, above the head of the female occupant, it can perhaps be considered as some kind of tomb guardian, perhaps with a role similar to that of the tall bronze bird found in the tomb of the Marquis Yi of Zeng (no. 63). Few root carvings of this type have survived. One other

66

ancient example is known, also from the state of Chu, found in tomb M2 at Baoshan in Jiangling county, Hubei province.[1] This piece is carved in the shape of three stags, a monkey, a bird and several snakes. These two carvings would appear to indicate a lively tradition of root carving from which little has survived; in later times root carving also proved very popular.

Published: Beijing 1985f, pl. 43: 1; Goepper 1995, no. 75.

1 Beijing 1991b, vol. 1, p. 261, fig. 174: 3.

67 Four pieces of silk

Eastern Zhou, late Warring States period, Chu State, 4th–3rd century BC

a Ribbon with woven 'pagoda' pattern
Length 84 cm; width 23 cm (N3)

b Part of the body shroud
Length 70 cm; width 50 cm (N4)

c Sleeve of embroidered gauze
Length 113 cm; width at cuff 32 cm; width at shoulder 49 cm (N9)

d Collar braid with lozenge pattern
Length 47.5 cm; width 7.1 cm (N12)

Excavated in 1982 from tomb M1 at Mashan, Jiangling county, Hubei province
Jingzhou Regional Museum, Hubei province

The excavation of tomb M1 at Mashan brought to light a sensational collection of textiles. In the tomb were discovered the remains of a woman who was not only completely clothed, but also wrapped in further garments and covers.

This burial outfit, which is the earliest example of its kind known to date, is in such a fine state of preservation that it serves to illustrate the costumes, burial customs and advanced state of silk weaving and embroidery in the state of Chu at this early date. Although better preserved textiles have been found in the tomb of Lady Dai at Mawangdui near Changsha in Hunan province, these are of a later, Han period date in the second century BC.[1]

Examinations of the skeleton in tomb M1 at Mashan reveal that the tomb occupant was a woman about 1.6 m tall, who was probably in her forties when she died. She was laid to rest on her back, arms by her sides, on a carved bier inside a rectangular, box-shaped coffin, enveloped in brown silk and held by three hemp cords.[2] On top of this lay a well preserved branch of bamboo, a small painted silk cloth and, at the head end, a tassel of gauze strips held together by glass beads.

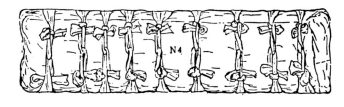

Fig. 67.1 *Drawing of the enveloped and tied body within the coffin of tomb M1 at Mashan, Jiangling county, Hubei province. After Beijing 1985f, p. 12, fig. 14.*

67a,b ▶

Fig. 67.2 *Drawing of the rolls of silk held in the hands of the deceased. After Beijing 1985f, p. 17, fig. 21.*

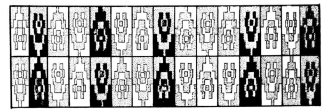

Fig. 67.3 *Drawing of the 'pagoda' pattern on the ribbon* **(a)**. *After Beijing 1985f, p. 38, fig. 31.1.*

Inside the coffin, between the coffin itself and the wrapped body, were several layers of textile: first, a cover of white gauze with a brocade hem; then a shroud of finely embroidered yellow silk; and finally a woven bamboo mat. Within these layers was the clothed and tightly wrapped body, tied with nine ribbons of 'pagoda' pattern (a, fig. 67.1).

Under the ties were thirteen further layers before the clothed body was reached. The outermost layer is illustrated (b). Both the quantity and quality of the woman's clothing indicate that she belonged to the upper echelons of society, and that she had been prepared to enter life in another world dressed in a manner appropriate to her daily existence. In this case the woman's dress consisted of two quilted silk outer garments over a lined garment. Under this was an unlined skirt and quilted trousers, the oldest example of their kind to be discovered in China. She also wore thick quilted shoes and a silk belt at her waist, from which hung, on ribbons, jade pendants and glass beads.

Textual evidence for the wrapping and clothing of the body can be found in the *Li ji*, a ritual text that describes the practices of the Zhou state although it was compiled in the Han dynasty. The fact that the present Chu burial seems to conform to Zhou practice is but one of many indications of the

close link between the northern central area of Henan and this more southern region. In the *Li ji* it is stated: 'When a person dies he becomes ugly . . . That is why there are garments for the dead, to conceal him, and the coffin covers to decorate the coffin so that people do not feel revulsion before death.'[3] The deceased was said to be entitled to as many as a hundred items of clothing, according to his or her rank.

In addition to the woman's clothing there were further textiles about her body. Her well preserved black hair was covered with a wig held by a headband and a wooden hairpin. Over her face was laid a protective cloth with openings at the eyes and nose.[4] Such cloths were common, but such openings were not. It was more common to cover the features of the face with jade plaques (no. 72) or to seal the orifices with jade or silk plugs (no. 81). One interpretation of the slits in the present face shroud is that they were to allow for the exit of the soul from the body, as postulated in the essay by Chen.

There were also ribbons and cords that had been used to tie together parts of the body: the arms were fixed at breast level with a ribbon, the thumbs and toes were wound with cord, and two long cords were knotted about the abdomen. This custom, which is seen in other burials,[5] may have been to hold the body together, although the tying of the thumbs and toes is unknown elsewhere. Another rare feature of the burial is the fact that the woman held in each hand a roll of silk, each about 20 cm long. One of these had been attached to her middle finger by a cord (fig. 67.2). Their function is not known. In a side chamber of the tomb, further textiles in the form of a mirror bag, a cap, a jacket and 452 pieces of cloth were contained in a small box made of woven bamboo. Even the four male and three female wooden figures, of 30 to 60 cm in height, which were buried with the woman and were probably intended to serve her in the afterlife, were clothed in silk (p. 142, fig. 2).

The four items illustrated here, representative of this extensive selection of silk textiles, show the advanced state of silk weaving and embroidery in the state of Chu during the fourth to third centuries BC.[6]

a Ribbon with woven 'pagoda' pattern

This ribbon is one of the nine that tied the covered and clothed body (fig. 67.1). Its width is almost half the total width of the material, which would have measured from 45 to 49 cm. The 'pagodas', which alternate in orientation, are

Fig. 67.4 *Drawing of the pattern on the body shroud* **(b)**. *After Beijing 1985f, p. 44, fig. 36.3.*

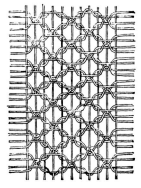

Fig. 67.5 *Detail of the sleeve of embroidered gauze* **(c)**.

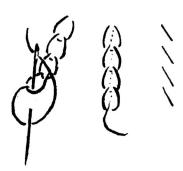

Fig. 67.6 *Drawing of the weaving technique used to produce the gauze* (luo) *of the sleeve* **(c)**. *After Beijing 1985f, p. 29, fig. 29.1.*

Fig. 67.7 *Drawing of chain stitch, front and back, used to embroider the sleeve* **(c)**. *After Kaogu 1989, p. 747, fig. 2.*

ranged in bands about a central, darker axis (fig. 67.3). To create the woven pattern, warp (lengthwise) threads of four different colours have been arranged in different combinations and weft (transverse) threads of a uniform dark brown colour have been passed through them. The use of a number of warp threads of different colours was the most advanced weaving technique of the Zhou period. As the majority of silk textiles with this kind of weave patterning that have been excavated recently have come from the provinces of Hubei, Hunan and southern Henan, it is thought that the technique was probably invented at the beginning of the Warring States period in the state of Chu.[7] The garments of the three wooden female figures found in the burial were decorated with similar 'pagoda' braids.

b Part of the body shroud

This piece of patterned silk was part of the outermost covering around the clothed body, immediately under the ties with 'pagoda' pattern. There were further garments of the

same material. The predominantly zigzag pattern is interspersed with animals, birds and figures which make up a pattern unit of eight pairs stretching across the entire width (fig. 67.4).

The zigzags themselves are decorated in alternate pairs with angular creatures and spiral patterns. The eight triangular sections in figure 67.4 show, from left to right, symmetrical pairs of, first, two dragons with long tails; then dragons turning away from each other; birds with raised wings; imaginary creatures with long tongues; another double set of dragons; birds with long tails and tufted heads; dancers with headdresses and very long sleeves; and finally dragons with elongated necks.

This pattern is one of the most complex woven figural designs so far discovered in China. Using warp threads of three different colours – brown, yellow and red – and a weft of brown thread, the weaver has created an immaculate design of exceptional quality.[8]

c Sleeve of embroidered gauze

This sleeve was formerly attached to the partially damaged garment that was the sixth of the thirteen layers enveloping the deceased woman (fig. 67.5). It is made of greyish white, unlined and embroidered silk gauze (*luo*), and six lengths of the same material had been sewn together to make the upper and lower parts of the garment. The cuffs, neck and lower hem were trimmed with brocade ornamented with tendrils.

The technique for making such gauze is highly complex. Rather than one weft thread passing over and under the warp threads, here two and then four weft threads are woven through the warp threads and caught together at intervals to create a delicate but extremely stable net-like fabric (fig. 67.6). Gauze like this had previously been found in the tomb of Lady Dai at Mawangdui, near Changsha in Hunan province, dating to the second century BC,[9] but the present find illustrates that the technique was known at least a century earlier.

Fig. 67.8 *Drawing of the braid with lozenge pattern* **(d)**. *After Beijing 1985f, p. 51, fig. 41.*

The garment was embroidered in chain stitch in a number of different colours (fig. 67.7). Dragons, tigers and phoenix-like birds parade amongst a swirling background of flowering tendrils. The use of embroidery to create such patterns suggests that the demand for intricate designs could not be met by weaving technology.

Chain stitch is the only one used in all the embroidered textiles found at Mashan. It is believed by some that chain stitch was in use as early as the Shang period,[10] and there is evidence of it in the Western Zhou period from impressions of embroidered textiles discovered at Rujiazhuang, near Baoji in Shaanxi province.[11] The pattern to be stitched was first drawn in with either a grey or a reddish ink. The variation in length and width of the chain stitch on the one garment suggests that more than a single embroideress was at work on each pattern.

d Collar braid with lozenge pattern

This braid once adorned the collar of an unlined silk garment, the eighth in the thirteen layers enveloping the body. Similar braid was used on other garments in the tomb.

Composed of two parts, the narrow right-hand strip is decorated with lozenges within zigzag lines. A more complex raised pattern of hexagons, triangles and lozenges decorates the wider left-hand band.

Published: Beijing 1985f; *Kaogu* 1985.1, pp. 88–95; Tim nerman 1986, pp. 221–3; *Kaogu* 1989.8, pp. 745–50; Kuhn 1991, pp. 224–8; Shen Congwen 1992, pp. 85–106; Goepper 1995, no. 78.

1 A Warring States burial similar to that of the present woman, but in a poor state of preservation, has been found at Baoshan, Jiangling county, Hubei province. See Beijing 1991b, vol. 1, pp. 166–89; Kuhn and von Eschenbach 1992, pp. 63ff; *Wenwu* 1975.2, pp. 49–52.
2 The coffin is described in detail in Beijing 1985f, pp. 4–18.
3 Wilhelm 1930, pp. 275–6.
4 Wenwu 1972.12, pp. 11–12; Höllmann 1986, p. 70; Beijing 1985f, p. 97.
5 For example, the arms and legs of Lady Dai, buried in tomb M1 at Mawangdui, near Changsha, Hunan province, had been tied together, as had those of a woman in tomb M48 at Mozuizi (*Wenwu* 1972.12, p. 11, fig. 3).
6 For more detailed discussion on silk weaving in ancient China see Kuhn 1995.
7 Kuhn 1995, pp. 84–5.
8 Kuhn 1995, pp. 88–9.
9 *Kaogu* 1972.2, pp. 17–19.
10 *Kaogu* 1989.8, pp. 746–7.
11 *Wenwu* 1976.4, colour pl. 1; Beijing 1979c, p. 176.

68 Dagger axe, *ge*

Eastern Zhou, Warring States period, 5th–3rd century BC
Bronze
Length 22 cm; width 6.8 cm

Excavated in 1963 from the banks of the Zhang River in Jingmen city, Hubei province (5:1855)
Jingzhou Regional Museum, Hubei province

This dagger axe was found in a grave near the Zhang River. Unfortunately the excavation has been only summarily reported, but the excavators who worked in the area and examined four or five pit graves were struck by two unusual weapons in one of them: the dagger axe blade illustrated here and a sword found with it.[1] The sword belongs to a category more usual in Sichuan than in the state of Chu, and it is possible that the dagger axe blade also originated further west or was copied from a weapon made further west.[2]

The weapon is very unusual. The blade would, like all dagger axes, have been mounted at right angles to a wooden shaft, and a small peg or pin through the hole in one end would have kept it in place. The general shape of the blade is quite close to, but not identical with, pieces used in Sichuan. The cast ornament is, however, unmatched anywhere. The same strange figure appears on both sides of the blade. It has a round head with staring eyes and open mouth, and plumes sprout from the top. Pendants from the ears are sometimes interpreted as snakes. The figure is dressed in clothes covered in small scales. Its arms are held at an angle and the feet are braced. In the right hand it holds a creature with dragon heads at both ends of its body; in the left hand is a lizard-like animal. An identical beast appears between the legs of the figure. The right foot stands on the disc of the sun and the left on the crescent of the moon.

Although the identification of the figure has been much debated, it is often regarded as Taiyi, the Supreme One or Supreme Unity. By the Han dynasty, Taiyi was recognised as a supreme deity among the spirits of heaven and had been endowed with cosmic force; star gods venerated in later times descended from the worship of Taiyi. Indeed, the pole star came to be regarded as the lodging of Taiyi. Pre-Han philosophical texts present Taiyi as a concept of cosmic oneness rather than as a deity, but we get some sense of a deity from texts such as records of divinations found in a Chu tomb at Baoshan in Hubei province, where Taiyi is named as one of several spirits who receive sacrificial offerings. As Li Ling has pointed out, Taiyi is depicted in an early silk painting from Mawangdui at Changsha in Hunan province.[3] In this painting the figure of Taiyi is juxtaposed with those of dragons, somewhat like the figure on the present dagger axe.[4]

Taiyi was considered to have powers to avert military disasters. A four-character inscription on the dagger axe, which has been read as *bingbi taisui* (weapon to repel the Grand

68

Year), adds weight to the argument that the figure on the axe is indeed Taiyi. The inscription has been interpreted by Donald Harper as meaning that the weapon was intended to avert the evil threatened by Jupiter's correlate Grand Year, an astronomical notion of the period.[5] In addition, the figure bears some resemblance to the Celestial Envoy, a heavily armed figure who delivered orders to the bureaucrats of the underworld.[6]

Published: *Wenwu* 1963.1, pp. 64–5; *Kaogu* 1963.3, pp. 153–5; *Kaogu* 1963.10, pp. 562–4; *Kaogu* 1964.1, pp. 54–7; *Kaogu* 1965.8, pp. 413–15; *Jianghan kaogu* 1991.2, pp. 35–9; Goepper 1995, no. 66.

1 For a brief report see *Wenwu* 1963.1, pp. 64–5, where rubbings of the sword and the blade are illustrated.
2 For swords from Sichuan, see Beijing 1994b, nos 159–61. A fragment of a dagger axe from Sichuan which has some features reminiscent of the piece under discussion is published in *Wenwu ziliao congkan* 3, 1980, pp. 207–9, fig. 1.
3 Li Ling forthcoming.
4 *Kaogu* 1990.10, pp. 925–8, pl. 5.
5 Donald Harper forthcoming; see Major 1993, pp. 39–40.
6 Seidel 1987, quoting Hayashi Minao. See also Introduction, p. 23.

69 Tools for preparing bamboo strips

Eastern Zhou, Warring States period, Chu state, 4th–3rd century BC
Bronze
Small hatchet, length 9.3 cm; width 4.7 cm (MI: *touxiang* 79)
Two splitting knives, length 17.6 cm each; width 2.7 cm (MI: *touxiang* 170)
Peeling knife, length 27 cm (MI: *guannei* 17)
Excavated in 1965 from tomb MI at Wangshan, Jiangling county, Hubei province
Hubei Provincial Museum, Wuhan

These four bronze tools would have been used to prepare narrow strips of bamboo so that they could then be written on with brush and ink (see no. 95). They come from one of three richly endowed Chu graves north-west of Ji'nan, where Ying, one of the early capitals of the Chu state, was located.

Tomb MI at Wangshan, from which the tools come, consisted of a large pit, almost 8 m deep. At the bottom was a wooden coffin chamber of several compartments, enclosing the coffin and numerous grave goods. As in a number of other tombs, more than twenty bamboo strips inscribed with over a thousand characters were found in a side chamber in the tomb. They referred to a sacrificial ritual (*jiyi*). All the tools for preparing the strips, except the peeling knife, had been deposited in what might be described as a rectangular tool box, 84 cm long, in the antechamber of the grave.

The small wedge-shaped bronze hatchet (*ben*) had originally been fixed to a curved wooden handle and resembled a hoe. It was presumably used for rough cutting to shape the bamboo pieces. The two double-edged splitting knives, which are almost identical in form, would originally have had

wooden handles. The character *wang* (king), executed in the elongated form characteristic of Chu script, is cast in one corner of the blade, close to the base for the handle. The slim peeling knife, with its slightly curved single-edged blade and extremely thin handle ending in a ring, was found in the coffin, rather than in the tool box, suggesting that it was one of the objects used by the tomb occupant himself. One of the uses of such knives was to scrape off old inscriptions. It is assumed that the other three tools had not been for their owner's personal use.

Published: *Wenwu* 1966.5, p. 50, fig. 22; Goepper 1995, no. 68.

70 Model of a house with musicians

Eastern Zhou, Warring States period, 5th century BC
Bronze with gold inlay
Height 17 cm; width 13 cm; depth 11.5 cm
Excavated in 1982 from tomb M306 at Shaoxing, Zhejiang
province (M306: 13)
Institute of Archaeology and Cultural Relics Bureau, Zhejiang
province

A change in burial patterns came about from the beginning of the Eastern Zhou period. Small human figures in ceramic, wood or bronze were now increasingly made for burial and would, in the course of time, replace the human servants, entertainers and charioteers. This small house, filled with musicians, may belong to this category of replicas. The house is the earliest architectural model known to date in China. It is highly unusual, being cast in bronze. At the same time, it is also the earliest bronze sculpture representing a musical performance, here including two singers and four musicians. This performance is likely to have had a ritual function.

The musicians have taken up their positions, kneeling in two rows one behind the other (fig. 70.1). Apart from the drummer on the right, who is facing the group and setting the beat (fig. 70.2a), all the other musicians face the open front of the building. Two figures kneeling in the front row, who are interpreted as female singers, have their hands crossed in front of them (fig. 70.2b). Their long hair is tied up in topknots, which distinguishes them from the musicians, who are probably male. Two of the musicians are playing four-stringed zithers (*qin*) (fig. 70.2c) and one is blowing into a mouth organ (*sheng*) (fig. 70.2d). In the mouth organ, the

Fig. 70.1 *Drawing of the house. After Beijing 1987a, no. 213.*

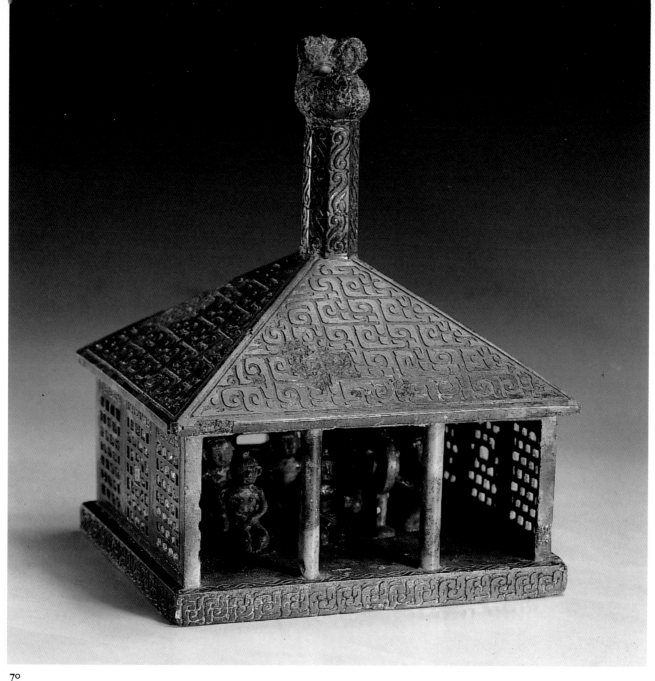

70

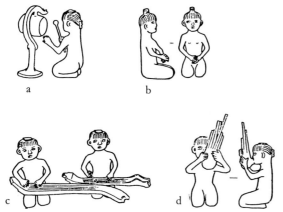

a　　　　　　　b

c　　　　　　　d

Fig. 70.2 *Drawings of the musicians in the house. After* Wenwu *1984.1, p. 17, figs 16, 17.*

air passes through a mouth piece into a gourd body, which usually holds thirteen bamboo pipes of different lengths; holes on these pipes can be covered by the fingers. As with a mouth organ, the sounds are formed by vibrating reeds. Suction and blowing thus result in different sounds.

None of the musicians appears to wear any clothing or headdress, which may indicate either the low social status of the musicians or the warm climate of the region. The open house may have been customary in the humid south. Three of its sides consist of pierced bronze plates in three sections and the front of the house is open, but also subdivided into three openings by columns. The structure stands on a solid base plate decorated around the sides with intaglio scrolls, which were formerly inlaid with gold. The same scrolls embellish the roof, which slopes steeply to a peak. Rising from the peak is an octagonal chimney-like shaft topped with a bird. In size and form the house bears a striking resemblance to the bronze antler stands discussed in the following entry (no. 71). On the present house the shaft supports a bronze bird rather than antlers.

This small building was among the unusual and sumptuous grave goods of a partially robbed tomb. The tomb also contained a set of bronze ritual vessels, a set of writing utensils, grinding stones and plumb bobs in a lacquer box, and, most unusually, a gold cup. Gold vessels are extremely rare in ancient China before the Han dynasty. The gold vessel alone indicates the very high status of the burial and hence, presumably, its owner.

Published: *Wenwu* 1984.1, pp. 10–29; Beijing 1987a, no. 213; Goepper 1995, no. 63.

71 Antler stand

Eastern Zhou, Warring States period, 5th century BC
Bronze, formerly inlaid with turquoise and copper
Height 16 cm; length 16 cm; width 13 cm; weight 10 kg
Excavated in 1982 from tomb M306 at Shaoxing, Zhejiang province (M306:18)
Institute of Archaeology and Cultural Relics Bureau, Zhejiang province

This bronze stand came from the same tomb as no. 70, and indeed was found next to the house. It is square at the base and slopes to a central apex, crowned by a square-sectioned shaft. This shaft may well have held antlers or an antlered figure of the types found in Chu tombs at Yutaishan near Jiangling in Hubei province. These antlered figures varied enormously in complexity, and have been mentioned in connection with no. 63 (fig. 63.2). The simple examples had a wooden stand of almost exactly the shape seen here, from which rose a vertical shaft supporting either real antlers or a head carrying antlers (fig. 71.1). More complex compositions included various creatures, often with long tongues.[1]

Various bronze versions of these stands have been found in central and eastern China. A seventh-century BC version in bronze has come from tombs of a small state by the name of Huang in southern Henan. This early piece takes the form seen here, comprising a truncated pyramid on a square base. Although an early piece, earlier than the surviving wooden sculptures, it is likely that the form, as well as the composition involving display of antlers, evolved from wood rather than from the bronze.[2] Use of bronze, on the other hand, indicates that the object was of sufficiently high value to be translated from wood into metal.

The present stand is later than the Huang state example and employs the idiom of its day. It carries cast decoration of leaping s-shaped bird-like figures. These were probably originally inlaid in copper. The fluid lines are reminiscent of

71

lacquerwork, from which the decorative style may have been derived.[3] The four crouching figures that support the stand are unusual additions. These figures squat, supported by their hands and feet, their fists turned outwards and their feet rolled inwards. Their bodies are covered with dense intaglio lines, which may be taken to indicate clothing tied at the waist with a belt. The hair dressed in the shape of a pair of horns is similar to the form of hairdressing seen on the jade figures at no. 75.

Published: *Wenwu* 1984.1, pp. 10–29; Goepper 1995, no. 64.

1 Beijing 1984c, p. 110, fig. 88.
2 Discussed in Mackenzie 1991.
3 See So 1995, no. 44, for a vessel similarly inlaid and for references to discussions of the category, especially to techniques of casting.

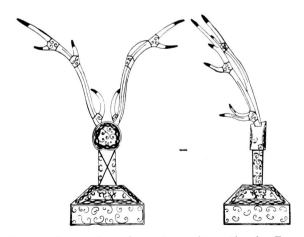

Fig. 71.1 *Drawing of a stand supporting a sculpture with antlers. From Chu tombs at Yutaishan near Jiangling, Hubei province. Eastern Zhou period, 4th century BC. After Beijing 1984c, p. 110, fig. 88.*

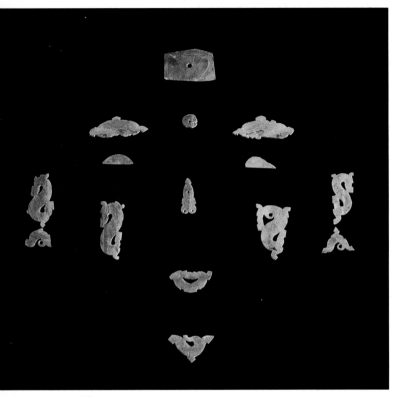

72

72 Face coverings for use in burial

Eastern Zhou, Warring States period, 5th–4th century BC
Jade
Fifteen parts, lengths 2–6 cm
Excavated in 1955 from tomb M3, western end of Zhongzhou Street, Luoyang, Henan province (M3: 1–14, M3: 170)
Luoyang City Museum, Henan province

A belief in the continuation of life after death was evident in the Shang period in the ancestor cult. Concern with the afterlife may have led to the use of jade in tombs, as the unchanging qualities of the stone perhaps suggested, by association, the promise of eternal life. From about 900 BC the dead came to be clad in jade plaques (no. 57) and face coverings. The most elaborate examples have come from tombs of the eighth century BC belonging to the Jin state (fig. 57.1). Splendid sets of jades have been excavated, comprising up to forty separate parts, with decorative patterns. These plaques were presumably sewn on to a textile placed over the face cover. They were only a small fraction of the extraordinarily prolific number of jades in the grave, which covered almost the entire body of the deceased.

This practice developed and reached its most advanced form in the Han period, with jade plugs for the nine body apertures and jade garments for the dead (no. 81). The jade plaques shown here come from one of the thirty-five Eastern Zhou graves, with similar stone or jade face coverings, which

were discovered in the mid-1950s during roadworks in Luoyang, within the area of the former Eastern Zhou city. Only a proportion of the jade plaques in the set shown here reproduce the features of a face: amongst these are the narrow eye plaques with smooth contours; a nose plaque, with curved contours and diminishing in size towards the top, with three holes bored in it; and a pierced, smiling mouth piece with a toothed external contour. Because of its position above the eyes, a pair of small plates of nearly identical form can be identified as a representation of two relatively powerful eyebrows. Between these, in the middle of the brow, is a small disc with a hole in the middle, below a larger rectangular jade plate which similarly has a hole in the middle. Presumably these two geometric plaques, as well as the mostly s-shaped cheek and ear plates in the shape of dragons, were purely decorative. The wealth of different forms and styles of jade face coverings found in the graves of Luoyang suggests that, in contrast to the regimented sets of ritual bronzes, for example, the numbers and forms of the various burial jades were not subjected to official regulation.

Published: Beijing 1959e, pp. 111–24; Goepper 1995, no. 71.

1 *Wenwu* 1994.1, p. 24, fig. 33; *Wenwu* 1994.8, pp. 4–21, 22–33, 68.

73 Figure of a kneeling man

Jade
Eastern Zhou, Warring States period (475–221 BC)
Height 7.5 cm
Excavated in 1987 at the western end of Zhongzhou Street, Luoyang, Henan province
Luoyang City Museum, Henan province

Very few jade carvings of human beings survive from the Zhou period. Of those that exist, most are about 3 cm high and are in a kneeling or standing position. Many have a hole bored in them, evidence that they functioned as beads or pendants. Others are slightly larger and carved in the round; the kneeling figure from Luoyang belongs to this second category. It was placed with the deceased, together with jade rings, beads, small bronze bells (*ling*), bronze knives and five ritual bronzes of the *ding* type. Their owner, accordingly, must have held a position of fairly high rank.

The block-like figure is represented in a kneeling position characteristic of Shang period figures (no. 49). Such a position was adopted when eating or receiving guests and when making ritual offerings. What may appear at first glance as designs tattooed on the skin are in fact the hatched geometric chequered patterns on a close-fitting, knee-length garment with half sleeves, similar to the dress worn by the figures in no. 75. This garment is folded from left to right over the chest and closed high at the neck. From the hip belt it hangs in several folds, also covered in the chequered pattern, but

73

these are slit at the back to reveal a striped undergarment. As with most Zhou period figures, the hands are folded over the belt, from which hangs a simple jade ornament consisting of a small jade disc and an arched pendant. The figure wears no shoes, which is quite commonplace for jade figures of the Shang and Zhou periods (no. 49). It is known that from the Han period it was customary to remove one's footwear inside a building.

The man's head is disproportionately large, with prominent ears and broad curved eyebrows which emphasise his almond-shaped eyes. Between them is a narrow, flat nose with spiralling flared nostrils. Above the narrow closed mouth, a moustache is represented by hatched engraving. This identifies the figure as male. Over his centrally parted hair is a close-fitting headpiece, held in position by a ribbon tied below the chin. A similar headpiece can be seen more clearly in bronze at no. 74.

This headpiece and the chequered clothing, which are char-

acteristic of the early Warring States period, and the jade ornaments, which occur on painted wooden figures of the Han period, suggest that the figure represents a high-ranking servant in a deferential posture, perhaps waiting to serve his master in the afterlife. At present there is neither archaeological nor literary evidence to suggest that such jade figures had any specific part to play in the funeral cult. They may have served a purely decorative function or may even have represented the tomb occupant.

Published: Luoyang 1990, no. 37; Goepper 1995, no. 70.

The royal tombs of the state of Zhongshan

The state known by the name of Zhongshan was established in Hebei province, in Pingshan county, south of Beijing and west of the modern city of Shijiazhuang. The kings of Zhongshan ruled over the Baidi or white Di, a non-Chinese people who had threatened the Chinese borders for some centuries before settling near Pingshan in the fourth century BC. Thirty tombs and two chariot burials have been excavated in the area. Tomb M1 belonged to King Cuo of Zhongshan, who died in about 310 BC, and tomb M6 probably belonged to a predecessor of a generation or so earlier.[1]

These two tombs are large constructions with pairs of access ramps. Indeed, the tomb shape is of Chinese type and demonstrates the degree to which these peoples had assimilated Chinese practices and beliefs. Tomb M1 was surmounted by a large mound, on which there had once been constructions of wood and tile. A plan of three structures was shown on a bronze plate recovered from the tomb, and from this plan a reconstruction has been proposed (fig. 1). Tomb M1 had four coffins, one inside the other, and also three further chambers holding burial goods. To the north of tomb M1 were accompanying burials, interred over a period of time, and to the south were two chariot pits with horses, a pit with sacrificial animals and a boat burial. Tomb M6, also a large tomb, was slightly apart from this first complex. As in tomb M1, the tomb furnishings were found in separate compartments around the main coffins.

The contents of these tombs are very fine and include sets of inscribed ritual vessels detailing the history of Zhongshan and the genealogy of their kings. As Li Xueqin has pointed out, these inscriptions include quotations from the ancient Chinese classics, such as the *Shi jing (The Book of Poetry)*, testimony to the degree to which the Di had been sinicised.[2] In addition, the quality of the workmanship in bronze and jade indicates a command of resources and techniques specific to the

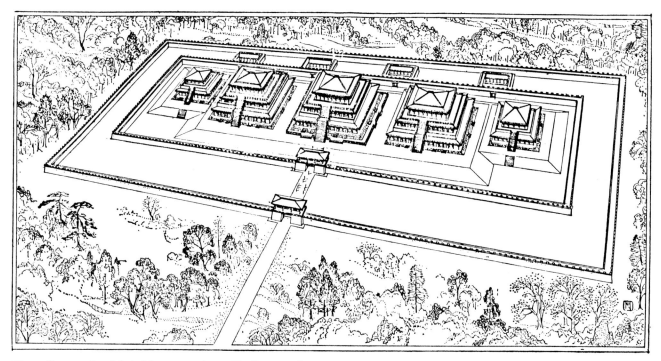

Fig. 1 *Reconstruction of the buildings over tomb* MI. *After* Kaogu xuebao *1990.1, p. 110, fig. 10.*

Fig. 2 *Bronze figure of an imaginary winged beast inlaid with silver. From the royal tombs of the Zhongshan state, Pingshan county, Hebei province. Height 24.6 cm. After Tokyo 1981, no. 43.*

Chinese cultural sphere. Famous figures of winged beasts (fig. 2) and a tiger devouring an ibex were cast in bronze and enhanced with gold and silver inlay. Such pieces were either stands or fittings for furniture.[3] While the craftsmanship is Chinese in character, the subject matter has affinities with the images of winged beasts

and animals in combat that were popular in Central and Western Asia. The pieces shown are, however, representative primarily of Chinese interests.

1 For a brief description of the tombs in English see So 1995, p. 429.
2 Li Xueqin 1985a, pp. 106–7.
3 Paris 1984.

74 Lamp bearer

Eastern Zhou, Warring States period, Zhongshan state,
4th century BC
Bronze with lacquer and silver inlay, black gemstone
Height 66.4 cm; diameter of lamp ring 17.3 cm; weight 11.6 kg
Excavated in 1976 from tomb M6 of the royal Zhongshan tombs, Pingshan county, Hebei province
Institute of Archaeology and Cultural Relics Bureau, Hebei province

This lamp bearer is an outstanding example of the art of early Chinese bronze casters and silversmiths. It was found in one of the subsidiary chambers to the east of the coffin chamber of tomb M6, which belonged to one of the rulers of Zhongshan. The head of the lamp bearer, which was worked separately in silver and then inserted into the torso of the figure, cast in bronze, is extremely well preserved. Shining eyes with dark pupils, inlaid with black gemstones, give the face a lively expression, intensified by a mouth that appears to smile and thus raise the cheekbones. The smiling mouth is exaggerated by the upward curving moustache. The heavy eyebrows are

carefully delineated with parallel lines, as are the winding strands of the hair, twisted inwards like horns above the temples, and pinned up at the back under a headpiece, which is pulled tight under the chin with the aid of a strap.

The lamp bearer is dressed in a long garment (*shenyi*) which is wrapped about his body several times, held by a wide waist-band and secured with a long narrow belt hook. This sumptuous garment, now corroded in places, is decorated with a complex pattern of volutes, straight lines and cloud motifs, in the recesses of which are traces of red and black lacquer. There is a double shawl collar with wide braids, and the sleeves terminate in wide openings. The bottom of the garment splays out over the low square pedestal, decorated with intaglio spirals and, in front of the feet, an animal mask.

The lamp bearer's outstretched hands clutch the tails of serpent-like creatures with horns. The serpent in his left hand balances a ring-shaped lamp groove, while that in his right hand supports a tall stave, at the tip of which is a second groove-like lamp ring. A small monkey climbs up this removable silver-inlaid stave and turns its head towards a dragon-like lizard creeping up after it from below. The base of the lower lamp has a further serpent twisted round it, its erect head supporting the upper snake. All three lamp channels, which would probably have been filled with vegetable oils, are provided with three spikes. These would have supported short torch-like wicks, which would have been tied together with hemp fibres or reinforced by narrow bamboo strips. Wax candles were not known at this period. When fully illuminated the lamp would have had nine flames burning on three levels.

The origins of Chinese oil lamps are not known. The earliest datable lamps come from Warring States tombs. Amongst these are lamp dishes on a high foot[1] and others held by a human figure – standing, kneeling or even riding on a camel.[2] Within the group of lamps with human figures, the present lamp is important for its inclusion of imaginary creatures. Lamps seem to have been valued for their mythological imagery, and they contributed to depictions of the cosmos within a tomb.

Published: *Wenwu* 1979.5, pp. 46–50; Paris 1984, no. 40; Thorp 1988a, pp. 132–5, no. 65; Beijing 1992a, no. 175; Beijing 1992b, no. 111; Goepper 1995, no. 65.

1 *Wenwu* 1983.7, pp. 78–86.
2 Rawson 1989a.

75 Four small plaques

Eastern Zhou, Warring States period, Zhongshan state, 4th century BC
Brown and black jade

a Female with jacket folded over on right
Height 3.4 cm; width 1.3 cm

b Slim female
Height 4 cm; width 1 cm

c Female with wide skirt
Height 3.4 cm; width 1.2 cm

d Child
Height 2.5 cm; width 1.2 cm

Excavated in 1974 from tomb M3 of the royal Zhongshan tombs, Pingshan county, Hebei province
Institute of Cultural Relics, Hebei province

These thin, flat standing figures with engraved decoration are all portrayed full face. Their arms and hands, clasped at the waist, give a rounded shape to the upper part of the body. On the three adult figures the curve of the arms is mirrored in the horn-like hairstyle or headdress. All the figures have round heads with summary features dominated by large triangular noses. Only the tallest figure and the child have ears. The most striking features of the group are the horn-like hairstyles or headdresses on the adult figures and the chequered pattern of the clothing. Lines engraved parallel to the horns of the headdresses on figures (a) and (b) may indicate strands of hair dressed upwards to the side. Between the so-called horns is a central band, which possibly served to fix the hair or to display jewellery. The child's hair consists of a central hairknot or tuft of hair on a smooth shaven head, a hairstyle that can still be observed on Chinese children today, particularly in rural areas.

Each figure is dressed slightly differently: figures (a) and (c) have 'waistbands', the former perhaps the braid along the bottom of a jacket, while the latter may be the waistband of a one piece garment; figure (b) wears a long undivided garment decorated on the upper arms and at the wrist with a narrow braid; and the child (d) wears a chequered skirt and appears to have a naked torso.

The function and significance of the group of figures are not clear. They were found in the heavily plundered medium-sized grave M3, in the rectangular grave pit, from which further smaller objects made of jade, as well as two *liubo* boards, broken into many pieces (no. 76), were recovered. This grave, like those at M4 and M5, was possibly that of a concubine of a Zhongshan ruler.

Published: *Wenwu* 1979.1, p. 13, and pl. 7: 4; Paris 1984, nos 70–4; Shen Congwen 1992, p. 38; Hebei 1991–3, vol. 3, no. 229; Goepper 1995, no. 69.

75a,b,c,d

76 Board for the game of *liubo*

Eastern Zhou, Warring States period, Zhongshan state,
4th century BC
Stone
44.9 cm × 40.1 cm
Excavated in 1974 from tomb M3 of the royal Zhongshan tombs,
Pingshan county, Hebei province
Institute of Cultural Relics, Hebei province

This board was used for a game most commonly called *liubo*
(six rods), played throughout élite Chinese society from the
6th century BC onwards. It is mentioned in the *Spring and
Autumn Annals*, although the great Han historian Sima Qian
(145–*c.* 86 BC) states that some earlier version of the game
was played during the late Shang.[1]

The excavation of tomb M3 among the royal Zhongshan
tombs recovered the broken fragments of this and a second
stone board (fig. 76.1). The present board is composed of
several stone slabs, bored with nine holes which probably
once enabled pins to secure the composite pieces to a backing
surface. The playing surface is framed by a three-row frieze
of whorls. Within this, the four arms of a cross are decorated
with intertwined snakes, and the remaining four quadrants are
each filled with a design of confronting masks, a twin-bodied
dragon and a tiger. The designs on the quadrants are diagon-
ally paired as mirror images. The central field, composed of
four adjoining triangles, uses a smaller version of the face
motif, flanked by snakes, which are not placed in a consist-
ently symmetrical arrangement. The game was played solely
along the 'roads' marked as L-shaped and single bars (fig.
76.2), and it is their presence which always identifies *liubo*
boards.

Tomb M3 contained no further gaming material, but it was
almost certainly once furnished with two complete sets of
liubo equipment. The basic equipment for *liubo* consisted of a
board, twelve pieces in the form of square or rectangular
blocks to move around the board, and either six rods or two

Fig. 76.1 *Drawing of the second* liubo *board discovered in tomb M3. After* Wenwu *1979.1, p. 26, fig. 32.*

dice to determine moves. Pieces made of ivory, bone, bronze,
jade and rock crystal have been discovered in excavations
throughout north and south China. The rods were split
bamboo canes, often strengthened on the concave side with
metal and lacquer. In the early history of *liubo*, these rods
were thrown rather in the manner of divinatory casting to
determine a score, but other forms of play replaced the rods
with eighteen-sided dice marked with numbers.

The earliest complete *liubo* games using six bamboo rods
are two sets discovered in two Qin dynasty tombs at Shuihudi

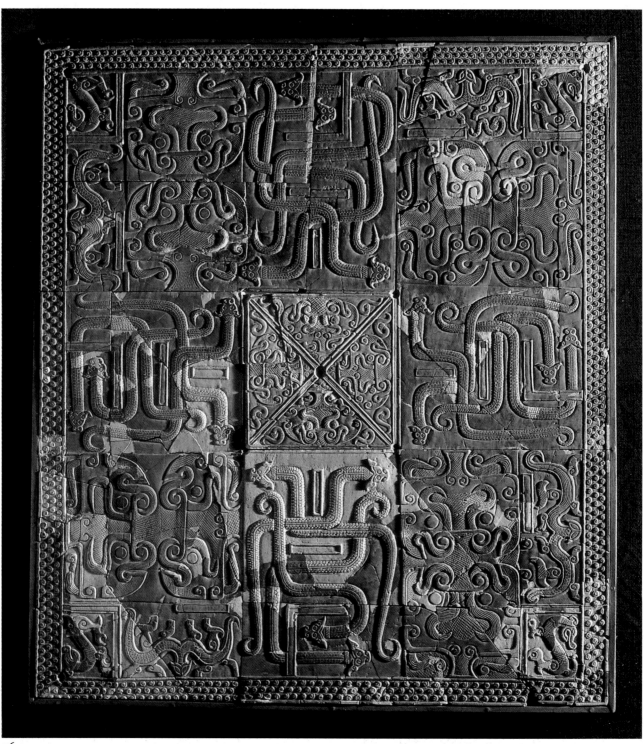

76

in Hubei province.[2] A complete Western Han set from a tomb at Fenghuangshan in Hubei province[3] contained six rods as well as an eighteen-sided die. However, another complete Han set, placed in an almost contemporaneous tomb at Mawangdui near Changsha in Hunan,[4] included an eighteen-sided die but lacked the six rods.[5] The Zhongshan board,

those of the four later complete game sets and all other Han *liubo* boards[6] bear a standard arrangement of 'roads', but a great number of playing rules must have developed over the long period of the game's history in different areas of China.

We do not know exactly how the playing pieces were moved around a *liubo* board, but it is quite plausible that the

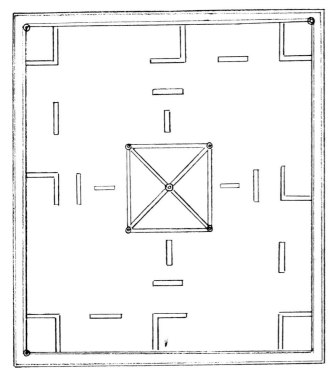

Fig. 76.2 *Drawing of the 'roads' on the* liubo *board.*

Fig. 76.3 *Rubbing of a tomb brick from Xinye, Henan province, showing immortals casting the six rods during a game of* liubo. *After Kaogu 1964.2, p. 91, fig. 1: 5.*

casting of rods and the moves made on the board were derived from ancient divination practices. The arrangement of the 'roads' and the ornamental designs of the Zhongshan board show an emphasis on the four directions, whilst the six pieces belonging to each player amount to the highly significant number of twelve. The twelve months of an annual cycle were divided into two sixes, in correspondence with the six *yin* and six *yang* tones of the Chinese gamut. These and many more parallels in cosmological imagery may be indications that *liubo* could be played as an allegory of the annual cycle and the regulation of the state.[7] This process was, of course, subject to the intervention of fate in the guise of rod or dice throws. Such an interpretation might explain why so many *liubo* boards and associated equipment have been found in the tombs of the ruling élite. The ancient Chinese also believed

that *liubo* was played by immortals (fig. 76.3). Apart from these serious concerns, however, *liubo* was a thoroughly entertaining game which featured at celebratory banquets and remained the favourite mental relaxation of rulers throughout the Warring States and Han periods. Its popularity declined soon after the fall of the Han.

Published: *Wenwu* 1979.1, p. 13 and figs 32, 33; Paris 1984, no. 45; *Gugong wenwu yuekan* 1986.11, p. 92; Goepper 1995, no. 76.

1 Sima Qian 1959, 3.104.
2 Beijing 1981d, pp. 55–6.
3 *Wenwu* 1974.6, pp. 50–1.
4 *Wenwu* 1974.7, pp. 45–6.
5 For the Mawangdui game see *Wenwu* 1979.4, pp. 35–9.
6 Six other Han finds are listed in Fu Juyou 1986, pp. 25–6.
7 For links between games and rulership see Lewis 1990, pp. 146–50.

77 Two dog collars

Eastern Zhou, Warring States period, Zhongshan state, late 4th century BC
Gold and silver
Diameters 38 cm; 36 cm
Excavated in 1978 from tomb M1, the grave of King Cuo of Zhongshan, Pingshan county, Hebei province
Cultural Relics Institute, Hebei province

Dogs were amongst the earliest domesticated animals of neolithic China. They were probably bred from the fifth or fourth

Fig. 77.1 *Excavation photograph of the dog skeletons with their collars.*

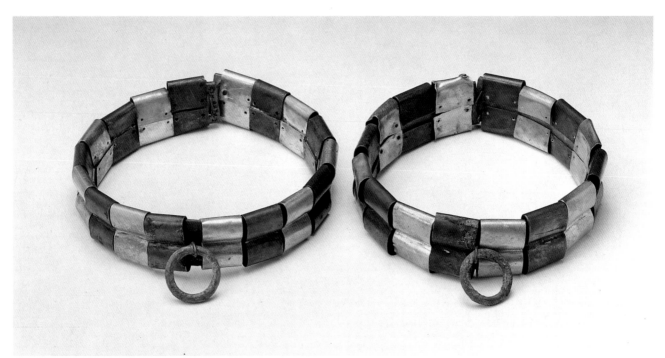

77

millennium BC as guard and hunting animals and they supplied humans with fur and meat. They were carefully buried at the feet of the deceased in the neolithic cemeteries of the Dawenkou and Longshan cultures (*c.* 4000–2000 BC), apparently to accompany the dead. Dogs were also frequently interred in Shang period graves, often beneath the body of the tomb occupant.

The precious dog collars shown here were found on the necks of two dog skeletons in a sacrificial pit to the south of the tomb of King Cuo of Zhongshan (fig. 77.1). Presumably they were the hunting dogs of the king which had followed their master into death, together with two or three hunting chariots and tents. In the southern part of the same badly plundered pit were the remains of ten sheep and six horses, which were probably animal sacrifices.

The two dog collars originally had a leather backing, to which were attached the alternating gold and silver sections. Each of these sections consists of a folded strip of metal, indented on the exterior to create the impression of two parallel narrow gold and silver bands. The holes in the strips suggest that they were originally fixed to the leather on the inside by four pins, or that they were joined by threads. There are no traces of the dog leads which were drawn through copper rings on the collar.

These splendid dog collars, together with many other items

in gold and silver in the Zhongshan tombs, are evidence of the wealth and luxury that existed at the court. At the same time, they also confirm the high esteem in which hunting dogs were held amongst the upper stratum of society, as described in a poem from the *Shi jing (The Book of Poetry)*, of *c.* 600 BC:

> Here come the hounds, ting-a-ling,
> And their master so handsome and good;
>
> The hounds, with double ring,
> Their master so handsome and brave.
>
> The hounds, with double hoop;
> Their master so handsome and strong![1]

A passage in the Tianwen chapter of the *Chu ci (The Elegies of Chu)*, a collection of poetry from the state of Chu dating from about 300 BC, illustrates the high value attached to hunting dogs: 'The elder brother had a hunting dog. Why did the younger brother not deserve it? The elder bestowed a hundred chariots on him, yet he ended by losing all his substance.'[2]

Published: *Wenwu* 1979.1, pp. 1–31; Paris 1984, no. 35; Goepper 1995, no. 77.

1 Waley 1954, no. 258.
2 Hawkes 1985, p. 134.

PART III

IMPERIAL CHINA

The Qin dynasty, 221–206 BC

The Qin state, which emerged the final victor from the conflicts of the Warring States period, had not initially been the dominant power, a position earlier claimed by the Jin and the Chu. The Qin had officially taken over the territory in the west abandoned by the Zhou in 770 BC, but they did not rise to political prominence until the fourth century BC. Qin is renowned for the ideology known as Legalism, which argued that the power of the state resided in its political and social institutions, and that a strongly enforced legal code should apply to all, regardless of rank.

During the fourth century BC the Qin embarked on a series of conquests, first annexing the prosperous basin of Sichuan, which may have given them the economic power essential to their later exploits. In 256 BC they obliterated the remains of the Zhou dynasty and, in the following decades, advanced across central China destroying states and their capitals. A crucial victory was the defeat of Chu in 223 BC. The King of Qin assumed the title of First Emperor, or Qin Shi Huangdi, in 221 BC with the conquest of the eastern state of Qi.

Control of this enormous territory was undertaken with efficiency and ruthlessness. The weapons of the former states were melted down, and a symbolic display of supremacy was made by building miniature replicas of the palaces of the defeated states in the grounds of the First Emperor's own palace. Qin is famous for unifying the script, currency, systems of measurement, the road system and even axle lengths in order to improve communications. The old feudal system was replaced by a hierarchical local government, with many officials directly appointed by the central government.

The authority of the First Emperor was proclaimed in texts and monuments. He travelled to major sites in his dominions and arranged for inscriptions detailing his achievements and ambitions to be set up. He is renowned, in particular, for major building projects: joining up large sections of defences on China's northern borders to make what is now known as the Great Wall; the construction of magnificent palaces; and, above all, the planning and execution of his large tomb, at which the famous terracotta warriors were found (no. 78). Discoveries at this last site have revealed material evidence of the conscription and the hardships of the workforce required for these vast enterprises.

Although these projects and administrative measures gave some coherence to the diverse parts of the Qin emperor's lands, the economic burden and political unrest they engendered were probably among the factors responsible for the rebellions that brought down the Qin state and led to the establishment of the following empire of the Han.

The Han dynasty, 206 BC–AD 220

The downfall of the Qin precipitated a bitter contest for the throne between two rebel groups, one led by a man called Xiang Yu and the other by the eventual victor and founder of the Han, Liu Bang. As the armies fought each other across the country, large areas were devastated.

The state established by the Han was to endure for nearly four hundred years, with only a short break (between AD 9 and 25) when a rebel leader, Wang Mang, established an alternative dynasty. This Xin dynasty separates the two parts of the Han dynasty, which are now known as the Western and the Eastern Han periods respectively. The terms Western and Eastern are used because, in the former period, the capital was in the west, near present-day Xi'an, and in the latter period the capital was moved eastwards to Luoyang. The Han perpetuated the hierarchical system of government instigated by the Qin, with large central and local bureaucracies. To serve this administration, the Han encouraged the development of an educated scholarly class. From 136 BC certain texts were singled out to serve as a basis for training officials, and in AD 175 these texts were inscribed on tablets (no. 117).

Control of a large empire depended on these expert officials, versed in a standardised code of rules and laws. This corps shared not only a similar outlook and ideology, but also a similar standard of material life. By this date highly organised workshops, supervised by officials, mass-produced standardised weapons, bronze vessels, lacquers and dress for distribution to the official class (nos 92–94). As the area dominated by the Han increased, such items were sent as far afield as Korea and Vietnam.

Indeed, the Han greatly extended the unified state created by the Qin. They reinforced the government of central China, and then under the martial emperor, Han Wudi (141–87 BC), the Chinese armies brought not only Korea and parts of Vietnam under their control, but also more distant regions along the Silk Route in Central Asia. In part these conquests came about as China's neighbours pressed upon her borders, provoking a military response. To combat the semi-nomadic peoples of Inner Mongolia, the Chinese sought fine horses in order to fight their enemies on their own terms. One Zhang Qian was sent as an ambassador to the west, to search for a supply of fine Ferghana horses and to negotiate for allies against the nomads. Neither of these efforts was successful, but through his efforts the Chinese were able to construct an account of the western regions which remains to this day an important description of the area and its inhabitants. In later centuries the Han continued to have trouble in negotiations with the nomads and were compelled to barter large quantities of silk in exchange for the horses they required in their continuing struggles to control their borders.

While the Han dynasty was a time when material and political life were visibly organised, it was also a time when changes continued to evolve in views of the afterlife. The Eastern Zhou period had seen the beginning of notions of an underworld governed by a bureaucracy, and of lands inhabited by immortals. These notions were further developed by the Han and were to transform burial practices. Tombs were built to represent the universe in which the dead were expected to live. Several separate rooms were created within the tomb for different activities: stables and kitchens, banqueting halls and resting rooms. The rooms were decorated with paintings or low relief carvings of scenes that illustrated both the daily life of the occupant and the realms of other worldly deities. Such decoration not only depicted a whole universe but brought it within a tomb. Some aspects of the burial, such as jade suits (no. 81) and mirrors (nos 88, 89), focused on the search for immortality and illustrated a concern with deities who could bestow eternal life. The ranges of goods buried in tombs changed concurrently, with ceramic replicas taking the place of many more precious items. Ceramic figures replaced human servants and also provided entertainers (nos 108–112); the scope of tombs was increased by adding models of quite complicated buildings (nos 106, 107). At first sight it seems that the tombs of the Qin and Han simply continued the practices of the neolithic and Shang periods by supplying the needs of the tomb occupant. However, the emphasis on immortality, and the new interest in the lands of deities and in replicas of the real world rather than in actual objects, indicate significant changes in outlook and belief.

The terracotta army and the tomb of the First Emperor

When the First Emperor died in 210 BC, his tomb and the pits within an extended burial ground had probably been under preparation for more than a decade. The excavations over the last twenty years in the region of Lintong outside Xi'an have revealed a complex arrangement of tomb and accompanying burials. The mausoleum lies under a natural mound that was artificially raised to form a truncated pyramid. It was enclosed within two walls, an inner and an outer one, as though it were a palace.

Although the tomb has not been excavated and may indeed have been looted, it is renowned from a description given by the famous Han dynasty historian, Sima Qian:

As soon as the First Emperor became king of Chin [Qin], excavations and building had been started at Mount Li, while after he won the empire more than seven hundred thousand conscripts from all parts of the country worked there. They dug through three subterranean streams and poured molten copper for the outer coffin, and the tomb was filled with models of palaces, pavilions and offices, as well as fine vessels, precious stones and rarities. Artisans were ordered to fix up crossbows so that any thief breaking in would be shot. All the country's streams, the Yellow River and the Yangtse were reproduced in quicksilver and by some mechanical means made to flow into a miniature ocean. The heav-

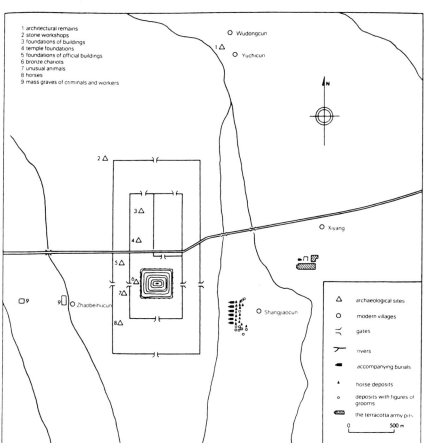

1 architectural remains
2 stone workshops
3 foundations of buildings
4 temple foundations
5 foundations of official buildings
6 bronze chariots
7 unusual animals
8 horses
9 mass graves of criminals and workers

○ Wudongcun
1 △
○ Yuchicun

2 △

3 △

4 △

○ Xiyang

5 △

6 △
7 △

□ 9   9 △ ○ Zhaobeihucun

8 △

○ Shangjiaocun

△   archaeological sites
○   modern villages
≍   gates
⅂   rivers
▬   accompanying burials
▴   horse deposits
○   deposits with figures of grooms
▦   the terracotta army pits

0   500 m

Fig. 1 *Plan of the mausoleum of the First Emperor.
Adapted from Ledderose and Schlombs 1990.*

Fig. 2 *Bronze chariots from the mausoleum of the
First Emperor.*

enly constellations were shown above and the regions of the earth below. The candles were made of whale oil to ensure their burning for the longest possible time.[1]

We thus know that the building in which the emperor lay was intended to be a microcosm of the world. What Sima Qian did not reveal was that the surrounding area was also filled with buildings and pits that complemented and extended the tomb (fig. 1). Buildings above ground acted as reception halls for those attending to the rites. Servants and officials serviced the area by preparing offerings to the dead emperor. Very near the tumulus itself was a small pit in which exquisite bronze chariots were buried. These highly detailed replicas are smaller than life size (fig. 2). Their fine detail and expensive materials and workmanship indicate that they were for the dead emperor himself to use. Other areas around the tomb contained clay coffins in which exotic animals and birds, probably from the emperor's zoo, were buried; an area in which several hundred horses were interred with terracotta figures of life-size grooms; and a series of burials of human beings, possibly of the princes and concubines, whom Sima Qian relates were buried at the time of the emperor's funeral.

The terracotta army may be viewed as part of this complicated microcosm. Several separate pits have been discovered and excavated. The largest pit, pit 1, held perhaps as many as six thousand figures of soldiers aligned in battle array, with archers and chariots at the front. They stood within a massive wooden building dug into the ground, creating rows of parallel corridors (fig. 3). When the invading forces of Xiang Yu reached this area, the building seems to have been burned and to have collapsed on to the figures. Pit 2 held over 1400 cavalry men and chariots. The third pit may have been a command group, as it held one chariot and a number of elaborate figures. A fourth pit was empty and may never have been completed.

The scale of the enterprise suggests that massive planning would have been required to achieve this multitude of figures, organised like a real army. The arrangement of the army must have been planned in advance, and then a scheme worked out to ensure that the figures were of a uniform type but that each had different dress or facial features, so that the final impression was one of an army of individuals. We have some notion as to how the task was carried out both from texts and archaeological evidence. Sima Qian indicates that

Fig. 3 *View of pit 1 near the mausoleum of the First Emperor.*

700,000 men from all over the empire were conscripted for work at the tomb. Summary burials have been discovered of such workers, who were recorded as criminals on pottery fragments buried with them.

The figures themselves were made of standard parts, many of which were moulded. Thus both the heads and hands were moulded in several sections. The hands were ingeniously made so that a limited number of parts could be combined in a variety of ways to create hands that could hold different weapon types and thus indicate soldiers of different ranks or functions. It is likely that the figures were made by small groups of workers acting together to make batches. The names stamped on some of the figures are probably those of foremen who supervised the gangs. Archaeologists argue that these foremen each controlled a group of ten to twelve workers. Once they had made the basic parts and fitted them together, they added the detail of the faces, armour, shoes and headdress.[2] Care and skill were required to fit the different parts together, so that the whole did not disintegrate while hardening or during firing. Vast quantities of fuel would have been required to fire these figures. They were also brightly painted to accord with the colours suitable for the different ranks. The pigments were embedded in lacquer, which has disintegrated since the pits were opened.

The care with which this replica army was planned and made is tribute both to the organisation of the Qin

state and to the beliefs and practices that sustained the Qin emperor and his subjects. It is noteworthy that the replica army stood alongside a tomb that was also supplied with real people and real objects. We can thus understand its function as similar to that of the depiction of deities and other worlds in Han dynasty tombs (Yu, fig. 3). As it would have been impracticable to bury the whole army, some sort of replica was needed if the emperor were to be supplied with an army in the afterlife. The fact that replicas were buried concurrently with real people and real objects suggests that quite a complex view of the afterlife was now current. We do not know exactly what sorts of theories were abroad. But just as the ancient Greeks, the Buddhists and the Christian church created images of gods and incomprehensible forces in an attempt to make them more accessible, so this terracotta army was probably the concrete representation of the army of the afterlife, enabling the peoples of the time to imagine what such an immortal army would be like and to provide it for the First Emperor's future existence.

1 Yang Hsien-yi and Gladys Yang 1979, p. 186.
2 Ledderose 1992.

78 Figure of a soldier

Qin dynasty, 3rd century BC
Brown and grey clay, originally painted
Height 187 cm
Excavated in 1974 at the mausoleum of the First Emperor, Qin Shi Huangdi, pit 1, Lintong county, Shaanxi province
Historical Museum, Beijing

This is one of the foot soldiers that formed the vanguard and the rearguard of the main troop from pit 1. In his right hand he presumably held a weapon, probably a hilted sword. He wears a wrap-around coat, flaring outwards at the bottom, over a soft undergarment. His wide trousers reach down to the knees. Puttees are wrapped around his calves and are held in position at the knee and ankle by slightly protruding ribbons tied with bows. On his feet the soldier wears shoes with blunt rectangular ends, which are tied by cords over the instep.

As the soldier seems to represent a comparatively low rank, he does not wear a hat or head covering, and his finely parted hair is clearly visible. The ends of the hair are restrained in plaits, one starting from the left temple and the other from behind the right ear. These two plaits are bound together behind the back of the head and their ends are tied up into a knot of hair.

The soldier would originally have been painted in brilliant colours to indicate both his physical features and his dress. But the pigment was held in a thin coating of lacquer, which has decayed, leaving only traces of colour. The soldier's main garment was a yellow or ochre colour, his face and hands were flesh coloured and his hair was black.

As discussed above, figures such as this one were made of mass-produced parts: the head, two hands, two arms, the torso, two legs below the garment, and the feet and the plinth usually made as one. The head and hands, in particular, were moulded, and the separate sections were put together in different combinations to make the various categories of soldier. For instance, the moulds employed for the half-closed right hand of the soldier, which here may have held a sword, might also have been used to produce a similar hand for a charioteer holding reigns. In both cases, hands with fingers curled in a semicircle were appropriate, but the arms would be in different positions for the two types of figure.[1]

An inscription is impressed into the clay at the back of the head and probably records the overseer of the group who made this soldier. Such inscriptions were not intended to proclaim the artistry of a particular man or his workforce, but probably served as a means of keeping count of the numbers of figures made by the different elements of a particular workforce.

The organisation of workers, directed by foremen, had been in force in China from the neolithic period. Bronzes from the tomb of the Marquis Yi of Zeng (Rawson, fig. 18) and the bells from another Zeng tomb (no. 62) were probably made by some sort of mass-production, using both mechanically decorated moulds and subdivision of labour. Such contrasting examples – the terracotta and the bronze – illustrate well how the ancient Chinese mobilised large numbers of people to create huge quantities of highly accomplished objects for widely different uses. As important as the skilled labour were the planning and organisation of the workshops producing these objects.[2]

Published: Goepper 1995, no. 79.

1 For general accounts of the find and some individual figures see New York 1980, pp. 353–73; Ledderose and Schlombs 1990, pp. 35–98, 249–325. See also Yuan Zhongyi 1990.
2 For a discussion of the mass-production of the terracotta figures see Ledderose 1992. For an account of mass-production in bronze casting see Bagley 1995.

79 Figure of a naked soldier

Han period (206 BC–AD 220)
Ceramic
Height 59 cm
Provenance unknown
Historical Museum, Beijing

This figure is unprovenanced, but belongs to a large category of simplified figures made for burial in pits alongside imperial tombs. It would have been one of a band of soldiers or ser-

vants, after the manner of the terracotta warriors (no. 78). A group of such figures has recently been unearthed near Xi'an at Yangling (fig. 79.1), the tomb of the Han dynasty emperor Jingdi (188–141 BC). These figures come from several large storage pits in which provisions and supplies of different types were buried alongside the main tomb. Like pit 1 at the tomb of the First Emperor, the pits were lined with a wooden structure in which the figures and other models were buried. The models included animals and waggons, bags of grain, cooking and serving dishes in bronze, ceramic and lacquer. While some figures were placed in these pits, perhaps as guards, other were massed in large six-metre-long boxes.[1] As this figure is unprovenanced, it is not certain that it came from the Yangling area. It could equally well have been in a storage pit near one of the other imperial tombs near Xi'an. However, it is likely to have come from a site very like those revealed at Yangling.[2]

The figures from Yangling and the present piece are much smaller and less elaborate than those of the terracotta warriors (no. 78). Indeed they demonstrate the ways in which, as the use of such massed figures developed, economies were made in scope and scale. In place of the varied moulded and carved features, hands and armour, the present figure is quite rudimentary and naked. But even these rather simplified figures were probably made in several separate moulded sections. The head of the present figure is neatly formed, with the features and hairstyle rendered in some detail. The rather flat body and legs are moulded, rounded sections of clay, that seem to divide at the waist. From the examples shown in figure 79.1, it seems that many of the figures have broken at the same place, suggesting that they were all made of several similar parts luted together.

Fig. 79.1 *View of the excavation of one of the storage pits at Yangling, near Xi'an, Shaanxi province.*

Small holes in the shoulders suggest that arms were pegged in here. They may have been made of cloth, and indeed such figures were almost certainly clothed in dress and armour made in some sort of organic material that has since rotted away. If this was so, the present figure and others like it recall the wooden figures clothed in silk and other textiles found in southern tombs, such as those from Mashan (p. 142, fig. 2) and from Mawangdui,[3] rather than the more elaborate and substantial pieces from the tomb of the First Emperor.

Published: Goepper 1995, no. 107.

1 For a description of Yangling see Mou Lingsheng 1992.
2 For accounts of the imperial tombs near Xi'an see *Kaogu* 1984.10, pp. 887–94; *Wenwu* 1992.4, pp. 1–13; *Wenwu* 1994.6, pp. 4–23, 30.
3 Beijing 1973b, vol. 2, pls 198–201.

80 Figures of an archer and a javelin thrower

Western Han period, 2nd century BC
Dark grey ceramic with traces of red, white, blue and black pigment

a Archer
Height 50.4 cm

b Javelin thrower
Height 42.5 cm

Excavated in 1950 at Langjiagou, Hanjiawan, near Xianyang, Shaanxi province
Historical Museum, Beijing

These two models are further examples of mass-produced figures from armies accompanying major Han tombs. They are said to have come from Hanjiawan, not far from Yangjiawan, where a pottery army was excavated in 1965 adjacent to

79

80a,b

The archer (a) has one arm stretched out to hold a bow, while the other draws the cord (now missing) behind his ear. He leans back to give a stronger pull to his weapon. While his body, dressed in a thick soft robe, faces the viewer, his face is turned to the side to watch his shot. A neat cap covers his hair. His companion (b) is similarly dressed, but has a yet more active pose. His body arches backwards from below the waist, with his legs strongly braced against the plinth on which he stands. Both hands are coiled around a weapon now missing. It is likely that the weapons were made of either wood or clay. The figures were painted, but only on the archer are there clear traces of colour.

Published: Goepper 1995, no. 108.

1 Los Angeles 1987, p. 106.

second-century BC tombs of ministers. Like the pits for the terracotta warriors, the trenches at Yangjiawan also held over a thousand figures in massed battle array. The soldiers from the pits at Yangjiawan, like the present figures, were shown fully clothed and carrying shields, and many were mounted on horseback.[1]

While the two figures thus belong to the lineage of the pottery armies mentioned in connection with the two previous items, they give a rather different impression. Both the figures from the tomb of the First Emperor (no. 78) and those at Yangling (see no. 79) appear to be standing ready prepared for battle, but not directly in action. These two soldiers, on the other hand, are hurling a javelin and shooting with a bow. The actual weapons have disappeared, but the angles of the bodies and the thrust of the arms leave us in no doubt as to what is happening.

The tombs of Liu Sheng and Dou Wan at Mancheng, Hebei province

The rock cut tombs of Prince Liu Sheng and his consort Dou Wan were discovered near Mancheng in 1968. Liu Sheng was the son of Emperor Jingdi (188–141 BC). In the early decades of the Han empire, the west was divided into administrative areas entitled commanderies, while the east was divided into kingdoms, each assigned to a son or relative of the emperor. Liu Sheng ruled the kingdom of Zhongshan, one of the most prosperous territories in the Han empire.

The Mancheng tombs were elaborately constructed and magnificently furnished. They were both hollowed out of rock at the end of long tunnels leading into the mountain. Both tombs had two long narrow chambers

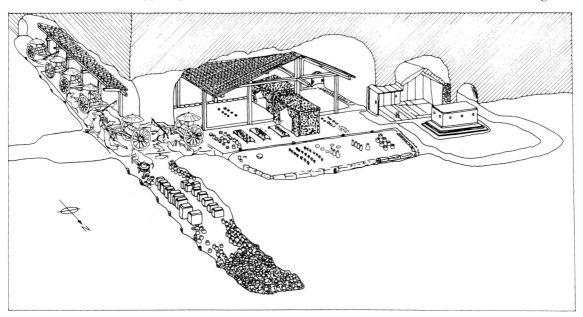

Fig. 1 *Reconstruction of the tomb of Liu Sheng at Mancheng, Hebei province. After New York 1980, fig. 112.*

either side of the main entrance, which held chariots, horses and wine and food (fig. 1). In Liu Sheng's tomb, a large central chamber enclosed a tiled structure, inside which were textile tents. This area was for formal banquets and possibly also for rituals. The rear private chambers of both tombs were the most elaborate being constructed of carefully fitted stone slabs, with their own doorways. Inside these inner rooms were the coffins within which the prince and his consort were encased in their jade suits (no. 81). These rear chambers were sumptuously equipped with fine inlaid wine vessels and lacquered furniture with gilded fittings. There were small stone figures of attendants in Liu Sheng's tomb.

The rock cut palace is a distinct variation on the multi-chambered tomb buried in the ground. From about this period, if not earlier, stone and especially jade seem to have had connotations of endurance and indeed immortality.[1] The intention in positioning a tomb within a mountain may have been to secure the enduring qualities of the stone to further the afterlife of the occupant. The special rooms within the caves created for the coffins, with neatly fitted stone slabs, and the jade suits of the royal pair, may also demonstrate preoccupations with the quest for eternal life.[2] To ensure complete protection, the tombs were carefully sealed, their entrances blocked with rubble and iron poured into the openings. The inner rooms were also separately sealed.

1 Ann Paludan 1991, p. 8.
2 For further discussion see a paper presented by Wu Hung at a colloquy at the Percival David Foundation, School of Oriental and African Studies, June 1995.

81 Jade suit, jade body plugs, and jade and gilt-bronze headrest belonging to Prince Liu Sheng

Western Han dynasty, 2nd century BC
Jade suit, length 188 cm
Head rest, height 17.6 cm; length 44.1 cm
Jade body plugs:
    pair of eye covers, length 4.5 cm
    pair of nose plugs, length 2.2 cm
    pair of ear plugs, length 2.2 cm
    mouth insert, length 7.2 cm
    anal plug, length 4.4 cm
    genital cap, length 6.8 cm; diameter 6.6 cm
Excavated in 1968 from the tomb of Liu Sheng at Mancheng, Hebei province
Hebei Provincial Museum

The suit crafted for Liu Sheng consists of 2498 small plaques pierced at the four corners and sewn together with a variety of knots of gold wire. The material has recently been identified as bowenite, which is a form of grey green stone softer than true jade or nephrite. Several distinct parts made up the suit, as indicated in figure 81.1, which obviously facilitated the dressing of the dead man. However, the excavators imagine from the way in which the suit was discovered that it had not been put onto the corpse properly. Although the suit was obviously intended to encase and seal the body, slits were provided for the eyes and mouth. A disc of the type known as a *bi* filled the top of the skull and thus left an opening at the top (fig. 81.2).

Jade suits are sometimes described as jade casings in Han texts. More than forty examples have been found, either com-

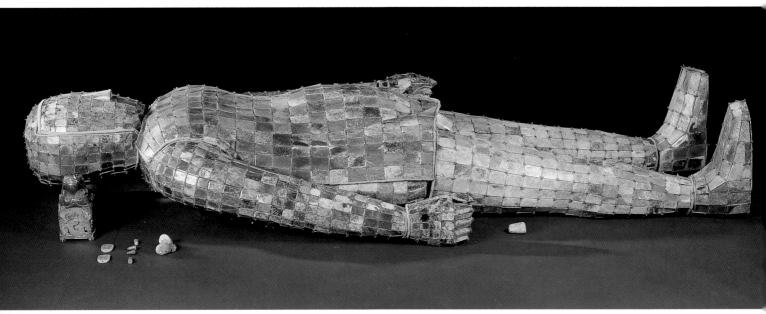

81

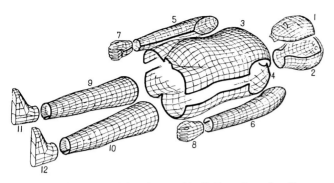

Fig. 81.1 *The sections of the jade suit. After Beijing 1980g, vol. 1, fig. 227.*

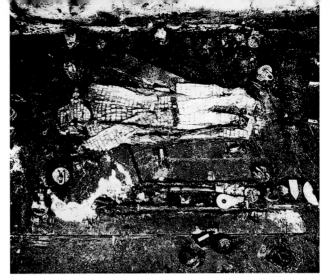

Fig. 81.4 *The jade suit as it was found in the tomb.*

Fig. 81.2 *The top of the head of the jade suit showing the jade disc.*

Fig. 81.3 *The jade and gilt-bronze headrest.*

plete or fragmentary.[1] The late Han history, the *Hou Han shu*, mentions the grading of the wires used to stitch the suits. The rank of the owner determined whether gold, silver or bronze wire was used.[2] However, such distinctions do not seem to have been observed at this relatively early stage in the Han period. The histories do not describe the motives for creating such suits. However, the link between jade and immortality seems to be the explanation for these painstaking means to preserve the bodies of their owners.

In addition to the suit, Liu Sheng's bodily orifices were sealed with plugs, and his head lay on a rest made of finely carved jade plaques set within a gilt-bronze frame (fig. 81.3). The prince was also surrounded by jades in his coffin (fig. 81.4).

Published: *Kaogu* 1972.2, pp. 39–47; Beijing 1980g, vol. 1, pp. 36–7, 344–57, vol. 2, colour pls 1–2 and pl. 13; Venice 1983, no. 104; Beijing 1990a, no. 88; Beijing 1992a, no. 27; Goepper 1995, no. 80.

1 For examples of jade suits see *Kaogu* 1981.1, pp. 51–8; *Wenwu* 1989.10, pp. 60–7.
2 See notes in the above articles; also Thorp 1991.

82

82 Incense burner of the Boshan *lu* type

Western Han period, late 2nd century BC
Bronze with traces of silver and gold
Overall height 32.4 cm; height of lid 13 cm
Excavated in 1968 from the tomb of Dou Wan, consort of Liu Sheng, at Mancheng, Hebei province (2: 3004)
Hebei Provincial Museum

The censer was found at Mancheng, in the tomb of Dou Wan, consort of Prince Liu Sheng, in whose tomb an even more elaborate example was interred.[1] Incense burners were

used from at least the fifth century BC, especially in southern China. A bronze openwork piece in the tomb of the Marquis Yi of Zeng of *c*. 433 BC may be among the earliest surviving examples, and during the fourth century BC such openwork bronzes were typical of the Chu state.[2] Only in the Han were incense burners made in the shapes of mountains. The source of the name Boshan *lu*, or burner in the shape of the Bo mountain, is a later term, meaning 'universal mountain'.[3]

An interest in mountains seems to be closely linked to the views about the other worlds that came to be elaborated at the end of the Warring States and in the early Han period. Among the concepts of the time was a view of the governance of the world in the afterlife. The central role was taken by the Yellow Emperor, the supreme deity who ruled the spiritual realm. He governed the five sacred peaks, including Mount Tai. In the reign of the emperor Wudi (141–87 BC), a major sacrifice was offered at Mount Tai, signifying imperial reverence for the mountain and the deities associated with it. Thus depictions of mountains should be seen in the light of a general reverence for the five sacred peaks, together with a special interest in Mount Tai and the Yellow Emperor.

Other venerated mountains included those inhabited by immortals – in the east at Penglai and in the west at Kunlun. Widespread beliefs linked mystical mountains with vapour and clouds or *qi*. Indeed, Han dynasty decoration displays many images and patterns of strange cloud-like forms that have been identified as embodying *qi* or vital forces of the cosmos. Examples of these swirling forces appear on bronzes and lacquers and, on a larger scale, on Han period lacquered coffins (Introduction, fig. 13a). Incense burners seem to represent a coalescence of the swirling clouds and, when filled with incense, the curling trails of smoke would re-emerge as *qi*.[4] In this way the mountain peaks of the burners, on which roamed the figures of miraculous creatures, would be enveloped in *qi* before the eyes of their owners.

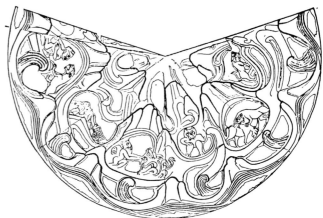

Fig. 82.1 *Drawing of the animals and figures on the mountain. After Beijing 1980g, vol. 1, fig. 171.*

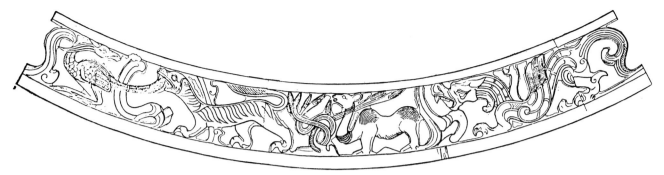

Fig. 82.2 *Drawing of the animals of the four directions. After Beijing 1980g, vol. 1, fig. 171.*

Here an openwork lid depicts a peaked mountain, the wild slopes of which are peopled by creatures: bears, armed warriors fighting with wild animals, and a tiger savaging a mountain goat; in another quarter a man drives along with his horse- or ox-drawn cart (fig. 82.1). Halfway up the slopes, a separate band is defined, within which are the creatures of the four directions, the Tiger of the West, the Dragon of the East and the Bird of the South. The position of the Northern Warrior, who is usually represented by a turtle grasped by a serpent, is here occupied by the rare representation of a camel (fig. 82.2). The incense bowl itself, in which presumably charcoal and incense were burnt, is held up effortlessly in the hand of a sturdily built figure. This figure, dressed in short trousers, appears to be a foreigner. He kneels on the back of a dragon-like creature, with wings growing out of its cheeks. On its underside, a nail holds the beast at the centre of a round bronze dish; this dish served to catch burning particles of charcoal.

Published: Watson 1973, no. 155; Beijing 1980g, vol. 1, pp. 256–7, figs

170–1; Venice 1983, no. 105; Beijing 1990a, no. 87; Munakata 1990, pp. 30–2; Sun Ji 1991, pp. 362–4; Goepper 1995, no. 82.

1 Beijing 1980g, pp. 64–5, figs 44–5.
2 For a discussion of early incense burners in Chu see Rawson 1989a.
3 For a discussion of the origins of the name Boshan *lu* see Munakata 1990, pp. 27–30; Erickson 1992.
4 For introductions to notions of *qi* in the Han period see Wu Hung 1984; Munakata 1990, pp. 20–34.

83 Figures of two storytellers

Western Han period, before 113 BC
Bronze
Heights 7.7 cm (MLM1: 4168); 7.8 cm (MLM1: 4169)
Excavated in 1968 from the tomb of Liu Sheng at Mancheng, Hebei province
Hebei Provincial Museum

These droll little bronze figures of two storytellers, who seem to belong together, appear in the midst of practising their art. They squat on the ground with their legs under them and

83

wear garments which are decorated with golden patterns and are draped so negligently that parts of their torsos remain uncovered. On their heads they wear tightly fitting caps with high pointed tips. Although both storytellers give the impression of being deeply immersed in their story, their expressions are quite different. The man on the right, whose left hand rests on his knee with the fingers stretched out straight, is full of temperament, with his head held high, and he appears to underline his words with the gesture of his right arm, raised at an angle. The storyteller on the left appears more reticent, with his bowed head, his forward-leaning posture, and his two arms lying carelessly on his knees.

The unusual physiognomy of the full faces with hollow cheekbones, wide mouths, tiny eyes, wide and emphasised nostrils, a low brow and an extremely small pointed chin presumably reveals the origin of these storytellers in a country lying to the south of China. During the Han period a multitude of foreign entertainers was employed at the imperial court or in the households of the nobility. Outside the great Han empire, south-western states, which were sometimes described as vassals, carried on an independent life, but had lively trading connections with the empire. In addition, the Han empire guaranteed protection from invaders, for which the imperial court was thanked by rich presents. In the year AD 120, a king by the name of Shan, who presumably ruled

a country in South-east Asia, is said to have sent the very considerable number of one thousand acrobats and jugglers to the court of the Han emperor Andi (AD 107–126). The members of this troupe not only mastered such conventional arts as juggling with several balls, but could also perform sensational magic tricks. Foreigners also came to the court along the Silk Route, or by sea across the Indian Ocean.

The bronze figures were discovered in Liu Sheng's tomb at Mancheng. Perhaps the prince appreciated the art of storytelling and did not wish to do without it in the afterlife. Such figures are, however, found in other tombs and may just have been conventional burial objects for high-ranking members of Han society. The two small sculptures were discovered in the middle of the approximately square central hall of Liu Sheng's tomb. The hall was intended for festivities in the afterlife and for the reception of officials and guests; here, too, the noble lord could enjoy himself alone or with friends at different games. Two tents, of which only the bronze parts of the support construction have survived, would have formed smaller private rooms within the main chamber; here the prince and his guests might be seated as they were entertained.

Published: Beijing 1980g, vol. 2, pl. 60: 1–2; Sun Ji 1991, p. 395, pl. 100: 13, 14; Goepper 1995, no. 81.

84 Model of a man with a millstone

Han period (206 BC–AD 220)
Bronze
Man, length 28.5 cm
Base of millstone, height 13.5 cm; width 17 cm
Millstone, diameter 11.6 cm
Excavated in 1964 in Zhongxiang county, Hubei province
Jingzhou Museum, Hubei province

Sweet cakes made of rice or millet flour were amongst the favourite dishes of many Han emperors, as reported in the Han dynasty history, the *Han shu*. As well as cakes, other foods made with flour were very popular in ancient China. Millstones required for the production of flour and clay models of complete mills are frequently found in the graves of the Han period.[1] What is much more rare is the use of bronze, from which our man with millstone is created.

Clothed only with a headcover and knee-length trousers, the man, standing with his legs apart, holds the handle of a long pole which, by being pulled backwards and forwards, would turn the heavy millstone. The pole is borne by a post supported by a tortoise. The round millstone, in two parts, is placed in a four-legged square box narrowing towards the bottom. Beside it stands a smaller, bellied vessel with ear handles. Presumably it contained the cereal, which was poured for grinding through two semicircular apertures in the upper stone. The grooved sides of the millstones, which facilitated the grinding, are visible. What is striking is the contrast between the nearly lifelike portrayal of the tortoise, which is raising its little head, and the relatively rigid depiction of the man.

Published: Goepper 1995, no. 83.

1 For models of milling equipment see Sun Ji 1991, pp. 15–18.

85 Hanging lamp

Late Eastern Han period, 2nd century AD
Bronze
Height 29 cm; length 28 cm
Acquired in 1974 in Changsha, Hunan province
Hunan Provincial Museum, Changsha

In the course of the expansion of the Qin and Han dynasties, Chinese troops and embassies penetrated beyond the boundaries of China to foreign lands, both in the south and to the west. Strange peoples from these regions are sometimes portrayed on objects of the time. Foreigners came to the imperial court as traders, servants or entertainers and as hostages; they served as slaves or servants in the households of the rich and are frequently depicted on oil lamps of ceramic or bronze. The lamp bearer, shown here almost naked, with curly hair, may represent a foreigner from South-east Asia.

Although we cannot identify the country to which this

lamp holder belongs, he has non-Chinese facial features, with large deep eyes and a high ridged nose, and his hair is dressed high in a knot. He wears a narrow loin cloth, quite unlike the clothes of the Han Chinese. The figure, which is suspended almost horizontally, is held by three bronze chains, the upper ends of which are attached to a domed bronze disc. On this disc sits a peacock-like bird, whose crown and tail feathers terminate in spirals. The topmost tail feathers finish in a loop, in which the lowest link of a short chain is engaged. This presumably ended in a hook. It is probable that a torch-like wick was placed on the spike of the lamp bowl, which is supported by the arms of the bronze figure (cf. no. 74). The lamp oil could be poured either directly into the bowl or into the figure itself through a flap at the back; from there it flowed into the lamp bowl through a small square aperture in its chest, the centre of gravity of the suspended construction. This innovation, which is as simple as it is effective, made it possible to guarantee a constant oil level in the lamp bowl.

Lamps were widely used during the Han period, being made of many different materials: bronze, iron, ceramic, jade, stone and wood. Many types, including some incorporating technical innovations such as flues, draft shields and dazzle shields, were developed. A new group of bronze lamps, in the form of cattle, sheep, birds, fish, peacocks, phoenixes, dragons, turtles, whose bodies were adapted as oil reservoirs, joined the wealth of shapes. The earlier tradition of multi-branched lamps (no. 74) was also developed (no. 97).

Published: *Wenwu* 1978.6, p. 88; *Kaogu yu wenwu* 1983.5, pp. 90–5; Li Xueqin 1985c, vol. 2, no. 246; Sun Ji 1991, pp. 355–7; Gao Feng and Sun Jianqun 1992, pp. 33–4; Goepper 1995, no. 84.

86

86 Winged immortal

Middle Eastern Han period, 2nd century AD
Bronze with gilt
Height 15.5 cm; width 9.5 cm
Excavated in 1987 from a tomb in an eastern suburb of Luoyang,
Henan province
Cultural Relics Bureau, Luoyang City

The first descriptions of deities, immortals and their dwellings in remote and distant places date from the Eastern Zhou. The Queen Mother of the West, Xi Wang Mu, seen below on the money tree (no. 87), a mirror (no. 89) and a brick (no. 101), is mentioned in the philosophical text, the *Zhuangzi*, (which was composed during the fourth and third centuries BC).[1] She was believed to dwell in a paradise in the Kunlun mountains. The ancient Chinese hoped that the elixir of immortality could be obtained from one of these paradises of the immortals. The First Emperor is described by the Han historian Sima Qian as ordering his servants to seek immortal potions, and he was much preoccupied by tales of immortals:

'The emperor, unable to find happiness, ordered the court scholars to write poems about immortals and pure beings, and wherever he went he made musicians set these to music and sing them.'[2] From these diverse traditions developed notions of attendant spirits and deities. Such spirits or immortals were often shown with feathered wings.

The kneeling bronze figure from Luoyang, the capital city of the Eastern Han period, is a typical example of a Han period winged immortal. We do not know what this piece was for, as no explanation has been found for the round and rectangular containers that the figure holds between its knees. One possibility is that these were supports for parts of lamps.

The figure is wrapped in a tightly fitting collarless garment, held by a belt at the waist and reaching down to bare feet. A feather motif is reproduced on the body in fine engraved lines. The feathers over the lower legs, as well as the wing feathers extended behind the back, are picked out in slight relief. Whereas the body and, in particular, the hands and feet are well proportioned, the facial features are exaggerated, and the strange large ears projecting above the head are very striking. A long drawn face, set off sharply against the neck by the bearded chin, has a pointed nose, below which the slightly open mouth appears to smile archly. The curved eyebrows protrude over small depressions for the eyes, which may possibly have been inlaid. A well preserved gold surface is visible in places, particularly on the torso, which must originally have been completely gilt.

The figure was discovered in a brick tomb lying under a mound about 7 m high. This quite substantial tomb had been almost completely plundered at an early date. The tomb robbers had presumably not discovered the figure in the antechamber, because the structure had collapsed and buried it. Scattered jade plaques and the copper wires of a jade garment indicated that the tomb occupant was of noble birth or high rank. An almost identical bronze figure was found about 5 m from the northern wall at the Chang'le palace, in present-day Xi'an, the capital of the Western Han dynasty.[3]

Published: Singapore 1990, p. 67; Luoyang 1990, no. 49; Beijing 1992a, no. 207; Imperial China 1992, no. 52; Goepper 1995, no. 85.

1 Yü Yingshih 1964–5, p. 87; Loewe 1979, p. 89.
2 Yang Hsien-yi and Gladys Yang 1979, p. 182.
3 *Wenwu* 1966.4, pp. 7–8; compare *Kaogu yu wenwu* 1981.4, inside front cover, fig. 2.

87 Money tree

Eastern Han period (AD 25–AD 220)
Ceramic and bronze
Height 105 cm
Excavated in 1972 in Pengshan county, Sichuan province
Sichuan Provincial Museum, Chengdu

'Money trees' or 'money shaking trees', so called after the coins distributed amongst their branches, rank as some of the most mythologically charged Han period archaeological finds. They are typical of south-west China and are without exception dated to the late Han period, although they are given no mention in Han period literature.

Many of the bases of stone or clay have survived the centuries relatively well. The fragile, finely cast bronze perforated branches, with dense leaves composed of mythical animals, human and divine figures and coins, on the other hand, are generally found only in fragments. One of the few complete examples is this money tree from Pengshan county in Sichuan, which was still standing on its pedestal, untouched, when it was discovered in an otherwise completely plundered simple rock tomb. Apparently the ancient tomb robbers had no understanding or use for this symbol of eternal wealth.

The unglazed clay pedestal takes the form of a slightly splayed bell, which was presumably intended to represent a mountain. Its surface is covered with complex ornament. Around its base are scattered *bi* discs joined by cords. On the summit of the mountain are two wild fantastic animals, presumably intended to guard the tree. The upper creature, whose horned head projects from the mountain relief, has the body of a predatory animal, with wings flowing from its shoulders. It stretches out its claws and opens its mouth in a threatening manner. The lower creature, with its round curved horns, is reminiscent of a sheep.

The bronze trunk of the money tree rises out of the ceramic base. It has five pairs of branches, projecting sideways, and a bird like a peacock with a curved neck and long tail feathers on the top. A kneeling figure puts a 'pearl' in its beak. The bird, surrounded by four coins, also has a winged being standing at its side, who holds up a sun disc in its arms. On each of the ten lateral branches, the Queen Mother of the West, Xi Wang Mu, presides as the central deity. On the upper side of the two topmost branches, she has taken up her place on her dragon and tiger throne under a canopy, and wears her typical crown. To her right kneels a hare holding a pestle with which he crushes the herb of immortality. On the left of the Queen Mother stands the moon toad, who offers her the *lingzhi* mushroom, which also confers immortality. This group of three is extended by further human figures to the side, who entertain the queen with drum beating, dancing and acrobatics. At the furthest end of the branch sits a swan-like bird facing the entertainment. The lower sides of the two upper branches are embellished with six coins, which,

87

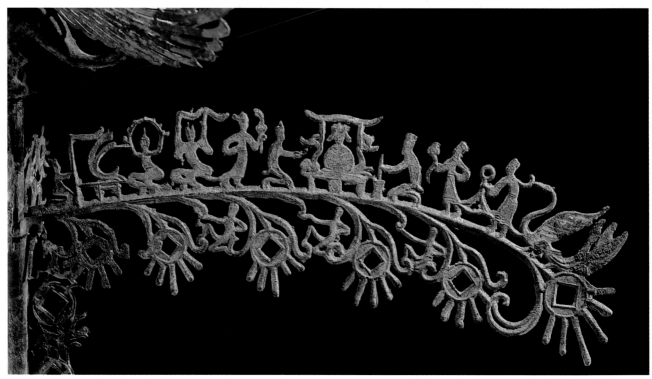

Fig. 87.1 *Detail of the topmost branch.*

surrounded by radiating wreaths similar to filaments, appear like blossoms hanging down from the tree (fig. 87.1).

The shorter branches, twisted into an s-shape, are identical in form and decor. The Queen Mother of the West, placed at the highest central point, is here flanked by two human beings below the throne, riding on animals, who appear to bear an offering in their raised hands. On the left of the Queen Mother is a galloping winged heavenly horse with raised mane and tail, whilst on her right are two goats with convoluted horns, facing each other. Between the lower sections of the branches, turned in volute manner, there also sit two musicians who beat drums or pluck a *qin* (zither). Two further humans, difficult to identify, can be seen among the eight densely intertwined coins in the lower part of the branch. One of them is pulling an ox, the other holds a shovel in his hands.

The earliest mention of the Queen Mother of the West is thought to be a reference in the philosophical text, the *Zhuangzi*, which was composed during the fourth and third centuries BC, where the deity is said to be an exemplary being who had achieved the *dao*. She was living in the Shaoguang Mountain, and no one had knowledge of her beginning or her end. The Han dynasty text, the *Shan Hai jing*, says: 'Three hundred and fifty *li* further west resides the Queen Mother of the West, dwelling on the jade massif. She has a human figure, the tail of a leopard, and the teeth of a tiger, she wears a *sheng* on her hair.' This *sheng* crown, which is often shaped

on a transverse rod with discs at its ends, is not shown clearly here, but is one of the principal ways of identifying the deity. Indeed she is frequently represented in Han tombs and on Han artefacts, such as mirrors, jades and bricks, often in partnership with the Ruler of the East, Dong Wang Gong.

Published: Sun Ji 1991, p. 405, pl. 102:16; Erickson 1994b; Goepper 1995, no. 86.

88 Mirror inscribed 'Sun, Moon and Kings of Heaven'

Late Eastern Han period, 2nd–3rd century AD
Bronze
Diameter 14.3 cm
Excavated in 1982 in Jingu Park in Luoyang, Henan province
Cultural Relics Bureau, Luoyang City

Flat discs, whose blank and polished surfaces acted as mirrors, are amongst the earliest bronzes found in China. Examples have come from neolithic Qijia sites. Mirrors of the Shang and Western Zhou periods are extremely rare, but numerous examples have been recovered from tombs of the Eastern Zhou period. At a time when ritual vessel manufacture was declining, mirror casting was strong. In addition to their everyday use, bronze mirrors had probably long been thought to have magical attributes, and to be talismans.

During the Han period in particular, the decoration on mirrors included cosmological symbols and images of mythical beings. Han period mirrors are often classified according to their decoration.

The mirror shown here was excavated in Luoyang from a spacious brick built double chamber grave with an antechamber 7 m long and 3 m wide. It is classified as a 'mirror with ring-shaped burls, wild animals and deities' and is typical of the Eastern Han period (AD 25–220). The front side has a slight convex curve. To achieve better reflection, the alloy employed has a high proportion of tin, silver or lead.

A large, semicircular, rounded knob, clearly defined decor zones and, above all, the high relief ornament are characteristic of the comparatively substantial bronze mirrors of the late Han period. Originally, a cord for holding the mirror passed through the knob, which may have been interpreted as the centre of the world. Around the knob is a circle of mythical animals, Daoist deities and feathered immortals, divided into four groups. Each of these figure groups is led by a long-necked fantastic animal, whose head recalls a dragon, a tiger or a bird of prey. On each of their backs sits a deity. These deities are flanked by two feathered immortals, who appear to be squatting on eight burls arranged in a circle. The four deities can not be identified unambiguously without accompanying inscriptions, but there are some indications of who they might be. One of them shows the characteristic attributes and the typical posture of the Queen Mother of the West (Xi Wang Mu), differing, as she does, from the others by her frontal seated posture, by her hands folded before the breast, and by her horn-like head or hair decoration. The deity opposite her could be her traditional partner, the Ruler of the East (Dong Wang Fu or Dong Wang Gong). Who the Southern and the Northern deities are meant to be remains uncertain at present. This field of figures is framed by two narrow ribbons, on each of which stand out thirteen semicircular fields decorated with volutes, alternating with thirteen square fields, on which the four graphs *ri* (sun), *yue* (moon) and *tianwang* (Kings of Heaven) are repeated in intaglio lines.[1]

Published: Luoyang 1990, p. 75, fig. 57; Imperial China 1992, no. 53.3; Goepper 1995, no. 87.

1 For a discussion of the Daoist connotations of mirrors and their inscriptions see Cahill 1986; see also Loewe 1979.

88

89 Two mirrors

Eastern Han period (AD 25–220)
Bronze

a Mirror with four mythical creatures
Diameter 23.8 cm

b Mirror with deities, chariot and hunting scene
Diameter 20.1 cm

Said to have been found at Shaoxing, Zhejiang province
Historical Museum, Beijing

The two mirrors illustrated here are characteristic of the mirrors of Zhejiang province. They both have wide rims and high relief designs at the centres of the main decorative fields around the central knobs.

The earlier of the two mirrors (a) displays four creatures prancing around a large central knob enclosed in a square field. Four much smaller bosses supported on four-petalled flowers separate the creatures from one another. The imaginary creatures cast in fine relief are a leopard, a tiger, a dragon and a stag. The beasts have fine feathered wings and are attended by figures of immortals, barely visible among the dense fine lines of the background.

The second mirror (b) also has four subjects in the main decorative field, separated by knobs. The most conspicuous of these is a roofed chariot drawn by four galloping horses; opposite it is a hunting scene. The two seated figures between these scenes are the deities, the Queen Mother of the West (Xi Wang Mu) and the Ruler of the East (Dong Wang Gong); the latter is named by three characters. Both deities are

89a

89b

flanked by attendants. A long inscription in seal script frames the decorative field. Inscriptions of similar content are known from a number of examples. It records the casting of the mirror at a time of political change, when hostile forces have been subjugated and the state has regained power. Wind and rains have come at the appropriate seasons and have guaranteed a rich harvest. The inscription concludes with a prayer

for the protective and long lasting blessing of the powers of heaven, who are asked to grant limitless joy to the descendants.[1]

Published: *Zhongguo lishi bowuguan yuankan* 1993.1, pp. 116, 118; Goepper 1995, no. 88.

1 For mirror inscriptions see Karlgren 1934; Loewe 1979.

90 Large dish, *pan*

Early Western Han period, 2nd century BC
Lacquered wood
Diameter 46.7 cm; height 4.2 cm
Excavated in 1975 from tomb M167 at Fenghuangshan, Jiangling county, Hubei province (M167: 58)
Jingzhou Regional Museum, Hubei province

This dish comes from the same tomb as the wooden figures in the following entry (no. 91). The tomb, belonging to a lady of noble birth who died between 179 and 141 BC, contained more than a hundred high-quality lacquered objects, including fourteen identical *pan,* which were placed in pairs and tied with silk cords. The tomb's wooden inventory tablets listed these *pan* as intended for use as serving dishes, in particular for roasted and pickled meats. Although the large size of the dish suggests a serving tray, rather than a dish, analysis of similarly-sized pieces in a nearby contemporaneous grave has revealed traces of chicken and beef on them, therefore confirming their use as described on the inventory slips.

This *pan* was found, together with many other tomb goods, in a small room next to the coffin chamber at the head of the body. The lacquered objects represented the largest group

90

amongst the grave offerings. Besides the *pan*, there were also wine containers (no. 93) and boxes, all of which had wooden cores and were decorated in red and black lacquer with similar designs.[1]

The decoration consists of a black undercoat and the interior has a circular black centre onto which the so-called cloud and phoenix decoration is painted in red. Five rings, alternately red and black, and of differing widths, surround the black circle.

The considerable similarity of the lacquered objects found in this grave, and those in other graves in the Fenghuangshan area, suggests that such wares were made in the same lacquer workshop. Many lacquerwares found in tomb M168 have marks on them, in the form of burnt-in seals or finely engraved characters, 'Chengshi *cao*' and 'Chengshi *bao*',[2] which translate as 'produced in the town of Cheng' and 'lacquered in the town of Cheng'. We know that Cheng is Chengdu, the capital city of Sichuan province.

The lacquer tree (*Rhus verniciflua*), is native to China and grows profusely in Sichuan. Chengdu and Guanghan seem to have been the main centres within Sichuan for the manufacture of lacquered objects, and these wares were renowned and prized throughout the empire and beyond. Inscribed, lacquered wares from Sichuan have been found in tombs in many parts of China, and also particularly in Korea, where they had been sent by the emperor and the imperial court as gifts or in lieu of payment of salary. The British Museum possesses one such object, an eared cup with an inscription dating it to AD 4, which was apparently found in a grave near Lelang, in Korea, an area brought under Chinese control during the reign of Wudi (141–87 BC) of the Western Han period. Several such dated lacquered objects, including the one in the British Museum, list the names of the craftsmen who worked on the pieces. On the cup are the names of six craftsmen and seven production inspectors who would have examined it at every stage. Objects in other materials carry inscriptions naming craftsmen who were obviously working in a production team.[3]

Published: *Wenwu* 1976.10, pp. 31–7; Goepper 1995, no. 90.

1 *Wenwu* 1976.10, p. 33.
2 *Wenwu* 1976.10, p. 33, mentions that the lacquers in tomb M167 have burnt-in marks and incised characters.
3 Michaelson 1992.

91 Group of seven servant figures

Early Western Han period, 2nd century BC
Painted wood

a Male servant
Height 49 cm; shoulder width 11 cm (M167: 2)

b Female servant
Height 45.5 cm; shoulder width 11 cm (M167: 7)

c Female servant, *zeshi*
Height 42.5 cm; shoulder width 11 cm (M167: 12)

d Female servant
Height 36.5 cm; shoulder width 9.5 cm (M167:18)

e Agricultural labourer
Height 38 cm; shoulder width 8.5 cm (M167: 21)

f Agricultural labourer
Height 38 cm; shoulder width 8.5 cm (M167: 28)

g Agricultural labourer
Height 39.5 cm; shoulder width 10 cm (M167: 17)

Excavated in 1975 from tomb M167 at Fenghuangshan, Jiangling county, Hubei province
Jingzhou Regional Museum, Hubei province

These seven painted wooden figures were part of a group of twenty-three servants, which were found together with horse-drawn carriages and ox-drawn carts and other animals in the same tomb as the dish, *pan*, described above (no. 90). The large number of servants indicates the status and wealth of the lady. The clothing and attributes of these figures give us some insight into the social structure of the Han period.

The intact grave consisted of a wooden coffin chamber and two rooms filled with grave gifts. The tomb contained groundwater, which may have penetrated over the years or may possibly have been deliberately inserted as some kind of preservative. Other grave goods included fine silk textiles, bamboo cups, bronze mirrors, ceramics, lacquered objects, clay models of a hearth and of a carriage, an iron sewing needle in a bag, and foodstuffs. The coffin containing the body was filled with a red liquid, and was surrounded by beans and cinnabar, all of which may have been intended as preservatives for the body.

The tomb also contained an inventory of the grave goods, written on seventy-four wooden strips (similar to no. 95). These strips have a hole at the top and were tied together with a hemp cord into book form. They were found in a layer of earth above the grave itself and so were protected from the water-logged grave; sixteen of these strips describe the wooden servant figures.[1]

The first in line (a) is one of two male guards or supervisors. He wears a v-shaped outergarment over two undergarments, whose collars are just visible, and his hands, clasped

91a–g

round a halberd, are hidden under the long sleeves. On his head he wears a cap which is fixed under the chin with ribbons. Behind him is a group of six further male and female servants. The first (b) is apparently of the highest rank, dressed in an orange outergarment with two further undergarments. Her clasped hands are also concealed under long sleeves. The next servant (c) has a black and red patterned outergarment, over two undergarments. The pattern of the outergarment suggests a finely printed or embroidered textile. She wears her hair in a style familiar to us from many Han models,[2] where the hair is parted in the centre and tied into a loose knot at the back below the shoulders, and from which, on one side, a few strands have slipped out. The knot is often carved separately but the strands of hair are merely painted. The inventory strip lists this lady as a *zeshi*, a servant woman who was a particular confidante of her mistress. The female servant behind her (d), with an outergarment over a round-necked undergarment and her hands outstretched, is of a lower rank.

The remaining three servants (e, f and g) are agricultural labourers on the lady's estate and are equipped with the tools of their trade, including axes, spades and hoes. These servants are not, however, as well made, detailed or finished as the household servants.

Published: *Wenwu* 1976.10, p. 33; Goepper 1995, no. 89.

1 *Wenwu* 1976.10, pp. 38–9.
2 *Wenwu* 1982.6, p. 79, fig. 3.

92 **Box, *he*, with ten eared bowls**

Early Western Han period, before 167 BC
Lacquered wood
Box, length 20.9 cm; width 17 cm; height 13.2 cm
Excavated from tomb M168 at Fenghuangshan, Jiangling county, Hubei province (M168: 79)
Jingzhou Regional Museum, Hubei province

This set of ten oval lacquer bowls, which are called eared cups (*erbei*) on account of the ear-like handles projecting from their longer sides, are either wine or food vessels. They were found in the tomb of an official, Sui Xiaoyuan, who was a district magistrate of the ninth rank and who died in 167 BC, aged about fifty-five. His body was as well preserved as was that of the wife of the Marquis of Dai who died in about 168 BC (for the banner from her tomb see Yang, fig. 3), and researchers have been able to analyse his blood group (AB) and work out that he died as a result of acute peritonitis. The red liquid in which he was found and preserved may have been injected deliberately or it may simply have accumulated over the years.

The coffin, as well as the tomb, was immersed in groundwater which had helped to preserve the lacquerwares. Whereas many of the 500 burial items found in the wooden rectangular chamber grave, comprising four small rooms, had suffered from being so immersed, the 160 lacquerwares were in a marvellous state of preservation. The other grave goods included jades, ceramics, bamboo, wooden model servants

92

and writing utensils, including brush, ink stone, rubbing stone and blank wooden tablets (no. 95), essential accoutrements for Sui Xiaoyuan's magisterial office. The contents of the tomb were listed on sixty-six wooden inventory tablets, the thirty-fifth of which included the ten eared cups.[1]

Of the 160 lacquered objects in this tomb, 110 were eared cups with a wooden core, lacquered red decoration on the inside, and black on the outside. The box into which these ten cups fit has a base and lid of identical size. These are painted with red lacquer on the inside and on the outside a black lacquered background is overpainted with various motifs in red. The top of the lid has cloud and phoenix decoration set within an oval band. Nine of the cups have thin wooden cores, but the tenth has a thicker wall. The cups were packed in two sets, four on one side and five on the other, separated by the thicker cup which acted as a wedge so that all the cups fitted snugly within the container. This was a very neat arrangement, but not unique; a similar arrangement of seven boxes was found in the tomb of the wife of the Marquis of Dai at Mawangdui.[2] Such eared cups were very popular in the Han dynasty, and many tombs contained several wine containers from which the wine would have been scooped with ladles into these eared cups. Examples of lacquered ladles and wine containers were also found in the tomb of Lady Dai.

Lacquered objects have a long history in China. The lacquer tree (*Rhus verniciflua*) is native to China and the sap obtained from it is a natural plastic which is resistant to heat,

acids and water. Lacquered decoration has been found on the walls of a Shang period coffin of the fourteenth century BC at Panlongcheng in Huangpi county, Hubei province.[3] The coffin belonging to Fu Hao, who died about 1200 BC, had red and black lacquer skin on the outside. The Marquis Yi of Zeng, who died about 433 BC, had twenty-three lacquered and painted coffins in his grave (Introduction, fig. 10).[4] The coffins from tomb M2 in Baoshan, in the Chu state area of Hubei province, dating to about 316 BC, were similarly decorated.[5] Thus by the Han dynasty the preservative features of lacquer had been well known for a long time. Lacquer had become a popular decorative material applied to vessels both for use in life and as burial items for use in the afterlife.

Published: *Wenwu* 1975.9, pp. 1–22; *Kaogu* 1976.1, pp. 24–7; *Jiangling chutu wenwu jingpin* 1991, pp. 25–6; *Kaogu xuebao* 1993.4, p. 476, fig. 19: 2–3, p. 478, fig. 21; Goepper 1995, no. 91.

1 *Kaogu xuebao* 1993.4, p. 476.
2 Beijing 1973b, vol. 2, pl. 164.
3 *Wenwu* 1976.2, pp. 5–15.
4 Beijing 1989c, vol. 2, pls 6–19.
5 Beijing 1991b, p. 61.

93 Large wine container, *bian hu*

Early Western Han period, before 167 BC
Lacquered wood
Height 48 cm; length 57 cm; width 13.5 cm
Excavated in 1975 from tomb M168 at Fenghuangshan, Jiangling county, Hubei province (M168:117)
Jingzhou Regional Museum, Hubei province

This lacquered wine container was found in the same grave, that of Sui Xiaoyuan, as the set of ten eared cups (no. 92). It is the largest such wine container of its type discovered so far and was placed in the grave with two smaller but similar ones. All the containers were listed on numbers 28, 29 and 30 of the grave inventory strips.[1]

The flattened flask, or *bian hu*, shape, with a footring and narrow neck, existed from the Western Zhou period. This particular vessel has an almost rectangular body but others

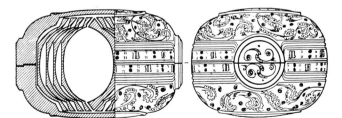

Fig. 92.1 *Drawing of the box with the eared bowls. After* Kaogu xuebao *1993.4, p. 475, fig. 21.*

93

are more rounded; it has a wooden core which was made in two parts, one for the front and one for the back. The lid is in the shape of a roof and the vessel has bronze rings on its shoulders which would have been fitted with cords for carrying purposes. On one of the smaller *bian hu* vessels in this grave remnants of the silk cord have been preserved.[2]

The decoration is predominantly of red lacquer painted on a black background. There are three leopards on either side, painted in red lacquer on a black background, within a frame outlined in red, and the seventh is on the knob of the lid.

Three of these leopards have wings sprouting from their backs; all are painted with elongated and arched bodies, very long tails and slender legs in the painterly, linear fashion typical of the Han period. The interior of the vessel is lacquered red, and there is also a red line painted round the base of the lid and on the top of the footring. Leopards were less frequently portrayed than tigers and only appear from the Warring States period. They can be recognised by their fur markings, indicated by dots or semicircles. Leopards seem to have been associated, together with tigers, with guarding the

Gates of Heaven and as such are seen on the silk T-shaped banner placed on the coffin of Lady Dai at Mawangdui near Changsha in Hunan province (Yu, fig. 3).[3] Leopards are also used as a decorative device on the coffin of Sui Xiaoyuan, in whose grave this container was found. It may have been believed that leopards on a coffin had powers to protect the body from evil forces, or that they acted as a vehicle for the deceased to ride on into the afterlife.

Published: Sun Ji 1991, pp. 319–21; *Kaogu xuebao* 1993.4, p. 472, pl. 16; Goepper 1995, no. 92.

1 *Kaogu xuebao* 1993.4, pp. 472–3.
2 *Kaogu xuebao* 1993.4, pl. 5: 4.
3 Beijing 1973b, vol. 2, pl. 75. In the *Zhaohun* (*Summons of the Soul*) section of the *Chu ci*: 'O soul come back, Climb not to the heaven above. For tigers and leopards guard the gates, with jaws ready to rend up mortal men' (Hawkes 1985, p. 225).

94 Eared dish with fish decoration

Early Western Han period, before 167 BC
Wood, with red, gold and yellow lacquer painting on black lacquer
Height 6.5 cm; width 15.5 cm; length 21 cm
Excavated in 1975 from tomb M168 at Fenghuangshan, Jiangling county, Hubei province (5: 1893 F233–1)
Jingzhou Regional Museum, Hubei province

This eared dish is one of the more than one hundred such vessels from tomb M168 at Fenghuangshan, where the box of eared bowls and the wine container (nos 92, 93) were also found. As indicated above (no. 90), such lacquerwares were clearly made by subdividing the process among a team of workers, demonstrating the early and widespread use of division of labour in China. Different workmen would have been responsible for making the wooden core, for applying the various coats of coloured lacquer, and for painting the design on the top coat; others would polish the item, and production

94

inspectors would examine it at each stage. However, despite the great numbers produced, lacquerwares were still expensive. Huan Kuan, in his *Yantie lun* (*Discourses on Salt and Iron*), compiled in the first century BC, recorded that the price of a lacquer vessel was ten times that of a bronze one.[1]

This cup is decorated with a combination of fish and leaves which had symbolic meaning for the Chinese: the fish was associated with fertility and wealth, and the four-leaf motif with longevity. As such eared dishes were often found in pairs, it is possible they were made as wedding presents.

Eared cups and dishes were commonly used as tableware in the Warring States and Han periods and are often described in contemporaneous texts. It has been calculated that more than 90 per cent of the lacquerware in tomb MI at Mawangdui consisted of tablewares.[2] We know from analysis of food remains in them that they were used both for liquids, such as wine, and for food. Inscriptions on eared cups found in the Mawangdui tombs include: 'May the Lord find pleasure in the wine' (*jun xing jiu*) and 'May the Lord find pleasure in the food' (*jun xing shi*).[3] The most elaborate, and presumably most expensive, of such lacquered cups had bronze and gilt 'ears'. The shape was made in jade as well, again only for the wealthy, and also in ceramic and undecorated lacquer for those requiring something less expensive.

Published: *Wenwu* 1975.9, p. 5, fig. 6 and pl. 5.1; Sun Ji 1991, p. 306 and fig. 77.3; *Kaogu xuebao* 1993.4, pp. 474–5 and fig. 18: 2; Goepper 1995, no. 93.

1 Huan Kuan 1979, p. 203.
2 Pirazzoli-t'Serstevens 1991, pp. 209–19.
3 Waley-Cohen 1984.

95

95 Writing equipment

Western Han period, before 167 BC
Stone, animal hair, bamboo
Ink stone, maximum diameter 15.3 cm
Grinding stone, length 3.5 cm
Pen and holder, length 24.9 cm
Writing strips, nos 14, 18, 21, 42, average length 22 cm
Excavated in 1975 from tombs M167 and M168 at Fenghuangshan, Jiangling county, Hubei province
Jingzhou Regional Museum, Hubei province

These implements were the standard equipment for writing and keeping records during the late Warring States and the Han period. They were discovered in two adjacent Western Han tombs, which also contained the lacquered wood objects described above (nos 90–94).

A black carbonaceous 'ink', as well as a red form comprising cinnabar (mercuric sulphide), were used sometimes as an embellishment on the surface of oracle bones in the Shang dynasty.[1] These substances were probably also used for writing on organic materials which have long since perished. By the Han period ink was produced in pellets formed of carbonised pine wood, lamp soot and glue extracted from boiled leather or horn.[2] Several pellets were included with the writing equipment discovered in tomb M168. The ink pellets would have been ground with water on the surface of the ink stone,

Fig. 95.1 *Historian seated behind his ink stone. Copy of a Han period (206 BC–AD 220) wall painting at Wangdu, Hebei province. After Boston 1976, pl. 12.*

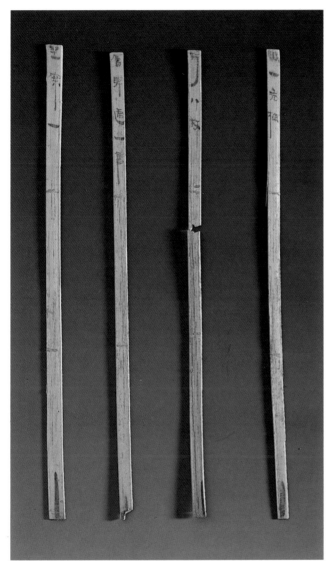

95 *writing strips*

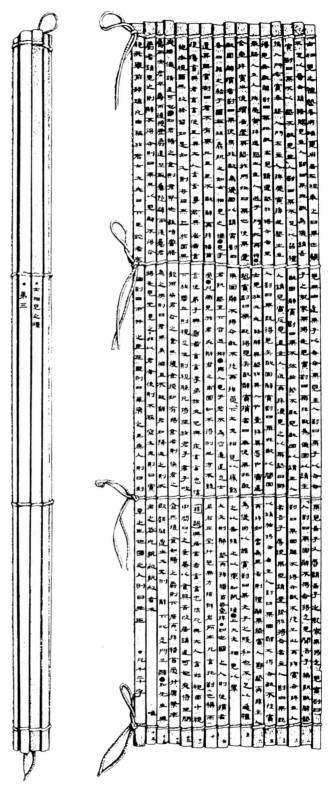

and the black liquid applied to the writing surface with hair pens. The present ink stone is a simple stone disc. Round inkstones were also made in the form of circular tripod platforms with a handled cover, as shown in a Han dynasty wall painting (fig. 95.1). More sophisticated clerical furniture, incorporating oblong ink stones in lacquered wooden secretaires with drawers, has been discovered in tombs of the late Han.[3]

Long strips for writing in vertical lines were made from bamboo, or from poplar or willow in regions farther away from the preferred sub-tropical habitat of bamboo. Equipment for dividing and splitting cane is described at no. 69. In order to provide a tenacious writing surface, the external skin of the bamboo was scraped off with a knife similar to the ring-handled specimen (no. 69). Strips which had been filled with consecutive passages of writing were bound with

Fig. 95.2 *Bamboo strips inscribed with the text of the* Yili *(The Book of Ceremonial). The length of text on each strip varies between sixty and eighty characters. From Wuwei, Gansu province. Eastern Han period (AD 25–220). Lengths 54–8 cm. After Hayashi Minao 1976, p. 223, fig. 11–19.*

cord and could be rolled for storage. Each strip of text was often numbered in sequence (fig. 95.2).

Lengths of writing strips varied. Archaeological evidence and Han comments reveal that literary etiquette ascribed various genres of writing to different lengths. Revered scriptures such as the *Yili* (*The Book of Ceremonial*, fig. 95.2) were often written on the longest strips, whereas shorter strips were employed for personal communications and administration.

The four strips shown are from a surviving total of sixty-six which once comprised an inventory of the objects placed in tomb M168. Today their numbering is only a sequence adopted by the excavators. Eight other strips of this inventory are discussed and illustrated (no. 91). During Han funerals, inventories such as this one were solemnly intoned before being placed and sealed inside the tomb.[4] The four inscriptions list the following: one standing tray (strip 42); two dishes for chopped meat (strip 21); eight bowls (strip 18); one mirror and container (strip 14). Significantly, tomb M168 contained five so-called chopped meat dishes, which is three more than the total listed in the inventory. This strongly suggests that the totals written in the inventory subscribed to conventions which were becoming outdated, deliberately flaunted or ignored.

Published: *Wenwu* 1976.10, p. 35, fig. 7; *Kaogu xuebao* 1993.4, pp. 499–507; Goepper 1995, no. 94.

1 Keightley 1978, pp. 54–6.
2 On the history of ink see Tsien Tsuen-hsiun 1962, pp. 164–74.
3 For the equipment discovered in a late Han tomb in Korea see Koizumi and Hamada 1934, pp. 45–6; Hayashi Minao 1976, p. 220, fig. 11–9.
4 Tsien Tsuen-hsiun 1962, pp. 92–6.

96 **Storage jar,** *hu*

Late Western Han period, 1st century BC
Painted ceramic
Height 48 cm; diameter of body 32 cm
Excavated in 1980 at Shaogou near Luoyang, Henan province
(M10: 46)
Cultural Relics Bureau, Luoyang City, Henan province

The low-fired ceramic of this jar suggests that it was made for burial rather than for everyday use, as it would not have been watertight. Its tall wide neck, rounded body, sloping foot and moulded *taotie* faces on the shoulders follow more or less exactly a form developed in metalwork and seen in such richly equipped tombs as that of Liu Sheng at Mancheng (no. 81).[1]

Ceramic replicas were always very popular. Bronze vessel types had, from as early as the Erlitou period (*c.* 1700–1500 BC), also been made in ceramic, probably to economise in bronze. Painted ceramic vessels in the shapes more usually associated with bronze were developed in the Eastern Zhou by the Qin state in Shaanxi province.[2] Indeed Qin willingness to bury replicas may have stimulated a general interest in ceramic copies, rather than real items, for burial, and from

this interest developed perhaps the multitude of different types of ceramic model interred in graves: vessels, buildings (nos 106, 107) and figures (nos 79, 80).

Ceramic had certain advantages. It was cheap, easily painted, and useful for making model figures and buildings. As we have seen, the First Emperor would have been unable to bury his whole army, but he could be accompanied by a carefully prepared replica. In the same way, the actual large buildings depicted as models (nos 106, 107) could never have been put into the grave. Ceramic replicas therefore greatly expanded the range of goods available for the afterlife.

While few could afford to be buried with elaborately decorated bronze vessels as owned, for example, by Liu Sheng, painted ceramics, such as we have here, could be used much more liberally. Indeed the several hundred similar examples found at the Shaogou cemetery at Luoyang are evidence of the ready access to such items by relatively minor members of the élite.

The imagery on painted or moulded burial ceramics frequently includes miraculous figures of the types found on contemporary bronzes.[3] For example, the animals of the four directions on this jar can also be seen on the bronze incense burner (no. 82). On the jar the four animals run around the shoulder band (fig. 96.1). A tiger with wings on its shoulders chases a bird reminiscent of a peacock and another very similar bird pursues a snake-like dragon. The tiger, dragon and bird symbolise respectively the East, the West and the South. The turtle and snake generally employed to represent the North are missing and have been replaced by the second bird. Many other painted jars from Shaogou show a similar phenomenon, which may have been a local custom.[4]

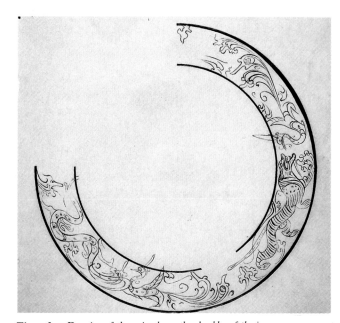

Fig. 96.1 *Drawing of the animals on the shoulder of the jar.*

During the Eastern Zhou and Han periods, both tomb objects and the walls of the tombs themselves were decorated with images of daily life, the cosmos and figures from mythology and history. Such images seem to have been intended to create a microcosm of the universe for the deceased to inhabit in the afterlife.

Published: *Zhongyuan wenwu* 1982.3, p. 62; Lu Delin 1986, p. 78; Singapore 1990, p. 102; Luoyang 1990, no. 38; Imperial China 1992, no. 54; Goepper 1995, no. 97.

1 Beijing 1980g, vol. 1, p. 50, fig. 23: 1.
2 Ledderose and Schlombs 1990, no. 26.
3 Sturman 1988.
4 A very early depiction of a tiger and a dragon in shells has come from a neolithic burial (*Wenwu* 1988.3, pp. 1–6, pl. 81). An early Eastern Zhou mirror from Shangcunling also carries the same figures (Beijing 1959c, pl. 41: 2). The next clear evidence of these figures is in the painting of one of the clothes chests from the tomb of the Marquis Yi of Zeng (Beijing 1989c, pl. 121; Introduction, fig. 11).

97 Lamp in the form of a tree

Late Eastern Han period, 2nd century AD
Painted ceramic
Height 92 cm; diameter of foot 40 cm
Excavated in 1972 at Jianxi Xilihe, near Luoyang, Henan province
Cultural Relics Bureau, Luoyang City, Henan province

The large and elaborate lamp was found in a substantial, untouched brick tomb, approximately T-shaped, with several side rooms. Its overall dimensions were 9.18 m in length, 5.9 m in width and 2.3 m in height. The lamp was placed in the western side chamber next to a ceramic table laid out for banqueting. It was evidently intended to illumine the feasts of the tomb owner. Below it were figures of musicians, jesters, acrobats and dancers, obviously to entertain and divert.

From the shape and ornament of the tree, it would appear that it was intended to be more than simply a replica of a lamp. It is itself a depiction of the worlds of the immortals. Its lower pedestal is shaped as a mountain, on which sits a pair of humans, their legs drawn up and their left arms raised. They wear flat caps. They are flanked by two of a total of five small sprouts, on each of which perches a cicada. Animals pursue one another across the slopes: hares, stags, toads, wolves, pigs, dogs, sheep, monkeys and tigers. The scene resembles those on the bronze incense burner (no. 82), and on decorated vessels and fittings that depict imaginary landscapes peopled by miraculous creatures.[1]

A pillar, standing on the back of a turtle and decorated with four cicadas, rises out of the mountain top and supports the base of the main part of the lamp. Four winged dragons ridden by immortals emerge from the shallow basin out of which the lamp rises. Twelve s-shaped stems, which spring from the basin or from the trunk of the lamp, form branches bearing flowers and support bowls in which flame-like ros-

ettes have been inserted. At the summit of the light are eight cicadas and eight winged beings. A large bird with a pearl in its beak flies over the top of the tree. Figures of cicadas and winged beings suggest immortality and rebirth – auspicious associations that were no doubt explicitly intended in the context of a tomb. The lamp lit up the feasts in the tomb, but at the same time contributed to the depiction of the immortal worlds within it.

As mentioned in connection with the bronze lamp bearer (no. 74), from the Warring States period lamps were made in many different and highly inventive shapes. Often these were animal forms – probably animals that were thought to be unusual or miraculous. An early example in the shape of a tree was found in the Zhongshan state tombs. On that tree, small monkeys playfully swing from branch to branch. In ceramic yet more elaborate compositions were possible, with yet more complex allusions to immortality.

Published: *Kaogu* 1975.2, pp. 116–23, 134, pl. 9: 1; Singapore 1990, p. 64; Luoyang 1990, no. 44; Taipei 1992, p. 134; Beijing 1992a, no. 77; Goepper 1995, no. 98.

1 Wu Hung 1984.

98 Imaginary tree

Late Western Han period, 1st century BC
Green and red glazed ceramic
Height 63 cm
Excavated in 1969 from tomb M8 near Sijian'gou, Jiyuan county, Henan province (M8: 10)
Henan Provincial Museum, Zhengzhou

The ceramic tree was found in a Han dynasty brick tomb, which also held more than forty different types of ceramic tomb model in the antechamber.

A number of different legends and myths have been cited to interpret the appearance of this tree. It is rather slim in relation to its height and is set upon a three-footed pyramidical base. This base is moulded in relief with animals and figures: three naked human beings, cicadas, horses, deer. While the mountain is relatively small, the tree appears top heavy by comparison. It has nine branches: the lower ones are decorated with three-petalled flowers; on the upper ones are flower-like elements with cicadas attached to them. On three of the branches are monkeys and on three are birds. While the branches are glazed, the monkeys and birds are not.

At the top of the trunk is a squatting figure and above it a cockerel. This cockerel may perhaps be understood as the Bird of the Sun or a bird of good fortune. A cockerel is mentioned in accounts of two different mythical trees: the Fusang tree and the Taodu tree. The Fusang tree was the home of the ten suns: nine suns would lodge in its branches and the tenth sun would rest on the top. The early legends

of the ten suns and the archer Houyi are described at no. 64. Later accounts give the following description: 'To the east of Penglai [one of the islands of the immortals] lies the Daiyu mountain, on which the Fusang tree grew 10,000 *zhang* into the sky. The Cockerel of Heaven often settles in its branches and has built his nest there. Every night, when the morning dawns, he crows, and the Crow in the Sun replies to his calls, and finally all the cockerels on earth join in.'[1]

It is possible that the later, post-Han, myth about the Taodu tree developed out of the account of the Fusang tree. The parallel account of the Taodu tree runs as follows: 'On its pinnacle [Mount Taodu], there rises an enormous peach tree by the name of Taodu, the branches of which extend over 3000 *li*. In its crown sits the Cockerel of Heaven. When the sun rises and its rays of light strike the tree, he crows and all the cockerels of the world join in.'[2]

Earlier than the account of the Taodu tree is the description of another peach tree, or Dushuo tree, by the Han period philosopher and sceptic Wang Chong. He says: 'In the midst of the eastern sea there is the Dushuo [Crossing the New Year] Mountain, on which there is an enormous peach tree, which twists and coils its way over a distance of three thousand *li*. Between its branches, on the north-east, there is what is called the Gate of Demons (*gui men*), in and out of which pass a myriad demons. Above there are two divine beings, one called Shen Shu, the other Yü Lü. They watch and con-

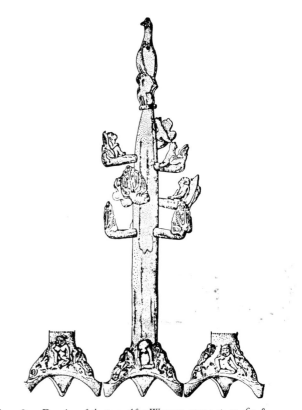

Fig. 98.1 *Drawing of the tree. After* Wenwu *1973.2, p. 51, fig. 8.*

◀ 98

trol the myriad demons, and those that are evil and harmful they seize with rush ropes and feed to tigers. This being so, the Yellow Sovereign (Huang Di) has prepared a ritual for their seasonal expulsion, in which large peachwood figures are set up.'[3] Indeed, peachwood figures were regarded as protective and have been found in tombs.

Published: *Wenwu* 1972.3, pp. 7–10; *Wenwu* 1973.2, pp. 46–53; Loewe 1979, p. 111; Los Angeles 1987, no. 28; Singapore 1990, p. 72; Beijing 1992a, pp. 85–6, no. 71; Taipei 1992, p. 156; Goepper 1995, no. 99.

1 Discussion of the Fusang legend and some of its sources are given in *Wenwu* 1972.3, pp. 8–9; see also Allan 1991, chapter 2.
2 This legend is described in Los Angeles 1987, no. 28; *Wenwu* 1973.1, pp. 2–3.
3 After Bodde 1975, p. 128.

99 Model of a well

Eastern Han period (AD 25–220)
Ceramic
Length 24.5 cm; width 17 cm
Found in 1960 in Yanshi, Henan province (0278)
Henan Provincial Museum, Zhengzhou

This model of a well has a roof and a spindle-shaped winch system from which two buckets dangle for drawing the water. One side of the well has a representation in relief of a drinking buffalo and a fish, and the other side shows a peasant carrying agricultural tools on his shoulders, flanked by the inscription 'The eastern well quenches the fire' (*dong jing mie huo*) (fig. 99.1). One end of the well shows a tethered ram, while the other bears a design of diamond shapes flanked by fish. The fish suggest the idea of plenty, as the character for fish is a homophone for that of abundance.

The earliest example known so far of a well in China is one found in the Longshan culture in Henan province dating to about 2000 BC.[1] It was 11 m deep. The earliest wells were round with a square frame made of logs at the bottom (fig. 99.2), and it is possibly this shape that is represented in the character for well, *jing* (the bottom left-hand character of the inscription on the well) (fig. 99.3).[2] The *Shuowen jiezi*, the earliest Chinese dictionary, compiled in the first century AD, describes wells as having a roof and a fence.

The Eastern Han period was a time when many families

99

built up huge estates. These are is reflected in the many representations of great estates and their component parts in the tomb models of the period (no. 106) and on the walls of the tombs themselves. Wells were dug in the courtyards of the great housing compounds, as well as in the fields. The tomb models, the paintings, and the painted and impressed bricks all clearly show wells with roofs and also often with the winch system, in use from the Warring States period, which would have been necessary when the groundwater was low or the well was particularly deep. Large buckets for holding the

Fig. 99.1 *Rubbings of the decoration around the well.*

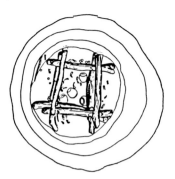

Fig. 99.2 *Drawing of a neolithic well with wooden frame. After Lindqvist 1990, p. 178.*

Fig. 99.3 *The graph for 'well' in oracle bone and bronze inscriptions. After Wang Hongyuan 1993, p. 77.*

water[3] are often depicted in tomb murals, as the water from the wells was used not only for human consumption, but also for irrigation and for putting out fires. Chinese buildings have always been built primarily of wood, so fire was a constant hazard.

Published: Sun Ji 1991, pp. 11–12; Goepper 1995, no. 100.

1 *Kaogu* 1980.3, pp. 200–2.
2 Lindqvist 1990, pp. 177–8.
3 Pirazzoli t'Serstevens 1982, fig. 135.

100 Two hollow bricks

Western Han period, 2nd–1st century BC
Ceramic

a Brick with tree motif
Height 51 cm; width 134 cm

b Brick with warrior motif
Height 53.9 cm; width 133.7 cm

Provenance unknown
Nanjing City Museum, Jiangsu province

Brick tomb chambers began to replace wooden tomb structures during the late Warring States period. The early bricks consisted of slabs of clay jointed together. In the Han period the bricks were made from clay moulded around a wooden core, the core being withdrawn before firing. The hollow forms were employed to reduce the weight of clay to be fired and to avoid the fractures and fissures that might have resulted on a solid brick.

We do not know where these bricks came from. However, it is likely that they were part of a tomb such as those dis-

covered at Luoyang in Henan province. These moulded bricks formed the walls of the tomb and provided the triangular sections that supported a sloping ceiling. Both these triangular slabs and a doorway lintel were supported on pillars. Hollow bricks, which could be as much as 1.6 m in length, were also employed outside the main tomb structure, in the construction of stairways for example (fig. 100.1).

As the tomb structures became more complex, with additional subsidiary rooms and doorways between the chambers, the large, long hollow bricks perhaps began to be impracticable. From the middle of the Western Han, smaller solid bricks were produced in two standard sizes. Some hybrid structures were made in which the hollow bricks retained pride of place in the main chamber with the small solid bricks being used in the subsidiary rooms. Gradually all hollow bricks were eliminated, and the solid bricks in their turn were decorated.

Both bricks display scenes in intaglio lines. On the first brick, a large fruiting tree divides the field. A winged horse, surrounded by birds, faces it, and to the left of the tree is a man twisting to fight off a tiger as he runs away from it. Another bird appears above this figure.

The second brick displays similar figures, differently arranged. A horse and a large figure leaning on a stick appear in the right-hand corner. A tiger at the centre of the field looks back to the left over its tail, and above it is a peacock with a plumed tail. On the left the horse, figure and peacock are repeated. This repetition shows that the designs have been stamped into the bricks.

The scenes of animals and figures in a landscape are perhaps related to the Western Han pictures of a mountainous universe peopled with miraculous creatures, seen already on the incense burner (no. 82), the lamp (no. 97) and the tree (no. 98), and on bronze fittings and vessels of the same period.[1]

Published: Goepper 1995, no. 101.

1 Wu Hung 1984. Discussed also in the Introduction.

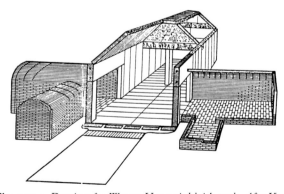

Fig. 100.1 *Drawing of a Western Han period brick tomb. After Kaogu xuebao 1964.2, p. 110, fig. 4.*

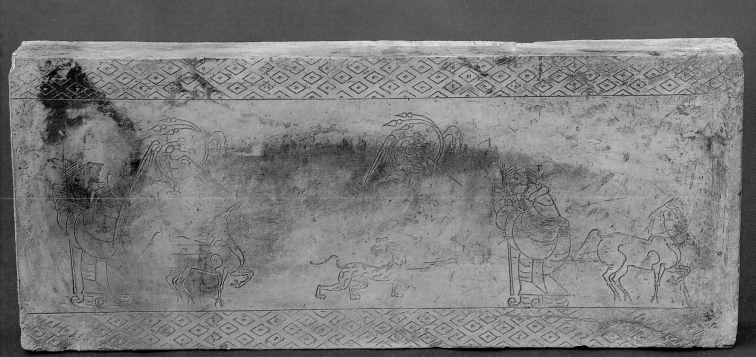

101 Three bricks decorated in relief

Eastern Han period (AD 25–220)
Ceramic

a Brick decorated with the Queen Mother of the West (Xi Wang Mu)
Height 41 cm; width 47 cm
Excavated in 1954 from tomb M1 at Qingbaixiang, Xindu county, Sichuan province

b Brick with a figure of the moon deity (yueshen)
Height 49 cm; width 28 cm
Excavated in 1965 near Chengdu, Sichuan province

c Brick with a figure of the sun deity (rishen)
Height 49 cm; width 28 cm
Excavated in 1965 near Chengdu, Sichuan province

Sichuan Provincial Museum, Chengdu

The Queen Mother of the West is depicted on a moulded brick, which presumably once formed part of a tomb chamber. She is seated on her throne consisting of a tiger and a dragon beneath a billowing canopy. Creatures symbolising the sun and the moon appear below her throne: a three-legged crow and a toad holding a branch. To the left of the deity is a nine-tailed fox with wings, who was interpreted in the Eastern Han period as an omen for numerous descendants. In front of the fox kneels a hare, who holds in its hand a plant known as the 'tree of the three pearls'. On the right the deity is protected by a guardian figure, who holds a halberd. A further male figure, holding a tablet in his hands, kneels in front of the deity and kowtows. This last figure may represent the owner of the tomb, who is seeking the deity's help. Between him and two further figures, who may represent the man's parents or may be members of the deity's retinue, is a long low table, which was perhaps used for the game of liubo (no. 76).

The relief bricks from Sichuan usually show the Queen Mother of the West, as here, as a sole and central deity. Occasionally she is supplemented by two winged beings, one on each side, representing the sun and the moon, such as those shown here on separate bricks. Their feathered garments were presumably intended to explain how these celestial bodies moved through the sky.[1] Whereas the female moon deity is identified by a hairknot, the male sun bird wears a cap on his head. The round discs at their bellies are the sun and the moon. A bird flies across the sun disc, and it would be usual for a toad to appear on the moon disc, dancing below the moon. On the present example the toad is missing.

The sun, the moon and the Queen Mother of the West are linked by one of the versions of the myth of the archer Houyi, already mentioned in connection with the clothes chest (no. 64) and the imaginary tree (no. 98). This myth explains how, in former times, ten suns followed their paths across the sky in succession. One day all of them rose simultaneously and would have scorched the earth if the archer Houyi had not shot down nine of them. As thanks, he received the elixir of immortality from the Queen Mother of the West. But his wife Chang'e drank it in secrecy and, fleeing to the moon, changed into a toad.

Published: *Wenwu cankao ziliao* 1956.6, pp. 37–8; Finsterbusch 1971, vol. 2, no. 44; Kominami Ichiro 1974, p. 65; Lim 1987; Munakata 1990, p. 104; Goepper 1995, no. 105.

102 Brick decorated in relief with acrobats

Han period (206 BC–AD 220)
Ceramic
Length 62.0 cm; height 32 cm; thickness 5 cm
Excavated in 1981 at Xinye, Henan province (0385)
Henan Provincial Museum, Zhengzhou

The grey hollow brick is broken off at the right-hand side. The acrobat scene is bounded at the top by a band of cloud tendril, and at the lower and the left edge by a band of net pattern. Within the frame a procession of a rider and two horse-drawn chariots moves towards the broken edge. All that remains of the broken off scene are two fluttering flags, part of a back wheel and possibly the end of an arched bridge.

The rider carries a pole with a loosely dangling rope over his shoulder. Above him is a second rider, who turns round at full gallop to shoot an arrow. The two horse-drawn chariots are each occupied by two people: the person at the front guides the chariot and the one behind holds the tall post on which the acrobats perform their feats. On the right-hand bar

Fig. 101.1 *Rubbing of brick (a) showing the Queen Mother of the West.*

◀ 101a,b,c

102

of the T-shaped post on the first chariot, a man hangs by his feet, with his arms spread out horizontally. He apparently has so much strength that he can hold a further man in each hand, one squatting with his hands on his rounded belly, the other standing on one leg. Almost more amazing than this acrobatic feat is that of the tightrope dancer: a rope inclined at 56 degrees is held by the post bearer in the first chariot and at the top by an acrobat, who is squatting at the top of the post on the second chariot. The latter holds the rope in one hand, while using the other to balance himself. The tightrope dancer moves gracefully, balancing himself with his raised arms.

The ways in which the individuals are dressed are striking: the riders and the men in the chariots appear to be wearing, as far as can be made out, garments with wide sleeves and high caps on their heads. The acrobats, on the other hand, display their bare torsos: the tightrope dancer wears wide

trousers, while the acrobats on the posts appear to have tight trousers. The hair of the acrobats is tied into a high knot above the head and fixed by a long ribbon. The artist has devoted particular attention to the portrayal of the chest muscles and the mostly fully rounded bellies of the acrobats. The entire scene is given further vigour by the horse drawing the first chariot, which, as it gallops, throws back its head and appears to be neighing loudly.

This brick can be compared with a contemporary and fully preserved one discovered in the Nanyang area of southern Henan (fig. 102.1). The comparative piece, with a counterpart, acted as the door lintel of two adjacent tomb doors, framed

Fig. 102.1 *Rubbing of a brick showing an acrobat scene. After Beijing 1990e, no. 116.*

Fig. 102.2 *Drawing of moulded bricks from a lintel from tomb M39 in Nanyang, Henan province. After Beijing 1990e, fig. 7.2.*

a

b

Fig. 102.3 *Scenes of acrobatics on posts.*
a *Rubbing of a brick. After Xiao Kangda 1992, p. 299, fig. 194.*
b *After Sun Ji 1991, p. 392, fig. 99: 8.*

by three pillars (fig. 102.2). The present brick may have occupied a similar position.

The left-hand side of the comparative brick is ornamented with an acrobat scene. Here, a tightrope dancer hangs by his foot from a horizontal rope which is held on the right by an acrobat squatting on a post, and is fixed on the left to a further post. The posts are once again fitted to two horse-drawn chariots rolling at full speed. To the right of the acrobat scene, a bridge spans an area of water, in which a fisherman poles his boat. Two further horse-drawn chariots with umbrellas cross the bridge and are received by two people bowing before them. Above these two individuals are two fighting swordsmen. A hunting scene above the chariots with umbrellas completes the picture. The obvious similarities of theme, composition and style on the two bricks allow the conclusion that the present damaged one had, on its right side, a similar bridge with further chariots and other comparable motifs.

Most probably the decoration on the bricks was more than purely decorative. The acrobat scenes may have been intended to provide entertainment in the afterlife.

Acrobat scenes were in general a popular theme during the Han period. Amongst the many representations, the art of gymnastics on posts is particularly striking. Post acrobatics can be graded according to three levels of skill. Acrobatic tricks were doubtless easiest to master on posts firmly anchored in the ground (fig. 102.3a). The challenge increased when acrobats performed on a post held by a strong man on his shoulders (fig. 102.3b). The example shows three tiny figures, the one at the top resembling a flying bird, while the other two perform their tricks on the horizontal crossbeam. The greatest feat in post acrobatics was surely to perform on posts held in moving chariots, as here. Whether the posts are

firmly anchored to the chariots or simply held by one person is not clear. The acrobatic virtuosity of the tightrope dancer is almost beyond belief, but similar skills survive to the present day and show the perpetuation of an ancient tradition.

Published: *Zhongyuan wenwu* 1981.3, pp. 12–14; Fu Qifeng 1985, pp. 7–28; Singapore 1990, p. 53; Beijing 1990e, no. 115; Sun Ji 1991, pp. 391–3; Xiao Kangda 1992, pp. 298–310; Beijing 1992a, no. 81; Taipei 1992, pp. 152–3; Goepper 1995, no. 102.

103 Brick decorated in relief with scene of alcohol production

Eastern Han period (AD 25–220)
Ceramic
Length 50 cm; height 28 cm
Excavated in 1979 at Xinlongxiang, Xindu county, Sichuan province
Sichuan Provincial Museum, Chengdu

The long rectangular brick from a tomb at Xinlongxiang in Sichuan is decorated in relief with a scene showing the production of alcohol. Perhaps such images were intended to guarantee the deceased a life in which such activities continued. Han period reliefs from Sichuan province frequently illustrate scenes of salt extraction, alcohol production, harvest, fishing and hunting. For the tomb owners they may have provided natural settings for the afterlife, and for us they offer information on the economy and trade of the time.

The production of distilled liquor is said to have been established during the Han period. The relief brick, together with a further one from Peng county in Sichuan province, is evidence of this development. Both bricks show an almost identical representation of distillation: to the right can be seen the production of alcoholic drinks; at the bottom left the liquor is being carried away by a man with two jugs hanging from a shoulder pole; and at the top left a man is transporting a wine chest on a wheelbarrow. The production of alcohol takes place in a roofed building and is watched by a man standing at the left, perhaps a buyer. Above him, a man ladles

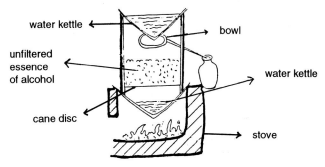

Fig. 103.1 *Drawing of the distillation process. After* Sichuan wenwu *1989.4, p. 29, fig. 3.*

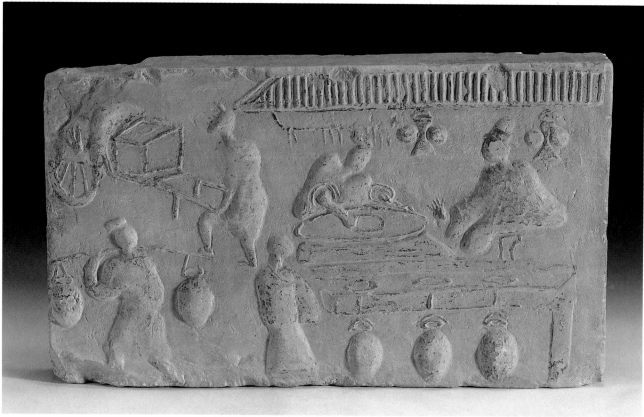

103

or stirs with a bowl in a wide cauldron. At the right sits a man on a bench, who appears to watch the process. In the foreground there is a counter, into which three bowls are placed. From each opening, a tube runs down to a large container which is set up before the counter.

According to Chinese scholars, this is one of the earliest representations of alcohol distillation. The plant and process were as follows (fig. 103.1): a large funnel-shaped water kettle was placed on an open hearth. Inside the kettle stood a tall wooden steamer with a woven bamboo base, onto which the unfiltered alcohol mash was placed. A second, funnel-shaped water kettle fitted neatly into the top of the steamer. Under this kettle was a small bowl, with an outflow into a large container at the side. When the water in the lower kettle came to the boil, it released steam which rose up through the mash, thereby extracting the alcohol. The water in the upper kettle was constantly changed to keep it cool, and thus cause the steam to condense on the underside of the kettle. This liquid would then drip into the small bowl, whence it was ducted into the container to the side. The large kettle on the present brick would thus correspond to the upper one in the distillation plant; the man with the bowl would be in the act of cooling the water. The lower parts of the plant are not visible on the brick. Presumably, however, there was a connecting tube from the bowl in which the alcohol collected to the

counter, from where the finished product would run through the pipes into the three containers that stand in readiness.[1]

A distillation vessel of bronze, from the Han period, which served for the extraction of alcohol, is today in the Shanghai Museum. Scholars have attempted to use it for the production of alcohol, and have extracted liquids with an alcohol content of 14 to 26 per cent.

The development of the distillation technique for alcohol portrayed on the brick is thought to have benefited from Daoist alchemical experiments. For example, from the Qin period, alchemists had attempted, under the direction of the First Emperor, Qin Shi Huangdi, to produce from jade, gold, mercury, cinnabar and other minerals, potions that would confer immortality. The practitioners hoped to gain thereby properties of these materials, such as immunity to change or indestructibility. From 144 BC onwards the use of real gold was prohibited for such processes and artificial gold was sought.[2] Drinking liquid gold was considered to be the most effective means to acquire immortality. It is possible that the alchemical pursuit of such elixirs led to the development of the distillation of alcohol.

Published: Gao Wen 1987, no. 15; Lim 1987, p. 103; *Sichuan wenwu* 1989.4, pp. 27–30; Goepper 1995, no. 103.

1 Sun Ji 1991, pl. 85:11.

2 *Sichuan wenwu* 1989.4, p. 30; Needham 1980, pp. 210–323.

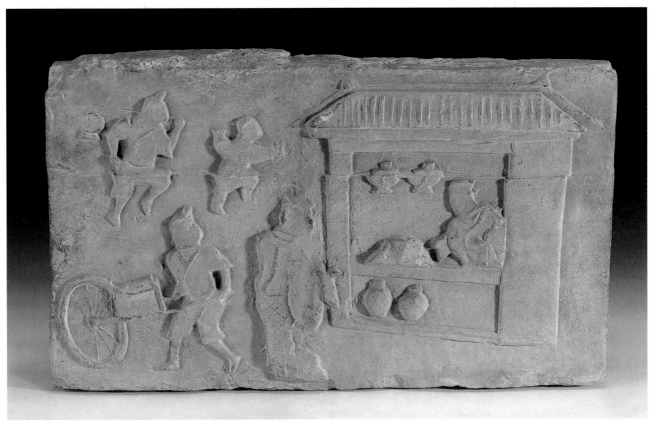

104

104 Brick decorated in relief with scene of the sale of alcoholic drinks

Eastern Han period (AD 25–220)
Ceramic
Length 42 cm; height 34 cm
Excavated in 1985 at Yihexiang, Peng county, Sichuan province
Sichuan Provincial Museum, Chengdu

The brick shows a merchant selling his alcoholic drinks to several customers, from a small shop. In the Han period it was believed that alcohol could transport man to the pleasurable state of an immortal. 'He who drinks wine assumes its good and its bad qualities,' reports the *Shuowen jiezi*, the earliest Chinese dictionary, compiled in the first century AD.

Alcoholic drinks were consumed in such great quantities and by all strata of the population that the state was able to set up a lucrative alcohol monopoly. The chapter on the reign of Emperor Wudi (141–87 BC) in the *Han shu* (*The history of the Han dynasty*) describes wine stalls on the street, which were checked officially, and whose profits were pocketed by the state.

It is presumably such an officially-run wine stall that is shown on the brick, in a rather coarse relief. The small shop on the right-hand side is open at the front. The merchant is shown behind the counter, and he offers his goods to a pos-

sible customer, who is standing in front of the shop on the left. Two flasks are set up under the counter; two further ones, which are presumably filled with different alcoholic drinks, hang in the background. The left half of the brick shows further customers. At the bottom, a heavy box is being rolled away on a wheelbarrow. Two men in the background give the impression of being cheerful: both leap away in high spirits; the larger one, on the left, carries the goods on a shoulder pole.

Published: *Kaogu* 1983.10, pp. 897–902; Lim 1987, p. 103: *Kaogu* 1993.6, pp. 534–42; Goepper 1995, fig. 104.

105 Brick decorated in relief with erotic scene

Eastern Han period (AD 25–220)
Ceramic with traces of reddish and black paint
Length 50 cm; height 29 cm
Excavated in 1979 at Xin longxiang, Xindu county, Sichuan province
Cultural Relics Bureau, Xindu county, Sichuan province

During earthworks on a mountain slope in Sichuan province in 1979 a worker came across a brick grave of the Eastern Han period with more than ten bricks decorated in relief with various themes. These include the planting of rice seedlings

105

Fig. 105.1 *Second brick decorated with an erotic scene.*

in spring, the production of alcohol, performances of dance and acrobatics, and the Queen Mother of the West with the sun and moon deities, scenes that appear on bricks from many other Sichuan tombs. Two bricks depict a much less common theme: the copulation of men and women in the open air.

The erotic scenes on the two bricks are similar, yet differ in their details. The brick in the exhibition shows three naked men and one naked woman in the open air beneath a mulberry tree in full leaf. The woman, her hair in a high topknot, lies on her back on the ground, her belt and her basket for mulberry leaves cast carelessly aside. She is about to be penetrated by the largest male, who is being given some assistance by the smallest male. The latter is also in a state of sexual arousal, as is the third man who appears to be queuing up behind the tree. This is not intimate sexual union but more like a public event. It is further witnessed by birds in the tree and by a couple of playful monkeys who hang from a branch. Further down the branch is slung what appears to be the clothing belonging to the four individuals.

The second brick may be interpreted as showing the continuation of the erotic scene on the first brick (fig. 105.1). The woman appears more relaxed as her present partner withdraws from her and stretches his left arm towards the clothing on the tree. The other two men seem to have concluded their involvement in the act: the tall man squats to one side, resting; the shorter one leans against the trunk of the tree. The birds and the monkeys have gone from the scene, another indication that the event is over.

The import of these scenes in juxtaposition with bricks illustrating more conventional subjects remains a matter of speculation. It seems likely that the erotic event was also a conventional scene, referring either to a well known story or legend or to a local custom. It may be the case that it is the depiction of such an event that is so unusual, rather than the event itself.

Published: Goepper 1995, no. 106.

106 Model of a manor

Early Western Han period, 2nd century BC
Ceramic with traces of paint
Height 89 cm; width 114 cm; length 130 cm
Excavated in 1981 at Yuzhuang, Huaiyang county, Henan
province (MI: 7)
Henan Provincial Museum, Zhengzhou

This exceptionally large and complete model was excavated from a multi-chambered Western Han tomb at Yuzhuang in Henan province.[1] Models and bricks illustrating buildings, especially in a farming context, were typical of the late Western and early Eastern Han period. It would appear that their

owners expected the afterlife to embrace these wider areas of their lives.

The model depicts a strongly fortified building, the walled boundaries of which enclose fields as well as the house of a wealthy man. The outer wall has only one entrance, located on the south side, to control entry and exit. After passing through the entrance gate with its raised gable roof, the visitor would encounter two stables, one on each side, possibly intended for sheltering horses and carts; he would cross a first court to a second gate in a two-storey wall, which forms the rear side of storage and corridor-like transverse rooms. Above this second gate rises a two-storey tower, with window slits and pierced stonework for light and air; this tower marks the start of the residential area proper. From the first floor of this tower there is access to the four-storey, approximately square watchtowers on each side. The second gate controls the access to the central residential courtyard, which dominates the overall design. It is flanked to the west and to the east by two-storey buildings, whilst a mighty hall, several storeys high, runs along its northern side. This is the main building of the entire complex and is open to the south. It can be reached from the courtyard up two staircases. It was presumably built on a stone foundation.

Models of six musicians, as well as several dishes, plates and a jug show that this hall was intended for feasting and banqueting. Two large doors in the southern side of the first storey, which presumably served as a living room, lead out to a long balcony, which is protected by a heavy hipped roof, adding to the monumental effect of the building. A small room attached to the western flank of the main building presumably served as a toilet, whilst on the eastern side is a further building which leads both to an eastern range and also to the rear courtyard. Here, located next to the pigsty, is a toilet, and further to the west a kitchen with hearth, table and cooking pot. At the western corner of the north wall is a further toilet.

Access to a vegetable garden, located separately to the west, is given through openings in the southern and northern walls. At the front is a field with twenty-two raised beds, watered from a well lying to the north, which also irrigates the rear vegetable beds through a central ditch.

In spite of very careful attention to detail, such as in the reproduction of the different types of roof and roof tiles, there were limits to the faithfulness with which wooden constructions could be reproduced in clay.

The owner of such a magnificent building with several storeys was presumably a major landlord. Such figures had assumed an increasingly powerful role in the economic and political life of their time towards the end of the first century BC and under the Eastern Han dynasty.[2] Members of this gentry, who played an innovative role in agriculture, were very prosperous. Many were directly or indirectly related to the

106

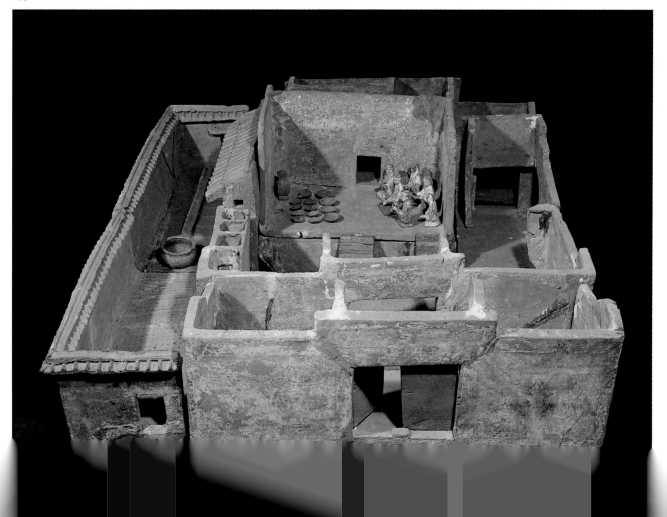

imperial family. This new gentry also produced a number of high officials, who represented a new social stratum, providing both political and financial support for the government. The great wealth of this class has been illustrated by Gernet with the example of the high minister Liang Ji, a relative by marriage of the emperor and executed in the year AD 159. The sale of his property is said to have provided the state exchequer with three thousand million coins, a sum sufficient to fund half the annual grain tax for the whole country. It may well have been the wealth and power of this social group that led to the use of elaborate models of farm buildings in later tombs of the Eastern Han. Such models transformed the pictures presented previously by tombs, drawing the wider farming landscape into them.

Published: *Zhongyuan wenwu* 1983.1, pp. 1–3; Taipei 1992, pp. 158–9; Goepper 1995, no. 95.

1 *Zhongyuan wenwu* 1983.1, pp. 1–3.
2 Gernet 1987, p. 151.

107 Model of a grain silo

Eastern Han period, 2nd century BC
Painted ceramic
Height 148 cm; width 76 cm; depth 59 cm
Excavated in 1984 near Mazuocun, Jiaozuo county, Henan province
Henan Provincial Museum, Zhengzhou

The five-storey building is impressive for its height and for its careful detailing, both modelled and painted. It is thought to represent a grain silo. The building is entered through a confined courtyard, which has a substantial roofed gateway and a tower on either side. A dog lies in front of the gateway. The small tiled roofs of these towers lift off. While the roof of the gateway is supported by representations of the brackets typical of Chinese wooden architecture, it is not clear how the roofs of the small towers are held in their cantilevered position.

The building itself is tall and narrow front to back. A figure, perhaps the owner, surveys the outlook from a balcony on the first floor. The beam above him is supported on three sets of brackets and behind him is a wall with four windows. The next storey has two much wider openings beneath a broad sloping roof. Below the three sets of brackets that support this roof are two tiers of trellis patterns forming a balustrade. The next two storeys diminish in size. Both have highly decorated openings or windows. The lower of the two storeys has a wide roof, but that on the top is small, with a bird perching on its apex. Both the front and the sides are painted with geometric patterns.

The Eastern Han period, to which this model is dated, was a time when varieties of building types were employed as burial goods. In any one area, at any one time, these models seem to

107

be somewhat stereotyped. Thus an almost identical model of a silo has been found at Jiaozuo in Henan province.[1] Obviously such large fragile pieces were not traded any significant distance. Models from tombs at Jiaqu in Shan Xian in Henan are of a different character, with more precise detailing of a wooden structure and many additional figures. More flamboyant buildings again come from tombs in Hebei province.[2]

Published: Taipei 1992, pp. 162–3; Goepper 1995, no. 96.

1 See *Wenwu* 1974.2, pp. 70 and 14; compare *Wenwu* 1966.3, pp. 6–7, fig. 2.
2 For the tomb in Shan Xian see *Kaogu xuebao* 1965.1, pp. 107–68; for Hebei see *Wenwu* 1990.1, pp. 19–30. Different styles of building again are found in central and southern China.

108 **Figure of a dancer**

Eastern Han period (AD 25–220)
Painted ceramic
Height 50 cm
Excavated in Baijiakou, near Xi'an, Shaanxi province
Historical Museum, Beijing

Graceful dancing figures, such as this one, are frequently found among the burial goods of the Han period. They were intended to entertain the tomb occupant in the afterlife, as presumably he was entertained during his lifetime. Dancers carved from jade survive from the Warring States and Han periods. The long sleeve dance (*changxiu*), which this dancer seems to be performing with her hands hidden in her excessively long sleeves, was one of the many dances that guests were treated to at banquets and court entertainments. Dancers were accompanied by musicians playing reed or stringed instruments.

The dancer has her knees slightly bent, her right leg extended, and the hem of her close-fitting garment spreads out around her feet. She bends forward and her head is inclined. Her left arm is stretched out backwards and her sleeve floats out behind her. Her right arm is raised to head height and forms another arc. Her dress is an overgarment, beneath which can be glimpsed two further robes. The dancers' dresses were frequently made of fine, patterned or embroidered material and were tied at the waist with a silk belt. Silk robes found in several Han tombs, such as those at Mawangdui, and fragments found on wooden and lacquered models of servants have enabled us to form a very good idea of what the textiles of this period were like.

The art of dance in China may have had its origins in rituals connected with cults of fertility and ancestor worship. During the Zhou and Han periods especially, dancing was regarded as playing an important role in imperial ritual ceremonies, together with music and mime. It was thought that the ancient kings established ritual practices to maintain cosmic harmony, and that they also sponsored music for its similar, beneficial effect. Emperor Wudi (141–87 BC) of the Western Han summoned poets and musicians to his court and also instituted the Yuefu bureau to collect folk songs and local music that might otherwise be lost. The 'Metropolis Rhapsody' by Zhang Heng (AD 78–139), a late Han poet, includes a description of dancers, probably similar to the present figure:

> Their vermilion slippers danced between plates and goblets
> And they waved their long, dangling sleeves
> With a curvaceous, cultivated bearing
> Their lovely dresses fluttered like flowers in the wind.[1]

Until the end of the Warring States period dancing performances were limited to banquets and festive occasions held by the royal court and the upper classes. A large number of dancers was a prerogative of the emperor, and, according to the *Li ji*, there were strict rules about how many dancers each noble could have, regulated according to his rank and merit. However, gradually over the Han period these rules were relaxed and dancing reached a wider public.

The Han emperor Chengdi (32–6 BC) favoured a dancer, Zhao Feiyan, whom he eventually made his consort and empress. She was supposedly so thin and slight that she could 'dance in the palm of the emperor's hand'; she was known as the Flying Swallow. Han dynasty fashion tended towards the willowy and very slim physique, whereas ladies of the Tang dynasty (AD 618–906) were decidedly more Rubenesque and plump.

Published: *Kaogu tongxun* 1955.2, pl. 3.1; *Gugong wenwu yuekan* 1994.1, no. 130, p. 130, fig. 73; Fu Tianchou 1985, no. 61; Goepper 1995, no. 109.

1 Knechtges 1982, vol. 1, p. 237.

108

110

109–110 Figures of two entertainers

Eastern Han period (AD 25–220)
Painted ceramic

109 Squatting drummer

Height 48 cm
Excavated in 1982 at Majiashan, Sanhexiang, Xindu county,
Sichuan province
Cultural Relics Bureau, Xindu county, Sichuan province

110 Standing drummer

Height 66.5 cm
Excavated in 1982 in Pi county, Sichuan province
Sichuan Provincial Museum, Chengdu

These two figures are entertainers who specialised in a genre of storytelling whereby their stories were both spoken and sung. Made of reddish brown clay, the first one (no. 109) squats on the ground and merrily beats his drum, which is cradled under his left arm. His full stomach hangs pendulously almost to the ground. He balances on his left leg, the right one thrown upwards as he strums and sings in time to the beat, his whole body vibrating with emotion. He raises his powerful short arms: with the left hand he clutches his instrument and with his right hand he would have held a drumstick which is now lost. His large head between his hunched up shoulders sports a hat capped by a scarf. He appears to be laughing merrily, and his open mouth and protruding tongue emphasise his comic, caricature-like stance.

The second entertainer (no. 110) beats his drum while standing. The story he is telling is, we suppose, lugubrious, causing his face to register a most realistic grimace. His posture suggests that he is swaying in time to his own musical accompaniment. His shoulders are hunched up, his legs bent, his torso slightly twisted and his back arched. His hair is rolled up into a pointed bun. The two entertainers seem to be wearing nothing more than a pair of trousers which, on both of them, appear to be falling down. Both are also wearing a bangle pushed high up their left arms. Both figures are of short stature, with disproportionately long limbs. Many such entertainer figures were probably dwarfs who traditionally in China, as in many other parts of the world, played an important role in court entertainment; certainly Qin Shi Huangdi kept dwarfs at his court, as did his son, the Second Emperor.[1]

Many such figures have been found in graves of Sichuan province in south-western China; it is therefore thought that these models were a specialised form of local art. The economy of this province in the Han period was particularly flourishing as it was one of the most fertile areas in the empire and was a great trading entrepôt. The Han empire greatly extended the empire's boundaries, particularly during the reign of Wudi (141–87 BC). This expansion provided communications and transport between the court and a variety of non-Han frontier areas. As a result, musicians and their instruments, conjurers, acrobats and dancers circulated from region to region, entertaining the public at various levels from Han urban centres to the mansions of the nobility and the imperial court. There was a general fascination during both the Han and the later Tang dynasties (AD 618–906) for the exotic, and particularly for foreign music and entertainment.

The diverse cultural elements of Han music and entertainment are well documented in these Sichuan figures of entertainers.[2] Tomb bricks portray acrobatic displays and a variety of performing acts (no. 102), as part of the hundred forms (*baixi*) of entertainment popular in the Han dynasty.[3] The wealthy people of Sichuan province seem to have particularly relished these singing and talking entertainers, taking models of them to the grave so that they could continue to enjoy their services in the afterlife. A large number of fragments of such figures have been found in a ceramic workshop in the vicinity of the capital of Sichuan province, Chengdu.[4] These figures were probably therefore mass-produced in large quantities.

Published: *Chengdu wenwu* 1985.3, p. 45; *Sichuan wenwu* 1987.3, pp. 4–10; Beijing 1992a, no. 80; Los Angeles 1987, no. 38; Singapore 1990, no. 76; Lim 1987, pp. 132–3, pl. 42; Xiao Kangda 1992, pp. 347–51; Beijing 1990a, no. 104; Goepper 1995, nos 110–11.

1 A chapter of the Qin dynasty annals, in the *Shiji,* is devoted to biographies of wits and humorists (Watson 1993, pp. 215–16).
2 Several examples are shown in *Kaogu xuebao* 1958.1, pls 5–8.
3 For example Lim 1987, pls 48 and 49, showing that, during the Han dynasty, dancers and other entertainers often combined for entertainment purposes, and acrobats, jugglers and dancers all performed simultaneously.
4 *Sichuan wenwu* 1987.3, pp. 5–6.

111–112 Figures of two women

Late Eastern Han period, late 2nd century AD
Ceramic, with red pigment on no. 111

111 Kneeling woman
Height 58 cm
Excavated in 1964 in Pi county, Sichuan province
Sichuan Provincial Museum, Chengdu

112 Standing woman
Height 63 cm
Excavated in 1982 at Majiashan, Xindu county, Sichuan province
Cultural Relics Bureau, Xindu county, Sichuan province

The kneeling female figure (no. 111) is wearing an elaborate costume with borders of zigzag decoration and scalloped sleeves. Her headband is intertwined with two chrysanthemum flowers, which were typical decorative motifs of the period and have been preserved on several other such models.[1] The flowers would have been formed in a mould and luted to the head, which was itself made separately and inserted into the body. Over her long-sleeved undergarment she wears an outergarment folded over on the right, held by

111

a belt and with half sleeves. Her right hand, with extended index finger, rests on her knee, while in the left hand she holds up a circular object. Her ears and fingers are much bejewelled. Similar costumes, headdresses and smiling expressions have been found on Sichuan pottery female figures that are clearly identifiable as entertainers. This figure may therefore represent an entertainer, or an attendant in a noble household.[2]

Her companion, the standing figure from Majiashan, wears

almost identical clothing. In her right hand she holds a circular object similar to that of her companion, while in her left hand she clutches a pair of shoes. According to literary sources there were strict rules governing the proper use of shoes: official shoes went with ritual costumes; ordinary shoes went with court costumes; and sandals made of hemp were for domestic use. When entering enclosed spaces it was customary to remove the shoes and walk around in socks; shoes would be recovered on departure.

There has been much speculation as to the identification of the circular object held by the two women. It may be a mirror, held with the knob from which it was suspended to the inside, so that the polished side would be visible to the lady on whom the women may be waiting. However, it is also possible that this round object is the short-stemmed, circular fan which was typical of the Han and Three Kingdoms period. Such fans had a gripping area, divided off at the lower part of the fan, and this may be what is represented by the horizontal line at the base of the objects held by the women. These fans are described in the literature of the period.

The ladylike appearance and splendid garments of these figures evoke the cultivated and comfortable lifestyle within the circle of the wealthy merchants and officials of Chengdu, the capital of Sichuan province. As Sichuan province was extremely fertile and also one of the main production centres in China for silk and lacquer, Chengdu was a flourishing trading centre.

Published: *Sichuan wenwu* 1984.4, p. 63, fig. 2; *Chengdu wenwu* 1985.3, p. 45, fig. 3; Fu Tianchou 1985, no. 115; Goepper 1995, nos 112–13.

1 For example Lim 1987, colour pl. 1.
2 See *Wenwu* 1985.7, pp. 66–72 for many similar figures.

113 Figure of a farmer with spade and shovel

Eastern Han period (AD 25–220)
Ceramic
Height 83 cm
Excavated in 1957 in Xinjin, Sichuan province
Sichuan Provincial Museum, Chengdu

This reddish coloured ceramic figure, holding a spade and a handleless shovel, is a typical farmer of the Eastern Han period and contrasts with the warriors, musicians and domestic servants found in many Western Han tombs. The figure was discovered in a tomb which had been hewn into a rock wall. In the recesses of the four grave chambers there were scattered human bones and six coffins which had been broken or damaged by grave robbers or desecrators. The farmer figure was one of the 156 objects left behind by the robbers.

112

He wears a knee-length undergarment with a slightly shorter overgarment, and he has a short knife and a long sword attached to his belt. A cap protects his head from the elements. Several similar figures are known, such as the one found in Mian county, Shaanxi province, in 1978.[1]

The farmer's wooden spade has a reinforced iron tip. The Chinese began casting iron in about the sixth century BC, and many such iron tips have been found in excavations. These iron tips would have been used on wooden implements, such as the spade, and transferred from one tool to another as the wood wore out. For much of the Han dynasty iron was a state monopoly and some of these iron spade reinforcements have inscriptions on them, such as 'Shujun Chengdu' (Chengdu in Shu district) or 'Shujun *qian wan*' (for Shu district, a thousand times ten thousand). Spades such as this with reinforced tips would be used not only to till the soil, but also to build dams for irrigation purposes and flood prevention, both of which were major concerns of the time.[2]

By the Eastern Han period the contents of tombs portray a belief in the afterlife that was significantly different from that of earlier dynasties.[3] Firstly there was a gradual change during the Han period in the equipment provided in the tombs. During the earlier part of the Han, the real objects used in life were put in the tomb. However, gradually substitutes, such as models, were seen to be quite sufficient. Therefore in the Western Han period the tombs of nobles and royalty contained the actual possessions required at court. Tombs of the Eastern Han period, however, were generally supplied with models which depicted the necessities of the countryside. These would include the tenant farmer to till the soil.

In the ideal Confucian social hierarchy farmers were ranked above merchants, and agriculture held a position of supreme value in the Chinese scheme of things. Agriculture was considered an honest and productive activity, in contrast to commerce and industry.[4] This did not of course stop the government exploiting the small tenant farmer and taxing him sometimes out of existence, as well as calling him up for military service. However, the occupation of farmer was often idealised, and the agricultural life, away from the hurly-burly of the metropolis, was seen as an escape from the cares of government. Much poetry was written about this idealised existence, in tilling the soil and living off one's own land without having to be dependent on others, though doubtless the lives of many tenant farmers were hard indeed.

Published: *Kaogu tongxun* 1958.8, pp. 31–7; Goepper 1995, no. 114.

1 Los Angeles 1987, colour pl. opposite p. 17 and cat. no. 30; Paludan 1991, pp. 48, 49, figs 43, 44.
2 *Wenwu* 1989.10, pp. 47–8; Finsterbusch 1971, vol. 2, pl. 17, fig. 56 and pl. 19, fig. 69.
3 Rawson 1995, pp. 75–85.
4 Mote 1971, pp. 4–5.

113

114 **Figure of a tomb guardian**

Eastern Han period (AD 25–220)
Ceramic
Height 44 cm
Found in 1965 near Chengdu, Sichuan province
Sichuan Provincial Museum, Chengdu

This figure from Chengdu is the best preserved example of a group of such ceramic figures designed to act as guardians at the entrance to the tomb. Such figures seem to be found only in Sichuan province and date from the end of the Eastern Han period. It is difficult to relate them to figures in Chinese mythology.

The figure has a frightening grimace, with two protruding bovine ears, small lateral horns, and incisor-like teeth growing obliquely from his upper jaw. His hair is drawn up into a topknot and he has a beard. His enormously long tongue extends as far as his stomach, but is interrupted between the top and bottom of the neck as the head and the body sections were made separately in moulds and fitted one into the other. He wears a long undergarment, over which is a coat and a shoulder cape. The decorative pattern on the clothing, scratched into the clay while it was still damp, indicates a belt from which a long knife is suspended. Like other guards of this type he carried an axe and a serpent in his hands. The long tongue may refer to serpent or phallic symbolism; the axe in the figure's right hand might be seen as illustrating the power and the will of the grim guard to act in a warlike manner against evil intruders.

Such creatures seem to be descended from the monsters holding serpents in their claws, which were put close to the heads of the deceased in Chu state tombs as some form of protection. In pre-Han China the task of protecting the grave from harm seems to have been entrusted to mythical, composite animals, rather than to humans. Demon faces showing their teeth and equipped with horns had been known in jade and bronze from the Shang and Zhou periods and were popular motifs on tomb doorways and door knockers of the Han period.[1] In the Chu state, hybrid guardians with strange faces and long tongues and antlers were carved from wood and placed as guardians in tombs (figs 63.2, 63.3, 71.1).[2] The present ceramic figure seems to be a late descendant of this tradition.

Published: Goepper 1995, no. 115.

1 For example, Beijing 1992a, no. 166.
2 The British Museum has such a wooden figure with a long, protruding tongue, and crowned by antlers made of dry lacquer (OA1950.11–15.1). As many as 155 tomb guardian creatures were gathered from the excavations of more than 500 Chu state tombs in Jiangling, Hubei province (*Wenwu* 1979.6, p. 87). In the Chu tombs excavated at Xinyang in northern Henan, a wooden tomb guardian creature, over 1 m was found buried in each tomb (Beijing 1986c, pp. 60–1, pls 58, 59; p. 114, pl. 109).

114

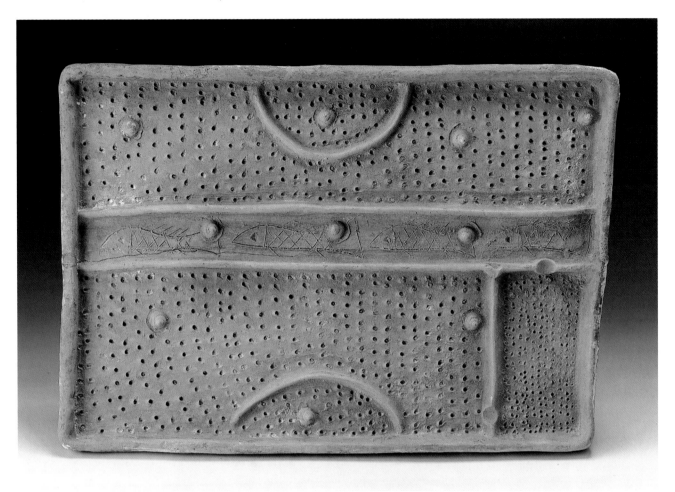

115

115 **Model of a rice field**

Eastern Han period (AD 25–220)
Clay
Length 55 cm; width 36 cm
Excavated in 1965 in Xinjin, Sichuan province
Sichuan Provincial Museum, Chengdu

This model represents a rice field divided into three main sections. A watercourse, identifiable by the fish scratched into it, runs through the middle. Low dams separate the watercourse and the rice fields from each other. The arrangement of the water inflows, indicated by small impressions in the dams, suggest that the larger field on the left lies lower than the small one on the right. A height gradation of rice fields, to allow the unobstructed flow of water, is often encountered in the Chinese countryside. Marsh snails are also depicted, in relief, distributed over the rice field. The regular pattern of dots in the fields suggests that the rice fields have been recently planted, and so it is springtime. The smallest field, with its closely spaced dots, may have been where the seeds were sown or pricked out. Some scientists have postulated that the two semicircular areas in the larger fields may

represent compost areas; others believe that they are ponds.

Rice has been cultivated in China since about 5000 BC. Some of the earliest evidence of rice cultivation has been discovered in Hemudu, the neolithic site near Hangzhou in Zhejiang province. Rice has acted as the staple diet of the southern Chinese for several millennia; the northern Chinese climate was better suited to growing millet and wheat. However, during the Shang and Zhou period rice cultivation spread into the area of the Yellow River in the northern Chinese provinces of Henan and Hebei. This model indicates the change in rice cultivation techniques which occurred during the Han dynasty. During the Western Han period the rice seeds were scattered directly on to the field, but during the Eastern Han period the seeds were germinated first in a more confined space. Once the extremely sensitive rice seedlings had grown to a certain size, they were then transplanted into larger fields. Rice fields tended to be smaller than other agricultural fields, as the water temperature was of great importance and this was easier to control in a restricted area.

Sichuan province, where the model was found, has a subtropical climate, ideal for growing rice. Indeed, the cultivation

116

of rice was a major agricultural activity in the Han dynasty. The Chengdu plain is extremely rich in water resources: its intersecting rivers and canals promoted the growth not only of rice but also of other crops, such as taro.

Irrigation was regarded as an essential undertaking by Qin Shi Huangdi and was continued by the Han emperors. Canals were built connecting Chang'an to the Yellow River, thus providing both irrigation for the fields and transport of essential foods to the capital and the provinces of Henan and Hebei. Small businesses were set up by the side of the canals making use of the hydraulic power. Other forms of irrigation were provided by wells (no. 99), and by natural and artificial ponds. Dammed rivers and lakes served as water reservoirs, from which water was ducted to the fields via canals and ditches. This in theory enabled good harvest yields even during the more extended periods of drought, although in practice such measures tended to be inadequate.

Other clay tomb models and many of the decorated bricks dating to the Eastern Han period tell us much about agricultural methods of the time, and as such are extremely valuable sources of information.

Published: *Wenwu* 1979.12, pp. 61–7; *Wenwu* 1985.8, pp. 41–8; Goepper 1995, no. 116.

116 Model of a pond

Eastern Han period (AD 25–220)
Clay
Length 51 cm; width 31.5 cm
Excavated in 1970 in Suining, Sichuan province
Sichuan Provincial Museum, Chengdu

This model shows a rectangular pond or reservoir. A boat, aquatic plants and two little ducks indicate that this aquatic area was also used for boating. Its regular, rectangular shape suggests that it is an artificially constructed reservoir, and the two areas separated off within it, with fish, may have been for fish farming or simply fishing. Between these enclosed areas is a water channel, possibly the beginning of an irrigation system. Proportionately the fish and the water plants, chestnuts and lotuses are over-large in relation to the boat, and the model is somewhat crudely made, as were many such models of the period.

Other models of clay ponds are placed next to what are apparently rice fields, with a small dam acting as a boundary into which a small lock gate is fitted.[1] Contemporary decorated bricks and literary texts are perhaps more graphic and give us additional information about the scenes portrayed in models such as this one. Bricks illustrate scenes such as picking lotus plants, boating on a lotus pond, fishing and rafting.[2]

Fig. 116.1 *Rubbing of a brick from Chengdu, showing a rice harvest and a lakeside scene. After Gao Wen 1987, no. 4.*

A brick decorated in relief, from Chengdu, illustrates a rice harvest and, in the upper portion, the bank of a pond or lake (fig. 116.1). Lotus flowers grow in the water whilst hunters appear from under a tree to shoot at flying wild geese with bow and arrows.

The person who took this and other such representations of agricultural scenes to the grave with him would have been providing himself with the possibility to fish, hunt and eat the fruits of the soil and the water.

Published: *Wenwu* 1979.12, p. 61; Lim 1987, p. 82; Goepper 1995, no. 117.

1 Los Angeles 1987, p. 115, fig. 35.
2 Lim 1987, pp. 86–9.

117 Two fragments of the Xiping stone canon

Eastern Han period (AD 25–220)
Stone
Lengths 15 cm, 15 cm; widths 12.2 cm, 10.5 cm; thicknesses 4.8 cm, 4.5 cm
From a former collection
Luoyang City Museum, Henan province

These are fragments of a series of forty-six stone slabs erected in a U-shaped arrangement three rows deep, inscribed on both sides with the principal texts of Confucianism. The idea of engraving the canons on stone – the first project of its kind – was recommended in AD 175 during the Xiping reign period (AD 172–8) and took eight years to complete.[1] Each slab was approximately 2.3 m high, and the entire arrangement was

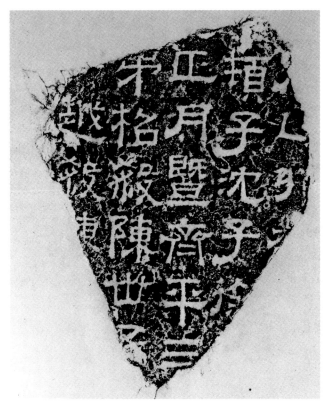

Fig. 117.1 *Rubbing of the fragmentary inscription from* The Spring and Autumn Annals.

Fig. 117.2 *Rubbing of the fragmentary inscription of the ode.*

117

sheltered by a walkway with a tiled roof and wooden balustrades.[2] The engraved scriptures were: *The Book of Changes (Yijing)*, *The Book of Poetry (Shi jing)*, *The Book of History (Shangshu)*, *The Book of Ceremonial (Yili)*, *The Spring and Autumn Annals (Chunqiu)*, *The Gongyang Commentary (Gongyang zhuan)* and *Analects (Lunyu)*. These seven texts represented the state-prescribed orthodoxy of Confucian learning and the official syllabus for teaching the sons of the imperial family and other children of the nobility. The stones stood in the state university at Luoyang, capital of the Eastern Han, and their presence was as much a political symbol of the state's existence as it was a practical reference to texts set in a version considered and approved by the authorities.

The engravers of the stone canons were skilled artisans whose names are unknown to us. According to the traditional story of the stone canon's creation, the famous Confucian scholar Cai Yong (AD 133–192) wrote the texts in ink on the slabs ready for the engravers to cut the characters and match his handwriting. Close study of the surviving fragments reveals that Cai Yong did not write out the entire corpus of over 200,000 characters single-handed, despite claims to the contrary in his official biography.[3] He was probably in charge of a commission of scholar-writers who shared this enormous task. Cai Yong was one of the most accomplished men of his generation, and his legacy in the form of these epigraphical monuments was immediately hailed as one of the dynasty's greatest cultural achievements.

The larger fragment shows some characters from a passage in the *Spring and Autumn Annals*, the history of political events during the period 770 to 475 BC, allegedly edited by Confucius (fig. 117.1).[4] The smaller fragment is filled with characters from an ode entitled 'Mang' in the *Book of Poetry* (fig. 117.2).[5] The text of the 'Mang' ode transmitted to us today shows that the intervals of text between characters at an equal altitude in

the four columns of this fragment were 69, 69 and 70 characters. The height of four characters is close to 10 cm, which allows us to estimate the total height of the inscribed portion of the stone in the region of 175 cm.[6] Significantly, a column length of, say, 70 characters is extremely close to the range of 60 to 80 characters on each strip of the *Yili* written on the bamboo strips discovered in a late Han tomb at Wuwei in 1958 (no. 95, fig. 95.2). This close parallel may suggest that during the late Eastern Han a standard text arrangement of canonical scriptures was used for both writing on bamboo strips and engraving on stone.

The stones' existence intact was brief. Already by AD 190 nearly half of them had been broken during a violent insurrection which destroyed most of Luoyang, and even more serious damage was to follow. Cai Yong joined this political movement and died afterwards in prison for his part in it. During the medieval period and afterwards, engraved stone fragments like the present specimens were avidly collected by residents of Luoyang. Moreover, in the minds of later governments, the short-lived Han achievement of engraving a complete canon on stone was to become a revered model of both political and scholarly consensus. The last of six further undertakings to engrave the Confucian canons on stone was carried out in the late eighteenth century, during the rule of the Manchu Qing dynasty.

1 For discussions of the Eastern Han stone canon see Tsien Tsuen-hsiun 1962, pp. 73–9; *Wenwu* 1986.5, pp. 1–6; Goepper 1995, no. 118.
2 On sizes of stones see *Wenwu* 1988.1, pp. 58–64.
3 Fan Ye 1971, 60B. 1990.
4 For the *loci* of the four columns of characters see *Chunqiu* 1937: 359.V.8, 362.VII.1, 367.VIII.1, 369.VIII.9; Legge 1872, pp. 600–23.
5 *Mao shi* 1934, 12.58.2, 13.58.2, 13.58.5, 13.58.8; Legge 1871, pp. 97–101.
6 For an important reconstruction of the stone-engraved *Shangshu* with a full column length of 74 characters, see *Kaogu xuebao* 1981.2, pp. 185–98. The author of this study, Xu Jingyuan, estimates the height of the main text inscription as 176 cm.

118 Guardian animal

Eastern Han period (AD 25–220)
Stone
Height 114 cm; length 175 cm; width 45 cm
Excavated in Yichuan county, Henan province
Guanlin Stone Sculpture Museum, Luoyang City, Henan province

Large stone carvings of animals like this one were set up along avenues, often known as Spirit Roads, leading to major tombs. This development seems to have been the result of ritual changes made by the Han dynasty emperor Mingdi in the first century BC. During the early part of the Han dynasty routine sacrifices to the dead had taken place in small temples near their tombs, while major ceremonies were held at the ancestor temples in the palaces or city. In AD 58 the emperor abolished the temple sacrifices and transferred them to the tombs. Over the following 160 years the tomb areas became the focus for all ancestral sacrifice. It has been suggested that the motivation for this change was political, that is, to concentrate all activity at the tombs of the ancestors of the ruler,

ignoring thus all extraneous problems of political legitimacy. Two changes seem to have followed from this move: a large sacrificial hall in which ceremonies could be held was built adjacent to, or in line with, each tomb, and stone statuary was set up to line the roads to the tombs.[1]

Stone statuary had been used at tombs earlier in the dynasty. The mound above the burial of the Han dynasty general Huo Qubing (d. 117 BC) was covered with large stone carvings of the creatures of the universe.[2] This composition of a mountain covered with strange and marvellous beasts parallels the depiction of imaginary and real creatures in the landscapes of hill censers (no. 82) and lamps (no. 97). The formal arrangement of the stone animals along an avenue was a new development. In the initial stages the avenue was entered between stone towers (fig. 118.1), which were representations of the wooden towers that flanked the entrances to important buildings.[3]

The creatures carved from stone tended to be the powerful beasts of the unseen spirit world. Thus, like the bronze hill

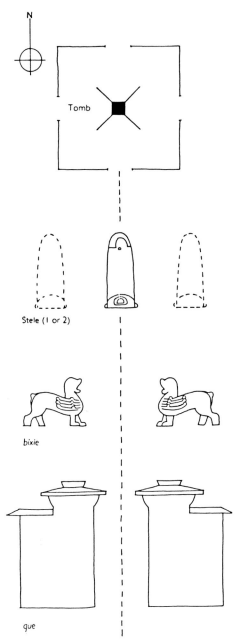

Fig. 118.1 *Reconstruction of the organisation of the Spirit Road to an Eastern Han tomb. After Paludan 1991, p. 242, fig. 2.*

censer (no. 82) or carvings of jade (Yang, fig. 4), the avenues brought the forces of the world before the eyes of those attending the ceremonies. In addition to winged beasts, felines and the occasional elephant are known from the Han period.

The use of stone might seem natural to those in the West, long familiar with sculpture of all sorts carved in stone. But in Han China the development was relatively new. Stone was used increasingly from the Qin and early Han periods, simply because it was durable and was thus probably thought to carry with it connotations of permanence and perhaps immortality. The tombs of Liu Sheng and Dou Wan, as well as their jade suits, also engage the permanence of stone in their pursuit of immortality (no. 81).[3] Dug deep into a mountainside, the coffin chambers were further sealed with stone slabs (p. 169, fig. 1).

The present beast is a magnificent example of the stone sculptures employed at Eastern Han tombs. Its head, with bulging eyes and wide open jaws as it roars, gives the feeling of force and power. The creature has two horns, a beard and wings on both shoulders and thighs, which indicate its supernatural powers. In other respects the animal is shown as a strong tiger-like feline, with powerful legs and a long tail. The feather patterns of the wings are repeated on the body and the tail. Because such creatures were placed at right angles to the avenue, they were carved to be seen from the side as family and officials proceeded along the avenue to the tomb.[4]

Published: Singapore 1990, p. 116; Paludan 1991, fig. 36; Imperial China 1992, no. 21; Beijing 1992a, no. 38; Luo Zhewen 1993, no. 199; Goepper 1995, no. 119.

1 For a discussion of the changes see Paludan 1991, pp. 28–9, and citations of Yang Kuan 1985. Further discussion is in Wu Hung 1988.
2 For the tomb of Huo Qubing see Paludan 1991, pp. 15–27.
3 For a discussion on the use of stone see Paludan 1991, pp. 29–31.
4 For a note on the standpoint of the viewer see Paludan 1991, figs 32, 33.

Neolithic Sites of Religious Significance

Lei Congyun

It is only by looking carefully at the archaeological remains of neolithic China that we can attempt to make tentative suggestions about the early beliefs of peoples which may or may not have had relevance for the later religious concepts of a more unified Chinese culture. The remains described here are from some of the most spectacular neolithic sites excavated in the last two decades, principally in north-eastern and south-eastern China. From them we can gain an impression of the ritual and religious practices, and hence some of the beliefs, of the peoples of these areas (fig. 1).

The first traces of religious beliefs

In China the first hints of some form of religious beliefs are to be found at Zhoukoudian, near Beijing, in the burial places of the Upper Cave Man, more commonly referred to as Beijing or Peking Man (*Sinanthropus pekinensis*), dating from about 16,000 BC.[1] Archaeological finds suggest that the deceased were buried in close proximity to the living, and a finely ground reddish mineral powder was scattered over the body. The fact that jewellery and objects of everyday use were placed by the sides of the deceased indicates that these prehistoric people already believed in the continuation of life after death: a person had to be equipped in death with those items that had been essential in life.

Archaeologists argue that around 9000 BC, after the last Ice Age, prehistoric man became sedentary, began the cultivation of fields and developed new forms of social, cultural and religious life. A further, more fundamental change in agricultural practices is thought to have occurred around 6000 BC in present-day Liaoning province, in the cradle of the Daling and Liao rivers. Here, at Chahai, an area of more than 3000 square metres was excavated to reveal the remains of a settlement thought to date from about 5000 BC. The foundations of twenty buildings, evenly distributed over the area, were uncovered. Also found were an adze and, in one place, a group of more than ten jade objects. These

included split jade rings, of the type later used as ear ornaments, and grooved implements used perhaps for eating.[2] From these finds we may infer that jade and other translucent coloured stones were already held in high esteem by a neolithic people known (after the area) as the Chahai. The site also revealed two ceramic sherds with simple decoration of a creature which may be the earliest representation of a Chinese dragon.

A little further west, in the eastern part of Inner Mongolia, at Xinglongwa near Aohanqi, another discovery dating from about 6000 to 5000 BC was made. Near the remains of a settlement, a stone carving of a kneeling human figure, with round open eyes and arms folded across the chest, was brought to light.[3] Because the figure was on a pedestal it has been interpreted by some as a deity. Not far away, a comparable stone figure was discovered at the centre of a neolithic dwelling at Baiyinchanghan in Linxi county.[4] The first of these two figures is rather crudely carved, but the second, a standing female, is well formed with distinctly projecting breasts. It was found half-buried in the middle of the room, not

Fig. 1 *View of Niuheliang, Liaoning province.*

far from the fireplace, with its head turned to face the entrance. The figure has been considered by some to be a goddess of the hearth, provider of food and warmth.[5]

Later figures that may have had some religious significance are ceramic. The earliest thin-walled ceramic vessels belong to the Zhaobaogou culture (*c.* 4500–4000 BC). They were made of clay mixed with sand, or of fine striated clay. Dating from this time is a ceramic head, 5.1 cm in height, with half-closed eyes and clearly modelled features, which was found in the foundations of a house at Zhaobaogou near Aohanqi.[6] Ceramic figures have also been found in a number of the northern Chinese provinces, and they may have had some religious function.

Ceramic vessels, which may have been for ritual or sacrificial purposes, were unearthed at Xiaoshan, another Zhaobaogou site.[7] One of these is decorated in outline with three imaginary creatures: each has a different head, in the form of a stag, a pig and a bird, and all three have plumes or winged bodies (fig. 2).[8] Although it seems rather far-fetched to suggest that these creatures were in any way related to the much later beasts of the four directions (nos 82, 96), they do bear some similarity to them.

However, it is not only the far north of China that has yielded discoveries hinting at early religious beliefs. In the south-east, along the Yangzi River, a number of sites also indicate early religious practices. Ceramic jar coffins that presumably once held the bones of the dead, and of children in particular, have been found near Yuyao in Zhejiang province. These belong to the Hemudu culture (*c.* 5000–4500 BC), in the region south of Hangzhou Bay. They are similar to the somewhat

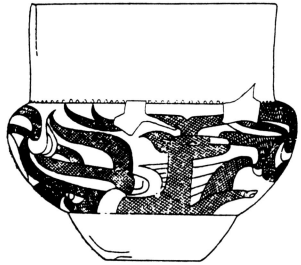

Fig. 2 *Vessel with zoomorphic decoration. Neolithic period, Zhaobaogou culture, c. 4500–4000 BC. After Eggebrecht 1994, fig. 26.*

later jar coffin illustrated in the catalogue (no. 9). What is believed to be the earliest sacrificial platform in southern China was also discovered at Hemudu. Built of reddish burnt earth, it is about 70 cm high and covers an area of about two square metres. In the second culture stratum of Hemudu the clay head of a figure, about 4 cm in height, was unearthed, and in the third stratum a complete clay figure.[9] These may have had some religious significance.

Over the course of the following millennium (4000–3000 BC) great progress was made among the agricultural communities of the Liao, Yellow and Yangzi rivers. The population expanded, accompanied by a certain degree of cultural interaction between the three areas, and new manual skills were developed. The innovations of the period have been grouped under five main headings by the archaeologist Su Bingqi. First, the smelting of metals began, which in due course would make possible production of bronze vessels; second, a fast rotating potter's wheel stimulated an increase in the number of vessels and permitted the manufacture of fine black eggshell ware; third, production of silk began; fourth, jade working and the making of lacquer objects reached new levels; and, finally, progress was made in the field of architecture.

Su Bingqi also sees great religious changes taking place during the fourth millennium BC. He believes that the altars, temples and grave tumuli of the north-eastern Hongshan culture and the large ritual buildings of the later Yangshao culture near Dadiwan in Gansu province point to the early establishment of religious practices and ceremonies, probably conducted by special priests who had been chosen by laymen. By about 3500 BC, however, he imagines that there was an organised body of professional priests. Also dating from this time are the first oracle bones (found near Lingtaiqiao in Gansu province), clay vessels marked with graphs of the Dawenkou culture, and altars in the burial grounds of the Liangzhu culture in Zhejiang province.[10]

The Hongshan culture and its religious sites

Our knowledge of the Hongshan culture (*c.* 3500–2500 BC of north-east China has been substantially increased by the excavation of sites in Liaoning province. The first of these to be discovered, in May 1979, was at Dongshanzui in Kezuo district. Here a rectangular stone structure, flanked on all sides by stone walls, was unearthed. At the centre was a round altar and there were also three round mounds of stone. All the foundations of the buildings were of heaped-up stones. In the area of the rectangular structure were found some small

Fig. 3 *Face from a life-size statue from the temple structure at Niuheliang, Liaoning province. Hongshan culture, c. 3500 BC. Height 22.5 cm; width 16.5 cm. After* Wenwu *1986.8, colour pl. 1.*

clay figurines of women, possibly pregnant women (no. 10), some fragments of larger figures and some articles of jade, including carved animals.[11]

Then, in October 1983, after many years' searching, archaeologists discovered at Niuheliang in Lingyuan-Jianping the foundations of a structure that they termed the Temple of a Goddess. In the initial stages of digging, a layer of reddish burnt earth yielded fragments of a clay figure (fig. 3). The removal of a subsequent layer of reddish burnt particles revealed the outline of a temple complex: along a north–south axis lay two buildings, the larger, northern one consisting of various smaller rooms (fig. 4). Near this building were recovered painted ceramic figures, clay vessels, a mask and architectural fragments. Nearby on a hilltop the archaeologists also discovered, under tumuli, four stone-lined graves covered by stone slabs (fig. 5). These graves contained various items of jade, such as hoops and rings, cloud-shaped objects, pig-dragons and *bi* discs.[12]

That these complexes at Dongshanzui and Niuheliang served some kind of tribal or religious purpose seems beyond doubt. They are of sufficient magnitude too to suggest that the roots of northern Chinese civilisation are to be found here.[13] Now that the sites and the material found there have been evaluated scientifically and the findings published, it is possible to propose a few theories.[14]

The form of the altar at Dongshanzui and of the

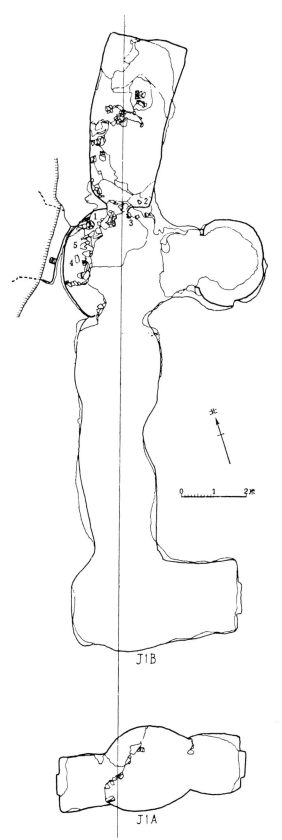

Fig. 4 *Plan of the ritual site at Niuheliang, Liaoning province. After* Wenwu *1986.8, p. 2, fig. 2.*

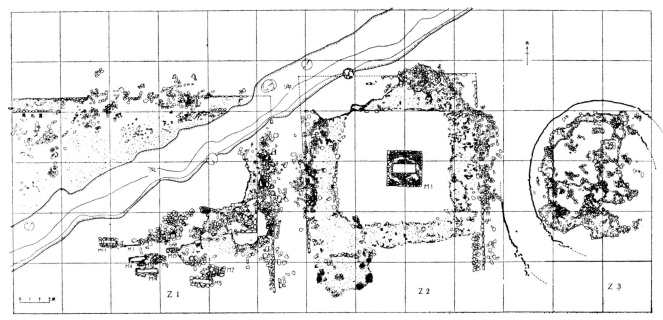

Fig. 5 *Plan of stone grave mound at Niuheliang* II, *Liaoning province. After* Wenwu *1986.8, p. 8, fig. 9.*

temple and graves at Niuheliang appear to be representative of traditional Chinese sacrificial sites, altars and temples. The architectural remains at Dongshanzui allow us to reconstruct an altar area with two main characteristics. In the first place, the various buildings seem to be grouped about a central altar. The complete complex of central and lateral buildings is aligned symmetrically along a central north–south axis. Along this north–south axis, rectangular and circular architectural forms face each other. This arrangement of buildings may foreshadow some Chinese principles concerning the distribution of buildings. The second point of interest about the structures at Dongshanzui is that they are all built of stone, a material that may have been chosen for a religious structure in order to mark its importance and make it more permanent. The complex at Dongshanzui has been compared by some scholars to the Temple of Heaven in Beijing: 'The southern end of the complex with its round altar may be compared with the round altar at the southern end of the Temple of Heaven; and the rectangular area to the north of the complex may be compared with the original Qinian Temple [one of the buildings at the Temple of Heaven] which was a large rectangular hall.'[15]

The foundations of the religious complex at Niuheliang also seem to presage later Chinese architectural principles of layout. The complex may even be the oldest of its kind, composed of principal halls aligned along a central axis, with smaller secondary buildings arranged symmetrically about this axis. At Niuheliang the buildings appear to have been constructed not of

stone but of clay mixed with plant fibres, the surfaces smoothed and some parts painted in colour. The grave tumuli, which were either round or angular and formed by heaped stones, contained stone coffins of varying sizes. The discovery of fragments of one or more large clay figures in the temple area suggests that the statue of a deity may have been worshipped in the main hall.

If indeed this building with its clay statues was employed for religious rituals, then it is likely that the Hongshan peoples practised some form of intercession whereby priests were responsible for communication with spirits and deities. Ancient Chinese literature abounds with descriptions of intercession and the role of priests, and such practices can still be observed amongst some groups in northern China and Korea. For example, among the Ewenke people of Heilongjiang province, such priests or shamans carry out sacrifices for members of the tribe, ward off evil spirits, heal people and administer funeral rites. The neolithic Hongshan peoples may well have had similar priestly roles, but we have only their material remains from which to propose such theories. The clay figurines (no. 10) and jade pig-dragons (Introduction, fig. 2) may have been objects of worship within some form of religion.[16] The clay figures may even suggest an early form of ancestor worship.

There is a school of thought that considers the Hongshan culture to be the cradle of Chinese civilisation and the point of interaction between early civilisations of northern central China. Neolithic period ceramics from the two regions already display designs of dragons and flowers, so prevalent in later Chinese ceramics.[17] Traces of bronze casting discovered in a Hongshan period settlement may be the earliest indications so far of bronze casting in China, and the remains of a settlement, covering an area of almost 500 square metres, to the west of Chifeng Xiaohe in Inner Mongolia, point to the possible origins of organised townships.

The Liangzhu culture and its religious sites

In parallel to the two Hongshan sites of Dongshanzui and Niuheliang, the two sites that best represent the religious beliefs of south-east China in the neolithic period are Fanshan and Yaoshan, both dating from the Liangzhu period (c. 3500–2500 BC). Fanshan and Yaoshan are in Yuhang county, about 30 km north-west of Hangzhou in the coastal province of Zhejiang. They form part of a huge prehistoric settlement covering about 80 square km.[18] The sites are similar, each with a sacrificial altar and a burial ground, probably for people of high rank.

Fanshan lies on a man-made earth mound of almost 3000 square metres and at a height today of about 4

metres. Initial digging revealed no traces of neolithic settlement, but subsequent removal of a layer of compacted earth brought to light eleven large earth pit graves, carefully aligned in two rows, and, nearby, a man-made earth platform.

At Yaoshan the earth platform is in a better state of preservation. Rectangular in plan, it is divided into three zones: at the centre is a raised platform of reddish soil; the intermediate zone is of greyish soil and is clearly demarcated from the outer zone, which slopes towards the area of the altar, with gravel laid over yellowish brown mixed earth. The square sacrificial area is 20 metres long on each side and covers an area of 400 square metres. In the southern half of this altar area were eleven graves (fig. 6), aligned east to west.

The sizes of the graves at Yaoshan, and the quantity of grave goods in each, vary. As the majority of the grave goods are of jade, these must have been the graves of high-ranking people, or possibly shamans. It has been suggested that the presence of ritual jade tubes (*cong*), as well as axes of stone and jade, in the graves to the south indicate that these were male burials, whereas the graves to the north may have been for females. That

Fig. 6 *Aerial view of Yaoshan, Yuhang county, Zhejiang province. After* Wenwu *1988.1, colour pl. 2.2.*

the altar area had been reserved for the separate burial of male and female members of the élite suggests that they formed an identifiable social group.[19]

The similarities between the sites of Fanshan and Yaoshan allow us to make certain suggestions about Liangzhu beliefs. It appears that the sites chosen for the sacrificial altars were on naturally high ground, which was then further raised by labour, perhaps to make the altar closer to heaven. If we are to believe later written sources on Chinese cosmology, the altars themselves may have been made four-sided. That these altars and graves were set apart from domestic habitation is indicated by the absence of any remains of human settlement in the vicinity.

Even the graves at Fanshan and Yaoshan are remarkably similar. At both sites they form part of the altar area and lie in two rows. The graves closest to the altar centre are the largest. Each grave consists of an earth pit with a specially prepared floor, on which was placed a wooden coffin. The larger pits had both an outer and an inner coffin. The heads of the deceased all faced south.

What is most astounding about these graves is the sheer quantity and combination of grave goods distributed over the floor of each pit. Over 90 per cent of these grave goods were of jade: at Fanshan, of the 1200 grave goods, 1100 were of jade; at Yaoshan the 707 items recovered included 635 jades. The remaining objects consisted of ceramics, stone implements and lacquerware with turquoise inlay.

Among the jades were large numbers of tubes or *cong* (no. 16), discs or *bi* (no. 17) and plaques (nos 18, 19). Many of these are characterised by the relief or incised decoration of a creature composed of human and monster elements (no. 16, fig. 16.1). This has been interpreted by some as representing a deity worshipped by the Liangzhu population, but at present we have no means of ascertaining this. According to later historical sources as well as ethnological research, shamans wore elaborate garments and headdresses when conducting rituals or sacrifices, and communicated with spirits and deities with the aid of a magical rod. The fact that the crown-shaped jade plaque and the three-pronged jade plaque – both of which bear the man and monster decoration – were found as unique specimens close to the head of the cadaver, flanked by awl-shaped jades, has given rise to speculation that these objects formed part of some special ritual headgear, worn by the tomb occupant. Such a splendid headdress would have been worthy of a shaman.

Speculation about the existence of shamans among the Liangzhu population has been further fuelled by the presence in each of the large graves at Fanshan and Yaoshan of one jade battle axe (*yue*), which, from its position near the hand of the deceased and from its decoration, has been interpreted as a magical rod similar to that used by present-day shamans in north-east Asia. One of these axes, originally about 70 cm in length, had a wooden handle, no longer extant, inlaid with fragments of jade. Moreover, the top and bottom ends of the handle were protected by jade caps, and two small *cong* hung from the handle.

The man and monster motif has been seen as the predecessor of the *taotie* masks of Shang period decoration. If the two motifs are in some way related to the religious beliefs of both the Liangzhu population and the Shang people, then it is possible that some aspects of Shang religious practices – as distinct from beliefs – originated in Liangzhu. However, it must be pointed out that while the Shang may indeed have borrowed the Liangzhu motifs, they may well have attributed to them their own beliefs.

The Hongshan and Liangzhu cultures are only two of the many highly complex neolithic societies of ancient China. They were succeeded by equally diverse bronze-using societies, represented in the catalogue by the finds from Sanxingdui in Sichuan province (nos 22–35) and by some of the contents of the tomb of the great Shang queen Fu Hao (nos 39–50).

1 Radiocarbon analysis dates Peking man to 18,865 ± 420 years old.
2 Su Bingqi 1994, p. 127. For a discussion in English of the cultures of the north-east see Nelson 1995.
3 Zhang Nairen 1989.
4 Guo Zhizhong 1991.
5 *Liaohai wenwu xuekan* 1993.1, pp. 49–57.
6 *Kaogu* 1988.1, pp. 1–11.
7 *Kaogu* 1987.6, pp. 507–18.
8 Su Bingqi 1994; *Liaohai wenwu xuekan* 1993.1, pp. 49–57.
9 *Kaogu xuebao* 1978.1, pp. 39–94.
10 Su Bingqi 1994.
11 *Wenwu* 1984.11, pp. 1–12.
12 *Wenwu* 1986.8, pp. 1–17.
13 *Liaohai wenwu xuekan* 1989.1, pp. 428–31.
14 *Liaohai wenwu xuekan* 1993.1, pp. 49–57; Zhang Xiying 1994; *Wenwu* 1986.8, pp. 1–17.
15 Su Bingqi 1994.
16 *Wenwu* 1986.8, pp. 1–17.
17 Su Bingqi 1994.
18 *Wenwu* 1988.1, pp. 1–31; pp. 32–51.
19 Su Bingqi 1994.

THE CHINESE JADE CULTURE

Yang Yang

Jade is found and used in each of the five continents of the world. Quite why its use should have been developed in particular by peoples whose lands border on the Pacific Ocean – the Chinese, the Maya of Central America and the Maori of New Zealand – remains a mystery. Yet, while the Maya made tools, figures and animals of jade, and the Maori made tools and ritual figures from predominantly green jade-like stones, among them jasper, the Chinese not only used jade to make similar utilitarian and ritual objects, but they treated jade with such veneration in many aspects of life that it assumed a position of inestimable importance in Chinese culture. In no other part of the world has such a jade culture developed.

Jade has always been regarded as extremely precious by the Chinese. The principal mineral named by the Chinese as jade, or *yu*, is nephrite, a tough translucent stone that is often white, grey-green or green in colour. Early written evidence in inscriptions on bronze vessels of the Western Zhou period (*c.* 1050–771 BC) points to its high value: the Chinese character for 'precious', *bao*, signifies a treasury in which jade as well as shell currency is stored (寶). And even today the Chinese have a saying: 'There is a price for gold, but jade is priceless' (*jin you jia, yu wu jia*). Because it has to be quarried from deep in the crust of the earth, jade is considered by the Chinese to be the 'essence of the mountains' (*shanyue zhi jingying*), and as such to have the power to act as an intermediary between earthly and spiritual spheres. Moreover, the intense beauty of the stone has made it synonymous with purity and beauty, and has given rise to numerous descriptive phrases that include the word jade: a jade heart means a pure heart, or a heart of gold, and a jade countenance is the attribute of a beautiful woman. The graph for jade used in the Chinese writing system is one of over two hundred radicals under which all Chinese characters can be classified. The majority of the five hundred or so characters incorporating the jade radical, such as the characters for many of the precious stones and for ruler and rank, have overtones of value, wealth, beauty or power. As well as being incorporated in characters and phrases, the term occurs in a great number of proverbs: 'To produce jade items with stones of some other mountain' means to try to perfect oneself through external powers; 'to burn jade and stone to ash' means to destroy both good and bad; 'better to be broken as jade than survive intact as brick' means that it is better to die honest than shamefully corrupted; and 'to have precious jades by the heart and in the hand' describes a noble man.

Why has jade always held a position of fascination for the Chinese? How and when did this Chinese jade culture develop?

What is the Chinese jade culture?

The Chinese jade culture can be described as embracing not only the development of jade working itself and the resulting jade objects, but also the metaphorical values ascribed to jade, and the ways in which the use of jade objects reflect different aspects and periods of Chinese civilisation. Jade and objects made from it have always been admired for their beauty and enduring quality. In the *Shuowen jiezi*, the earliest Chinese dictionary, compiled by Xu Shen in the first century AD, jade is defined as follows: 'Jade is beauty in stone (*shi zhi mei*) with five virtues: its warm glow stands for humanity; its purity for moral integrity; its pleasant sound for wisdom; its hardness for justice; and its permanence for perseverance and bravery.' This definition draws heavily on the physical and moral attributes ascribed to jade in a description attributed to Confucius, dating from some centuries earlier. Both descriptions point to the two most important characteristics of jade: its beauty, and the ways in which its beauty have become synonymous with human virtue. These two concepts are central to our understanding of the development of the Chinese jade culture.

The origins of the Chinese jade culture

There are jade objects dating from the end of the palaeolithic period, but it was not until the neolithic period (*c.* 6000–1700 BC) that the techniques of jade working were developed to produce objects that were probably associated with some sort of ritual ceremonies: jade tools and weapons, ornaments, and items whose uses we cannot fathom. Different objects were made by different peoples, although a certain degree of borrowing occurred. A multitude of local cultures developed within six main cultural areas: in northern China, to the north and south of the Yan Mountains, centred on a stretch of the much later Great Wall; in eastern China, mainly in Shandong province; in the central Chinese provinces of Shaanxi, southern Shanxi and western Henan; in the south-east around Lake Tai in Jiangsu province; in the south-west in Sichuan province and around Lake Dongting in Hunan province; and in southern China along an axis from Lake Poyang in northern Jiangxi province to the Pearl River in Guangdong province.

Since the 1950s more than a hundred neolithic sites have been excavated in these six main areas, and even further afield in the north-eastern province of Liaoning and the north-western areas of Xinjiang, Gansu, Ningxia, Qinghai and Tibet. The fact that items of jade have been unearthed in so many parts of the Chinese landmass points to the importance of jade and to the neolithic beginnings of the jade culture. The jade culture owes its development to two phenomena in ancient China: the technical abilities to quarry and to work the stone, and the early division of labour within groups or societies. The importance of jade in the neolithic period has caused some later writers to insert a 'jade age' between the Stone and the Bronze Age, but as jade working was not universal throughout the Chinese landmass, this term is inappropriate. The jade culture should be seen rather as developing in specific areas, each with its own religious beliefs and practices. These areas were predominantly on the east coast, stretching from the north-eastern province of Liaoning to the south-eastern province of Guangdong. Within this crescent-shaped 'jade belt' we can look in particular at the Hongshan culture of the north-east and the Liangzhu culture of the south-east, of which the latter is represented in the catalogue (nos 16–20). Jade was used at many intervening sites between these two areas (no. 21).

Jades of the Hongshan culture (*c.* 3500–2500 BC) have been unearthed in the north of Liaoning province, at a large ceremonial site near Niuheliang. Excavations at this site revealed platforms of stone, a shrine with mud-brick images of women, and complex burials. Fifteen small graves to the south of grave mound number one yielded a huge variety of jades: objects in the form of hooked clouds (fig. 1), in the form of dragons with heads reminiscent of pigs (the so-called pig-dragons), hoops and rings, rod-shaped jades, and plaques with

Fig. 1 *Jade pendant in the form of a cloud. Neolithic period, Hongshan culture, c. 3000 BC. After Beijing 1993b, pl. 40.*

double animal masks and three holes. Some graves contained as many as five jades, whereas others had none at all. The discovery of the pig-dragons (Introduction, fig. 2) caused the greatest excitement: here, to some scholars, lay the origin of the Chinese dragon, in the humble pig sacrificed in the hope of a rich harvest. If such a theory holds any truth then it points to an early society with some form of religious beliefs.

The deposits of jades in graves of the south-eastern Liangzhu culture (*c.* 3000–2000 BC) were even more prolific. The tomb M3, of a young man, for example, discovered in the late 1970s at Sidun in Wujin county, Jiangsu province, yielded more than a hundred jade objects (fig. 2). Both on top of and beneath the skeleton lay twenty-four jade discs (*bi*) and all around the body were thirty-three jade tubes (*cong*). Some of these jades showed traces of fire, and, on the basis of the arrangement of the remains of the bones of the body, it is believed that the body had been burned before the positioning of the ritual jades.

Further graves of the Liangzhu culture, at Fanshan and Yaoshan in Yuhang county, Zhejiang province, have produced even larger numbers of jades, although the quantity varies from tomb to tomb. Some small tombs contained fewer than ten jades, whereas the large tomb M14 at Fanshan held 260 jades. In some of the larger graves there were several tens of *bi* discs, sometimes placed next to each other, sometimes piled one on top of the other, but usually in the area of the legs of the deceased. Other jade objects in the graves included plaques, axes, semicircular jades, pendants, hoops, jades in the shapes of crowns, awls and rods, three-pronged jades, amulets, rings, belt hooks, beads, tubules and small carvings of birds, cicadas, turtles and fish (no. 20).

But by far the most frequently occurring type of jade

Fig. 2 *Tomb M3 at Sidun in Jiangsu province, showing the arrangement of the jades. Neolithic period, Liangzhu culture, c. 2500 BC. After Zhejiang 1990, pl. 4.*

was the ritual tube, *cong* (no. 16), whose use and meaning are as yet unknown, despite the many opinions on the subject. Is the *cong* a symbol of the vulva and hence Mother Earth, or is it a phallus and thus an embodiment of the ancestors of the tomb occupant? Or does it represent a part of the weaving loom, or an arm decoration? We do not know, but there is general consensus on its ritual properties. All Liangzhu *cong* are decorated with an incised or relief motif of a human figure or an animal mask, or a combination of the two, and some also bear designs of birds and geometric cloud patterns (fig. 16.1). But it is the motif of the human figure and animal mask that distinguishes the Liangzhu *cong* from those of other neolithic cultures. This motif suggests some supernatural being and hence some associated religious belief or ritual ceremony. It has even been suggested that the deceased with whom a particular jade was buried had been clothed in a manner similar to that of the human figure in the motif.

The development of the jade culture in the Erlitou, Shang and Western Zhou periods

The coming of the Bronze Age in China was to bring about great changes in the jade culture. Bronze tools, which were first used by the Erlitou culture from about 1700 to 1600 BC in the central province of Henan, gave rise to more sophisticated production techniques for jade. Bronze fretsaws, such as those excavated from the Erlitou layer at Yanshi in Henan, would have been used with abrasive sands and in conjunction with stone drills and cutting discs to reduce the effort and time needed to make items of jade. The specialised production of jade and bronze was centred in large cities such as Yanshi, where high-quality goods could be made for the élite.

Before this period, jade production had predominated on the east coast, which makes the large quantity of high-quality jades produced by the central Erlitou culture a notable change. Ritual sceptres known by the later names of *gui, zhang* and *yue* have been found, as well as jade knives with as many as seven holes drilled in them, blades of the *ge* or halberd type, and handle-shaped objects.

The Erlitou culture was the predecessor of the first of the great dynasties, the Shang (*c.* 1500–1050 BC), which was centred first at present-day Zhengzhou and then at Anyang, both in Henan province. To the Shang, sacrificial rituals and burial ceremonies, in which both humans and animals were sacrificed, assumed great importance. By the time of Fu Hao, consort of the Shang king Wu Ding, who was buried about 1200 BC, the quantity of goods placed in tombs was astounding. Fu Hao was buried with nearly two thousand items of bronze, jade, bone, ivory, ceramic and shell, the jades representing about 750 of these (nos 48–50). This huge number of jades serves to illustrate the high esteem in which jade was held, especially at the royal court and amongst the élite. Their demands were assiduously catered for by the state. In 1915 the foundations of a building at Yinxu, near Anyang in Henan province, were excavated, revealing six hundred awl-shaped stone implements, over two hundred stone grinding heads and a number of jade objects. These are assumed to be the remnants of a jade workshop, possibly subject to bureaucratic control by the Shang court. Moreover, it was not just the élite who were buried with jade goods, as jades have also been discovered in tombs of lower-ranking members of society at Yinxu.

The Shang jades discovered at Yinxu fall into three main categories: ritual jades, objects of daily use and ornaments. Among the multitude of jades are the ancestors of the so-called ritual or ceremonial jades, which include *cong, bi, gui, zhang, huang* and *hu* and were described as the six 'ceremonial jades' in the *Zhou li*, a much later text, probably compiled towards the end of the Western Han period (see below). Other ritual or ceremonial jades include vessels of the *gui* type (no. 48), and weapons such as axes, spears and large knives. The everyday items, many of which show traces of use, include cups, plates, combs, ladles, spoons, earscoops and belt hooks, as well as musical instruments such as sounding stones (*qing*), some of which were decorated with paint or with engraved designs. Among the jade ornaments were semicircular arcs, bracelets, hairpins, beads and hangings, and figurines of men, birds, and wild and imaginary animals (no. 49).

There seem to have been certain customs or conventions for the placement of jade objects in burials at Yinxu. The jades in the shapes of sceptres or discs were found in the coffin chamber, either between the inner and the outer coffin or on the coffin lid. From the positions in which the ornamental jades were found on the deceased, we can begin to understand how such ornaments might have been worn in life. Other jades had been placed in the mouth or hands of the dead, including the blades, *zhang* (no. 34).

After the fall of the Shang dynasty, jade production declined somewhat under the new ruling dynasty, the Western Zhou (*c.* 1050–771 BC). It was not until the middle of the Western Zhou (*c.* 900 BC) that a new style of jades, characterised by lively surface decoration, made its appearance (nos 55–57).

Metropolitan Shang jades tend to be of whitish, yellowish or greenish tones. Mineralogical research suggests that the majority of the jade came from Hetian in the north-western territory of Xinjiang, although a small proportion seems to have come from Xiuyan in the north-eastern province of Liaoning and from Dali in the south-western province of Yunnan. It is possible that already by the Shang period there may have been a well trodden 'jade route' between Central Asian jade sources and the heart of China.

The Shang and Western Zhou periods saw the rise of a system of rites or rituals in which offerings were made to the gods, spirits and ancestors. As we have seen, many of the items associated with these rituals were made of jade, and, amongst jade objects, ceremonial jades made up the largest number of categories. By the time of the subsequent Eastern Zhou period, the jade types in use had changed once more.

The Eastern Zhou period

The collapse of the central Zhou state in 771 BC heralded a period of warfare and political unrest. Because the centre of Zhou power moved from the area of Xi'an to a new eastern capital near present-day Luoyang in northern Henan province, the period from 770 BC to 221 BC is named the Eastern Zhou. This period is often further subdivided into the Spring and Autumn period (770–475 BC) and the period of the Warring States (475–221 BC), when China was divided politically among more or less powerful royal courts. Against this background of political turmoil there emerged an atmosphere of intellectual activity which produced the first philosophical texts, and artistic creativity seems to have thrived.

Progress in jade carving had much to do with the technical innovations brought about by the use of iron tools with the abrasive sands essential for jade carving. Grinding heads and the speed at which they could be turned, as well as the use of corundum sand, which is even tougher than jade itself, contributed to the refinement of jade working and created a new era in the production of jade.

The political competition between the various states was probably a major incentive to devote time, energy and wealth to the production of luxury goods, and rulers were buried with some of the finest and most precious jades. These include specimens unearthed from the grave of the ruler and consort of the small state of Huang near Guangshan, in southern Henan province, as well as from the élite tombs of the state of Guo near Sanmenxia Shancunling, also in Henan province. Further specimens have been excavated from the royal tombs of the state of Zhongshan in Hebei province (see p. 155) and from the tomb of the Marquis Yi of Zeng near Suixian, Leigudun, in Hubei province (see p. 132). The feudal states seem to have competed to produce the best jades: jade ornaments were worn as a sign of rank by the élite, and certain jades were of supreme importance to their owners, who saw them as symbols of status. The *Shi ji*, written by the Han historian Sima Qian in the second to first century BC, recounts a famous story of diplomatic exchange: with an offer of fifteen towns in its own territory, the powerful state of Qin in the west attempted to gain possession of a *bi* disc, carved out of Hetian jade from Xinjiang, from the small eastern state of Zhao.

During this period of incessant struggle between the various states, some extraordinary individuals put forward widely different proposals for effective government. These proposals gave rise to conflicting philosophical schools, some of which also voiced opinions on the manufacture of jade objects. The philosopher Mo Zi, who was born at about the time of Confucius' death in the early fifth century BC, condemned jades as mere luxury goods belonging to a small élite. He regarded the production of such goods as a waste of labour because they contributed nothing to the common good. Another critic of jade objects was Han Feizi (*c.* 280–233 BC), who was an advocate of legalism, the need for laws as the basis of order in society. Han Feizi considered jades purely from a utilitarian standpoint: 'All potters' wares, even the simplest forms, may serve to pour wine, as long as they are watertight. Vessels of gold and jade, however costly they may be, are useless objects if they are not watertight, for who can do anything with them then?'

But philosophers' attitudes to jade were not all critical. In fact, the man generally regarded as the first and arguably the most influential of Chinese philosophers, Confucius (*c.* 551–479 BC), is said to have developed the metaphor in which human virtues are equated with and explained by the qualities of jade (see p. 230). The high esteem in which Confucius is said to have held both the material and the objects made of jade was to have a lasting effect on the development of the Chinese jade culture.

Even the Chinese theory of *yin* and *yang*, the opposing yet harmonising principles of nature, was to exert an influence on the social significance of jade. In the *Zhouyi (Book of Changes)*, compiled at some time in the third to first century BC on the basis of older texts, it is stated in the chapter on the eight oracle diagrams: 'The diagram *qian* stands for heaven, for the round, for the ruler, for the father, for gold, for jade.' This identification of jade with the male principle *yang* was basic to many later expressions of the association between jade and ruler.

The preoccupation of Eastern Zhou and Han texts with the qualities associated with jade and with the use of jades to display rank seems to have coincided with a change in the uses of jades. Most apparently, the ancient neolithic *cong* was used less, and blades were more limited in type. *Bi* discs, however, began to acquire new functions. The *Zhou li*, probably compiled in the Han dynasty, describes the use of jades as indicators of rank within the government: 'The *rui* [ceremonial] jades correspond with the ranks in the state. The king (*wang*) is entitled to *gui* [sceptres] jades of the *zhen* type; the highest ranking noble (*gong*) to *gui* jades of the *huan* type; the second in rank marquis (*hou*) to *gui* jades of the *xin* type; the third in rank earl (*bo*) to *gui* jades of the *gong* type; the fourth in rank viscount (*zi*) to *bi* [discs] jades of the *gu* type; and the fifth in rank baron (*nan*) to *bi* of the *pu* type.' These six ceremonial jades are distinguished

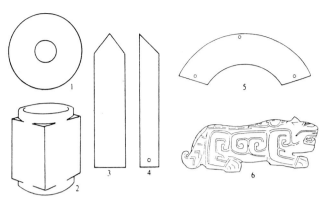

Fig. 3 *The six ritual jades: 1 bi, 2 cong, 3 gui, 4 zhang, 5 huang, 6 hu. After Xia Nai 1983, p. 129, fig. 1.*

from the six ritual jades used to serve heaven, earth and the four points of the compass: Heaven is venerated by the dark blue *bi* jade, earth by the brown *cong* jade, east by the dark green *gui*, south by the red *zhang*, west by the white *hu*, and north by the black *huang'* (fig. 3).

It is all too easy to accept the above descriptions as some sort of definitions of the functions and meanings of different types of jades. What they may be, however, is a later attempt by writers to codify ancient objects whose purposes were no longer known, in a way that made them comprehensible to their own and later generations. Considered in this light, the definition of the six ritual jades may have been composed to fit with Eastern Zhou concepts of the heaven as round (hence the notion of the *bi* disc representing sacrifices to heaven) and the earth as square. These suggestions, however, were undoubtedly made long after the neolithic period when these jade types had first been developed and used (*c.* 3500 BC). Indeed, by the time of the historic dynasties, the Shang and the Zhou, the ancient *cong* was little used and probably hardly understood at all.

The display of rank extended far beyond the six *rui* jades that were worn to indicate hierarchy at court or at meetings between dignitaries of the five upper ranks. For example, status could be indicated by jade ceremonial weapons such as axes (*yue* and *fu*), sceptres (*zhang*), by jade table utensils such as *gui* vessels or plates (*pan*), and by the large variety of ornamental jades that were sewn on garments or worn as jewellery or pendants.

This last category, the jade pendants (*quanpei*), demonstrates most clearly the extraordinarily complex types of jade worn by high officials and assistants. A set of ornamental jades (*peiyu*) consists of a multitude of individual pieces which were, by the late Western or early Eastern Zhou, thought to embody and reflect the moral values of their wearers. The earliest evidence of this is in the *Shi jing (The Book of Poetry)*, which was compiled around this time and which already points to the moral values attached to jade that were later to be classified by Confucius. The *Li ji*, one of the Confucian classics, explains this classification with reference to a conversation between Confucius and Zi Gong:

> Zi Gong turned to Confucius with the words, 'Permit me to ask why jade is esteemed so highly and alabaster is not. Is it because jade is so rare and alabaster found so much more readily?'
>
> To which Confucius replied, 'If the wise in ancient times did not think much of alabaster whereas jade meant so much to them, this has nothing to do with the availability or rarity of alabaster or jade. It is rather that the wise compared their virtue to jade: it stands for goodness (*ren*) because it is soft and smooth to the touch; it stands for righteousness (*yi*) as it hangs down from the body but does not injure it; it stands for decorum (*li*) as it appears to bow down when hanging down from the belt; it stands for music (*yue*) as it gives off clear and noble sounds which end abruptly; it stands for loyalty (*zhong*), as its glow neither veils imperfection nor is it veiled by imperfection; it stands for trust (*xin*), because its good inner qualities can be seen from the outside; it stands for heaven (*tian*) as it is like a *white* rainbow; it stands for earth (*di*) as it embodies the powers innate in mountains and rivers; it stands for virtue (*de*), as do the *gui* and *zhang* ritual jades employed at audiences; it stands for the path of virtue (*dao*) as there is no one on earth who does not esteem it. In *The Book of Poetry* it says, "I think of my lord, he is mild like jade". It is because of this that jade is esteemed so highly.'

According to the *Li ji*, the real value of jade lies not in its external beauty but in its inner virtues. The chapter on jade ornaments states: 'Jade ornament is an essential component of clothing. It should be left off only in cases of mourning. The noble man will never appear without jade ornament and his virtue is like his jade ornament.'

The same chapter stresses the importance of the tinkling sounds emitted by pendent jades. When a person moves while wearing jade, the sound of the jade should bring the person's behaviour into balance. Certain movements should cause the jades to make certain sounds that purify his thoughts. It was, therefore, important when assembling sets of pendent jades that the sound of each jade was tuned to follow a certain sequence, and that the sounds made a certain rhythm when the wearer walked at a measured pace. It was believed that a combination of ritual movements and the tinkling sounds of jade would ensure a clear frame of mind.

A person with a clear frame of mind would in turn be expected to act in a morally upright manner. The emphasis on moral perfection within society was clearly a Confucian concept which relied on order. The association of jade with human virtue and the hierarchical ranking of jade ornaments therefore fitted well with Confucian philosophy, and this interaction between objects and the beliefs of the society that used them was of paramount importance for the development of the jade culture. However, with the political upheavals and intellectual rivalry between the different schools of philosophy during the late Eastern Zhou, Confucian doctrines were not always to the fore, although Confucianism was eventually to triumph.

Qin was to emerge as the most powerful of all the states of the late Eastern Zhou period. By 221 BC King Zheng of Qin declared himself the ruler of China and changed his name to Shi Huangdi, the First Emperor. But the success of the dynasty was shortlived and by 206 BC a new dynasty, the Han, was founded by Liu Bang.

The climax of the Chinese jade culture

During the Han dynasty, the rise to prominence of Confucianism had a positive effect on China's developing jade culture. Acceptance of Confucian doctrines involved acceptance of Confucius' comments on jade and its metaphorical associations. Moreover, conditions under the mighty Western Han empire were ripe for the further development of the jade culture, in that ceremonies and extravagant sacrificial rituals were numerous and new burial customs had been adopted. A wide variety of jade objects were produced: ritual jades, imaginary animals possibly to ward off evil powers (fig. 4), ornamental jades, everyday jades and burial jades. It is these burial jades that are perhaps the most fascinating as, so far, over 10,000 have been recovered from Han period tombs. Tombs containing such burial jades are usually the burials of feudal rulers or their relatives: for example, the tomb of the King of Nan Yue in Guangzhou in Guangdong province; the tombs of Prince Qing of Zhongshan, otherwise known as Liu Sheng, and his consort (no. 81), and of the princes Huai, Jian and Mu of Zhongshan in Hebei province; the tombs of Prince Guangyang and his consort at Dabaotai near Beijing; the tomb of the Prince of Chu near Xuzhou in Jiangsu province; and the tomb of the Prince of Liang in Shangqiu in Henan province.

Fig. 4 *Jade carving of an imaginary winged animal. From Baoji in Shaanxi province. Eastern Han period (AD 25–220). After Beijing 1992b, pl. 78.*

Although the practice of burying jade objects with the deceased had existed since the neolithic period, the sheer quantity of jades buried with the élite of the Han period points to the growing importance of the custom. One of the distinguishing features of the Han burial jades is the emphasis on jades intended to protect the deceased and perhaps confer immortality. These protective jades were to culminate in the magnificent jade suits made to cover the body completely and the nine jade plugs that were inserted into the body's orifices. One of the finest examples of a jade burial suit is included in the catalogue (no. 81). It covered the body of Prince Liu Sheng, who was buried with his consort Dou Wan in a tomb hewn deep into the rock near Mancheng in Hebei province. He also had the nine jade plugs, as well as a semicircular disc of the *huang* type in each hand. The sheer cost of making such suits of jade meant that they were reserved for individuals of the highest rank. These suits may in fact have their origins in the shrouds with jades attached to them that were used from at least the middle Western Zhou. The jade plaques from such a shroud, dating from the Warring States period of the Eastern Zhou, are also included in the catalogue (no. 72).

The Western Han period (206 BC–AD 9) can be regarded as a climax of China's long jade culture. After the collapse of the Eastern Han dynasty in AD 220, China was once again to undergo a long period of disunity until the Sui reunification of 581. Under the Three Kingdoms (AD 221–80) Confucianism experienced a gradual decline, and in the subsequent Jin dynasty Confucianism had to hold its own against the enthusiasm generated by the steady import of Buddhism from India and Central Asia. The temporary obscuring of the Confucian tradition did not, however, bring an end to the jade culture. With the development of religious Daoism from the second century AD, jade began to satisfy new demands. Another repertoire of jade objects made its appearance in response to Daoist beliefs, including new types of vessels and magic implements. But these are topics beyond the scope of the present catalogue.

THE SACRIFICIAL PITS
AT SANXINGDUI

Zhao Dianzeng

The finds from Sanxingdui are perhaps the most remarkable to have come out of China in recent years. Although the site, near Guanghan in China's south-western Sichuan province, had previously been earmarked as important, it was not until 1986 that two pits filled with magnificent objects of bronze, jade and gold were unearthed.[1] There is no doubt that these were sacrificial pits.

The nature of these pits is therefore as interesting as their contents. Here is evidence of a people in a remote area who practised rituals that we cannot yet fathom, and who made offerings, although we do not know to whom or on behalf of what power. We know from later texts that sacrifice was one of the most important duties of the later Chinese states, and this is confirmed for the Shang and Zhou periods by inscriptions on oracle bones and bronze vessels which mention such acts and rites. Any act of sacrifice is an attempt to communicate and mediate with deities, to seek appeasement or offer gratitude. The finds from Sanxingdui give us an insight into what was sacrificed. Remaining unanswered are how such sacrifices were made, what kinds of ritual ceremonies were conducted and what the beliefs were of the people involved in such forms of worship.

The archaeological site of Sanxingdui and its significance

For over sixty years, the area around Sanxingdui has been recognised by Chinese archaeologists as a potential site for archaeological investigation. Since the early 1980s the site has been excavated scientifically by the Institute of Archaeology of Sichuan Province and other organisations, and the resulting finds have been remarkable. These finds show not only that Sanxingdui must have been the centre of an independent local culture, with a large city, but that there was also a hitherto unknown state established there.

The site of Sanxingdui lies about 40 km north of Chengdu, the provincial capital of Sichuan province,

and about 10 km west of the county town of Guanghan. The site, which covers a total area of about 17 square km, is bounded to the north by the Yazi River and crossed by the Mamu River (fig. 1). Among over thirty find sites, the most important are Sanxingdui itself in the south, Shizinao in the east, Hengliangzi in the west and Dongshengsi even further west. All these sites appear to have shared a common early culture.

A combination of stylistic and radiocarbon analysis of the numerous finds enables us to date the site and its culture to the period between about 2800 and 1000 BC. The four phases of its development from a neolithic society to an early state can be equated with the periods of the Longshan culture on the Yellow River, and then the Erlitou, the early Shang culture at Erligang, and the later Shang culture at Yinxu, near the present-day town of Anyang. Although there is evidence that an independent local culture extended well across Sichuan province, the name Sanxingdui is here applied to this complete culture, as the site at Sanxingdui seems to have been at its centre.

Excavations begun in 1984 on high earth mounds to the south, east and west of Sanxingdui indicated that these were the man-made boundaries of a town. Further excavations in 1989 confirmed that parts of the mound had been supported by man-made piles and that there had been a ditch on the outside of these mounds. Gaps in the mounds, with holes for foundation posts and longitudinal foundation ditches, may well indicate town gates. The mounds or walls are, however, by no means complete, and the absence of a mound to the north suggests either that the Yazi River washed it away or that the river itself served as the northern boundary of the town. The methods of construction and the dimensions of the mounds vary considerably (the 1100-m stretch of the eastern mound is 4 m high, 40 m wide at the base and 20 m at the top, whereas the remaining 180 m of the southern mound is 6 m high with a base width also of 40 m), but this is not uncommon for early town enclosures. There is certainly no doubt that the

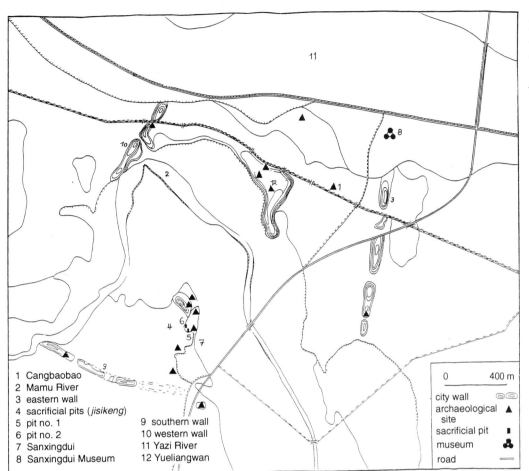

11

10
2
12
1
3
8
4 6
5 7
9

1 Cangbaobao
2 Mamu River
3 eastern wall
4 sacrificial pits (*jisikeng*)
5 pit no. 1
6 pit no. 2
7 Sanxingdui
8 Sanxingdui Museum

9 southern wall
10 western wall
11 Yazi River
12 Yueliangwan

0   400 m

city wall
archaeological site
sacrificial pit
museum
road

mounds were built for the fortification of a town.

Analysis of the earth layers of these mounds has shown that they were begun during the second phase of the development of Sanxingdui, that is, around the time of the Erlitou period (*c.* 1700–1500 BC) in Henan, and that they protected a town of 2.6 square km until it was abandoned about 1000 BC. In addition to having obvious boundaries, the city seems to have been laid out around a central, elevated north–south axis, along which the most important finds have been made, at Zhenwugong and Xiquankan in the north, Yueliangwan in the centre and Sanxingdui to the south. Such a layout can be compared with that of the roughly contemporaneous Shang metropolis of Erligang near Zhengzhou in Henan province, a comparison which highlights the importance of Sanxingdui during this flourishing period of its history in the early second millennium BC.

Excavations both inside and outside the city at Sanxingdui have revealed the foundations of numerous buildings, many of them in layers, one on top of the other. The buildings took various shapes – round, angular, rectangular – and seem to have been constructed of interlocking wooden beams with clay infill. The largest building covered an area of 200 square metres and had several rooms. This was obviously no ordinary residential building but must have served as a meeting place. Most of the buildings date from the second and third phases of Sanxingdui, that is, from approximately 2000 to 1400 BC.

Within the town itself, closely packed buildings indicate a high population density in a flourishing metropolis. The remains of craftsmen's workshops and kilns suggest the production of items requiring specialisation, and indeed the numerous finds of jade, stone, bronze and gold substantiate this view. Such costly objects must have far exceeded the needs of ordinary people in their everyday lives. But the presence of these objects, as well as of the sets of bronze and jade implements, which were obviously for ritual use, make it almost certain that Sanxingdui was more than just an ordinary city: it may have been a ritual centre, possibly even a city of pilgrimage.

Objects such as a rod covered with sheet gold (fig. 8) and the many ritual implements may even point to a centre of royal, as well as religious, power. Chinese archaeologists are now of the firm opinion that Sanxingdui was the centre of an ancient state, possibly named Shu, which had developed from a loose association of local tribes.

The finds themselves and the way many of them were buried in sacrificial pits are the most remarkable of the discoveries at Sanxingdui.

The form and contents of the sacrificial pits

The most spectacular of the finds from Sanxingdui were discovered in a number of rectangular pits. Finds of some jade and stone implements in 1929 first indicated that Sanxingdui might be an interesting site. A further six sites of valuable offerings were discovered over the following decades, both inside and outside the town. These sites have yielded several thousand items of gold, bronze, jade and stone, many of them quite unlike anything hitherto discovered in China. Among them is a life-size human figure in bronze (no. 22), some bronze figurines (no. 30), bronze human-like heads (nos 23, 24), some of them partly coated in gold, strange masks (fig. 5) and trees of bronze (fig. 6), a gold rod (fig. 8), bronze ritual vessels of the *lei* and *zun* types (nos 27, 28), ritual weapons such as halberds and spears, and ritual jades (nos 33–35). The unusual nature of many of these objects suggests a culture with a great deal of independence and individuality.

Fig. 2 *Pit 1 at Sanxingdui.*

Most of the richly filled sacrificial pits lie along the raised central north–south axis of the town (fig. 1). Four pits have been scientifically excavated: pits 1 and 2 on the south side of the town (excavated in 1986); the pit known as Yueliangwan in the town centre, which yielded stone and jade artefacts (discovered in 1929 and published in 1933); and the pit known as Cangbaobao at Zhenwucun, to the east of the central axis (excavated in 1988). Other sites within the town have yielded stone and jade objects: these include a site at the southern end of the eastern mound near Shizinao (excavated in 1987), a pit near Yueliangwan (excavated in 1964), and another at Suozitian (excavated in 1974). As all of these sites had at some time in the past been disturbed, their shape is no longer clearly visible. However, comparison of the jades from them with those from documented pits suggests that all were buried in pits of the same type. The form of the pits can be determined more closely from the four that have been scientifically excavated.

Pit 1 was rectangular and relatively shallow, with well delineated sides. Its length (4.64 m), width (3.48 m) and depth (1.64 m) show its measurements were in the ratio 9:6:3. The pit was filled in with earth compacted in layers, the middle one containing a high proportion of burnt bones, probably of animals sacrificed by burning. The floor of the pit was covered with ritual jades such as various sceptres, known by their later names of *zhang, ge, fu, gui* and *zuo*, ritual bronzes of the *zun* and *lei* types, and bronze heads and masks, intermingled with a few ceramic vessels (fig. 2). Some heads and other articles, such as a rod, a tiger and a face protector, are decorated with gold leaf. This pit has been dated to the end of the second phase of Sanxingdui, *c.* 1300–1200 BC.

Pit 2 was discovered 30 m to the south-east of pit 1. It was also rectangular, with a length of 5.3 m, a width of 2.3 m and a depth of 1.68 m, corresponding to an approximate ratio of 10:4:3. This pit was filled with yellowish soil and the finds were distributed in three layers. The top layer contained over sixty elephant tusks (fig. 3), while the middle layer (fig. 4) yielded the large bronze items such as the complete standing figure (no. 22), the human-like heads (nos 23, 24), the mask (no. 25), the tree (fig. 6) and the ritual vessels (nos 27, 28). In the bottom layer were jade and stone implements, jade blades and discs, small animal masks, small bronze birds and animals, and seashells. Although some of the finds from pit 1 are similar to those from pit 2, the latter is distinguished by the enormous number of impressive bronze items. An evaluation of these bronze objects, as well as of the earth layers, supports a slightly later date than that of pit 1, corresponding to the transition from the Shang to the Zhou period, *c.* 1200–1000 BC.

The pit at Yueliangwan, excavated in 1929, was documented by the museum at Huaxi University. It records a length of about 2.1 m, and a width and depth of about 0.9 m, which is a ratio of 7:3:3. This pit contained almost four hundred ritual jades, amongst them a large number of discs (*bi*) piled one on top of another, as well as *cong*, *zhang*, *gui* and *fu* placed in layers. The jade types and the way in which they were buried invite comparisons with pits 1 and 2, but closer examination of the jades supports an earlier date of *c.* 1500–1400 BC.

To the east of Yueliangwan, near Zhenwucun, is a hillock known in the area by the interesting name of Little Trove Mound (Cangbaobao). Excavations here in 1988 produced forty items of stone, bronze and jade, including twenty jade discs (*bi*) piled one on top of another, just as they were reported to have been at Yueliangwan. There were no jade blades of the *zhang* or *ge* type, and the *bi*, *huan* and *fu* are so coarsely worked that an early Shang date for them has been proposed by some. Further ritual jades of the *huan* and *zuo* types were recovered, as well as stone axes and two bronze plaques which are so similar to those from Erlitou, dated to *c.* 1700–1500 BC, that they are ascribed to that period.

In addition to these four main excavations, two related finds must also be mentioned. First, a group of jades and bronzes was discovered in a pit 1 m deep at Gaopianxiang to the west of Sanxingdui. These objects included lozenge-shaped jades, axes (*fu*), rectangular stone knives, stone spearheads and an oblong bronze plaque, measuring 12.3 cm by 7.3 cm and decorated with turquoise inlay, of an animal mask and geometric patterns. Almost identical plaques inlaid with turquoise *taotie* masks have come from Erlitou (no. 36). This plaque and the other finds from Gaopianxiang suggest even closer affinities with Erlitou culture, and their date is most probably earlier than that of the objects recovered from Cangbaobao, that is, somewhere in the period 2000 to 1600 BC.

The second find of related interest was a sacrificial pit at Mayangxiang in Yanting county in the north of Sichuan province. According to the author's own investigations, this pit was 3.32 m long, 1.6 m wide and 1.3 m deep, giving a ratio of 8:4:3, which is roughly approximate to the pits of Sanxingdui. A set of ten jade *bi* discs was discovered here, so close in type to those of Sanxingdui – especially those from Yueliangwan and Cangbaobao – that they must be of similar date, that is, *c.* 1500 BC.

Close examination of the above pits allows us to draw certain conclusions, although these are by no means definitive. The large numbers of rectangular pits of sim-

Fig. 3 *Upper stratum of pit 2, Sanxingdui.*

ilar proportions, filled with precious goods, are characteristic of the city of Sanxingdui and probably also of the surrounding province of Sichuan. Although the pits vary in date, their layout and the systematic ways in which they were filled suggest a common purpose. The fact that they all contained ritual items and animal bones or tusks, but no everyday objects or human bones, demonstrates that these were not the graves of human beings. It seems that these pits were dug to receive ritual items and the charred bones of animals which were sacrificed, presumably to deities and spirits. Thus the pits are known as sacrificial pits. It is possible, based on finds of mortice-joined beams in the vicinity of some of the pit openings, to speculate that there were structures built above ground over the pits. These would no doubt also have served a ritual purpose, or may even have been halls similar to that found above the tomb of Fu Hao, dating to *c.* 1200 BC (Zheng, fig. 4), in the central Shang state, where it is well known that ritual ceremonies were conducted, and comparable rituals may have been practised at Sanxingdui. However, the presence of sacrificial pits and the numerous enigmatic items that they contained point to religious or spiritual beliefs at Sanxingdui quite unlike those of the central Shang state. There seems to have been at Sanxingdui a very obvious attempt to perform animal and material sacri-

Fig. 4 *Middle stratum of pit 2, Sanxingdui.*

fices in order to mediate between earth and heaven. This is the most salient feature of the Sanxingdui finds.

The life-size bronze figure, bronze heads and figurines

The life-size bronze figure and the bronze heads and figurines make up the first of the four major groups of objects recovered from the sacrificial pits at Sanxingdui (nos 22–24). The second group comprises the human-like masks (no. 25) and diamond-shaped fittings (no. 32); the third consists of bronze trees (fig. 6; Introduction, fig. 8), birds and animals (nos 29, 30); and the fourth includes all the other items of jade, stone, gold and bronze (nos 33–35; fig. 8). Each of these groups gives us some clues about the culture and beliefs of the people of Sanxingdui, but not until further related discoveries are made will we be able to piece together these clues to create a picture of a specific cult or religion.

It is the single life-size bronze figure and the group of fifty-four life-size bronze heads that have caused the greatest excitement, eliciting comparison with the vast terracotta army of the first emperor of China, Qin Shi Huangdi, interred almost a thousand years later (no. 78).

But apart from the bronze standing figure, which is clothed in a realistic manner, and the fifty-four heads, the scale of the Sanxingdui figures is generally much smaller. There are a number of figurines between 10 and 20 cm high, which may represent worshippers.

The function and significance of the figures and heads are completely unknown, and we can suggest only tentative interpretations. Does the tall standing figure (no. 22) represent a cult figure, grasping a ritual implement in the act of mediating between man and the spirits? His crown-like headdress and garments decorated with dragons, animal masks and clouds certainly set him apart as the most splendid of the figures, the one who might lead such a ritual. Do the life-size bronze heads, perhaps once attached to bodies made of a less valuable material, depict lesser cult figures or priests, perhaps even clan representatives participating in the ritual? The variations in the headdresses, hairstyles and facial expressions may indicate different clans or different social ranks within a hierarchy. Those heads with overlaid gold leaf may have belonged to figures with prominent social roles (no. 23).

There were also several small and medium-sized figures in the pits, ranging in size from a few centimetres

Fig. 5 *Large bronze mask from pit 2, Sanxingdui.*

hooked nose – some with a projection – and the prominent pointed ears gives them a quite fantastic appearance. The second form of eye is notable not for its projecting pupil, but for its exaggerated size. These eyes are flat and almond-shaped. All the faces possess the rectangular holes for attachment.

Pit 2 also yielded a number of diamond- and hook-shaped fittings which, like the masks, have holes for attachment. The diamond-shaped fittings are made in one, two or four parts (no. 32). Chinese archaeologists have identified the twenty or so diamond-shaped fittings as eyes, and the thirty or so hook-shaped fittings as pupils. If this identification is correct, and there is as yet no way we can be sure, then it does not seem too far-fetched to suggest that the peoples of Sanxingdui had a particular veneration for the eye, and hence they exaggerated its form and size in the artefacts they made.

Attempts have been made to link this veneration for eyes with Cancong, the legendary first ruler of the state of Shu in Sichuan. According to an early history of Sichuan, *Huayang guozhi*, compiled in about AD 350, Cancong was known for his protruding eyes (*zongmu*). He was reputedly buried in a stone coffin, an event that the people of Shu are said to have turned into a custom by subsequently burying all men with protruding eyes in stone coffins. Such a tradition provides at least one helpful explanation for the existence of the human masks buried at Sanxingdui.

to between 20 and 30 cm in length. Some formed small kneeling groups, perhaps once arranged below the bronze trees (fig. 6; Introduction, fig. 8). The others, in various postures and expressions, seem all to be engaged in rites of homage. Were these members of different clans in the act of worship? We may be looking at a complex hierarchical group composed of a chief cult figure or priest, his acolytes and the common worshippers, which in turn may reflect the prevailing social conditions of Sanxingdui. But we cannot be certain.

The bronze human-like masks and diamond-shaped fittings

Speculation continues about the second group of objects, the group of large human-like masks and diamond-shaped fittings. For, whereas the bronze figures and heads have a certain degree of realism about them, these masks are stylised to an almost grotesque degree of fantasy.

All the twenty or so masks were found in pit 2, and all share a U-shaped structure when viewed from above (fig. 5; no. 25). They include the giant mask with protruding eyes which is 138 cm wide (fig. 5), the mask (no. 25) which is 77 cm wide with a projection rising from its nose, and other masks with widths ranging from 20 to 50 cm. Each has a pair of rectangular holes at each side, suggesting that they were attached to something else, perhaps part of a building or a body in another material.

The most astounding feature of these masks is their eyes, which take two different forms. One form is characterised by pupils which project like bottle corks to a distance of more than 10 cm from the eye. The eyes themselves, under powerful eyebrows, slant upwards at the outer edges. The combination of these eyes, the

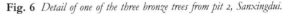

Fig. 6 *Detail of one of the three bronze trees from pit 2, Sanxingdui.*

Further suggestions have been made concerning the human-like masks. The fact that they are obviously not purely human, only human-like, has led some to believe that they represent a combination of man and spirit, perhaps even a deified ancestor, particularly since the concept of ancestor worship in China is archaic. But it must be emphasised that such interpretations are purely speculative.

The bronze trees, birds and animals

Just as the bronze figures, heads, masks and fittings are so elusively peculiar to the art of Sanxingdui, so too is the third category of object, the magnificent bronze trees decorated with birds and fruits. As with the life-size bronze figure (no. 22), it is the enormous scale of these trees that is so impressive. So far, three trees have been pieced together from the broken and charred remains discovered in pit 2. None is complete, and they vary in height from approximately 1 and 2 to 4.2 m. This last specimen is the tallest bronze sculpture from the period contemporaneous with the Shang (Introduction, fig. 8).

This tallest tree has a straight, slender trunk composed of four pole sections, the lowest one fitted into an openwork pedestal that may represent a mountain. The tree is crowned with a four-leaf stand that once supported a bronze bird, now preserved only in fragments. The gracefully curving branches emerge from the trunk at three different levels and support leaves and peach-like fruits. Sitting on nine of these fruits are birds with hooked beaks and outstretched wings. The tree has nine branches, nine birds and twelve fruits, but holes in the branches indicate that further decorations would have been suspended from them. Extending from the base in a sinuous curve similar to that of the branches is the body of a dragon whose angular, horned head and front claws rest on the base. This dragon originally reached to the top of the tree, but only half of its body has been recovered.

The 2-metre tree differs only slightly from the tallest one. It, too, has a straight trunk resting in a pedestal, and nine branches with nine fruits and birds. Instead of a dragon, however, there are three kneeling figures set between the three legs of the base. These figures face out from the tree and appear to have held some implement in their outstretched hands.

We can only assume from the badly destroyed remains of the smallest tree that it was similar to the other two. Some of the birds that were fitted to this tree are unusual, however, in that they have crowned human-like heads (no. 30).

The birds were perhaps believed to fly between heaven and earth as intermediaries between men and higher powers. Later Chinese mythology includes trees that represent ladders between heaven and earth, although we should be wary of applying later concepts to these early artefacts when so little is known about them. The trees could equally have been objects of worship, or they may simply have been part of a spiritual landscape, a background to the figures, heads and masks already described.

Related to these trees and their birds are the numerous other birds, animals and imaginary creatures recovered from the sacrificial pits. These take the form of pendants, belts and ornaments. Many of the birds are characterised by their hooked beaks, and one in particular stands out for its sheer size (no. 29). As high as 43.3 cm, this magnificent three-dimensional bird's head has holes at the base of the neck, suggesting that it was attached to a body or a fixture. As well as birds, the pits contained many other creatures in bronze – tigers, dragons, serpents, fish and insects – and fruit, flowers, leaves and branches. All of these may have been part of the spiritual landscape suggested above.

Ritual items

The fourth large group of finds from the sacrificial pits of Sanxingdui comprises the ritual items of jade, stone, gold and bronze. In contrast to the first three groups of unique fantastical objects peculiar to Sanxingdui, the ritual items in the fourth group resemble quite closely those of the Shang culture in Henan province. They provide evidence of a degree of contact between the remote western areas of China and the central Shang state.

Pit 1 yielded over two hundred ritual items of stone and jade, while pit 2 held 130. Of the more than twenty different types of ritual jades, the most numerous are discs and rings. Also of particular note are the many ceremonial blades, sceptres (*zhang*), which occur in a variety of forms (fig. 33.1). Clues as to the uses of such jades can be gleaned from the engraved scenes on a jade sceptre (*bian*) also found in pit 2 (fig. 7). These scenes may perhaps be interpreted as representing some form of worship or sacrifice. Against a background of sixteen mountains with eight hands pointing down from the sky are eight imposing upright *zhang* blades, four horizontal tusk-shaped objects, four boat-shaped objects and twenty-two standing or kneeling figures who appear to be performing some act of worship or sacrifice. Their clothing and headgear are similar to that of the large bronze standing figure.

The other two main sites within Sanxingdui, Yue-liangwan and Cangbaobao, also yielded ritual jades, but of different types from those in pits 1 and 2. The predominant types are discs (*bi*), rings (*huan*) and tubes (*cong*), many of which are very large.

In contrast to the range of ritual jades found at Sanxingdui, the ritual bronze types are very restricted: all are vessels of either the *zun* or *lei* type (nos 27, 28). While these correspond quite closely with the *zun* and *lei* made at the central Shang city of Yinxu (near Anyang), they are distinguished by differences in their decoration, such as the three-dimensional animal heads and small birds on the shoulders of the vessels. It is possible that *zun* and *lei* held a particular significance for the peoples of Sichuan province, as the majority of bronze ritual vessels excavated in the area belong to these two types.

As well as the finds of ritual jades and bronzes, there is a splendid rod covered in sheet gold which was discovered in pit 1. This rod (fig. 8) would originally have had a wooden core, which has now disintegrated. It is 14.2 cm long and engraved with two human faces wearing tall headdresses, and four groups each composed of one fish and two birds linked by a feathered arrow shaft. It has been suggested that this rod was held by a cult figure or priest during a ritual ceremony, or that it was a sceptre held by a ruler to demonstrate his power. As yet there is no certain explanation of its function.

As mentioned already, if we are to believe later historical records, such as the *Huayang guozhi*, the first ruler of the state of Sanxingdui may have been Cancong, who was succeeded by Bohu and then by Yufu. It is said that Yufu was immortal and that an ancestor hall was erected for him. The *Shu wang benji* (*Chronicles of the Shu Kings*), contained in the *Shi ji*, an historical text of the Han dynasty, states: 'Each of the three royal houses ruled for many hundreds of years; all were declared to be gods and immortal'. Such texts indicate that the ruler of a state was considered to be endowed with both political and religious power.

Whether or not Sanxingdui was the capital of the

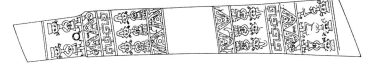

Fig. 7 *Drawing of figures holding grave sceptres engraved on a jade blade from pit 2 (K2: 201–4). After* Wenwu *1989.5, p. 18, fig. 38.*

state of Shu is, however, still open to question. There seems no doubt that Sanxingdui was an important ritual centre, although any attempt to reconstruct the religious beliefs and ritual ceremonies can only be hypothetical. Chinese archaeologists have proposed that at Sanxingdui there were sacrificial sites on raised platforms, decorated with bronze trees bearing fruit and hung with jade discs and rings. Imaginary creatures and birds sat on the branches, and kneeling men protected or worshipped the trees. The splendidly attired priest may have stood on a pedestal, holding in both hands some ritual implement, and he may have been surrounded by important priests, shamans or clan representatives, as well as by the common people. Ancestor deities, perhaps represented by bronze masks with protruding eyes, may have been worshipped, and the bronze birds and animals may have served to communicate the prayers and messages of the worshippers from the world of men to the realm of the spirits. Ritual bronzes and jades, symbolic of the power of the priest and the ruler, may have been used in ceremonies of sacrifice and then buried in sacrificial pits along with animal bones, the human-like heads, masks and trees, which were all first broken and burned. The pit may then have been filled with soil and a building constructed to mark the site above ground. But, however appealing this description may be, only further archaeological discoveries in the area will help to clarify what at present is only a hazy picture of the beliefs and practices of a mysterious people. The search has just begun.

1 For discussion of the pits in English see Bagley 1988; Bagley 1990. For interim reports see *Wenwu* 1987.10, pp. 1–15, 16–17; *Wenwu* 1989.5, pp. 1–20. For articles on various aspects of the finds see Sichuan 1989 and Sichuan 1992.

Fig. 8 *Detail of gold rod from pit 1, Sanxingdui.*

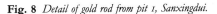

THE ROYAL CONSORT FU HAO AND HER TOMB

Zheng Zhenxiang

Fu Hao must rank as one of the most charismatic of ancient China's heroines. One of several consorts of the Shang king Wu Ding, under whom the power of the dynasty reached its zenith, Fu Hao combined the qualities of wife and mother, victorious military leader, influential politician, and principal performer in ritual ceremonies of a magnitude that decided the fate of the empire. The esteem in which she was held is reflected in her richly equipped tomb and the traces of a hall that may have been used for offering sacrifices to her ancestors.

Excavations at the late Shang period site of Yinxu (literally, the Yin ruins, fig. 1) were begun as early as 1928, but it was not until the spring of 1976 that the tomb of Fu Hao was discovered at Xiaotun, a village 3 km north-west of present-day Anyang in Henan province. By comparison with all the Anyang period royal tombs of the Shang dynasty excavated prior to 1976, this one was by far the best preserved. Its identification as the tomb of Fu Hao was made possible by the numerous mentions of her name, long known from Shang period oracle texts, in inscriptions on ritual bronzes found in the tomb.

These ritual bronzes are only a few of the enormous number of items, almost two thousand, that were buried in the tomb. The extremely good state of preservation of many of them makes this one of the most significant archaeological finds of the Shang dynasty. Not only do the objects give us a number of clues about the deceased, but they also permit us, by stylistic comparison with other archaeological finds, to date Fu Hao's tomb to the middle of the Anyang phase of the late Shang dynasty, c. 1200 BC (sometimes known as Yinxu II). The dating of the tomb thus also provides a rough date for the reign of King Wu Ding, whose existence had previously been known only from oracle texts. The objects furthermore provide some evidence of the relationship between the central Shang state and surrounding local cultures. Also of great importance was the discovery above Fu Hao's tomb of the remains of a building, probably her ancestor hall, which is the oldest of its kind to have come to light so far.

Evidence from oracle bone inscriptions

Information about King Wu Ding and his wives or consorts can be gleaned from the oracle bone inscriptions of the late Shang period. The system of divination by inscriptions on bone extended to many aspects of life and exerted considerable influence in matters of war, agriculture, hunting, the weather, illness and childbirth (no. 37). The inscriptions reveal King Wu Ding as one of the greatest rulers of his dynasty, who expanded the Shang empire through the conquest of local tribes and brought its economy and culture to a position of great strength.

The oracle bone inscriptions also throw light on Wu Ding's numerous wives or consorts, and give them credit for more than simply bearing and bringing up his children. Over twenty of his consorts were involved in the organisation of agriculture, fishing and animal breeding, and a few are mentioned as participating in military activities and ritual ceremonies.[1]

Fig. 1 *Aerial view of Yinxu, near Anyang, Henan province.*

The duties performed by Wu Ding's royal consorts appear to have gone far beyond those normally assigned to women. From the late neolithic period, it is generally believed, women were expected to rear children and take care of the home, while men applied themselves to working in the fields or hunting. Participation in military activities and ritual ceremonies was probably the preserve of men. One aspect of Wu Ding's legendary wisdom is thought to have been that, unusually, he allowed his wives or consorts to contribute to court life.

The discovery of Fu Hao's tomb has gone a long way to solving the uncertainties surrounding the names on many oracle bones. A number of these names are preceded by the character 'Fu': for example, Fu Hao and Fu Jing. These names have been explained by the great twentieth-century philologist and historian, Tang Lan, who has suggested from his studies of oracle bone inscriptions that the consort of the ancestor to whom an offering is made is called *bi*, the consort of the father of the individual making the offering is called *mu*, and that the ten individuals who bear the symbol 'Fu' in their names are to be understood as principal consorts of Wu Ding.[2]

The identification of Fu Hao as a royal consort from inscriptions both on oracle bones and on many of the bronzes in her tomb has been reinforced by the work of a number of scholars. Some of the bronzes (no. 39) bear the inscription 'Si Mu Xin' (which is the ritual title for the consort of the father of the individual making the offering) or 'Mother Xin'. 'Xin' is probably the posthumous name for Fu Hao, a name known from oracle bone inscriptions as referring to a deceased wife of Wu Ding. The bronze vessels inscribed 'Si Mu Xin' were probably commissioned by the sons of Fu Hao for the occasion of her burial.

The two names that occur most frequently on the oracle bones are Fu Hao and Fu Jing, who appear to have enjoyed positions of equal status, although, it would seem, in different spheres. Fu Jing's area of influence was agriculture: she is said to have controlled an area where millet (*shu*, or *Panicum miliaceum*) was cultivated. One oracle inscription mentions an occasion on which Fu Jing received the harvested millet, and another records a period when harvests were poor. Fu Jing's name is sometimes mentioned in connection with military activities, but in the main these were the preserve of Fu Hao.

The high esteem in which Fu Hao was held by both king and state is frequently mentioned in oracle texts. So too, however, is concern for her well-being, in terms of childbirth and the rearing of children, illnesses and concerns for her speedy recovery. But her position of power seems to have been so strong that she was allowed to participate in the ritual and military affairs of state, which, as later texts would have it, were cardinal principles of dynastic survival.

The significance of ritual ceremonies during the Shang period cannot be underestimated. Almost certainly the Shang believed that the deceased were not extinguished but lived on in another world, where, as past ancestors, they watched over the fate of the surviving family and indeed of the state. The ancestors were consulted at ritual ceremonies, as were the gods. The *she* cult, or veneration of rivers, mountains and rainbows, was also practised. Ancestors and spirits were consulted on all affairs of state, great and small, and animal and human sacrifices were presented by those eager to ingratiate themselves or to express their gratitude.

Although the Shang king exercised ultimate control over ritual matters, he could transfer the performance of the ceremonies to worthy persons. Fu Hao obviously enjoyed the confidence of her husband and was repeatedly instructed to conduct special rituals and offer sacrifices. Her name appears in one oracle text, for example, in which an enquiry is being made as to whether she should offer wine to the ancestral mothers at the *you* and *gao* sacrificial services.[3]

Inscriptions on oracle bones provide evidence of Fu Hao's participation not only in ritual ceremonies but also in military affairs. King Wu Ding and Fu Hao lived in turbulent times, and military actions were the order of the day. It would seem that, with her presumed strength of spirit, ability to assert herself, capacity for strategic thinking and physical strength, Fu Hao became one of the greatest military leaders of the Shang state.

Oracle texts recording Fu Hao's involvement in military activities are numerous. She is mentioned frequently as the leader of campaigns against the neighbouring Tu, Ba, Yi and Qiang tribes. On the *yiyou* day, for example, it is asked whether Fu Hao should gather soldiers before an attack.[4] On the *xinsi* day, it is reported that the king had assembled soldiers whom he wanted to send into battle under Fu Hao against the Tu tribe, if Fu Hao were to be given the protection of the gods.[5] In another inscription on a day with the same cyclic name, the question is posed as to whether Fu Hao could defeat the Qiang with the army of 13,000 soldiers that she had assembled for the purpose.[6] The blessing of the gods is sought again, on the *renshen* day, as Fu Hao prepared to conquer the Ba tribe. In another text the king enquires whether he might give his consort Fu Hao the order to attack the Yi tribe.[7]

As well as attacking surrounding tribes, the Shang

sought to protect themselves from invasions by local states. In their eagerness to enlarge their own state and gather booty, the Shang appear to have sent Fu Hao on endless campaigns, and the fact that they continued to do so can surely only point to her success as a military leader at the forefront of Shang expansion.

Fu Hao's tomb and ancestor hall

Fu Hao's tomb and what appear to be the remains of a hall for offering sacrifices to her ancestors were discovered in 1976. The tomb consists of a rectangular earth pit, measuring approximately 5.6 by 4 m, with vertical walls under which there was a smaller pit. Within the partially preserved wooden grave chamber were found the remains of a lacquered wood coffin, in which Fu Hao had presumably been buried, and the skeletal remains of sixteen people and six dogs. Directly above the eastern and western walls of the grave chamber were two long niches (fig. 2), and between the grave and the surface of the earth was a shaft filled with compacted earth.

The grave has yielded an extraordinarily rich and varied selection of grave goods, the high quality of which testify to Fu Hao's royal status. Among the approximately two thousand items recovered were 468

Fig. 3 *Drawing of an archer's thumb ring in jade. After Beijing 1980a, pp. 194–5.*

of bronze, over 750 of jade, about 560 of bone, over 110 of stone and semi-precious stone, a few of ivory and ceramic, and over six thousand cowrie shells which would have served as currency in the Shang period. A taste for luxury is seen in many of the items, such as the jades shaped as animals and humans (no. 49), a rare jade bowl (no. 48) and an ivory cup inlaid with turquoise (no. 47). Judging from the collection of 527 hairpins and three combs that were discovered with Fu Hao (no. 50), lavish hairdressing must have been a notable mark of high status.

As well as these personal items, there were a number of vessels and weapons that seem to have been used in ritual ceremonies. The splendid bronze vessels (nos 39–45) were almost certainly used in ritual ceremonies, whereas the weapons may also have been used in battle. Among the weapons were four bronze axes (*yue*) (no. 46), over ninety dagger axes (*ge*), six implements like bows and an archer's thumb ring of jade (fig. 3). Weapons in a tomb usually identify the occupant as male, and the discovery of such a large number of weapons in the grave of a woman is most extraordinary. It can only be assumed that the presence of weapons in Fu Hao's tomb was a reflection of the power she wielded in military affairs.

Directly above the grave shaft could be discerned the outline of a rectangular building, the position and dimensions of which suggest that it was an integral part of the tomb complex (fig. 4). With a length of 5.5 m and a width of 5 m, it corresponded approximately with the proportions of the underlying grave and shaft. A slightly depressed and compacted earth floor had been well preserved, and round it, except on the destroyed south side, was a double row of fairly evenly spaced holes, six on the inner and seven on the outer row, which presumably once held wooden columns. The heavy stones at the foot of each hole probably served as foundation supports for these columns.

This building was probably the ancestor hall of the Xin matriarch, Mu Xin Zong, which is mentioned in

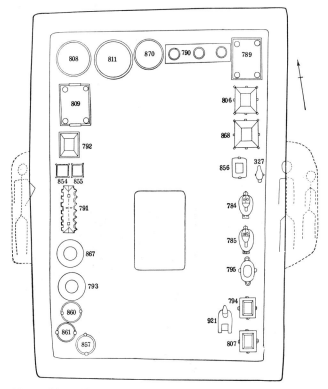

Fig. 2 *Plan of Fu Hao's tomb, showing lateral niches, the smaller pit and grave goods. After Beijing 1980a, p. 14.*

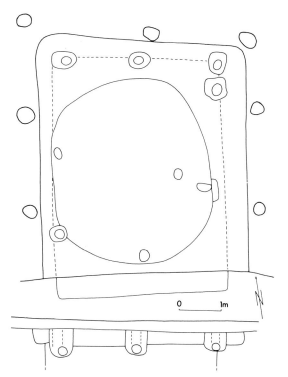

Fig. 4 *Outline of building above Fu Hao's tomb, showing holes for wooden columns.*

oracle texts as a place where sacrificial ceremonies were carried out. This conclusion is based on the assumption that the Xin matriarch is indeed the posthumous title of Fu Hao. Certainly, following her death, Fu Hao would have been elevated to the status of an important ancestor, on whose behalf lavish sacrifices would have been performed in a specially dedicated space or building. Her descendants would have believed that she guarded the safety of her family and of the Shang state from an exalted position in another world.

Ritual bronzes as an aid to dating

The numerous bronze vessels uncovered in Fu Hao's tomb are extremely well preserved and provide an invaluable aid to understanding the period of King Wu Ding within the Anyang phase of the Shang dynasty, that is, between 1300 and 1050 BC. The name Wu Ding (well known from later texts) appeared on a group of inscribed oracle bones that were excavated from a small pit south of Xiaotun village near Anyang in 1973. It was thought that Wu Ding reigned during the middle of the Anyang period, but excavators were surprised at the highly developed bronze casting seen in Fu Hao's tomb, dating, it seemed, to a comparatively early stage in the Anyang period. The advanced state of bronze casting at this early stage was confirmed by the discovery of

tomb 18 (the tomb of a noble) at Xiaotun.[8] The ceramics and bronzes in tomb 18 were originally thought to be slightly later in date than those of Fu Hao, but a comparison of the bronze vessels of the *gui*, *zun* and *you* types from both tombs points to striking similarities (Rawson, fig. 1). Furthermore, inscriptions on Fu Hao's bronzes include the names 'Fu Hao' and 'Ya Bi', and 'Zi Yu' appears on those from tomb 18 (fig. 5); all of these, according to the oracle texts, were individuals who were alive during the reign of King Wu Ding. Thus the contents of both tombs were shown to belong to the same period.

Bronze casting was obviously undergoing a change at this time, with the production of new ritual vessel types including very large vessels of the kind represented in Fu Hao's tomb. The sheer quantity found in her tomb enables us to see which vessels may have been used together in ritual ceremonies (figs 41.2, 42.2). Technological progress is evident in the forms of bronzes cast with the aid of ceramic moulds, exemplified in the *zun* and *gong* (no. 45) made in the shapes of birds and animals. Animal heads, mythical birds and other fantastic creatures further adorn the shoulder sections of many vessels (no. 44). The relief decoration on the bronzes is also exceptionally fine. Prior to the discovery of the bronzes in Fu Hao's tomb, it was assumed that relief decoration of the type found on these vessels had not been developed before the late Anyang period, around 1100 BC; Fu Hao's bronzes demonstrate, however, that such decoration was already being executed around 1200 BC. Inscriptions, which appear only rarely on bronzes of the first phase of the Anyang period, become more numerous in the second phase, with two or three characters appearing on vessels and weapons. This new proliferation of bronzes dating from the period of King Wu Ding is evidence of advances in casting techniques that were to herald a new chapter in the history of bronze art.

Fig. 5 *Inscription 'Zi Yu' on a bronze from tomb 18 at Xiaotun, near Anyang, Henan province.*

Decorative motifs on ritual bronzes

The bronzes from Fu Hao's tomb display all the decorative motifs typical of the Shang period: the so-called *taotie* (monster face), the *kui* (dragon), and birds similar to the phoenix (*feng*).[9] What distinguishes the decoration of Fu Hao's bronzes, however, is a new emphasis on tigers and dragons.

Both creatures had been known in China since the neolithic period, when it is assumed they held an important place within certain religious beliefs in some areas. A clear neolithic instance of a dragon and a tiger appearing together was uncovered in a rectangular earth pit grave (M45) at Xishuipo near Puyang in Henan province. This grave dates from the Banpo phase of the Yangshao culture, *c.* 5000 BC. The dragon and the tiger, each composed of snail shells, flanked the occupant of the grave (the dragon on the right, the tiger on the left), both with backs turned towards the deceased. The head of the deceased faced south, whereas those of the dragon and tiger faced north. On all sides of the grave, except the south side, were further skeletons, probably of persons buried with the deceased. It is believed that this was the grave of a man who had played an important role in his clan, yet the significance of the dragon and tiger is still subject to debate. This example of a dragon is certainly thought to be the oldest portrayal of the creature known so far.

Dragons recur throughout the neolithic period, in widely dispersed areas: there are coiled 'pig-dragons' of jade from the Hongshan culture of north-east China, *c.* 3500 BC (Introduction, fig. 2), and painted dragons on ceramic plates of the Longshan culture, *c.* 2500 BC (no. 7). This latter painted dragon bears a close similarity to dragons on bronzes dating from the Anyang phase of the Shang period, which can be seen on large dishes (*pan*) from Fu Hao's tomb and from tomb 18 at Xiaotun near Anyang. From the placing of these dragons in water basins of the Shang period it could be argued that at this time the dragon had an association with water.

Despite changes in appearance, dragons of later periods seem to have had one consistent feature: an ability to fly to heaven and, much later, to accompany the soul on its journey there. This divine quality is described in the *Shuowen jiezi*, the earliest Chinese dictionary, compiled in the first century AD, which says: 'The dragon is a long scaly animal; sometimes it is light in colour, sometimes dark; it can transform itself and is sometimes large, sometimes small. In spring it rises up to heaven and in autumn it settles in deep water'.

The dragon motif appears only relatively late on ritual bronzes, that is, in the Yinxu or Anyang phase of the Shang period. As symbols of both royal and political power, these bronze vessels played a significant role in the affairs of the Shang state, being used in ritual ceremonies at which prayers for protection, support or blessing for the state were made to the ancestors or deities. On the bronze water basins of the Shang period the head of the dragon is usually portrayed full face, though occasionally in profile, with horns and a wide open mouth.

As well as displaying dragons in their decorative schemes, many Shang ritual bronzes bear a mysterious motif, sometimes compared to a wild feline, which has been known as a *taotie* since the Song period (AD 960–1279). The Eastern Zhou historical text, *Lüshi chunqiu*, records: 'A *ding* vessel from the Zhou period shows a *taotie*. The being has a head, but no body, and it eats up men'. This so-called *taotie* motif, with or without a body, assumes many forms on Shang bronzes, yet many of its features are constant (Rawson, fig. 6). Neither the Chinese character for *tao* nor for *tie* is found in Shang oracle texts.

The character for a tiger (*hu*) is found, however, and occasionally the character can be interpreted as a tiger eating a man. There are rare examples of a tiger and a man appearing together on Shang ritual bronzes, such as the handles of the Si Mu Wu *fang ding* from Wuguancun in Henan province (fig. 46.4c) and the ceremonial axe (*yue*) from Fu Hao's tomb (no. 46). As some versions of the *taotie* motif look very similar to a mask of a tiger face, it may be that the tiger motif was the inspiration for the *taotie*. *Taotie* tend to have wide open mouths, like those of the tigers in the oracle bone characters, as well as the protruding eyes and sharp teeth associated with a tiger.

During the Anyang phase of the Shang period the tiger was used to decorate bronze vessels and weapons, presumably to confer upon the owner of the object those qualities associated with the tiger, such as courage, fearlessness and a fighting spirit. The hunting of tigers was an important activity in the Shang period. An oracle inscription dated to the *renwu* day bears the question whether a tiger should be caught, indicating that the king must have ordered such a hunt. It is believed that, in general, tigers and dragons acted as protectors of clans and their kings and leaders in ancient China.

The relationship between the Shang state and its neighbours

The bronzes from Fu Hao's tomb are a magnificent example of the culture of the central Shang state. Other items in Fu Hao's tomb, however, point to the relationship of the Shang state to its predecessors and neighbours.

The Shang state is generally believed to have evolved from various neolithic cultures. For example, the small coiled jade dragons found in Fu Hao's tomb appear to be based on the jade 'pig-dragons' of the neolithic Hongshan culture (Introduction, fig. 2), and the ritual jade discs (*bi*) and tubes (*cong*) can be traced back to the southern Liangzhu culture (nos 16, 17). Thus the Shang peoples must have inherited some cultural aspects of their neolithic predecessors.[10]

Study and discussion of the relationships between the Shang state and neighbouring cultures are relatively recent. As we now know, links between the Shang and their neighbours were to bring about exchanges in both directions: bronzes and jades from neighbouring states show traces of central Shang influence; weapons in Fu Hao's tomb are similar to those used in the north-western periphery of the central Chinese area and are, along with axes found in Henan, typical of pieces introduced to the Shang centres from the steppes. Even some jades in Fu Hao's tomb came from distant areas (Rawson, fig. 8).

Central Shang influence at the time of King Wu Ding extended as far as the Chengdu plain in south-west China. Evidence of contact with states in that area, which were later known by the names of Shu and Ba, has come to light through recent excavations and information on oracle bones. Chinese scholars have identified a particular character as 'Shu', and one oracle text reads: 'The military power at the time of the rule of King Wu Ding reached from the west as far as the [states of] Ba and Shu'.[11]

Objects excavated in 1986 from the site at Sanxingdui near Guanghan in Sichuan province have caused a sensation (nos 22–35). Two pits yielded bronzes and jades of a quality rarely seen elsewhere. On the one hand, they appear to be quite independent of outside influence, yet on the other they bear similarities, for example, to central Shang bronzes of the period of King Wu Ding. A bronze *lei* from Sanxingdui (no. 27) is similar in both form and decoration to *lei* dating from the end of the first phase of the Anyang period (fig. 8), that is, the early reign of King Wu Ding, and a lidded vessel from pit 1 bears oblique *leiwen* decoration typical of the central Shang. Pit 2 at Sanxingdui yielded a *zun* (no. 28) very similar to one from tomb 18 at Xiaotun near Anyang (fig. 8), and several jades which resemble those found in Fu Hao's tomb. Such comparisons allow a tentative dating of pit 2 at Sanxingdui to the later phase of King Wu Ding's reign.

Only a very few of the bronzes from Sanxingdui show the influence of central Shang culture. Indeed, most have striking features that point to the independence of the culture. There is an elongated life-size human figure (no. 22), and there are masks with protruding eyes (no. 25) and strange trees (Introduction, fig. 8; Zhao, fig. 6). Nothing like these bronzes has ever been discovered elsewhere. Such magnificent objects show the mastery of bronze casting techniques by a culture seemingly independent of the Shang empire.

The independence of southern bronze casting, including the Sanxingdui finds, is highlighted by certain differences between the southern and Shang methods of casting. The differing use of moulds by the casters is a case in point. This contrast can be illustrated by examining the bronze vessels of the *lei* and *zun* types, of which three and ten respectively were recovered from Sanxingdui. A *lei*, such as no. 27, is made from a four-part mould, the seams falling at the points where there are animal or bird heads on the shoulder of the vessel. This *lei* is generally similar to one found in a pit in Zhengzhou, dated to the Erligang phase of the Shang period (fig. 6).[12] The moulds used for Shang culture bronze *lei* and *zun*, however, are generally formed of only three parts.

A further difference between the *lei* of Sanxingdui and other southern areas and those of the Shang cultures can be seen in the design of the animal heads on the shoulders of the vessel. On *lei* and *zun* of the Shang culture (figs 6, 8) the heads are flattened on the shoulders of the bodies, whereas the heads on a *lei* from the south are placed vertically (no. 27). On vessels from Sanxingdui and on a *lei* excavated in 1982 at Yueyang in Hunan province are four and three similar animal heads respectively, between each of which is a bird instead of a flange (fig. 7). Birds also decorate the shoulders of a *zun* from pit 2 at Sanxingdui (no. 28), but they are not found on equivalent Shang culture bronze vessels from Anyang.[13]

The *zun* from pit 2 at Sanxingdui fall into two groups. The first is characterised by a low, bulging body and shoulders decorated with three bird and three ram heads (no. 28); the second type is taller with shoulders adorned with eight bird and four buffalo heads. *Zun* of each of these two types have been found in tomb 18 at Xiaotun near Anyang (fig. 8). A *zun* similar to the second type, but from a non-Shang culture, was found at Sucun, Chenggu, in southern Shaanxi province. This *zun*, with a tapered standing ring, is decorated on the shoulders with birds rather than seam ridges (fig. 9), as is the *lei* from Yueyang described above. It belongs, therefore, to the southern tradition and is distinct from the principal Shang types from Anyang.

Fig. 6 *Wine vessels,* lei *(above left) and* zun *(above right), from Sanxingdui (nos 27, 28).*

Fig. 7 *Drawings of two wine vessels,* lei *(below left) and* zun *(below right), from Zhengzhou in Henan province. Early Shang period,* c. *1500–1300 BC. After* Wenwu *1983.3, p. 53, figs 10, 13.*

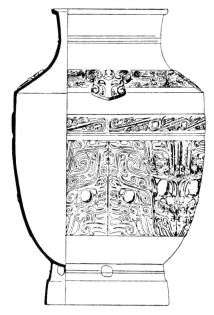

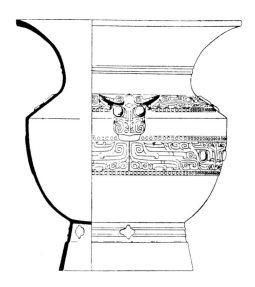

As *lei* and *zun* from the Sanxingdui and Shang cultures exhibit both similarities and differences in shape and decorative style, it is likely that peoples of the Chengdu plain in present-day Sichuan province were in contact with the central Shang state in Henan province but that they had closer links with the southerly local cultures of Hunan and Hubei. These exchanges of material culture suggest that the political and cultural influence of the Shang state reached well beyond adjacent areas to places as far away as the Chengdu plain. The idiosyncratic objects discovered at Sanxingdui, however, such as the bronze men, masks and trees, do indicate that, at least in terms of religious or spiritual beliefs, the Sanxingdui culture stood apart from the central Shang state.

The importance of the discovery of the tomb of Fu Hao cannot be overestimated. The tomb itself and the remains of the ancestor hall provide valuable evidence of the relationship between these two structures, while the enormous quantity of well preserved grave goods illustrate diverse aspects of Shang social, political and religious customs. These objects also help to illuminate matters known previously only from oracle texts; they serve as an aid to tracing and dating the evolution of Shang bronzes; and they indicate the relationship of the central Shang state with its neighbours. But, above all, the tomb and its contents confirm the powerful position held by Fu Hao as a royal consort as well as the great respect accorded her, in death and probably in life.

Fig. 8 *Bronze vessel* (lei) *excavated in 1982 at Yueyang, Hunan province.*

Fig. 10 *Bronze vessel* (zun) *from Sucun, Chenggu, Shaanxi province.*

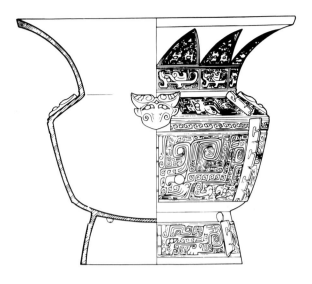

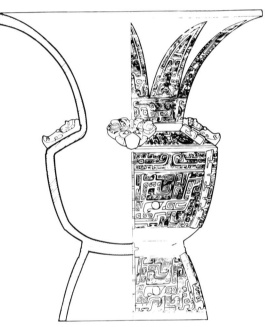

Fig. 9 *Two types of bronze* zun *from tomb 18 at Xiaotun, near Anyang, Henan province. After* Kaogu xuebao *1981.4, p. 498, fig. 18.*

1 Guo Moruo 1982, p. 423.
2 Tang Lan 1981, p. 27.
3 Jin Zutong 1974, *juan* 1, 2a, rubbing no. 7.
4 Luo Zhenyu 1912, *juan* 7, 30b, left.
5 Guo Moruo 1978, p. 942, rubbing no. 6412.
6 Couling-Chalfant 1935, rubbing no. 310.
7 Guo Moruo 1937, rubbing no. 1230.
8 *Kaogu xuebao* 1981.4, pp. 491–518.
9 See the essay by Rawson.
10 Discussed in Rawson 1995, section 2.
11 *Wenwu* 1987.10, pp. 1–15; *Wenwu* 1989.5, pp. 1–20.
12 *Wenwu* 1983.3, pp. 49–59.
13 These features are discussed in Bagley 1987, pp. 32–6.

THE RITUAL BRONZE VESSELS
OF THE SHANG AND THE ZHOU

Jessica Rawson

The ancient Chinese kings and nobles made magnificent cast bronze vessels for offering food and wine to their ancestors in ceremonial banquets. Evidence for such use of the vessels can be gleaned from the inscriptions on some of them and from texts, most of which were written long after the bronzes were made. These extraordinary vessels are among the most impressive pieces catalogued here (nos 39–45) and they display the aesthetic and technological skills of their makers. The great care with which they were produced and the large quantities of resources consumed indicate just how important they were to the ritual ceremonies of the time.[1]

The principal ritual act was a banquet held by the family with the participation of the ancestors. The meeting of worldly and spiritual guests is described in a poem of about 600 BC. Of course, we do not know how these ceremonies were perceived a thousand years before. However, as there is continuity in the use of such bronzes over two thousand years or more, it is likely that some of the essential elements remained the same, namely a ceremony with many participants at which food was offered to honoured guests, those guests being the ancestors and the spirits:

> We mind the furnaces, treading softly;
> Attend to the food-stands so tall,
> For roast meat, for broiled meat.
> Our lord's lady hard at work
> Sees to the dishes, so many,
> Needed for guests, for strangers.
> Health and pledges go the round,
> Every custom and rite is observed,
> Every smile, every word is in place.
> The Spirits and Protectors will surely come
> And requite us with great blessings,
> Countless years of life as our reward.
>
> Very hard have we striven
> That the rites might be without mistake.
> The skilful recitant conveys the message,

> Goes and gives it to the pious son:
> 'Fragrant were your pious offerings,
> The Spirits enjoyed their drink and food.
> They assign to you a hundred blessings.
> According to their hopes, to their rules,
> All was orderly and swift,
> All was straight and sure.
> For ever they will bestow upon you good store;
> Myriads and tens of myriads.'[2]

As well as such textual evidence, we also have the material evidence provided by the excavation of large intact burials dating from the early Bronze Age, *c.* 1700 BC, to the end of the first century BC during the Han period. Bronzes of all types play an important part in those tombs. The ancient Chinese seem to have believed that in some way or other they continued their lives after death more or less as they had always done. To do this properly they needed with them in their tombs all the most important possessions of their earthly lives; these tombs were in effect their dwellings in the afterlife. We can infer these notions from the very complete burials that have been recovered from all periods. The burial of so many fine utensils and ornaments seems to imply their future use. Indeed, tombs were equipped as were the fine houses or palaces of their day. But as times changed so did the functions and fashions, and these changes were, as we shall see, mimicked in the contents of tombs over the two-thousand-year period surveyed.

In all early periods, bronze vessels occupied a major position. Along with many other burial items they tell us of the priorities of their owners. Production of large numbers of bronze ritual vessels must have consumed large quantities of material resources and required a great deal of manpower. So too would jade weapons and ornaments. These jades seem to have been essential to the delineation of their owners, perhaps signifying their rank and personal associations. The bronzes, on the other hand, were instrumental in the delineation of the social organisation to which their owners belonged.

Employed in banquets that celebrated the roles of the ancestors in the lives of their descendants, such bronzes represented a society arranged in ranks and determined by a family structure in which earlier generations were senior to later ones.

The bronzes are outstanding, both in quantity and quality. The weight of bronze used is astonishing, as is the extraordinary level of craftsmanship. The number of vessels required was determined by the nature of the ceremony. As at any banquet, cups, goblets and dishes were needed for different beverages, foods and indeed complete courses. The wealth and status of an individual were displayed not only through the use of a great deal of precious material, a scarce resource, or by fine craftsmanship, but also in the consumption of abundant food and drink, requiring many vessels at any one time. No doubt the proper serving of many courses, with the appropriate gestures and movements, also served to highlight the power and prestige of the owners.

Again a much later text gives an impression of the way the goblets might have been used:

The host sits down in front of the wine holders and, taking a goblet from the cup-basket, descends the steps and proceeds to wash it. The guest also descends, the host declining the honour; but the guest does not decline the honour of having the goblet washed for him. He stands exactly in line with the west inner wall, and faces east.

When the washing is finished, they ascend with the usual salutes and yieldings of precedence, and the guest takes his stand at the head of the western steps in an attitude of expectancy. Then the host fills the goblet and pledges the guest.

Then, sitting down at the top of the east steps with his face to the north, he lays down the goblet and bows.[3]

This description, and the many movements it lists just for one toast, give us a glimpse of the many different gestures and actions that must have been linked to the offering of all the foods and drinks, each in its own special bronze vessel. Indeed, to the peoples of the day, the different vessels were probably recognised as being for particular foods and associated with particular stages in the ritual banquets. The set of vessels would have carried, as it were, coded instructions of what to do at different stages in the ceremonial meal. The vessels drawn in figure 1 (found in tomb 18 at Anyang) were made for a member of the ancient Chinese nobility in about 1200 BC. The different shapes were specific to particular uses. The tall beakers in the second row, known as *gu*, were for wine, for example, while the basins on three legs, known as *ding*, were for food.

Fig. 1 *Drawing of a typical set of Shang dynasty vessels from tomb 18 at Anyang, Henan province. Such a set would have belonged to a noble of high standing, but of lower status than the consort of a Shang king. Row 1: four jue (one is missing); row 2: five gu; row 3: two jia; row 4: two zun, one you, one lei; row 5: three ding, one gui; row 6: one pan, two yan, one shovel. Height of gu 28.5 cm. After Kaogu xuebao 1981.4, pp. 491–518.*

Experts in ritual and their patrons certainly knew how these different vessels were to be carried and offered to guests.[4] At all periods it is likely, indeed evident, that expertise in ritual determined what vessels were commissioned and how they were used.

As we shall see, components of the vessel sets changed over time. Such changes in the sets indicate changes not only in the actual rituals performed but also in the intellectual attitudes expressed by the rituals. There are in effect three major developments to be noted, followed by a fourth – the decline and effective disappearance of the ritual vessels. Bronzes began to be made from about 1700 BC, and for nearly a thousand years the range of shapes and the complexity of their decoration expanded enormously. There was a sudden change in both types and decoration from about 900 to 850 BC, suggesting some sort of ritual revolution. A less complete, but nonetheless important, transition occurred in the fourth and third centuries BC. But from at least the first century AD, and perhaps a little earlier, there was a further and, from the point of view of the bronzes themselves, catastrophic change. Religious and social factors probably precipitated all these changes, for all objects, especially those concerned with ritual and religious belief, are created within the contexts of beliefs and can therefore tell us something about those beliefs.

Before we review the range of shapes taken by bronze vessels, the kinds of banquets that required such vessels, and the religious beliefs implied by such banquets, we will consider the techniques of casting.

Casting technology

The Chinese cast their vessels rather than making them by hammering bronze, which was the practice in many other parts of the ancient world. This is remarkable because it implies a very great consumption of metal, metal that would also have been useful for weapons. For technical reasons a casting has to be much thicker and heavier than a hammered bronze of similar size: the outer mould and the inner core of a casting must be kept a reasonable, if not large, distance apart to allow the metal to run between them, making for a significant thickness. The fact that the Chinese were able to use such a quantity of weapon material for ceremonial use, and indeed to bury bronzes in such huge numbers, indicates both the enormous importance of the function of offering food in fine utensils and also the relative abundance of copper and tin.[5]

The ancient Chinese developed a most unusual method of casting bronze vessels. In place of the lost wax method common in the ancient West (in which the model of the item to be cast is first made of wax), the Chinese made their models out of something like clay. Around this model, which they carved with the required decoration, they packed clay for the moulds. As the model could not be melted out, the moulds had to be cut apart in sections and the model taken out of the centre. Figure 2 shows the number of mould sections

Fig. 2 *Drawing of the ceramic mould sections required for casting a bronze ritual food vessel,* ding. *The mould consists of three principal outer sections and a piece for the base, a core for the inside, three cores for the legs, a section between them, and a lid and base to contain the hot metal when poured. After Rawson 1992b, fig. 21.*

required for a bronze tripod vessel of the type known as a *ding*. The sides would have had to be made as three principal pieces, and then further sections would have been required for the top and bottom.

After the model had been removed, the pieces were then reassembled in the correct positions and reinforced with further clay to resist the impact of pouring in molten bronze. To derive the metal itself, copper and tin had to be mined, and the ore processed – probably far from the Shang and Zhou capitals – and transported there as bars. Some bronzes were of an enormous weight, so large quantities of metal must have been mined and refined in this way. Once the bronze had been poured into the moulds, it was allowed to cool before the moulds were removed. Very little finishing was required, so accurate and carefully made were the moulds. Indeed, ancient Chinese bronze casting was a triumph of ceramic technology.

The ritual vessels of the Erlitou, Erligang and Anyang periods

Bronze casting was first successfully developed on a significant scale in the Erlitou period (1700–1500 BC).[6] The Erlitou peoples, who preceded the Shang in Henan province, built large cities with palaces and temples and buried the dead with a few bronze vessels as well as ceramic ones, bronze weapons and jades. Their successors, the Shang, built yet larger cities in what are known as the Erligang (c. 1500–1300 BC) and the Anyang periods (c. 1300–1050 BC). In the discussion that follows, and indeed in the catalogue, the Anyang stage is represented principally by the contents of the tomb of Fu Hao, consort of the powerful king Wu Ding, who died in about 1200 BC.[7] The discovery of her tomb in 1976 was a milestone in our understanding of the lives of the Shang kings and other members of the élite.

The ritual vessel forms used in all these periods were derived from much earlier ceramic vessels employed by the neolithic predecessors of the Erlitou (c. 1700–1500 BC) and Shang cultures (c. 1500–1050 BC).[8] Tripods, basins, tall cups, pouring vessels – all had their proto-

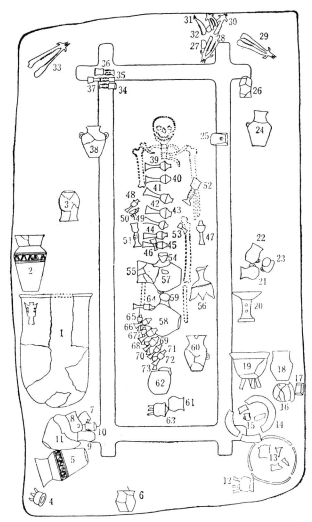

Fig. 3 *Drawing of tomb M17 at Dazhujia in Ju county, Shandong province, showing a large number of high-stemmed cups lying along the body of the dead. Neolithic period, Dawenkou culture, c. 3500 BC. After* Kaogu xuebao *1991.2, pp. 167–206, fig. 4.*

types in late neolithic ceramics. Indeed, the offerings to ancestors may well have begun at a very early stage in the neolithic. Tombs of the neolithic Dawenkou culture in Ju county in western Shandong are typical of many east-coast neolithic burials, in which the occupants were interred with ceramic pieces (fig. 3). In these burials were many cups on tall feet, between six and twenty in any one tomb, which would have been far too many for one person.[9] Either they were employed by the tomb occupant's relatives at the funeral or they were intended for the tomb occupant to share with his ancestors or other spirits. In any event, the ceramics in early tombs appear to have been the containers needed for sumptuous meals, just as the bronzes were to be.

Over more than three hundred years, that is, from the beginning of the Erlitou period until well into the Erligang period, these basic types of neolithic ceramic were borrowed and adapted for bronze casting (fig. 4). Figure 5 illustrates the bronze shapes found in a large hoard excavated from the Erligang period city site at Zhengzhou. Not all the vessel types of the period are represented in this hoard, but it does show some important developments. First of all, bronze made possible great variety in size: both very large and smaller, personal-sized vessels were cast. The two rectangular *ding* or cooking vessels, the predecessors of no. 39, are very large, being over 80 cm high. The small ones are only 31 cm high. In ceramic such large vessels would have been less likely to survive. The other significant feature of these immense food vessels is the rectangular form of some of them. Flat sides were relatively easy to cast in bronze by the piece mould section method, but would not have been stable in ceramic. Moreover, they had the advantage of being thereby distinctive, making it clear to the onlooker that the owner of these vessels possessed bronze rather than ceramic ones. In other words, the forms helped to identify the material and thus to express further the wealth and power of the owners.

Indeed, many of what we might regard as aesthetic developments are, perhaps primarily, changes made to differentiate bronzes from their ceramic prototypes. If the bronzes were to be effective in expressing both the status and piety of their owners, they had to display command of both material and craftsmanship. As a result, the forms of bronze vessels evolved from mainly rounded and barely decorated pieces to ever more ornamental vessels that presented to their best advantage the angular forms possible in bronze. For example, wine flasks, known by the name of *zun* (no. 28), were given pronounced shoulders and sharply articulated lids and footrings. All these details made the forms easy to

Fig. 4 *Bronze ritual vessel,* he *(left), compared with a ceramic one (right). Both from Henan Yanshi Erlitou. Erlitou period,* c. *1700–1500* BC. *Heights 24.5 cm; 25 cm. After Osaka 1993, nos 13, 16.*

recognise in dim light. Quick recognition was probably essential in ceremonies, in which as many as twenty different vessel forms had to be used at appropriate moments.[10] Further, these shapes became standardised, suggesting close control of the foundries.

As well as sharp horizontal divisions, bronze ritual vessels were given vertical flanges (nos 42–44). These are sometimes thought to have evolved as a way to cover up any defects caused by piece mould casting. But such an explanation is inadequate as, at all periods, the majority of bronzes did not have flanges. Instead, it is best to view the flanges as part of a system for articulating shapes and decoration. Together with the horizontal divisions created by the changes in the angle of shoulders and footrings, flanges served to define panels of decoration. Decoration in clearly defined units was a product of the piece mould system.[11] Moreover, it was a means by which vessels could be given more or less decoration, as the wealth of the patron and the function of the vessel demanded. A panel could either be filled with motifs or left blank. Even at a very early date the

ancient Chinese graded their possessions with minute distinctions. The wine vessel at the left of row four in figure 1 is covered all over with decoration and was presumably a highly valued vessel with a significant function. The rounded piece at the right of the same row, on the other hand, is completely undecorated. It was presumably much less prominent in the ritual and was therefore left plain.

The motifs, set within the panels delineated by the vessel form and sometimes by the flanges, are almost all based on the face of a creature known in later texts as the *taotie*. The function and associations, or 'meanings', of this creature have long puzzled scholars and still do today. In fact, much of the discussion of this creature has been confused by a search for a meaning.[12] Meanings alone cannot and do not determine visual images. Visual images are contrived and exploited, often by chance, for particular functions and uses; over time they acquire meanings through the associations of these functions with a particular image. Thus the meanings of the *taotie* are likely to have depended upon the func-

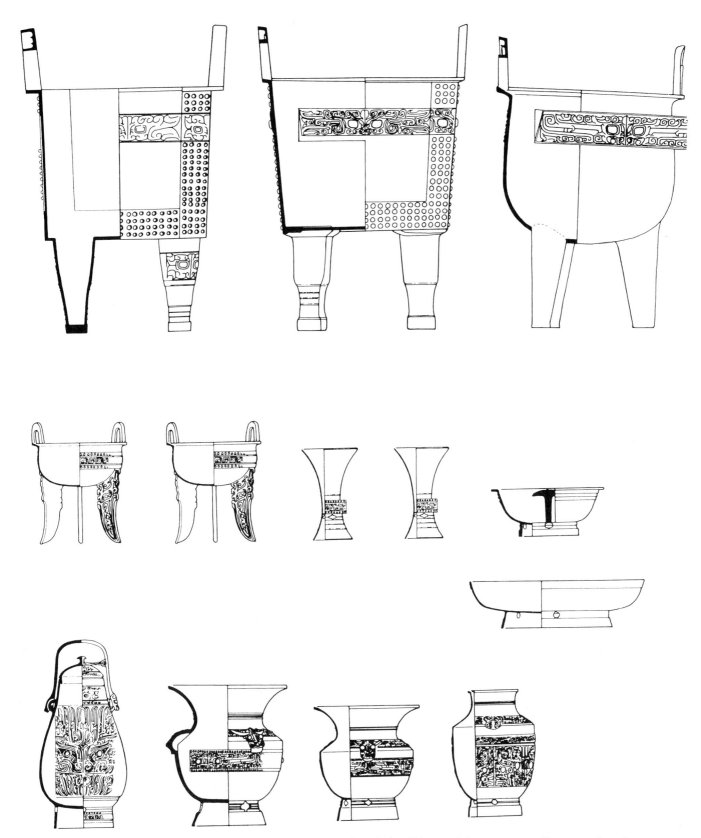

Fig. 5 *Drawings of bronze vessels from a hoard found at Henan Zhengzhou. Shang dynasty, Erligang period,* c. *1500–1300* BC. *Top row:* two fang ding, *one circular* ding; *row 2:* two ding *with flat legs, two* gu *and two* pan; *bottom row: one* you, *two* zun *and one* lei. *Height of* fang ding *81 cm. After* Wenwu *1983.3, pp. 53–7, figs 10, 14, 17, 18, 19, 21, 22.*

tions of the vessels on which it appeared; it was probably linked to the ritual offerings to the ancestors. We cannot say much more than that. It is very difficult to know whether the *taotie* had specific associations with the role of the ancestors, with other spirits or gods, life or death, food and wine, or prosperity. Indeed, it is likely to have been linked with all of these through its appearance on so many ritual vessels. We can also suggest that the variations in decorative detail, which are numerous, as we shall see, have little or nothing directly to do with specifying either these associations or any sort of specific ritual programme. Interactions between the visual effects and references to social and ritual qualities are likely to have been intricate and are very far from obvious to us today.

The earliest forms of the creature are abstract and consist of two large eyes, with sequences of scrolls on either side suggesting the body (fig. 6a). During the stages known as the Erlitou and Erligang periods, denser patterns were made of these scrolls (fig. 6b). The first stages are rather abstract, but then a more concrete

Fig. 6 *Rubbings of four different versions of* taotie *face decoration from Shang period ritual bronzes illustrate the decorative variety within a single motif over the period 1400–1200 BC. After Beijing 1984, nos 155, 156, 115, 31.*

creature emerged, with the features of the face prominent against a background of spirals (fig. 6c, d).

The origin of the face design appears to have been decoration employed in the Erlitou period. A rather abstract design of a face with large eyes can be seen on the Erlitou period bronze plaque with turquoise inlay (no. 36), and a jade baton excavated at Erlitou has faces carved on it that alternate in direction. This face pattern was almost certainly copied from late neolithic jade ornament from a distant area, namely the area around Shanghai, where the Liangzhu culture flourished.[13] Face patterns were clearly part of the Liangzhu culture and must have had specific meanings within that culture. A strange being holding a monster face was obviously essential to their interpretation of the world (fig. 16.1). Abbreviated versions of these complex images were employed on jades known as *cong* (no. 16). However, this series of faces was not transferred in its entirety to the Shang area, nor almost certainly were the ideas associated with the images. Indeed, as the functions of the faces and many of their attributes are completely different in the two areas, their associations and thus their meanings must also have been very different.

Designs and shapes can easily be borrowed from other areas without the meanings attached to them in their place of origin also being taken over.[14] Almost certainly this is what must have happened. Possibly a stray ancient Liangzhu period jade survived over a period of years to be found and copied in the Erlitou period, leading among other things to face patterns with which casters came to decorate bronzes.[15] These faces on bronzes probably had meanings quite different from those on the jades, as they do not reproduce the combinations of features that were evidently essential to the jade designs. The bronze casters copied some of the outlines of the face motifs on the jades, but not enough to suggest that they understood the original meanings of the faces.

Instead the Shang developed a whole range of variations of their face design, quite unlike anything seen in the Liangzhu culture. While the Liangzhu faces had some animal and some human characteristics, those on the bronzes were almost exclusively animal (fig. 6; no. 43). Associations no doubt accrued to these bronze motifs over time, adding further qualities and notions to any principal meaning that the face may originally have had. These associations must have been primarily linked with the uses of the ritual bronzes, as it is in this context, and this context alone, that the face patterns were fully elaborated.

Here, too, single-eyed creatures evolved. All the faces were divided down the centre. Additional, rather abstract creatures with single eyes and appearing, there-fore, in profile might be tucked in behind them on either side. These additional minor creatures seem to have provoked the separation of the features of the cen-tral face, so that it could be read as two separate dragons (fig. 6c). As a next stage, a variety of ingenious new creatures could be created by reusing horns as dragon bodies and so on. For example, a dragon with two paral-lel sections of body, displayed on the shoulder of a *fang lei* in the Shanghai Museum, is made up of parts of the original central *taotie* face on the vessel (fig. 7).[16] The creatures devised by fragmenting existing motifs and recombining the features in new ways may, of course, have acquired associations and meanings. However, the main reason for inventing these new types of imaginary beast seems to have been to fill the units of decoration on a bronze (fig. 7).[17]

These units of decoration could be used separately or together to create simple or complex decoration. More than any other people, the Chinese developed their forms of decoration in a systematic way, with small increments creating numerous stages between a com-pletely plain and a fully decorated vessel. These numer-ous grades of ornament could then be used to define the relative importance of vessels belonging to any one rank or individual. Further, the small differences in den-sity of decoration could be used to define ranks within a society. Such a system was readily adapted by work-shops to comply with the prevailing ritual and social framework. The key to the success of the decoration is that it was produced in large workshops which could respond to these social and ritual demands because, we surmise, they operated a sophisticated system of sub-division of labour.[18]

During the Anyang stage these essentially non-realistic creatures were supplemented with a few motifs based upon real creatures, especially birds and cicadas. This change occurred just as new vessel shapes in the forms of imaginary creatures were introduced at the time of the royal consort Fu Hao (nos 39–45). The con-tents of her tomb give us a glimpse of the wealth of both bronzes and jades at the height of the Anyang period of the Shang dynasty.

These new designs were not a natural extension of the existing repertory, but rather the intrusion of a for-eign or exotic range of designs and vessel shapes. Such realistic creatures entered the repertory because the Shang, an energetic and aggressive power, came into contact at this stage with the many peoples around them, who were manufacturing a wide range of goods in both bronze and jade.[19]

The historical texts portray the Shang as the domin-

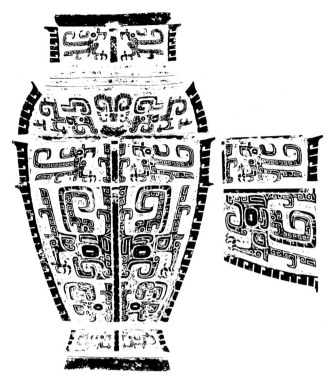

Fig. 7 *Rubbing of the decoration on a bronze ritual vessel,* fang lei, *illustrating the use of parts of the* taotie *motif to create dragons. Shang period, c. 12th century BC. Height 53 cm. Shanghai Museum. After Shanghai 1964, vol. 2, p. 11.*

ant power in the Chinese landmass. But we know today from archaeological evidence that they were surrounded by equally influential peoples, all with their own social and religious organisations. The bronzes and jades from Sanxingdui in Guanghan county, Sichuan province, dis-played here in the West for the first time (nos 22–35), are the products of one such competing society.[20] It is evident from the jades and bronzes used by the two peoples that the culture of Henan, where the Shang cap-ital was situated, differed markedly from that of Sichuan where Sanxingdui lies. The different uses to which jade and bronze were put by these peoples show that their religious preoccupations and spiritual beliefs were also different. Thus the typical ritual vessel set of the Shang, illustrated in figure 1, was unknown outside the Henan area. In Sichuan, for example, only *zun* and *lei* (nos 27, 28) were used. Without tripods and wine cups the peoples of Sanxingdui could not have practised the same rituals as the Shang. Whereas the *taotie*, mainly in very abstract forms, was a recurrent design among the Shang, it was much less popular with the bronze-using peoples around them. These other peoples, in Jiangxi, Hunan and Sichuan provinces, used images of people or anthropomorphic gods and real animals (nos 22–30). At the point when these images of men and real animals

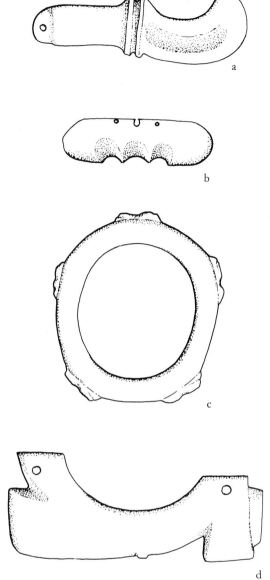

Fig. 8 *Drawings of neolithic period jades found in Fu Hao's tomb at Anyang. While the tomb dates from c. 1200 BC, some of the jades date from more than a thousand years earlier.*

a *Sickle-shaped jade. Hongshan culture, c. 3500 BC.*

b *Notched jade. Hongshan culture, c. 3500 BC.*

c *Ring. Possibly Liangzhu culture, c. 2500 BC.*

d *Part of a notched ring. Possibly Longshan culture, c. 2500–2000 BC. After Beijing 1980a, pls 164, 162, 93.*

crept into the bronze and jade repertory of the Shang (no. 46) we assume that the peoples of Henan province were probably in contact with these distant areas.

The contents of Fu Hao's tomb illustrate well the impact of exotic objects, both in bronze and jade. The jades present a phenomenon that may be paralleled in her ritual vessel set. Fu Hao had a collection of foreign jades, some ancient survivals from the Hongshan and Liangzhu cultures, for example (fig. 8). She also possessed locally made copies, notably coiled dragons based upon the dragons of the Hongshan culture. The figures of human beings (nos 49a, b) and the small tigers and elephants (nos 49c, d) were based upon southern models. Such jades were probably recognised as foreign and carried unusual associations.[21]

This exoticism was paralleled in bronze. Among the bronzes in the catalogue, an axe decorated with a human head between two tigers is an example of an exotic design (no. 46). This subject was borrowed from the south.[22] It is likely that, in its transferral to Anyang, the design was interpreted differently than in its place of origin.

Bird-shaped containers with small dragons and birds on their heads were also copied from southern prototypes, as probably were the animal-shaped vessels and pouring vessels known as *gong* (no. 45). The position of these vessels within Fu Hao's set is instructive. The exotic vessels are not among the basic components, those essential to all rituals (they were not generally placed in lesser tombs). They appear among the wine vessels additional to the main complement. Only the very wealthy and powerful seem to have had access to the exotic, and only members of the élite could display these contacts. The noble who owned the vessels drawn in figure 2 did not have any of these exotic, animal-shaped containers.

While the exotic was kept for additional and sometimes very large and rare pieces (nos 44, 45), quite different, highly conservative designs were reserved for such ancient vessel types as the wine goblets (*gu*) and wine cups (*jue*) (no. 41). Fu Hao had fifty-three *gu* and forty *jue*, all in standard if not archaic forms. In addition, her principal large vessels for serving wine, the *jia* and the *pou*, were decorated in elaborate up-to-date styles, namely in densely arranged relief (nos 42, 43).[23] Thus vessels with different roles within the ritual were differentiated not only by their shapes but also by their decoration. Such use of decoration to indicate the importance of the vessel type continued throughout the Shang and early Western Zhou. The decor also indicated the owners' contacts, both with the exotic and the foreign and with the past and the traditional – all, we may surmise, viewed as sources of power and influence.

Some links were elaborated in vessel inscriptions. From the period of Fu Hao or perhaps a little earlier, vessels were cast with names of either individuals or families. The vessels in Fu Hao's tomb carried a number of different names – those of Fu Hao herself, including her name in life and her supposed posthumous name, Si Mu Xin (no. 39). In addition, there were other clan and personal names on her vessels. Indeed, she had whole subsets of *gu* and *jue*, for example, that bore other names, probably those of their previous owners.[24] It is very unlikely that the individuals whose vessels appeared in Fu Hao's tomb were unknown to her. They were probably relatives or associates, or perhaps enemies, whose bronzes had been appropriated in some way. As the rituals were celebrated and foods and wines were offered in the vessels originating from these different sources, the interrelationships of these individuals may have been implicitly commemorated. A set of bronzes as complex as Fu Hao's thus offered not only the bronzes necessary for highly elaborated ceremonies, but in addition made possible references to many aspects of Fu Hao's world, both material and spiritual. By participating in the ceremonies, Fu Hao and all those present would have been conscious of references to the present and the past, to distance in space and time, and to a variety of different individuals, no doubt related in some way.

The bronzes of the Western Zhou period

In about 1050 BC the Shang were conquered by the Zhou from a position of relative obscurity, as their power lay in the west, perhaps in present-day Shaanxi province. Long texts, poems and other documents proclaim the ancestry, wisdom and potential statesmanship of the Zhou before the conquest. However, from their material remains, the pre-conquest inhabitants of Shaanxi appear to have been at a generally lower level of development than the powers that ruled in, say, Sichuan or Jiangxi province at a somewhat earlier stage. An important factor in the Zhou victory and their subsequent rule of the north China plain may have been the similarity of some of their attitudes and beliefs to those of the Shang.[25]

As already mentioned, the bronzes from Sichuan Guanghan Sanxingdui (nos 22–35) and Jiangxi Xin'gan Dayangzhou (fig. 52.4) suggest that the peoples of these areas had complex societies with beliefs and practices different from those of the Shang. Before the conquest the Zhou, on the other hand, may well have followed Shang practices of making sacrifices to their ancestors and burying bronze ritual vessels in tombs. We can infer from this characteristic that they also shared two essential Shang beliefs: first, that the ancestors were a force to be reckoned with and needed to be included in all family ceremonies; and, second, that life continued after death, and that the dead would continue to carry out ancestral rites. These are major elements that do not seem to have been part of the world view of the other peoples in the area, mentioned above.

The Zhou followed the Shang so intimately and effectively that, until the recent excavations in Sichuan and Jiangxi, we did not know what alternatives to Zhou rule there might have been. What is more, their written and presumably spoken propaganda was extraordinarily pervasive. They proclaimed their own legitimacy in terms of a succession of dynasties, and this idealised inheritance has remained the model right up to the present day. Before the discoveries in Sichuan represented in the present catalogue (nos 22–35), few scholars questioned the truth of what the Zhou wrote. As a result, the existence of a mosaic of competing states, perhaps equal to and certainly quite distinct from the Shang, has only recently been recognised.[26]

The ways in which the Zhou climbed to power are well displayed in their ritual bronzes. Before the conquest they seem to have used some Shang bronze types, but these were rather limited in range and decorative detail. Indeed, most ritual vessels assigned to the pre-conquest Zhou period are poorly cast and carry little decoration. After the conquest the Zhou immediately took command of their heritage and made wide use of the technological and artistic traditions of the areas they now ruled.

The range of bronze ritual shapes cast by the Zhou increased dramatically. They seem to have used the majority of Shang forms, suggesting that either they were or became familiar with Shang ritual. If anything, they reduced the number of vessels for wine and increased those for food – a trend that was to be reinforced later, as we shall see. The stages in the ritual that concentrated on food would, therefore, have been emphasised at the expense of those for wine. In other ways the Zhou also developed Shang traditions in vessel casting. They adopted elaborate shapes for wine, such as the *gong* and the *fang yi*, which they do not seem to have used before (see below fig. 15a). They also covered them in designs that were Shang in style. Indeed, the level of design and craftsmanship rose steeply, perhaps because the Zhou had captured Shang craftsmen (fig. 9).[27] By taking over Shang ritual practices and ritual vessels the Zhou emphasised their legitimate inheritance of Shang rule.

In addition to their imitations of mainstream Shang bronze shapes and decoration, the Zhou continued the rather conservative casting traditions associated with pre-conquest Shaanxi. Following the conquest, more types were made in the smooth rounded forms with narrow bands of decoration.

Another type of bronze provides evidence of Zhou contacts with the south-west. Indeed, the Zhou are

Fig. 9 *Bronze ritual vessel, the Li* gui, *from Shaanxi Lintong xian. Early Western Zhou period, 11th century BC. Height 28 cm. After New York 1980, no. 41, and the inscription mentioning the conquest of the Shang.*

renowned for their almost barbarously decorated vessels, such as a *lei* from Peng xian (fig. 10), in the region formerly dominated by the peoples of Sanxingdui. Outstanding features of such bronzes are their bold hooked flanges and small birds within the flanges, and designs of small buffaloes and coiled dragons, motifs rarely, if ever, found on Shang bronzes. It has been shown that these motifs come from a southern bronze casting tradition that entered Shaanxi perhaps from the west.[28] But the Zhou also used such motifs on bronzes cast at the capital. They cannot have been unaware of these references, and probably prized them.

We know that these rather exotic bronzes were not made by a forgotten provincial section of the Zhou empire because they carry inscriptions on them. These give accounts of their owners' successes in assisting the king in warfare and other court activities and thus describe the events that led to some specific reward. A food basin on a square stand, known as the Li *gui*, refers to the Zhou conquest of the Shang.[29] Inscriptions in such vessels as the He *zun* refer to events central to the success of the Zhou state, including the conquest of the Shang. Such inscriptions on vessels must have been an

essential feature, reporting these crucial moments in the history of the family to the ancestors (fig. 11). As these inscriptions were important records for powerful Zhou families, they would never have been cast on bronzes that were deemed in any way inferior. Vessels such as the He *zun* (fig. 11) are likely to have been highly prized, the hooked flanges recognised as a sign of prestige rather than as a flamboyant barbarism.

Two further phases of Western Zhou bronze casting can be mentioned. The first followed another burst of contact with the south, which brought changes to ritual practices and especially to aesthetic conventions. Contact with the south is most evident in jades and in such bronzes as bells and animal-shaped containers made about 900 BC. Jades decorated with birds and human-like heads, which suddenly appeared in Zhou territory, seem to have been derived from southern neolithic jades in which birds and human-like heads were combined (fig. 12). Such motifs had been used in the neolithic Shijiahe culture of Hubei province (*c.* 2000 BC). A very fine jade face of this southern culture has been found in a Zhou tomb at Zhangjiapo in Chang'an county, Shaanxi province, and indicates that the Zhou were

Fig. 10 *Bronze ritual vessel,* lei, *from Sichuan Peng xian Zhuwajie. Early Western Zhou, 11th century* BC. *Height 69.5 cm. After Higuchi and Enjōji 1984, no. 195; rubbings of decoration after* Kaogu *1981.6, p. 498, figs 3: 2–4.*

Fig. 11 *Bronze ritual vessel, the He* zun, *and its inscription, from Shaanxi Baoji. Early Western Zhou, 11th century* BC. *Height 38.3 cm. After Higuchi and Enjōji 1984, no. 49.*

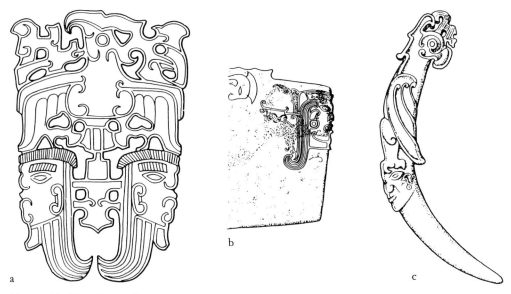

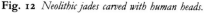

Fig. 12 *Neolithic jades carved with human heads.*
a *Bird with wings outstretched around two human heads in profile. Palace Museum, Beijing. After Wu Hung 1985, fig. 24.*
b *Detail of one end of a large ceremonial blade, showing a human head in profile. Freer Gallery of Art, Washington, DC. After Dohrenwend 1975, fig. 32.*
c *Bird with a human head in its claw. Metropolitan Museum of Art, New York. After Salmony 1963, pl. 11: 6. All neolithic period, c. 2500–2000 BC.*

Fig. 13 *Rubbing of the decoration on a jade handle, showing a human-like head with a crouching body, a bird and dragons. Western Zhou period, 10th century BC. Height 26.2 cm. Metropolitan Museum of Art, New York. After Salmony 1963, pl. 13: 2.*

familiar with such exotic pieces (no. 55).[30] These motifs frequently appeared on jades, especially on the multitudes employed in burial (fig. 13).

From about this period quite elaborate jade coverings for the body of the deceased were developed. These had hardly existed before. The fine jades of this period are exemplified by no. 57. Similar pieces have been found in late Western and early Eastern Zhou tombs from the Tianma Qucun area near Houma in Shanxi province (fig. 57.1). The masses of jades from tombs of this date are in complete contrast with the rather restricted numbers buried in the early Western Zhou,[31] a development which marked a major ritual change and was part of a whole complex of new developments.

At the same time, very fine bird decoration was evolved for bronze ritual vessels (fig. 14). These designs seem to have paralleled the use of birds on jades. The human heads employed on jades were not transferred to ritual bronze vessels and seem to have been excluded by convention (although they were permitted on weapons and chariot fittings). A renewed interest in animal-shaped bronzes did not affect the overall direction of the bronze development. On the other hand, bells, which came from the south, certainly did. A few bells are known from Shang tombs, but had little use, and were perhaps an exoticism that did not last. Bells

Fig. 14 *Bronze ritual vessel, the Gong zun, decorated with birds. Middle Western Zhou, 10th century BC. Height 24.3 cm. Pillsbury Collection, Minneapolis Institute of Arts.*

were reintroduced from the south, perhaps via the Han River, and are found in early Western Zhou tombs in western Shaanxi.[32] They did not at this stage achieve the size or magnificence of the southern examples, but came in sets of three, in graded sizes.

Following the so-called ritual revolution of the middle Western Zhou such bells became widespread. This revolution is marked by a dramatic change in the use of sacrificial vessels as well as bells (fig. 15b).[33] Perhaps stimulated by these southern examples and due to political instability, the whole repertory of ritual bronzes was dramatically altered in type, shape and decoration. The change was wholesale and so relatively sudden that it must have happened as the result of some sort of central decision.

While beliefs about the ancestors probably continued as before, practices changed. It would have been almost impossible to carry out the same ceremonies as those in the early Western Zhou once many of the earlier vessel types had been discontinued (fig. 15a), which they were. The wine vessels, *jue* and *gu*, were abandoned. There were also some new vessel types, which must have been required for new stages in the ritual. The traditional food vessel types, on the other hand, multiplied and were made in identical sets (fig. 15b). Such changes in ritual objects would have had repercussions on practice. Whereas in the Shang and early Western Zhou periods the majority of nobles had several tripods (*ding*) and food basins (*gui*), all of which were slightly different in shape or decoration and easily distinguished from one another, now such bronzes were usually identical, so there might be nine almost indistinguishable *ding* and eight identical *gui* in a set. These very similar vessels, almost impossible to tell apart, were also probably very like the bronzes belonging to other nobles of the same rank. Actions connected with one individual *ding* or *gui* could no longer be distinguished by the differences between the objects. So these vessels may have been used in ritual actions that were repeated. Indeed, there seems to have been an emphasis on mass and repetition (fig. 15b). Identical basins in any particular set were likely too to carry inscriptions of identical content, again the repetition seemingly in some way important. Repetition of the inscription may have been one of the benefits of the change. Certainly much more effort was put into the calligraphy of the inscriptions than into the decoration.

Such a change cannot have been the result of lack of artistic imagination. The jades, for example, show a wide range of new and inventively used motifs, including interlace.[34] It seems that there were deliberate restrictions on the decoration of bronzes. Indeed, the

15a

Fig. 15 *Drawings of the vessels belonging to the Wei family found in a hoard at Shaanxi Fufeng Zhuangbai.*

a *Vessels of early and middle Western Zhou date. These predate the burial of the hoard and were probably treasured antiquities.*

b *(overleaf) Vessels that belonged to Wei Bo Xing, probably the main set owned by the family in the 9th and 8th centuries BC. Top left: set of eight identical food basins, gui. Bottom: several sets of bells (see Rawson 1987, fig. 12; Rawson 1992b, fig. 231).*

After Beijing 1980g, nos 14–33.

15b

have been a view that simplified and repetitive bronze ritual vessel shapes and decorative motifs were desirable. Music, it would seem, was also officially endorsed.

The Eastern Zhou and Han periods

Nothing like this ritual upheaval took place when political catastrophe actually struck. In 771 BC the Zhou were defeated by the Quan Rong tribes from the west and fled to their eastern capital at Luoyang. The area dominated by the Zhou fragmented into many states.[35] In the two or three hundred years following the fall of Xi'an the ancestral sacrifices continued to dominate ritual life, but over this period display became paramount as an aspect of the competition that inevitably arose between major states, all striving for power.

Immediately after the defeat in 771 BC there was a dearth of bronze. The princes and nobles had left most of their principal pieces behind in Shaanxi, buried in pits. No doubt they hoped to return to unearth them, but they never did. In eighth-century BC tombs of the Guo state at Sanmenxia are buried many wonderful jades, but the bronzes are inferior. Indeed, many are small non-functional replicas, perhaps because there were no spare bronzes to be buried.[36] Everything available had to be kept in use above ground; some small pieces were quickly improvised. Other tombs further south are better equipped, perhaps because the area was richer and had been less devastated by the eighth-century upheavals.

There are signs of considerable improvement in bronze-casting quality in the seventh century BC, and the art of bronze casting flowered in the sixth and fifth centuries. A growth in all luxuries stimulated dramatic improvements in the quality and overall design of bronzes. One of the factors leading to this change may have been the steady introduction of gold, which had been surprisingly little used in ancient China, when greater value was placed on jade.

During the eighth century BC, perhaps because the tribes to the west were having such an impact on the Chinese heartland, gold items started to appear in élite tombs. The first pieces look as if they might have been belt ornaments; over the next two centuries more elaborate work began to appear in the forms of belt hooks and sword hilts. Such items are particularly well represented in Qin state tombs in western China. The impact on jade was immediate, with jade copies of the gold belt hooks and sword hilts appearing at the same time: both forms and decoration were copied.[37]

Both gold and jade were decorated with very fine motifs, often in relief and with patterns that imitated the

more inventive motifs, such as interlace, developed first on jades and appeared on bronzes only in obscure positions, on handles and bases.

We can, therefore, imagine the ritual changes being associated with two different types of development. First, it would seem that major decisions were made centrally, at court, about ceremony and objects for the ceremonies, involving a change in ritual practice. Many bronzes were cast as royal gifts to the Zhou élite and were thus under royal control. In addition, there may very finest and most elaborate goldwork. Fine stippled surfaces were easy to produce in gold, because it is a soft metal. We can recognise the imitations in jade and bronze from the care with which gold surfaces were reproduced in these much less tractable materials. The influence of this fine work is evident in the casting techniques developed at Houma, the foundry site of the Jin state in southern Shanxi province. Here a remarkable array of moulds and models has been found.[38] Many are decorated with strange creatures, whose wings and claws seem to have Central Asian elements (fig. 16). In addition, these creatures carry fine striated and stippled patterns that refer back to the gold already mentioned. Here is a striking example of an outside contribution to a native industry.

What is more, the refinement of detail possible in gold may also have stimulated the development seen at Houma of the mass-production of bronze moulds for casting. A mould for a bell handle is shown in figure 16. Both the griffin-like creatures and the fine detailing are probably derived from work in gold that may have come from further west. To generate this mould, a pattern or model was first carved in the positive. Several negatives or moulds could then be impressed from one fine positive and used for casting several different bronzes. This method of creating mould segments from highly worked positives, or pattern blocks as they are usually called, was well developed at Houma, where several stages of replication were involved. The reasons for this complexity were perhaps twofold. First of all, large numbers of similar if not identical bronzes had to be cast to produce the sets of food vessels, *ding* and *gui*, and the bells required for a small princely court (nos 58, 59, 62). As there were now many courts and princes, there was considerable demand for such bronzes. In addition, standards of finish had risen greatly with the influx of gold and the creation of jades to match. Within each state and in each material, whether jade, bronze or gold, there was an upward spiral of endeavour towards spectacular visual effects. Bronze casting reached a high point which it was to sustain for only a century or so, before declining in the face of new casting techniques and new preoccupations.

The bells and *ding* vessels from the sixth-century BC tombs at Xiasi in Henan province belong to this period of visual opulence (nos 58–60).[39] The vessels are magnificent large castings, which must have impressed both by their size and the intricacy of their ornament. In this case the ornament includes sections cast by the lost wax process. Here too is another important technological innovation, again spurred on by decorative imperatives. As mentioned above, ancient Chinese craftsmen were

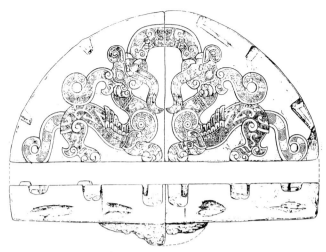

Fig. 16 *Drawing of the design on a section of the mould for a bell handle. The creatures have wings and claws like Western Asian griffins. From the Jin state foundries at Shanxi Houma. Eastern Zhou period, 6th–5th century BC. After Beijing 1993f, fig. 67.*

Fig. 17 *Bronze ritual vessel,* zun, *standing inside a basin,* pan, *from the tomb of the Marquis Yi of Zeng (see fig. 18). Eastern Zhou period, c. 433 BC. The two vessels are remarkable for their filigree decoration executed in lost wax casting (compare nos 58, 59).*

generally conditioned to make their models from a material that could not be melted out of the clay wrapping used as moulds (fig. 2). Their whole repertory of shapes and designs depended on this factor. In the sixth century rare examples of lost wax casting appeared, almost all on unusual pieces and in small appendages (fig. 17). This technique allowed filigree, as on bronzes from Xiasi in southern Henan (nos 58, 59). It is possible that this development, like the mass-production of moulds at Houma and probably other foundries, was the outcome of the need to emulate the fine qualities of gold. Gold, a soft and pliable material, is quite easily worked into openwork and filigree. Lost wax casting gave the bronze casters the means to reproduce some of the same effects.

However, lost wax casting did not catch on. The magnificent set of bronzes from the tomb of the Marquis Yi of Zeng (fig. 18) had a full range of *ding, gui* and bells, but only one item with lost wax appendages, a very rare wine flask, or *zun*, standing in a basin or *pan* (fig. 17).[40] This form was unusual, coming originally from the east coast, and was no doubt specially decorated to emphasise its outlandish qualities.[41]

The marquis's tomb contained a wide range of objects in different materials, including many lacquer items (nos 64, 65). Brilliantly coloured lacquer may well have inspired the next technical innovation, inlay set in bronze. A wide variety of inlays was experimented with (no. 71): copper and stone, then gold and silver. These bright gleaming metals had been used much earlier for inscriptions on bronze weapons and a few vessels, but they were not drawn from this specific role into more general use for over a century (fig. 19).

The use of inlay coincides with another important development: the burial (and therefore the use in life) of many more kinds of bronze objects than ever before. Meanwhile, standard ritual vessels were in relative decline. Indeed, ritual vessel sets in both southern tombs of the Chu state and the northern Zhongshan tombs are often undecorated. Alongside them lamps (no. 74), stands (no. 71) and incense burners (no. 82) were intricately decorated. Although the change is not mentioned in any texts, it is likely that attention to these new types of bronzes reflects new religious interests.[42]

New beliefs seem to have grown up in parallel with the ancient notion that after death the ancestors continued to exert influence in the world and had to be drawn into social life through the ceremonial banquets. New deities, of both the underworld and the heavens, were gaining increasing recognition. At first the interest in these deities, who included the immortals of the islands of Penglai in the Eastern Sea and the Queen Mother of the West (no. 101), with her palaces in the Kunlun mountains, did not involve the notion that the dead might join them; incense burners (no. 82), lamps (no. 87) and exotic wine vessels may have been intended for ceremonies connected with these distant immortal realms.[43] Previously unknown imaginary creatures were drawn into the visual repertoire. Winged beasts were represented as part of the universe among the objects

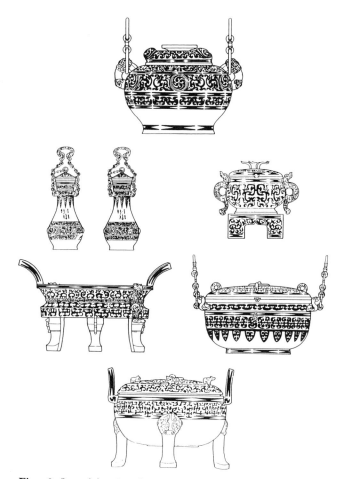

Fig. 18 *Some of the principal ritual vessels from the tomb of the Marquis Yi of Zeng, buried at Hubei Sui xian Leigudun in* c. *433 BC. After Beijing 1989c and Rawson 1992b, fig. 232.*

Fig. 19 *Bronze ritual vessel,* dou, *inlaid with gold. Eastern Zhou period, 5th century BC. Height 15.5 cm. Freer Gallery of Art, Washington, DC.*

buried in the fourth-century BC tombs at Zhongshan in Hebei province. The gaming boards from the same tombs, used perhaps for divination, also suggest that there were immortal worlds to which mankind hoped to have access (no. 76).

It is possible that changes in beliefs about the afterlife were responsible not only for the decline in the quality of bronze ritual vessels, but even for their disappearance from tombs. During the Western Han period ritual vessels had gradually diminished in importance, and in the Eastern Han they and other goods buried in tombs were made as ceramic copies. It is sometimes suggested that pottery replicas were an outcome of the economic impoverishment of the Han state (nos 78–86, 108–114). However, the one expenditure that no one would have wished to save on would have been the proper equipment of the dead for the afterlife. If burial goods changed so dramatically, the reasons for this change are more likely to have been religious and intellectual rather than purely economic.

The folk religious beliefs, which we today know as religious Daoism, were coming to dominate, with the effect that new religious practices quite distinct from the ritual offerings to ancestors now attracted attention and resources. The changes we see simply as differences in burial patterns were actually much more than that. Decline in the quality of the ritual vessels and the use of substitutes in tombs signal completely new attitudes to spirits, deities and the afterlife. There could hardly have been more fundamental changes in the outlook of the ancient Chinese (see Introduction). Just as the magnificence of the early bronzes (nos 39–45) is evidence of both the central role of ancestors in the minds of the Shang and Zhou and their belief in the continuation of life in the tombs, so too the decline in the use of bronze and its disappearance from burials present us with visual evidence of a complete change in the beliefs of the later Zhou and Han periods.

1 For a general discussion of ritual bronzes see Rawson 1987b.

2 Waley 1954, pp. 209–11.

3 Steele 1966, p. 57.

4 *Kaogu xuebao* 1981.4, pp. 491–518.

5 For a discussion of ancient casting techniques see Bagley 1987, introduction.

6 For a discussion of the Erlitou period and its Shang successors see Rawson 1987b, chapters 1–3; and the catalogue, nos 39–45.

7 For the contents of the tomb of Fu Hao see the archaeological report (Beijing 1980a); Thorp 1988b; and the catalogue, nos 39–45.

8 The one outstanding exception is the *jue* vessel (no. 41), which does not seem to have a neolithic origin.

9 *Kaogu xuebao* 1991.2, pp. 167–206.

10 For a discussion of such purposes of the ornament see Rawson 1993a.

11 The question of the origin and purpose of flanges has given rise to much discussion. The most convincing account of the definition of modules of decoration is given in Bagley 1987, pp. 26–8.

12 For a discussion of the *taotie* in the light of casting technology see Bagley 1987, pp. 19–20; for the range of issues raised by a search for meaning see essays in Whitfield 1993. It is becoming ever more evident that most writers on the subject of meaning have sought an oversimplified iconographic meaning, when discussion of a range of associations would be more appropriate.

13 The Liangzhu culture is discussed in the present catalogue (nos 16–20).

14 Rawson 1992c considers the appearance of exotic items in the Shang repertory.

15 Rawson 1995, introduction, discusses the durability of jade and the survival of ancient examples over several millennia, to be reproduced at much later periods.

16 This topic is discussed and illustrated in Rawson 1990, no. 50.

17 Lothar Ledderose has treated these as modules in a decorative system (Ledderose 1992).

18 The origins of the subdivision of labour have yet to be fully explored. Fruitful examinations are found in Ledderose 1992 and Bagley 1995; see also Keyser 1979.

19 The role of foreign exoticism in Anyang design is discussed in Rawson 1992a and 1994. For a study of exoticism in European art and design see Pomian 1990, pp. 1–64.

20 For a discussion of the way Shang power has been magnified and the cultural achievements and power of contemporaneous peoples obscured see Bagley 1992; on the role of the Zhou in this distortion see Rawson 1989b.

21 Rawson 1994.

22 Bagley 1987, pp. 32–6.

23 For illustrations of the vessels from Fu Hao's tomb see Beijing 1980b.

24 Beijing 1980a, pp. 235–8.

25 For a discussion of the Western Zhou see Rawson 1987b, chapter 5; Rawson 1989b; Shaughnessy 1991.

26 The best account of the distortion of the record that was the consequence of Zhou writing is given in Bagley 1992; see also another aspect of Zhou propaganda in Rawson 1989b.

27 A detailed account of Zhou ritual vessel shapes and designs is to be found in Rawson 1990, introduction.

28 Bagley 1987, pp. 32–8.

29 Shaughnessy 1991 gives a full account of Western Zhou inscriptions; for the Li *gui* see Shaughnessy 1991, pp. 87–105.

30 Uses of faces on Shang and Zhou bronzes and jades are summarised in Rawson 1993b.

31 Tombs of the Yu state near Baoji illustrate the contrast between early and middle Western Zhou use of jades (Lu Liancheng and Hu Zhisheng 1988).

32 Rawson 1987b, no. 28; Falkenhausen 1993.

33 Rawson 1990, pp. 93–110.

34 Rawson 1990, pp. 113–25.

35 Li Xueqin 1985a.

36 The recent excavations at Sanmenxia have been inadequately published; for a tomb at Shangcunling see *Wenwu* 1995.1, pp. 4–31. For some of the jades see Hebei 1991–3, vol. 2, nos 230, 231, 249, 273, 296.

37 This topic is considered in Rawson 1995, introduction and sections 21, 23. For gold and jade examples see *Wenwu* 1993.10, pp. 1–14.

38 For the moulds at Houma see Beijing 1993f; Bagley 1993b and 1995; Keyser 1979.

39 The excavations at Xiasi are discussed in the catalogue at nos 58–60; for an archaeological report see Beijing 1991c.

40 For the excavation of this tomb see Beijing 1989c.

41 Mackenzie 1991.

42 Rawson 1989a.

43 The question of the changes in beliefs during the late Zhou and Han period is a large subject, unfortunately little discussed in Western languages. Major contributions have been made by Anna Seidel (for example, Seidel 1982; Seidel 1983). See also Wu Hung 1984; and the Introduction to this catalogue.

THE STATE OF CHU

Yu Weichao

The extent of the ancient state of Chu should not be underestimated, nor should aspects of its culture. By the time of the Warring States period of the Eastern Zhou, from the fifth to the third century BC, the state of Chu occupied almost the entire southern half of the Chinese landmass.

The Chu people originated in the Yangzi River basin and seem to have gradually absorbed the smaller, less powerful surrounding cultures. In their early days they may have been dependent on the central Zhou state: the Han period historian Sima Qian, albeit writing much later, in the second to first century BC, records that the ancestor of the Chu people, Yuxiong, considered himself a descendant of the Zhou king, Wen. Later texts name the Chu capital as Danyang in the south of present-day Henan province, and recent archaeological finds relating to the Chu people discovered near the Danjiang reservoir in the far south of the province lend weight to this location (fig. 1).

By the seventh century BC the state of Chu was sufficiently powerful to begin its campaign of expansion. In 689 BC King Wen of Chu moved his capital to Ying, near the present-day town of Ji'nan in Jiangling county, near the Yangzi River in southern Hubei province. All that remains of this city are traces of a city wall (fig. 2). The Chu state then gradually expanded until it covered an area whose boundaries would today pass through the western province of Sichuan, the southern provinces of Yunnan, Guangxi and Guangdong, and as far north as Henan. Archaeological remains in the form of Chu burials of the late Spring and Autumn period (770–475 BC) have been found near the Xi River in southern Henan province. Later burials, of the Warring States period (475–221 BC), are concentrated around present-day Ji'nan. After the invasion of Ji'nan by forces of the state of Qin in 278 BC, the capital was relocated several times before the ultimate capital, Shouchun, in present-day Shou county in Anhui province, was finally laid waste by Qin troops in 223 BC.

By this time, however, the culture of the Chu state had achieved an identity powerful enough to manifest itself in the succeeding consolidation periods of the Qin

(221–206 BC) and the Han (206 BC–AD 220) dynasties. Elements of Chu cultural influence can be identified in the early Western Han period, particularly in the area of the present-day town of Changsha in Hunan province.

The peoples of the Chu state seem to have made specific and highly individual contributions to the development of ancient Chinese thought and belief. As the catalogue illustrates (nos 58–69), large tombs containing exceptional finds have been discovered in Hubei and Hunan provinces. Among the finds are bronzes that exploit and develop the central Zhou traditions of the manufacture and use of ritual vessels and bells. For example, the Marquis Yi of Zeng, who died in about 433 BC (Rawson, figs 17, 18), seems to have possessed vessels and bells which would have enabled him to practise ritual sacrifices similar to those performed in other areas of China. However, his tomb also contained highly unusual objects rarely if ever seen outside the south: among these a long-necked bronze bird with antlers (no. 63) is a spectacular example.

The antlers that crown this tall elongated bird indicate

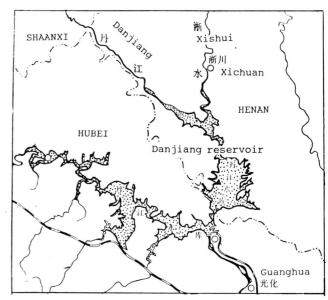

Fig. 1 *Map of area around the Danjiang reservoir, Henan province. After Beijing 1991c, p. 2, fig. 1.*

that it belongs to a large category of sculptures found in Chu state tombs. These sculptures were usually carved in wood, and indeed the state of Chu supported a strong tradition of carving in wood, perhaps due to the availability of the material.[1] Chu wooden sculptures may have developed from the simple carved wooden stands made to support real antlers. A large number of such wooden stands have been found in Chu tombs dating to the fifth century BC. In some cases the antlers are replaced by stylised elongated wooden birds and other creatures, some bearing real antlers as wings or horns (figs 63.2, 63.3). The long-necked bird, reminiscent of a crane, in the present catalogue (no. 63) is an example in bronze of such a fantastic creature. An example in root and bamboo is the beast from Mashan in Jiangling county, Hubei province (no. 66). Many of these sculptures have been found positioned near the head of the tomb occupant, and it is possible that they were regarded as tomb guardians. It is tempting to speculate that this early interest in crane-like birds and deer antlers was the beginning of the more intense focus on these two creatures by later adherents of religious Daoism.

Some of the Chu animal sculptures, both in wood and in bronze, are squatter and more solid and served as stands and supports for musical instruments (no. 61; fig. 71.1). Many of the wooden sculptures were painted in brightly coloured lacquer.

An ancient text known as the *Shan Hai jing* (*The Classic of the Mountains and Seas*) describes many strange and miraculous beings, often with attributes of several creatures. Although the text in its present form was probably compiled no earlier than the Han dynasty and perhaps later, some parts of it may date to the late Warring States period. The compilation of this text is sometimes linked with the Chu state and may reveal the interest of its peoples in strange creatures. At the same time, texts such as the poetry gathered together in about the fourth century BC as the *Chu ci* (*The Elegies of Chu*) reveal the interest of the inhabitants of the southern area in *wu*, that is, priests who acted as intermediaries between mankind and the spirit world. The term *wu* is sometimes translated as 'shaman', but perhaps this use of a term more commonly applied to quite different cultures is misleading. The *wu* are described in the *Chu ci* as interceding with spirits and gods. In addition, long journeys through the universe are described:

I bade heaven's porter open his barrier,
And stand by his gate awaiting my arrival.
I summoned Feng Long; I made him ride ahead
And ask the way to the Palace of Mystery.

Fig. 2 *Remains of the city wall of Ying, the former Chu capital, near present-day Ji'nan, Jiangling county, Hubei province.*

Passing through the Bright Walls I entered the House of God,
Visited the Week Star and gazed on the Pure City.
In the morning I set off from the Court of Heaven;
In the evening Wei-lü came in sight below.

I marshalled in order my ten thousand chariots
And moved slowly forwards in splendid procession.
Eight dragons drew my car, coiling and curvetting;
Over it a cloud-banner flapped upon the wind.[2]

Also to be found in Chu are traces of other religious and philosophical ideas, especially those associated with the school known as Huang-Lao, that is, an amalgam of interest in the legendary Yellow Emperor and in Laozi, to whom the foundation of philosophical Daoism is credited. Little was known about this school until a cache of manuscripts on silk was discovered in 1973 in tomb M3 at Mawangdui, near Changsha in Hunan province. The manuscripts revealed the strength of this school of thought in the area of the former Chu state.[3] Such ideas contributed to the rise of Daoism, the name given to the folk religious beliefs that developed into a series of concepts of the afterlife and of the deities who were believed to direct both the underworld and the celestial spheres.

Further evidence for the role of Chu in the gradual development of a new concept of the afterlife, including the paradises of the immortals, comes from another find

from Mawangdui, a banner painting found in the tomb of the wife of the Marquis of Dai (tomb MI), dating to the second century BC (fig. 3). This banner is literally a picture of the universe as conceived at that date in central China, in ancient Chu territory. At the centre of the silk banner stands the tomb owner, Lady Dai, supported on a stick and attended by servants. Below her is the underworld with its strange monsters, and above her are the heavens with the moon and sun. Large dragons prance beyond the gates of heaven.

Other parts of the tomb also contribute to the depiction of a universe.[4] For example, spirits and creatures of the spirit world are illustrated on two of Lady Dai's coffins (Introduction, fig. 13). It seems likely that these images of the universe were a particular contribution of Chu, as so much in this tomb is modelled on earlier Chu practice. For example, the shape of the coffin structure and the way in which the corpse was wrapped in the burial are both very similar to the Chu tomb at Mashan (no. 67), which dates from the third century BC.

The influence of the powerful state of Chu does not seem to have abated with the overthrow of its capital in 223 BC. This is nowhere more evident than in the finds from Mawangdui, which date from the century following the downfall of Chu. If, as is generally accepted, the coffins and banner painting at Mawangdui are a product of changes in Chinese attitudes to the afterlife which became linked with religious Daoism, it is likely that a number of the features of religious Daoism were already germinating in the influential state Chu during the preceding centuries. Although Daoism probably acquired features from many parts of ancient China, there is early evidence for a number of them in the state of Chu.

1 Mackenzie 1987.
2 Hawkes 1985, p. 196.
3 The school of thought known as Huang-Lao is discussed in Peerenboom 1993.
4 The concept of the whole tomb is discussed in Wu Hung 1992.

Fig. 3 *Drawing of the silk banner from the tomb of Lady Dai at Mawangdui, near Changsha, Hunan province. Han period, 2nd century BC. After Beijing 1973b, vol. 1, p. 40, fig. 38.*

THE ANCESTOR CULT IN ANCIENT CHINA

Chen Lie

In searching for the origins of any religious cult, the first task is to examine the response of primeval humans to the supernatural forces of nature. Their reaction may be divided into three phases: finding themselves faced with the incomprehensible animated forces of nature; then personifying these forces in the form of deities; and finally, worshipping these deities and developing this into varying forms of religion. All three phases are evident in the development of China's religions, but in China the second phase shows certain peculiarities. Not only did the ancient Chinese turn the forces of nature into deities, but they also developed a powerful veneration of the human soul, which they believed to be immortal. This was the beginning of the ancestor cult in ancient China.

The origins of the ancestor cult

As discussed in the essay by Lei above, there are indications of a belief in the afterlife as early as about 16,000 BC. This is the conclusion of the archaeologists who in 1939 discovered the remains of the Upper Cave Man, more commonly referred to as Beijing or Peking Man (*Sinanthropus pekinensis*), at Zhoukoudian near Beijing. At the rear of the dwelling cave were found three complete skulls and several bones, surrounded by red mineral powder, flints, stone beads, perforated teeth and shells.

The excitement of this discovery led to comparisons with the burials of Neanderthal man in Europe, who lived between 40,000 and 100,000 years ago. Neanderthals appear to have been buried with their heads to the east and their feet to the west, with red mineral sand scattered about the body and tools placed beside it. Scholars attribute the parallels between these widely separated burials to a common approach by early humans to the phenomena of nature and life. As the sun rises in the east, early man may have believed that the origin of life lay in the east, and conversely that the setting of the sun in the west meant that the realm of death lay in that direction. By placing the feet of the deceased to the west, the survivors were preparing a body for its journey to the realm of the dead. The scattering of red mineral powder on the body may have represented a desire to provide life-giving blood for the corpse, and the placing of tools beside it may have symbolised the deceased's need for equipment necessary for life in another world. This type of attention to the dead suggests a belief in the afterlife. It has even been suggested that Peking man buried his relatives in the dwelling cave so that the souls of the deceased could continue to exist as members of the living family along with subsequent generations.

Signs of religious beliefs become more widespread by the neolithic period. Red mineral powder is found in a number of burials of the north-western Yangshao and Qijia cultures (*c.* 5000–2000 BC), and there is evidence that provision may have been made to assist the passage of the soul out of the body of the deceased. A ceramic jar coffin (no. 9) of *c.* 3000 BC, excavated in Henan province, has a small aperture which may have been intended as an exit for the soul. Similar jar coffins have been found in the provinces of Shaanxi and Yunnan.

By the Han period (206 BC–AD 220), the concept of protecting the body and soul of the dead had been elaborated to the extent that certain individuals of high rank were buried in jade suits that completely encased the corpse. The crowns of both heads of the jade suits belonging to Prince Liu Sheng and his consort Dou Wan – buried at Mancheng in Hebei province in the second century BC – incorporated a *bi* disc, with a central hole through which it may have been thought that the soul could depart (no. 81, fig. 81.2). *Bi* discs have also been found incorporated into the head of the jade suit of King Liu Sui of Liang, buried at Yingcheng in Henan, and within a jade garment found in Xuzhou in Jiangsu province. The higher the deceased's rank, the greater the attention bestowed on the individual in death. A high-ranking person would in general have been considered an important contributor to the state and society, and his or her soul would, therefore, have been all the more worthy of veneration after death. It was hoped that, by appeasing such mighty souls, great rewards would later emerge in the affairs of daily life.

Early forms of the ancestor cult

The ancestor cult can be regarded as the natural consequence of the veneration of the souls of the deceased. Some theorists, including Marxist interpreters, have suggested that early society was matriarchal. In such a society the venerated ancestors would, of course, have been female. This premise has been used to explain the various discoveries of ceramic and stone female figures dating from the neolithic period.[1] The most significant of these are discussed in the essay by Lei, and one specimen is illustrated in the catalogue (no. 10). Two more, from a group of six discovered at Houtaizi in Luanping county in Hebei province, are illustrated here. Dating from *c.* 5000 BC, the largest is 34 cm in height (fig. 1), and the other is shown in the position of childbirth (fig. 2). Such figures may have been made to embody the soul of a female ancestor considered worthy of veneration, or they may have represented female deities worshipped in some form of fertility cult.

The veneration of a female ancestor has been suggested by some scholars based on the assumption that early peoples knew only their mother and not their father. It is assumed that these people imagined their mothers had conceived them through union with totemic species of animal or plant life or other inanimate phenomena. The painted fish on neolithic vessels of the Yangshao culture (*c.* 5000–4000 BC) of Banpo near Xi'an have been variously interpreted as such totems, or as symbols of the female sexual organs, or as representatives of the desire for fertility through the sacrifice of fish (no. 1).[2] The important status of women at Banpo has been argued on the basis that rich grave goods have been found in the graves of immature females, and in certain graves sons and daughters have been buried with their mothers.

Chinese legends also stress the role of women and recount the fantastical births of the male leaders of the mythical first peoples. Scholars in China suggest that during the Shang and Zhou periods there was a gradual transformation from a matriarchal to a patriarchal society, and that the procreative role of the male became a subject of worship. Archaeological evidence, however, points to a much earlier worship of the phallus. A ceramic phallus has been unearthed from a neolithic site of the Qujialing culture of *c.* 3000 BC (no. 11), and a conical human head in ceramic from Houwa in Liaoning

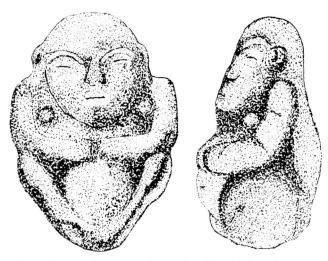

Fig. 1 *Drawing of a stone female figure from Houtaizi, Luanping county, Hebei province. Neolithic period,* c. *5000 BC. Height 34 cm. After* Wenwu tiandi *1993.6, p. 5, fig. 1.*

province bears striking similarities to a phallus. The ambiguity of gender in the human decoration on a ceramic vessel from a site of the Majiayao culture at Liuwan in Ledu county, Qinghai province (no. 5), may indicate a cultic emphasis on the roles of both sexes in procreation.

Because Chinese legends and historical writing have tended to focus on the ruling classes, in which succession was determined by blood relationships, it is tempting to assume that the ancestor cult was practised and exploited mainly by the ruling classes. Shang period oracle inscriptions from Yinxu near Anyang in Henan province often refer to a deity (*di*) who appears to have been considered as a remote ancestor. The Shang could, therefore, be said to have been claiming spiritual or superhuman ancestry in an attempt to buttress their rule.

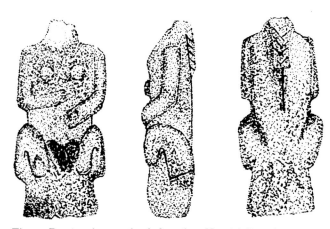

Fig. 2 *Drawing of a stone female figure from Houtaizi, Luanping county, Hebei province. Neolithic period,* c. *5000 BC. Height 20 cm. After* Wenwu tiandi *1993.6, p. 5, fig. 2.*

By the Zhou dynasty (*c.* 1050–221 BC) the system of hereditary rule is more apparent: a king was succeeded by the eldest son of his principal wife, and the offspring of secondary wives were granted land and official positions. During the Eastern Zhou period (770–221 BC) rulers claimed descent from the highest deity, Huangdi, who was himself considered an emperor, namely the Yellow Emperor.

The ancestor cult of the Shang and Zhou periods

In early Chinese texts we are told that the two most important duties of the ruler were to make sacrifices and to wage wars. Of the two, it seems that making sacrifices to the ancestors was considered the more important.

In the Shang period the deceased was given a posthumous or 'temple' name (*miaohao*) which was selected according to the calendrical day on which the person died. Burial was accompanied by a prescribed ritual ceremony, and regular sacrifices were made thereafter. These points are confirmed by the tomb of Fu Hao, consort of the late Shang king Wu Ding, who died in about 1200 BC. Her tomb contained a large number of ritual bronze vessels which she probably used during her lifetime and which were inscribed with the name Fu Hao (nos 40–45). However, also included in her tomb were bronze vessels inscribed 'Si Mu Xin' (no. 39). The name Xin was probably a posthumous name for Fu Hao, and would indicate that such vessels were cast specifically for the occasion of her burial, for her use in the afterlife. A rectangular *ding* vessel, now in the Historical Museum in Beijing, bears the inscription 'Si Mu Wu', thought to be another of Wu Ding's consorts who died three years before Fu Hao.

References to females are also evident in oracle bone inscriptions of the Shang period (*c.* 1200 BC). Mentions of a deceased mother (*bi*) are more numerous than those of a father or male ruler, and it has been suggested that the predominance of female names points to a matriarchal society. This situation appears to have changed during the Zhou period, by the end of which no special sacrifices seem to have been directed at female ancestors.

To both the Shang and the Zhou rulers it seems that the construction of an ancestor hall had priority over the construction of a palace. Moreover, the architecture of the ancestor hall reflected the hierarchical system for the veneration of ancestors. According to the precepts of Han dynasty ritual, the ancestor temple of the Son of Heaven consisted of seven main halls and two side halls (fig. 3). The first ancestor (*taizu*) was venerated in the main central hall, which was flanked by two side halls (*jiashi*) devoted to the ancestors beyond the seventh generation. The remaining six halls were for the veneration of the ancestors of the second to seventh generations: the three *zhao* halls, named for the 'ritual display [of respect]', were for the second, fourth and sixth generations, and the three *mu* halls, for 'respectful piety', were for the third, fifth and seventh generations. With the passing of generations, they were moved between the halls, with the exception of the first ancestor who remained perennially in the central hall.

Han dynasty ritual also stipulated that princes were allowed five main halls, not counting the two side halls, and the highest officials were permitted three. Only the ruler could make an annual sacrifice to his ancestors. The lower levels of society were allowed to honour family ancestors, but slaves were forbidden to do so. As well as these later ancestor halls, there is archaeological evidence from the late neolithic period of large halls which may have served both as public meeting places and as places for making sacrifices to the ancestors.

The Chinese ancestor cult was not based solely on the veneration of the soul of the deceased. It was also concerned with the individual soul's well-being, so that the deceased had to be properly equipped for life in another world. The task of supplying these material

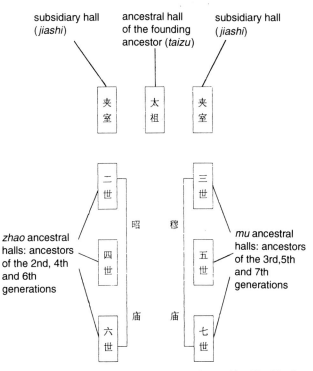

Fig. 3 *Plan of an ancestor temple of the Zhou kings. After Zhu Tianshun 1982, p. 211.*

requirements fell to the descendants, who would provide both grave gifts and subsequent sacrifices, so that the deceased could continue to live as he or she had on earth. The highest priority was nourishment, and we know from texts that food and wine constituted the greater part of sacrificial offerings. China's earliest lyrical texts, dating to the early Eastern Zhou period or perhaps earlier, reveal that sacrificial preparations were dominated by the obligation to lay out food and wine. Later ritual texts inform us that, during a sacrificial ceremony, various kinds of meat and wine were placed in bronze ritual vessels at several locations in the ancestor temple, and the souls of the ancestors were summoned by music and invited to accept these offerings.

The ancestor cult was entirely dependent on procreation. If a person had no descendants, the continued existence of his soul would be endangered. It was therefore considered worse to have no descendants than to neglect the performance of ancestral sacrifices.

The fusion of religious beliefs in China

Throughout the Shang and Zhou periods the veneration of ancestors underwent considerable change. During the latter part of the Eastern Zhou period, supreme power no longer resided in one ruler but was spread among numerous contending states. This situation was to have an effect on the ancestor cult, which for centuries had depended upon the strength of a hierarchical system of rituals culminating in a single supreme emperor.

During the reign of the Han emperor Wudi (141–87 BC), the philosopher and statesman Dong Zhongshu sought to combine the Confucian doctrine of the power of man with the spiritual power of the gods. He advanced theories of the unification of man and heaven, correlated to earthly rule by means of divine power. These theories were most welcome to rulers, who could thereby exercise the power of the gods, but were less acceptable to the lower ranks of society, who found themselves turning to the religions of Daoism and Buddhism, which by the Han period (206 BC–AD 220) were gaining widespread popularity.

Co-existence in China of the three major schools of philosophical and religious belief – Confucianism, Buddhism and Daoism – may seem remarkable. Indeed, it is likely that the deities and spirits of the three religions became fused to some extent. The reason can be found in the fact that all three accepted the overriding Chinese principle of veneration of the ancestors. Each was able to propagate its own doctrines in so far as these did not undermine the ancestor cult, ultimately the core of Chinese religious belief.

1 *Wenwu* 1986.8, pp. 1–17.
2 Zhao Guohua 1987.

Precursors and Early Stages of the Chinese Script

Roger Goepper

One of the most striking features of Chinese culture is its remarkable unity over such a vast landmass and such a long period of time. A contributing factor to this phenomenon may be China's unique writing system. A study of the evolvement of this system can help to illuminate some of the apparently alien characteristics of the Chinese, because it is this very system that has given form to the expression not only of daily activities but also of philosophical and religious concepts. The development of Chinese writing from neolithic marks and pictorial graphs to brush-written scripts of great aesthetic beauty in some ways reflects the consolidation of Chinese culture from local archaic traditions to the unified culture that is still clearly evident today.[1]

The Chinese language

Because the particular nature of the Chinese writing system is inseparably connected with the structure of the language, this should first be outlined briefly.[2]

First and foremost, the Chinese language is mono-syllabic, that is, each word consists of one syllable. This may be the result of a development that might have been complete by prehistoric times. It is possible that the language originally contained polysyllabic words which became monosyllabic due to changes in pronunciation and perhaps also under the influence of a particular writing system. A small pocket dictionary widely used in China today lists no fewer than eighty-six characters which are all pronounced *li*, but which have completely different meanings. The possibilities for confusion are to a large extent reduced by the tendency to create disyllabic words out of single-syllable synonyms, hence *shu* (tree) and *mu* (tree) are united to form *shumu* (tree).

The Chinese language can also be described linguistically as isolating, that is to say that single words do not change their form according to their position or function within a sentence. There is no inflection in any form, such as the declension of nouns or verbal conjugation. The position of a word within the sentence determines its function. Several words usually deemed essential for the structure of sentences in English, such as the pronouns 'I' and 'you', can be left out if they add nothing extra to the meaning of a sentence. Furthermore, without any alteration to their inherent form, many words can fulfil the functions of more than one part of speech: *ren* signifies not only 'a man' or 'men' but also the adjective 'human' and the verb 'to be human'.

Chinese is a tonal language, like other members of the Sino-Tibetan family. The speaker's pronunciation of any word is controlled by a variation of tones. Today's 'common language' (*putonghua*), based on the language of Beijing and its surrounding area, uses four tones, but Chinese languages using up to ten or more tonal inflections are common in southern China. Thus many homophonous syllables may be distinguished from each other and the appropriate meaning recognised. For example, *ma* pronounced in a high tone means 'mother', in a rising tone 'hemp', in a low tone 'horse' and in a falling tone 'to scold'.

These characteristics of the spoken Chinese language are important in considering the written Chinese language. In its literary form used by scholars and administrators, the written language has remained unchanged in its basic structure over a period of about two thousand years. A written language formed on the basis of the characteristics outlined above was destined to produce a writing system in which each syllable of its pronunciation was represented by a single written character.

The Chinese script

As in other forms of writing, such as Egyptian and Mayan hieroglyphs, pictures used for the representation of phenomena mark the beginning of the development of the Chinese script.[3] But in China these pictographic formulations were not ultimately transformed into abstract symbols representing the vocal sounds of an alphabet or a syllabary. Instead, they matured to become the written characters of the script, each representing a word and its meaning.[4] The resulting script is called logographic, which means in the case of Chinese that every sign represents a single-syllable word or – unusual in ancient China – the meaningful syllable of a word composed of two or more syllables. Logographs are what we observe in the earliest known form of Chinese writing, on Shang oracle bones of the thirteenth to eleventh centuries BC (no. 37).

By the Han period (206 BC–AD 220), a writing system whose origins were pictographic had long since completed a process of development into the complete system of signs which still exists today. In the earliest dictionary, the *Shuowen jiezi*, compiled in the first century AD, these signs are divided into six categories. The most easily recognised group of characters are pictographic representations (*xiangxing*) of phenomena which have been transformed into more or less abstract graphic complexes, such as the graphs for 'moon' (*yue* 月); 'sun' (*ri* 日); 'tree' (*mu* 木); and 'fish' (*yu* 魚). The second group comprises combinations of simple pictographs to make indirect symbols (*zhishi*, literally, suggestion of a situation), which express certain conditions, characteristics or situations. For example, the condition 'brightness' or 'bright' (*ming* 明) is expressed by uniting 'sun' and 'moon'; and 'early morning' (*dan* 旦) is evoked by placing 'sun' over a horizontal line representing the horizon. Associative compounds (*huiyi*, literally, corresponding to ideas) are formed by a similar combination of two or more simple characters. For example, the character for 'good' (*hao* 好) is formed by placing the signs for 'woman' and 'child' side by side; and 'man' (*nan* 男) consists of 'force' (*li* 力) and 'field' (*tian* 田) placed one above the other. Many such combinations may reveal early Chinese concepts and ways of thinking.

A further, more complex category of characters comprises mutually interpretative symbols (*zhuanzhu*, literally, transferred meaning), whereby the mirror-like reversion of a character or a slight alteration changes the meaning. When reversed, the character for 'official' (*si* 司) becomes 'empress' (*hou* 后); when slightly altered, the character for 'investigate' (*kao* 考) becomes 'old' (*lao* 老). There are also phonetic loans (*jiajie*, literally, borrowing) whereby a written character with one meaning is used for another pronounced with the same sound. For example, the character with the obsolete meaning 'to enter' (*ge* 各) is used as the pronoun 'each' or 'every'; the original pictorial representation of a sieve for grain (*qi* 其) is used for the pronoun 'this'; and the image of a scorpion (*wan* 萬), still recognisable to a cer-

tain extent in the present written character, is nowadays used only in the sense of 'ten thousand'.

However, by far the largest group, comprising about 90 per cent of all Chinese characters, consists of those made up of a least two components, one expressing the pronunciation, the other indicating the meaning. These are known as determinative phonetic characters (*xingsheng*, literally, image and sound). Examples include the combination of the verb 'to be able' (*ke* 可) and the graph for 'water' to compose the word 'river' (*he* 河); the juxtaposition of 'to divine' (*zhan* 占) with the character for 'to stand' to give 'to stop' (*zhan* 站); and the combination of 'to stand' with 'dark blue' (*qing* 青) to express 'quiet' (*jing* 靖). This system is based on the idea, probably developed during the early Zhou period (*c.* 1050–221 BC), that a word can be written with a graph suitable for its pronunciation and attached to a semantic signifier to clarify the meaning. This signifier is known as a radical or determinative. With this method the ancient Chinese were able to write, for instance, words for psychological attitudes and emotions by adding the radical 'heart' (*xin* 心) to any suitable phonetic graph. Many phenomena or conditions connected with fluidity could be expressed by the addition of the radical for water. In the Han period there were more than five hundred such radicals in use, but present-day dictionaries are arranged according to 214. This aspect of the writing system allowed early Chinese writers the potential of an enormously wide vocabulary.

Over the widespread area of Chinese culture the writing system was essentially invariable, even though long periods of time and vast geographical separations created the linguistic conditions in which different regional communities applied extremely varied phonetic readings to exactly the same written words. Variations of dialect, indeed spoken language, exist just as vigorously today, but the commonality of their speakers' written language still persists. All speakers of a Chinese language who were literate could communicate by writing with speakers of any other Chinese languages, provided that they too were literate. This extremely powerful unifying factor of Chinese culture is quite distinct from the difficulties still encountered by Europeans, who must learn each other's languages in order to communicate either in speech or by writing, or else adopt a common second language – once Latin, now English. That the ancient Chinese had apparently escaped the need for a second language gave rise to wild speculation in western Europe from the seventeenth century onwards that Chinese itself was communicated by means of images contained in ideographs which evolved and functioned totally independently of China's various spoken languages and their sounds.[5] Quite apart from misguided linguistic thinking, the conditions proposed by a system of ideographs would completely ignore the best modern psychological insights into how the human brain processes language.[6]

The scripts and functions of Chinese writing

Out of the early forms of Chinese writing, on oracle bones of the Shang period and on bronze vessels of Shang and Zhou times, there emerged around the middle of the Han period five basic scripts, some of which are still used today as ornamental or decorative scripts (fig. 1).

Seal script (zhuanshu) Ornament applies especially to this script, in which a strong pictographic element is still recognisable in many characters. On the so-called stone drums (shigu) of the fifth century BC this script was already fully developed (fig. 9). By the late Eastern Zhou period there existed local variants known as greater seal script (dazhuan), which were unified around 200 BC during the reign of Qin Shi Huangdi, the First Emperor, to become smaller seal script (xiaozhuan), which by imperial command was established as the orthodox script for the whole empire. Following the Han dynasty this script was used almost exclusively as a decorative script for the titles of commemorative stelae and tomb inscriptions. Today seal script is still deliberately applied as an archaistic variant. Its swinging strokes, with little visible difference of pressure from the writing instrument, make it especially suitable for engraving into hard materials and for writing with a brush on paper.

Clerical script (lishu) The pronounced and sometimes overemphasised differences in the thickness of strokes are characteristic of writing with a brush. Clerical script was developed during the last two centuries BC in the offices of imperial civil servants. It was soon acknowledged as the official script of the Han period, and may be found as an everyday script on narrow slips of wood or bamboo (no. 95) and on stone stelae. Even today it is often chosen for ceremonial occasions, especially in its refined form known as bafen.

Normal or regular script (kaishu, zhengshu or zhenshu) This script evolved some time between the late Han period and the fourth century AD. It was essentially a process of graphic simplification adopted in brush writing. It is still the most common script used in printed books today.

Cursive script (xingshu) This type of script, which might be described in the West as handwriting, employs many conventions which result from writing quickly, and speed provides its often highly individual character.

It was already fully developed by the fourth century AD.

Draft script (caoshu) This script, in which the characters are extremely simplified, was used in parallel with zhuanshu and lishu during the last centuries BC and quickly developed into a rapid style which allowed individual expression. In early forms of the so-called zhangcao (draft script for petitions), single characters were isolated graphic forms, unconnected with each other in the sequence of a line. Later, especially after the Tang period, whole vertical lines of a text were sometimes drawn together in one single, fluent, uninterrupted brushstroke.[7]

Each of these scripts had a special function determined by the content of the text and the occasion or purpose for which the text was being written. From historical times the most important texts were those transmitting a name or event to posterity and therefore they had to be handed down in an appropriate form (see fig. 40.2). For example, the inscriptions on sacrificial bronze vessels of the Western Zhou period are often placed on less visible parts of the vessel but, on the other hand, they clearly aim to impress by their formation and arrangement. Already at this stage the form and content of an inscription tended to aim for an effect of symmetry. Exemplary in this respect are the inscriptions on commemorative stone stelae of the Eastern Han period (no. 117), on portal-like buildings (que) and on pillars (zhu) marking the entrance to tomb areas, and on walls of natural rock (moyai) which, by their sheer size, attract the attention of the viewer. From about the fourth century AD commemorative inscriptions on Buddhist stone sculptures (zaoxingji) and, later, plaques designating the names of the halls of palaces or temples belong also to this category.

Closely related to this group are decorative inscriptions, which often form an integral part of the decoration of an object. Such inscriptions can be seen as early as the Eastern Zhou period on weapons (no. 68), on bronze mirrors of the Han period (no. 89) and later on the stone slabs covering tombs.

As far as longer texts and scriptures were concerned, legibility was of prime importance. The inscriptions on Shang period oracle bones (no. 37) may be regarded as precursors of longer texts, and it is possible that even at such early periods there existed texts written on more perishable materials which have since disappeared. A script for composing and transmitting scriptures was fully developed by the Western Han period and it was used for longer texts and treatises such as the medical works discovered in one of the second-century BC tombs at Mawangdui near Changsha in Hunan province. Such texts were originally written with the brush on

Fig. 1 *Four of the basic Chinese scripts. From top to bottom:* kaishu *(regular script),* caoshu *(draft script),* lishu *(clerical script) and* zhuanshu *(seal script). From the* Sanzijing *(Three Character Classics).*

narrow strips of wood or bamboo. These were held together with strings to form bundles which could be rolled up for storage (no. 95), in the manner of the later hand scrolls made of silk or paper.

Other forms of longer text were individual despatches and personal correspondence. The process of a more rapid execution with brush and ink led to an increasingly cursive script, of which there are examples datable to the Han period. It was such cursive scripts that resulted in the growth of an artistic form of brush writing in about the fourth century AD, which is today known as calligraphy. Although in its strict sense calligraphy means the execution of aesthetically pleasing characters, there is also in Chinese calligraphy a strong emphasis on personal expression.

The precursors of Chinese characters

China is of course not without its legends surrounding the invention of writing. It was believed that Fuxi, the first of China's three cultural heroes, had received the eight basic trigrams (bagua) of the later Confucian classic, the Yi jing (Book of Changes), from a dragon-like creature in about 3000 BC. Later, Cang Jie, an official serving the mythical Yellow Emperor (Huang Di), was said to have created written characters. Modern archaeology, however, presents us with more convincing theories.

Following the discovery in the mid-1950s of neolithic pottery dating to the fifth millennium BC at Banpo, near Xi'an in Shaanxi province, there was lively debate as to whether or not the marks on these sherds and other ceramics of different neolithic cultures should be regarded as precursors of the Chinese script (fig. 2).[8] Some of the Yangshao culture sites in Shaanxi province, such as Jiangzhai, have yielded pottery with marks similar to later written characters (fig. 2).[9] Pottery found

further east in Dawenkou, Shandong province, and dating from 3000 to 2500 BC, bears image-like marks composed of different graphic elements and thereby coming close to the so-called 'associative compounds' (huiyi) so characteristic of later Chinese writing. Typical is a graph documented in three versions, consisting of three components which could be interpreted as 'mountain', 'moon' and 'sun', and which is read by Chinese specialists as either 'morning' (dan 旦) or 'hot' (shu 暑). Other image-like depictions such as 'hoe' and 'hatchet' (fig. 3) are also documented.[10] From a total of some

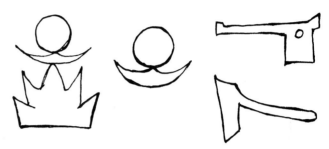

Fig. 3 *Marks on pottery from Dawenkou, Shandong province. Neolithic period, Dawenkou culture, c. 3000–2500 BC. After* Wenwu *1978.9, p. 75, fig. 2.*

twenty thousand sherds at the site of Chengziyai, also situated in Shandong but belonging to the Longshan culture and dating from about 2000 BC, eighty-eight sherds were found to bear graphic marks.

The Liangzhu culture in the coastal province of Zhejiang (nos 16–20) displays distinct differences from northern neolithic cultures, but the marks on its pottery resemble those on Longshan pottery, hinting at the possibility of intercultural diffusion. On some of the Liangzhu pottery there are simple signs similar to the later Chinese characters for numbers (fig. 4).

Fig. 4 *Marks on pottery from Zhejiang province. Neolithic period, Liangzhu culture, c. 3000–2000 BC. After* Zhongguo yuwen *1978.3, pp. 162–71.*

The marks or perhaps graphs of the late Erlitou culture (1700–1500 BC) in Henan province, shortly before the transition to the Shang period, may possibly be interpreted as precursors of the graphs appearing in Shang inscriptions on oracle bones (jiaguwen).

What distinguishes all of these neolithic marks from the archaic script of the Shang and Zhou periods is the fact that they almost always appear as isolated single

Fig. 2 *Marks on neolithic pottery. Top row: from Banpo, near Xi'an, Shaanxi province, c. 5000 BC. After* Zhongguo yuwen *1978.3, pp. 162–71. Bottom row: from Jiangzhai, Shaanxi province, c. 5000 BC. After* Wenwu *1975.8, p. 82, fig. 1.*

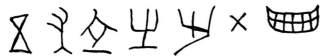

Fig. 5 *Marks on pottery from Wucheng, Jiangxi province. Erlitou period, c. 1700–1500 BC. After* Wenwu *1975.7, pp. 56–7.*

marks. They therefore do not represent the text of a living or extinct language, because one of the prerequisites for the definition of marks as writing signs is that they convey speech in visible form. They should not only be visual symbols, but must also be linked to a phonetic unit which represents a word or part of a word. The ceramics from Wucheng in Jiangxi province, datable to the period from 1800 to 1600 BC, present an interesting case. Although most of the graphs appear singly, there are also sequences of up to twelve characters which unfortunately cannot yet be interpreted as meaningful sentences (fig. 5).[11]

Although there have been attempts to match the marks on neolithic pottery with characters of the later Chinese script, or with those of the *Yi jing* (*Book of Changes*), and to attribute some meaning to them, it is more likely that the marks were made to distinguish certain pots within a larger lot, perhaps to indicate a pot's producer or owner, or even his or her position within a clan or tribe. K.C. Chang remarks that many of the characters in oracle and bronze inscriptions of the Shang and Zhou periods represent the names of social or political groups and not necessarily individual persons. The marks on neolithic ceramics should perhaps also be interpreted as emblems of the social group who owned the pots. Chang believes the marks were developed by craftsmen and not by scribes, and he sees the tradition continuing on Zhou ceramics. He has this to say on writing: 'The invention of writing in China was more associated with social identification than with economic transaction, and it was initiated by the common potters rather than by society's heroes and geniuses'.[12] This theory is backed by Guo Moruo, who realised that Chinese cursive scripts (*xingzhu*) predate the regular scripts (*lishu* and *kaishu*), the latter only emerging after writing had been monopolised by the ruling class.[13] Archaeological finds over the last few decades have shown that in the neolithic and even the Shang periods there existed several unrelated systems of marks and emblems which, in some cases, may have exerted an influence on each other and which eventually led, in the provinces of Henan and Shaanxi, to the origins of writing as we know it from inscriptions on oracle bones and bronze vessels.

Early forms of Chinese script

The basic structure of the Chinese writing system appears to have been developed during the second half of the Shang period, the so-called Anyang phase (*c.* 1300–1050 BC). At this stage the script appears, according to its function, in two rather different forms. There are inscriptions on bronze ritual vessels and there are oracle texts on bones and turtle shells. Writing which served other functions may also have been done on more perishable materials that have not survived.

The characters on bronzes (nos 39–46) are closer to pictographic images than those on oracle bones, and some of them form aesthetically appealing graphic structures. Many are marks or clan symbols similar to those on neolithic pottery and are only tenuously identifiable with later written characters.[14] In some cases they seem to depict the sacrifice of human beings (fig. 6), and occasionally they are placed inside a cross-like boundary

Fig. 6 *Characters inscribed on bronze vessels, showing two ritual scenes and a human sacrifice. Late Shang period, c. 13th–12th century BC. After Shimonaka 1954, pls 18, 23.*

which may correspond to the groundplan of the royal tombs at Yinxu or to the ancestor halls of the Shang period (fig. 7). Apart from dedicatory inscriptions stating the posthumous name of the deceased, a few longer inscriptions appear during the late Shang period.

Quite different in form and function are the texts inscribed on oracle bones (no. 37). The characters are in general engraved – only in rare cases written with a brush – on the hard and brittle surface of bones or turtle shells. With their simplified and increasingly abstract forms they were suitable for use as an everyday script, in this case the script of a social élite composed of nobles and priests. Many characters had several variants and no fixed form. About a third of the total of 2500 characters consists of phonetic combinations typical of the later writing system. The vertical arrangement

Fig. 7 *Character inscribed on a bronze lei, probably showing a ritual scene, inside a cross-like boundary. Shang period (c. 1500–1050 BC). After Shimonaka 1954, pl. 19.*

of lines can probably be attributed to the fact that much early writing was done on narrow strips of wood or bamboo (no. 95). Dong Zuobin distinguishes five different styles of script in a historical sequence, whereas in other classifications the styles are named after the clan names of leading oracle priests.[15] Although the texts deal with subjects of prognostication and were addressed in general to the ancestors or the spirits, their contents mostly appear as rather matter-of-fact record-keeping. Events that had already occurred, such as successful hunts, military campaigns, unusual weather phenomena and births and illnesses within the royal family, are all registered chronologically and thereby documented for posterity.

The Western Zhou period (c. 1050–771 BC) saw not only a decline in oracle texts but also an enormous increase in inscriptions on bronze vessels, commissioned at first mainly by the central Zhou court but in later times also by members of the nobility in local states such as Chu in the south. Military successes, enfeoffments and ceremonial events are documented in often quite long texts (fig. 9). To begin with Shang script was used, the size of characters often varying but becoming more unified over time. Occasionally the characters are placed within the squares of a grid.

In the Spring and Autumn period (770–475 BC) of the Eastern Zhou, local variants of scripts increase in number. In the south-eastern state of Chu characters formed of slender, swinging lines are often stretched into oblong vertical forms (fig. 8).

In the subsequent Warring States period (475–221 BC) the many local styles of script reflect the generally unstable state of Chinese civilisation at a time when the central Zhou dynasty reigned only nominally. The northern state of Qi continued to use a strictly conservative style, from which, after political unification, emerged the officially prescribed standardised small seal script (xiaozhuan). Well known examples of this script occur on stone drums (shigu) found in Shaanxi province and dating from the fifth century BC. They are covered in rhymed texts about hunting which are in parts difficult to read (fig. 9). In addition to this northern tradition there existed in southern China explicitly ornamental inscriptions on bronze vessels and weapons which were

Fig. 8 *Rubbing of inscription on a bell from the state of Chu. Eastern Zhou period, 5th century BC. After Shimonaka 1954, pl. 94.*

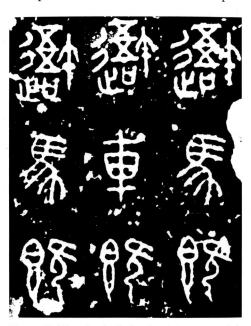

Fig. 9 *Rubbing of a detail of an inscription on one of the stone drums (shigu) from Shaanxi province. Eastern Zhou period, 5th century BC. After Shimonaka 1954, pl. 131.*

Fig. 10 *Rubbing of inscription in 'bird script' (niaoshu) on a sword hilt. Late Eastern Zhou period, 5th–3rd century BC. After Shimonaka 1954, pl. 108.*

often playfully enriched by the integration of small images of birds' heads into the characters. These gave rise to the name 'bird script' (*niaoshu*) (fig. 10). Such stylistic forms, which were obviously intended to create a decorative effect, are expressions of the material and cultural wealth of the south-eastern area, especially the state of Chu.

Within the same geographical area can be found the use of quite simple scripts on the seals of officials, on coins made of bronze and on lacquer objects. There also existed specific types of everyday writing on strips or slips (*jian*) made of wood or bamboo, and even on silk, accompanied by pictorial illustrations.[16] These different types and stylistic forms of writing must be seen in close connection with social changes. Writing was no longer the sole monopoly of the social élite, represented by the royal family and the nobility, but was also used by lords of lower feudal rank, by ministers and officials of the state and even by commoners trained as members of a clerical personnel.

Qin Shi Huangdi, the unifier of an empire and the first emperor of the short-lived Qin dynasty (221–206 BC), in response to a policy proposal by his chancellor Li Si in 213 BC and following the promulgation of his general regulations for the unification of measurements, weights and legal administration, ordered a standardisation of all local writing forms. The result was the so-called small seal script (*xiaozhuan*) which was stipulated for use in all government business throughout the empire. It was applied most effectively, and in a way that was visible to all members of the population, on the stone stelae known as *songdebei* (stelae for the praise of the emperor's virtues), which Qin Shi Huangdi had erected in all parts of the empire following his halts during inspection tours. Fragments of only two of them remain today.[17] Examples of this standard writing system can still be found on vessels for measurement and on weights (fig. 11). For the first time in Chinese history, a certain type of writing had become an instrument for the execution of a political programme. Its standardisation was meant to guarantee the functioning of administration, even in the most remote areas of the huge centralised empire where diverse Chinese languages and many other languages were spoken. At the same time, the destruction of scriptures which did not conform to Qin ideology aimed to secure the unification of intellectual culture.

During the four centuries of the Han dynasty (206 BC–AD 220) nearly all aspects of the Chinese script as it is used today were developed. The transformation of the slightly cumbersome *xiaozhuan* of the Qin period into the clerical script (*lishu*), the style characteristic of

Fig. 11 *Rubbing of inscription on a standard weight. Qin dynasty (221–206 BC). After Shimonaka 1954, pl. 138.*

the Han period, probably occurred in the offices of civil servants. The accentuated start of each stroke and its feather-like ends are obvious indications of the use of a brush. Clerical script reached its full aesthetic flowering towards the end of the Han period in the form known as *bafen*, but there also existed variants which were rather closer to the later regular script (*kaishu*). The development of writing styles can be traced through the great number of stone inscriptions of the period, many of them dated.

A parallel trend may be observed in the non-official texts on wooden tablets (*mudu*) and on bamboo strips (*zhujian*) which made up an early form of Chinese 'book' when bound in sequence by cords (no. 95). Decorative styles of writing persisted, for instance, on the round tile ends edging the roofs of palaces and on the seals of officials.

The central role played by writing within Han culture is evident from the fact that private individuals began to collect texts. Previously texts were collected only by the imperial library, which contained most of the existing works of literature, and by other official libraries. The eminent official Cai Yong (AD 132–92) is reported to have owned more than ten thousand texts in scroll form.[18] The growing role of writing in all aspects of Chinese civilisation led to the emergence of cursive scripts (*xingshu* and *caoshu*) which were to become so important in later times. These were created not from *kaishu*, which originated only after the Han period, but directly out of the *xiaozhuan* and *lishu* scripts (fig. 12). In its early form – *zhangcao* (draft script for petitions) – the single characters were placed one below the other in the line without any connection, whereas in the later *jincao* (modern draft script) several characters were often combined in one continuous brushstroke.

High-ranking officials such as Cai Yong (no. 117) won considerable career approval due to their writing ability. But critical voices also opposed, in particular, cursive forms of script as symptomatic of the decadence of Confucian values. In his *Disapproval of Draft Script (Fei caoshu)*[19] of about AD 200, Zhao Yi ascribes to such forms of writing the 'disregard of canonical authority and the pursuit of vulgarity' (*beijing qusu*). However, the later development of Chinese brush writing into one of the highest forms of art, on a par with poetry and paint-

Fig. 12 *Characters for* sui *(years of age, top) and* cheng *(to become, bottom), showing development from* lishu *(clerical script) at left to* caoshu *(draft script) at right.*

ing, was to prove such a statement untenable. Whereas in the fourth century AD only cursive scripts had been considered suitable for artistic expression, from the Tang period (AD 618–906) onwards theorists on the arts of writing judged the classical regular script equal in stature to the cursive scripts and therefore also worthy of artistic interpretation by the writer.

1 A comprehensive account of early Chinese scripts and books is given in Tsien Tsuen-hsiun 1962.
2 An excellent account of the peculiarities of the Chinese language and writing can be found in Needham 1961, pp. 27–41.
3 For a recent and highly readable acount of the transition from pictographic to phonetic writing forms in several civilisations see Coe 1992, pp. 13–45.
4 Indispensable sourcebooks for the formal and phonetic development of Chinese characters are Karlgren 1972, Lindqvist 1990, Wang Hongyuan 1993 and Guo Moruo 1991.
5 For a history and comparative considerations of this still common misapprehension of the workings of ancient Chinese see Boltz 1994, pp. 3–15.
6 Pinker 1994.
7 For a fuller discussion of the five scripts see Boltz 1994, pp. 143–55.
8 Keightley 1983, pp. 323–91.
9 *Wenwu* 1975.8, pp. 82–6.
10 *Wenwu* 1978.9, pp. 74–6.
11 *Wenwu* 1974.7, pp. 72–6; *Wenwu* 1975.7, pp. 51–76. A list of the characters found at Wucheng is given in Keightley 1983, pp. 340–1.
12 For comments concerning the marks on neolithic pottery see Chang Kwang-Chih, 'Prehistoric and Shang Pottery Inscriptions' (unpublished draft). For Western Zhou marks see *Wenwu* 1988.2, pp. 81–8.
13 *Kaogu* 1972.3, p. 3.
14 Chang Kwang-chih 1986b, pp. 141–206.
15 *Kaogu* 1979.6, pp. 510–14.
16 Barnard 1973b.
17 Shimonaka 1954, pls 135–7.
18 Tsien Tsuen-hsiun 1962.
19 Some of this text is translated in Acker 1954, LIV–LVIII.

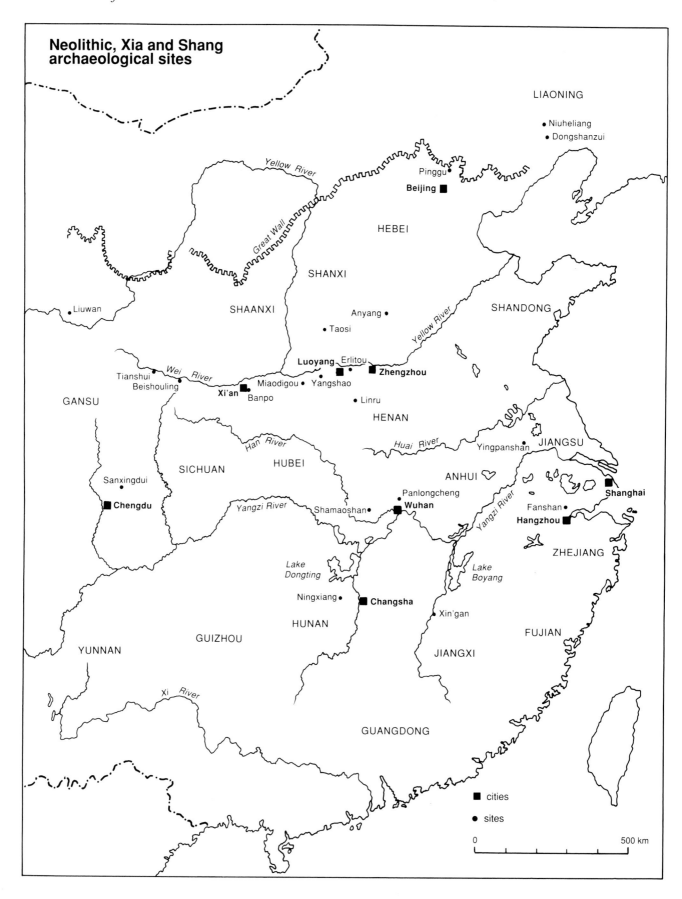

Neolithic, Xia and Shang archaeological sites

LIAONING

• Niuheliang
• Dongshanzui

Pinggu •
Beijing ■

Yellow River

HEBEI

Great Wall

SHANXI

SHANDONG

• Liuwan

SHAANXI

Anyang •

• Taosi

Yellow River

Tianshui
•
Beishouling

Wei River

Luoyang Erlitou
■ ■ **Zhengzhou**

Miaodigou • Yangshao
Xi'an ■
Banpo

• Linru

GANSU

HENAN

Han River

Huai River

Yingpanshan •

JIANGSU

SICHUAN

HUBEI

ANHUI

• Sanxingdui

Yangzi River

Shamaoshan •

Panlongcheng
■ **Wuhan**

Yangzi River

Shanghai ■

Fanshan •
Hangzhou ■

■ **Chengdu**

Lake Dongting

Lake Boyang

ZHEJIANG

Ningxiang •
■ **Changsha**

• Xin'gan

FUJIAN

HUNAN

JIANGXI

YUNNAN

GUIZHOU

Xi River

GUANGDONG

■ cities

• sites

0   500 km

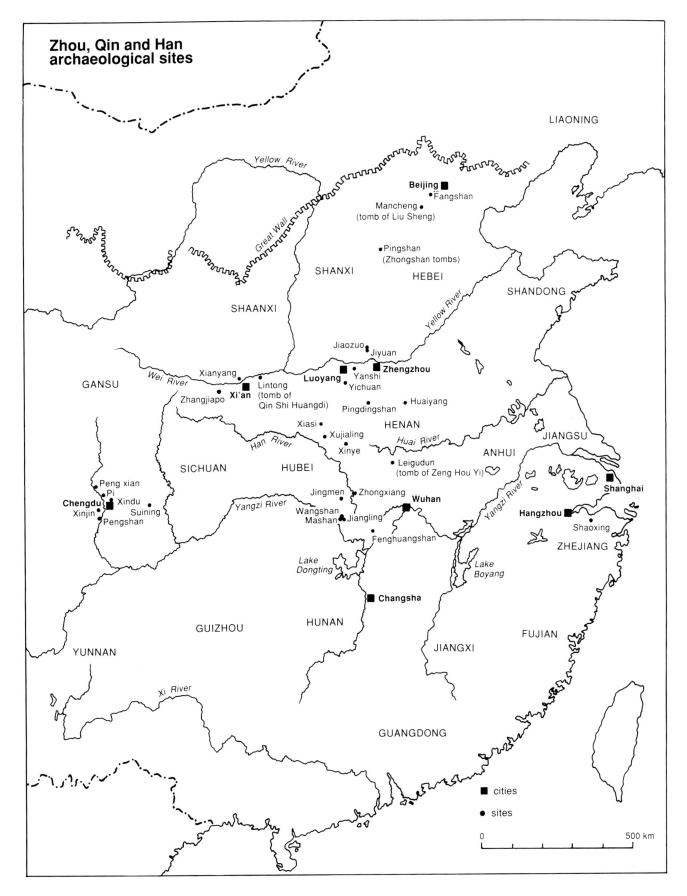

Zhou, Qin and Han archaeological sites

LIAONING

Yellow River

Great Wall

Beijing ■
• Fangshan

Mancheng
(tomb of Liu Sheng)

• Pingshan
(Zhongshan tombs)

SHANXI

HEBEI

SHANDONG

SHAANXI

Yellow River

Jiaozuo
• Jiyuan
• **Zhengzhou**

Wei River   Xianyang
• **Luoyang** Yanshi
• Yichuan

GANSU

Lintong
Zhangjiapo • **Xi'an** • (tomb of
Qin Shi Huangdi)

Pingdingshan

• Huaiyang

HENAN

Xiasi •
• Xujialing
• Xinye

Han River

Huai River

JIANGSU

ANHUI

• Leigudun
(tomb of Zeng Hou Yi)

Yangzi River

Peng xian •
Pi •
Chengdu ■ • Xindu
Xinjin • • Suining
• Pengshan

SICHUAN

HUBEI

Jingmen • • Zhongxiang
Wangshan • **Wuhan**
Mashan • • Jiangling

Yangzi River

■ **Shanghai**

Hangzhou ■
• Shaoxing

ZHEJIANG

• Fenghuangshan

Lake
Dongting

Lake
Boyang

GUIZHOU

HUNAN

Changsha ■

JIANGXI

FUJIAN

YUNNAN

Xi River

GUANGDONG

■ cities

• sites

0 _____ 500 km

283

CHRONOLOGY

UNKNOWN CHINA

Neolithic period   *c.* 6000–*c.* 1700 BC

North-eastern China

Xinglongwa	*c.* 5000 BC
Chahai	*c.* 4500 BC
Zhaobaogou	*c.* 4500–*c.* 4000 BC
Hongshan	*c.* 3500–*c.* 2500 BC

North-central China

Central Yangshao	*c.* 5000–*c.* 3000 BC
Gansu Yangshao	*c.* 3500–*c.* 1500 BC

Eastern China

Dawenkou	*c.* 4500–*c.* 2500 BC
Longshan	*c.* 2500–*c.* 1700 BC

South-eastern China

Hemudu	*c.* 5000–*c.* 4500 BC
Majiabang	*c.* 5000–*c.* 4000 BC
Songze	*c.* 4000–*c.* 3000 BC
Liangzhu	*c.* 3500–*c.* 2500 BC

South-central China

Daxi	*c.* 5000–*c.* 3000 BC
Qujialing	*c.* 4000–*c.* 3000 BC
Shijiahe	*c.* 2500–*c.* 2000 BC
Erlitou period	*c.* 1700–*c.* 1500 BC

GREAT DYNASTIES

Shang	*c.* 1500–*c.* 1050 BC
Erligang period	*c.* 1500–*c.* 1300 BC
Anyang period	*c.* 1300–*c.* 1050 BC
Western Zhou	*c.* 1050–771 BC
Eastern Zhou	770–221 BC
Spring and Autumn Period	770–475 BC
Warring States Period	475–221 BC

IMPERIAL CHINA

Qin	221–206 BC
Han	206 BC–AD 220
Western Han	206 BC–AD 9
Xin	AD 9–25
Eastern Han	AD 25–220

BIBLIOGRAPHY

Acker 1954 Acker, W. R. B. *Some T'ang and pre-T'ang Texts on Chinese Painting*, Leiden, 1954

Allan 1991 Allan, Sarah. *The Shape of the Turtle: Myth, Art, and Cosmos in Early China*, New York, 1991

Allan 1993 Allan, Sarah. 'Art and Meaning' and 'Epilogue' in Whitfield 1993, pp. 9–33, 161–76

Allen 1950 Allen, M. R. 'Early Chinese Lamps', *Oriental Art*, 1950.4, pp. 133–41

Anhui 1987 Anhui Sheng Bowuguan. *Anhui Sheng Bowuguan cang qingtongqi*, Shanghai, 1987

d'Argencé 1966 d'Argencé, René-Yvon Lefebvre. *Ancient Chinese Bronzes in the Avery Brundage Collection*, San Francisco, 1966

Bagley 1987 Bagley, Robert W. *Shang Ritual Bronzes in the Arthur M. Sackler Collections*, Washington, DC, and Cambridge, Mass., 1987

Bagley 1988 Bagley, Robert W. 'Sacrificial pits of the Shang period at Sanxingdui in Guanghan county, Sichuan province', *Arts Asiatiques*, vol. XLIII, 1988, pp. 78–86

Bagley 1990 Bagley, Robert W. 'A Shang City in Sichuan Province', *Orientations*, November 1990, pp. 52–67

Bagley 1992 Bagley, Robert W. 'Changjiang Bronzes and Shang Archaeology' in *International Colloquium on Chinese Art History, 1991, Proceedings, Antiquities, Part 1*, Taipei, 1992, pp. 209–55

Bagley 1993a Bagley, Robert W. 'An Early Bronze Age Tomb in Jiangxi Province', *Orientations*, July 1993, pp. 20–36

Bagley 1993b Bagley, Robert W. 'Replication Techniques in Eastern Zhou Bronze Casting' in Lubar and Kingery 1993, pp. 234–41

Bagley 1995 Bagley, Robert W. 'What the Bronzes from Hunyuan Tell Us about the Foundry at Houma', *Orientations*, January 1995, pp. 46–54

Barnard 1973a Barnard, Noel. 'Records of Discoveries of Bronze Vessels in Literary Sources and Some Pertinent Remarks on Aspects of Chinese Historiography', *Journal of the Institute of Chinese Studies of the Chinese University of Hong Kong*, vol. 6, no. 2, 1973, pp. 455–546

Barnard 1973b Barnard, Noel. 'The Ch'u Silk Manuscript, Translation and Commentary', *Monographs on Far Eastern History*, no. 5, 1973

Barnard 1990 Barnard, Noel. 'Some Preliminary Thoughts on the Significance of the Kuang-han Pit-burial Bronzes and Other Artifacts', *Beiträge zur allgemeinen und vergleichenden Archäologie*, 9–10, 1990, pp. 249–79

Bauer 1971 Bauer, W. *China und die Hoffnung auf Glück*, Munich, 1971

Beck 1990 Beck, B. J. Mansvelt. *The Treatises of Later Han: Their Authors, Sources, Contents and Place in Chinese Historiography*, Leiden, 1990

Beijing 1954 *Chu wenwu zhanlan tulu*, Beijing, 1954

Beijing 1956a *Hui Xian fajue baogao*, Beijing, 1956

Beijing 1956b *Shou Xian Cai Hou mu chutu yiwu*, Beijing, 1956

Beijing 1957a *Changsha fajue baogao*, Beijing, 1957

Beijing 1957b *Nan Tang er ling*, Beijing, 1957

Beijing 1958 *Wu sheng chutu zhongyao wenwu zhanlan tulu*, Beijing, 1958

Beijing 1959a *Zhengzhou Erligang*, Beijing, 1959

Beijing 1959b *Shandong wenwu xuanji – pucha bufen*, Beijing, 1959

Beijing 1959c *Shangcunling Guoguo mudi*, Beijing, 1959

Beijing 1959d *Luoyang Shaogou Han mu*, Beijing, 1959

Beijing 1959e *Luoyang Zhongzhoulu*, Beijing, 1959

Beijing 1959f *Shanbiaozhen yu Liulige*, Beijing, 1959

Beijing 1960 *Hunan chutu tongjing tulu*, Beijing, 1960

Beijing 1961 *Xin Zhongguo di kaogu shouhuo*, Beijing, 1961

Beijing 1962 *Fengxi fajue baogao*, Beijing, 1962

Beijing 1963a *Xi'an Banpo*, Beijing, 1963

Beijing 1963b *Jiangsu Sheng chutu wenwu xuanji*, Beijing, 1963

Beijing 1963c *Fufeng Qijiacun qingtongqi qun*, Beijing, 1963

Beijing 1963d *Nei Menggu chutu wenwu xuanji*, Beijing, 1963

Beijing 1964 *Qian Shu Wang Jian mu fajue baogao*, Beijing, 1964

Beijing 1965 *Chang'an Zhangjiapo Xi Zhou tongqi qun*, Beijing, 1965

Beijing 1972a *Xin Zhongguo chutu wenwu*, Beijing, 1972

Beijing 1972b *Wenhua da geming qijian chutu wenwu, di yi ji*, Beijing, 1972

Beijing 1973a *Zhonghua Renmin Gongheguo chutu wenwu zhanlan zhanpin xuanji*, Beijing, 1973

Beijing 1973b *Changsha Mawangdui yi hao Han mu*, 2 vols, Beijing, 1973

Beijing 1974a *Dawenkou*, Beijing, 1974

Beijing 1974b *Gugong Bowuyuan cang gongyi pinxuan*, Beijing, 1974

Beijing 1976a *Zhonghua Renmin Gongheguo chutu wenwu xuan*, Beijing, 1976

Beijing 1976b *Yinxu, nuli shehui di yige suoying*, Beijing, 1976

Beijing 1978a *Guangxi chutu wenwu*, Beijing, 1978

Beijing 1978b *Zhongguo lidai huihua Gugong Bowuyuan cang hua ji*, Beijing, 1978

Beijing 1979a *Wenwu kaogu gongzuo sanshi nian 1949–1979*, Beijing, 1979

Beijing 1979b *Shaanxi chutu Shang Zhou qingtongqi*, vol. 1, Beijing, 1979

Beijing 1979c *Shang Zhou kaogu*, Beijing, 1979

Beijing 1979d *Qinghai caitao*, Beijing, 1979

Beijing 1979e *Gansu caitao*, Beijing, 1979

Beijing 1980a *Yinxu Fu Hao mu*, Beijing, 1980 (see Beijing 1984i)

Beijing 1980b *Shaanxi chutu Shang Zhou qingtongqi wenshi*, Beijing, 1980

Beijing 1980c *Hebei sheng chutu wenwu xuanji*, Beijing, 1980

Beijing 1980d *Shaanxi chutu Shang Zhou qingtongqi*, vol. 3, Beijing, 1980

Beijing 1980e *Sui Xian Zeng Hou Yi mu*, Beijing, 1980

Beijing 1980f *Zhongguo Kaogu Xuehui di yici nianhui lunwen ji 1979*, Beijing, 1980

Beijing 1980g *Mancheng Han mu fajue baogao*, 2 vols, Beijing, 1980

Beijing 1980h *Bang Chang'an chengjiao Sui Tang mu*, Beijing, 1980

Beijing 1981a *Henan chutu Shang Zhou qingtongqi*, vol. 1, Beijing, 1981

Beijing 1981b *Guangzhou Han mu*, 2 vols, Beijing, 1981

Beijing 1981c *Zhongshan Wang Cuo muqi wenxue bian*, Beijing, 1981

Beijing 1981d *Yunmeng Shuihudi*, Beijing, 1981

Beijing 1982a *Zhongguo Kaogu Xuehui di erci nianhui lunwen ji 1980*, Beijing, 1982

Beijing 1982b *Yinxu yuqi*, Beijing, 1982

Beijing 1983a *Zhongguo kaoguxue zhong Tan shisi niandai shuju ji 1965–1981*, Beijing, 1983 (errata listed in *Kaogu* 1984.3, p. 288)

Beijing 1983b *Xin chu jinwen fenyu jianmu*, Beijing, 1983

Beijing 1983c *Baoji Beishouling*, Beijing, 1983

Beijing 1984a *Shang Zhou qingtongqi wenshi*, Beijing, 1984

Beijing 1984b *Shaanxi chutu Shang Zhou qingtongqi*, vol. 4, Beijing, 1984

Beijing 1984c *Jiangling Yutaishan Chu mu*, Beijing, 1984

Beijing 1984d *Zhongguo Kaogu Xuehui di sanci nianhui lunwen ji, 1981*, Beijing, 1984

Beijing 1984e *Xin Zhongguo di kaogu faxian he yanjiu*, Beijing, 1984

Beijing 1984f *Zhongguo kaoguxue nianjian, 1984*, Beijing, 1984

Beijing 1984g *Chu wenhua kaogu dashi ji*, Beijing, 1984

Beijing 1984h *Qinghai Liuwan*, 2 vols, Beijing, 1984

Beijing 1984i 2nd printing of Beijing 1980a, with additional material at pp. 241–88, consisting of four essays on the Fu Hao tomb reprinted from earlier publications: Xia Nai, 'Shangdai yuqi di fenlei, dingming he yongtu' (*Kaogu* 1983.5, pp. 455–671); Zheng Zhenxiang and Chen Zhida, 'Lun Fu Hao mu dui Yinxu wenhua he buci duandai di yiyi' (*Kaogu* 1981.6, pp. 511–18); Zhongguo Shehui Kexueyuan Kaogu Yanjiusuo Shiyanshi, 'Fu Hao mu tongqi chengfen di ceding baogao' (*Kaoguxue jikan 2*, 1980, pp. 181–93); and Zhang Peishan, 'Anyang Yinxu Fu Hao mu zhong yuqi baoshi di jianding' (*Kaogu* 1982.2, pp. 204–61)

Beijing 1984j *Yin Zhou jinwen jicheng*, vol. 1, Beijing, 1984

Beijing 1984k Zhongguo Yishu Yanjiuyuan Yinyue Yanjiusuo (ed.). *Zhongguo yinyue cidian*, Beijing, 1984

Beijing 1985a *Yinxu qingtongqi*, Beijing, 1985

Beijing 1985b *Chutu wenxian yanjiu*, Beijing, 1985

Beijing 1985c *Beijing Tushuguan cang qingtongqi mingwen taben xuanbian*, Beijing, 1985

Beijing 1985d *Zhongguo meishu quanji: Diaosu bian 2, Qin Han diaosu*, Beijing, 1985

Beijing 1985e *Nanyang Handai huaxiangshi*, Beijing, 1985

Beijing 1985f *Jiangling Mashan Chu mu*, Beijing, 1985

Beijing 1986a *Zhongguo kaoguxue yanjiu, Xia Nai Xiansheng kaogu wushi nian jinian lunwenji*, 2 vols, Beijing, 1986

Beijing 1986b *E'erduosi shi qingtongqi*, Beijing, 1986

Beijing 1986c *Xinyang Chu mu*, Beijing, 1986

Beijing 1987a *Quanguo chutu wenwu zhenpinxuan, 1976–84*, Beijing, 1987

Beijing 1987b *Songze, Xinshiqi shidai yizhi fajue baogao*, Beijing, 1987

Beijing 1987c *Ba Shu kaogu lunwenji*, Beijing, 1987

Beijing 1988a *Jiangzhai, Xinshiqi shidai yizhi fajue baogao*, 2 vols, Beijing, 1988

Beijing 1988b *Jiao Xian Sanlihe*, Beijing, 1988

Beijing 1989a *Xichuan Xiawanggang*, Beijing, 1989

Beijing 1989b *Beijing Dabaotai Han mu*, Beijing, 1989

Beijing 1989c *Zeng Hou Yi mu*, 2 vols, Beijing, 1989

Beijing 1990a *Zhongguo wenwu jinghua*, Beijing, 1990

Beijing 1990b *Wenwu kaogu gongzuo shi nian, 1979–89*, Beijing, 1990

Beijing 1990c *Ding Ling, The Imperial Tomb of the Ming Dynasty*, 2 vols, The Institute of Archaeology, CASS, Museum of Ding Ling, The Archaeological Team of the City of Beijing, Beijing, 1990

Beijing 1990d *Longgangsi, Xinshiqi shidai yizhi fajue baogao*, Beijing, 1990

Beijing 1990e *Nanyang Handai huaxiangzhuan*, Beijing, 1990

Beijing 1990f *Zhongguo gudai tuyutushuo*, Beijing, 1990

Beijing 1991a *Xi Han Nan Yue Wang mu*, 2 vols, Beijing, 1991

Beijing 1991b *Baoshan Chu mu*, 2 vols, Beijing, 1991

Beijing 1991c *Xichuan Xiasi Chun Qiu Chu mu*, Beijing, 1991

Beijing 1991d Xu Jialu (ed.). *Zhongguo gudai lishi cidian*, Beijing, 1991

Beijing 1992a China Cultural Relics Promotion Center (eds). *Treasures: 300 Best Excavated Antiques from China*, Beijing, 1992

Beijing 1992b *Zhongguo wenwu jinghua*, Beijing, 1992

Beijing 1992c *Xi'an, Legacies of Ancient Chinese Civilization*, Beijing, 1992

Beijing 1992d *Dengfeng Wangchenggang yu Yangcheng*, Beijing, 1992

Beijing 1992e Xiongi Huang Ti (ed.). *Treasures from a Swallow Garden*, Beijing, 1992

Beijing 1992f *Shuowen jiezi*, 12th edn, Beijing, 1992 (1st edn, Beijing, 1963)

Beijing 1993a *Kaogu jinghua*, Beijing, 1993

Beijing 1993b *Zhongguo wenwu jinghua*, Beijing, 1993

Beijing 1993c *Zhongguo kaoguxue luncong – Zhongguo Shehui Kexue Yuan Kaogu Yanjiu Suo jiansuo 40 nian jinian*, Beijing, 1993

Beijing 1993d *Han Duling Lingyuan yizhi*, Beijing, 1993

Beijing 1993e *Beiyinyangying – Xinshiqi shidai ji Shang, Zhou shiqi yizhi fajue baogao*, Beijing, 1993

Beijing 1993f *Houma zhutong yizhi*, 2 vols, Beijing, 1993

Beijing 1994a *Shangma mudi*, Beijing, 1994

Beijing 1994b Duan Shu'an (ed.). *Zhongguo qingtongqi quanji*, vol. 13 (Ba-Shu) in *Zhongguo meishu fenlei quanji*, Beijing, 1994

Beijing 1995 *Liulihe Xi Zhou Yanguo mudi 1973–1977*, Beijing, 1995

Berglund 1990 Berglund, Lars. *The Secret of Luo Shu: Numerology in Chinese Art and Architecture*, Lund, 1990

Birrell 1982 Birrell, Anne. *New Songs from a Jade Terrace*, London, 1982

Birrell 1988 Birrell, Anne. *Popular Songs and Ballads of Han China*, London, Sydney, Wellington, 1988

Birrell 1993 Birrell, Anne. *Chinese Mythology: An Introduction*, Baltimore and London, 1993

Bloch 1991 Bloch, Maurice. 'Language, Anthropology and Cognitive Science', *Man*, new series, 26, 1991, pp. 183–98

Bluett and Sons Ltd 1990 Wu Hung and Morgan, Brian. *Chinese Jades from the Mu-Fei Collection*, London, 1990

Bodde 1961 Bodde, Derk. 'Myths of Ancient China' in Samuel Noah Kramer (ed.), *Mythologies of the Ancient World*, New York, 1961, pp. 367–408

Bodde 1975 Bodde, Derk. *Festivals in Classical China: New Year and Other Annual Observances during the Han dynasty, 206 BC–AD 220*, Princeton and Hong Kong, 1975

Bodde 1991 Bodde, Derk. *Chinese Thought, Society, and Science: The Intellectual and Social Background of Science and Technology in Pre-modern China*, Honolulu, 1991

Boltz 1994 Boltz, William G. *The Origin and Early Development of the Chinese Writing System*, New Haven, Connecticut, 1994

Boston 1976 *Han and T'ang Murals Discovered in Tombs in the People's Republic of China and Copied by Contemporary Chinese Artists*, Boston, 1976

Brandt 1988 Brandt, Klaus. *Chinesische Lackarbeiten*, Stuttgart, 1988

Brinker 1979 Brinker, Helmut. *Zauber des chinesischen Fächers*, exhibition catalogue, Zurich, 1979

Brinker 1981 Brinker, Helmut. *Kunstschätze aus China*, exhibition catalogue, Zurich, 1981

Brinker and Goepper 1980 Brinker, Helmut and Goepper, Roger. *Kunstschätze aus China, 5000 v. Chr. bis 900 n. Chr., Neuere archäologische Funde aus der Volksrepublik China*, Zurich, 1980

Britton 1937 Britton, R. S. 'Oracle-bone Color Pigments', *Harvard Journal of Asiatic Studies*, vol. 2, 1937, pp. 1–3

Butz 1993 Butz, H. *Frühe Chinesische Bronzen aus der Sammlung Klingenberg*, exhibition catalogue, Berlin, 1993

Cahill 1986 Cahill, Suzanne E. 'The Word made Bronze: Inscriptions on Mediaeval Chinese Bronze Mirrors', *Archives of Asian Art*, vol. 38, 1986, pp. 62–70

Cahill 1993 Cahill, Suzanne E. *Transcendence and Divine Passion: The Queen Mother of the West in Medieval China*, Stanford, California, 1993

Chang Cheng-lang 1986 Chang Cheng-lang. 'A Brief Discussion of Fu Tzu' in Chang Kwang-chih 1986b, pp. 103–19

Chang Kwang-chih 1963 Chang Kwang-chih. 'Changing Relationships of Man and Animals in Shang and Zhou Myths and Art', *Bulletin of the Institute of Ethnology Academia Sinica*, vol. 10, 1963, pp. 115–46

Chang Kwang-chih 1977 Chang Kwang-chih. *Food in Chinese Culture*, New Haven and London, 1977

Chang Kwang-chih 1980 Chang Kwang-chih. *Shang Civilization*, New Haven and London, 1980

Chang Kwang-chih 1981 Chang Kwang-chih. 'The Animal in Shang and Chou Bronze Art', *Harvard Journal of Asiatic Studies*, vol. 41, 1981, pp. 527–54

Chang Kwang-chih 1983 Chang Kwang-chih. *Art, Myth, and Ritual: The Path to Political Authority in Ancient China*, Cambridge, Mass., and London, 1983

Chang Kwang-chih 1986a Chang Kwang-chih. *The Archaeology of Ancient China* (4th edn), New Haven and London, 1986

Chang Kwang-chih 1986b Chang Kwang-chih (ed.). *Studies of Shang Archaeology. Selected Papers from the International Conference on Shang Civilization*, New Haven and London, 1986

Chang Kwang-chih 1989 Chang Kwang-chih. 'An Essay on *Cong*', *Orientations*, June 1989, pp. 37–43

Chang Ping-ch'üan 1986 Chang Ping-ch'üan. 'A Brief Description of the Fu Hao Oracle Bone Inscriptions' in Chang Kwang-chih 1986b, pp. 121–40

Chang Tsung-tung 1970 Chang Tsung-tung. *Der Kult der Shang-Dynastie im Spiegel der Orakelinschriften: Eine paläographische Studie zur Religion im archaischen China*, Wiesbaden, 1970

Chase 1983 Chase, W. T. 'Bronze Castings in China: A Short Technical History' in Kuwayama 1983, pp. 100–22

Chase and Franklin 1979 Chase, W. T. and Franklin, Ursula Martius. 'Early Chinese Black Mirrors and Pattern-Etched Weapons', *Ars Orientalis*, 11, 1979, pp. 215–58

Chavannes 1987 Chavannes, E. *Les Mémoires historiques de Se-Ma Ts'ien*, Paris, 1987

Chaves 1977 Chaves, Jonathan. 'The Legacy of Ts'ang Chieh, The Written Word as Magic', *Oriental Art*, Summer 1977, pp. 200–15

Chen De'an 1994 Chen De'an. 'Shilun Sanxingdui yuzhang de zhonglei, yuanyuan ji qi zongjiao yiyi' in Hong Kong 1994b, pp. 87–99

Chen Shukui 1986 Chen Shukui. *Ya'an diqu wenwuzhi*, Chengdu, 1986

Chen Wenhua 1984 Chen Wenhua. 'Agricultural Science and Technology in Ancient China' in *Recent Discoveries in Chinese Archaeology*, Beijing, 1984, pp. 49–55

Cheng Chen-hsiang 1986 Cheng Chen-hsiang. 'A Study of the Bronzes with the 'Ssu T'u Mu' Inscriptions Excavated from the Fu Hao Tomb' in Chang Kwang-chih 1986b, pp. 81–102

Cheng Te-k'un 1959 Cheng Te-k'un. *Archaeology in China, Volume I, Prehistoric China*, Cambridge, 1959 (reprinted with corrections, 1966)

Cheng Te-k'un 1960 Cheng Te-k'un. *Archaeology in China, Volume II, Shang China*, Cambridge, 1960

Cheng Te-k'un 1963 Cheng Te-k'un. *Archaeology in China, Volume III, Chou China*, Cambridge, 1963

Cheng Zheng and Qian Zhijiang 1994 Cheng Zheng and Qian Zhijiang. *Huanghe caitao*, Taipei, 1994

Childs-Johnson 1987 Childs-Johnson, Elizabeth. 'The *Jue* and its Ceremonial Use in the Ancestor Cult of China', *Artibus Asiae*, vol. 48.3/4, 1987, pp. 171–96

Childs-Johnson 1988 Childs-Johnson, Elizabeth. 'Dragons, masks, axes and blades from four newly-documented jade-producing cultures of Ancient China', *Orientations*, April 1988, pp. 30–41

Childs-Johnson 1991 Childs-Johnson, Elizabeth. 'Jades of the Hongshan culture, the dragon and fertility cult worship', *Arts Asiatiques*, vol. 56, 1991, pp. 82–95

China Institute 1967 *Art Styles of Ancient Shang from Private and Museum Collections*, exhibition catalogue, New York, 1967

Chunqiu 1937 Harvard Yenching Institute Sinological Index Series, supplement no. 11, Beijing, 1937

Cleary 1990 Cleary, Thomas. *The Tao of Politics: Lessons of the Masters of Huainan*, Boston, 1990

Clunas 1991 Clunas, Craig. *Superfluous Things: Material Culture and Social Status in Early Modern China*, Cambridge, 1991

Clunas 1993 Clunas, Craig. 'Regulation of Consumption and the Institution of Correct Morality by the Ming State', *Sinica Leidensia*, vol. XXVII, 1993, pp. 39–49

Coe 1992 Coe, Michael D. *Breaking the Maya Code*, London, 1992

Cooper 1978 Cooper, Jean Campbell. *Illustrated Encyclopaedia of Traditional Symbols*, London, 1978

Cotterell 1982 Cotterell, A. and Yong Yap. *Das Reich der Mitte*, Frankfurt, 1982

Couling-Chalfant 1935 Roswell Britton (ed.). *Couling-Chalfant Collection of Inscribed Oracle Bones – Ku Fang er shi cang jiagu buci*, Shanghai, 1935

Creel 1970 Creel, Herrlee Glessner. *The Origins of Statecraft in China, Volume One, The Western Chou Empire*, Chicago and London, 1970

Croissant 1990 Croissant, Doris. 'Der unsterbliche Leib. Ahneneffigies und Reliquienporträt in der Porträtplastik Ostasiens' in Martin Kraatz *et al.* (eds), *Das Bildnis in der Kunst des Orients*, Stuttgart, 1990, pp. 235–68

Dewall 1990 Dewall, M. von. 'Wagen und Gespanne der Qin' in Ledderose and Schlombs 1990, pp. 49–57

Deydier 1980 Deydier, Christian (trans. Janet Seligman). *Chinese Bronzes*, New York, 1980

Dissanayake 1988 Dissanayake, Ellen. *What is Art for?*, Seattle and London, 1988 (paperback, 1990)

Dohrenwend 1975 Dohrenwend, Doris. 'Jade demonic images from Early China', *Ars Orientalis*, vol. X, 1975, pp. 55–77

Douglas 1970 Douglas, Mary. *Natural Symbols: Explorations in Cosmology*, New York, 1970 (paperback, 1982)

Du Jinpeng 1992 Du Jinpeng. 'Luelun Xingan Shang mu yu, tong shenxiang di jige wenti', *Nanfang Wenwu* 1992.2, pp. 49–54

Du Naisong 1980 Du Naisong. 'Si Mu Wu ding niandai wenti xintan', *Wenshizhe*, 1980.1, pp. 63–4

Dudbridge 1995 Dudbridge, Glen. *Religious Experience and Lay Society in T'ang China, a Reading of Tai Fu's Kuang-I chi*, Cambridge, 1995

Duffy 1992 Duffy, Eamon. *The Stripping of the Altars, Traditional Religion in England, c. 1400–c. 1580*, New Haven and London, 1992

Edgren 1984 Edgren, Soren. *Chinese Rare Books in American Collections*, catalogue of exhibition at China House Gallery, New York, 1984

Eggebrecht 1994 Eggebrecht, A. (ed.). *China eine Wiege der Weltkultur*, exhibition catalogue, Hildesheim and Mainz, 1994

Eichhorn 1973 Eichhorn, Werner. *Die Religionen Chinas*, Stuttgart, Berlin, Cologne, Mainz, 1973

Erdberg 1958 Erdberg, Eleanor von. *Das Alte China*, Stuttgart, 1958

Erickson 1992 Erickson, Susan, N. 'Boshanlu – Mountain Censers of the Western Han Period: A Typological and Iconographic Analysis', *Archives of Asian Art*, vol. XLV, 1992, pp. 6–28

Erickson 1994a Erickson, Susan N. 'Twirling Their Long Sleeves, They Dance Again and Again. . .: Jade Plaque Sleeve Dancers of the Western Han Dynasty', *Ars Orientalis*, vol. XXIV, pp. 39–63

Erickson 1994b Erickson, Susan N. 'Money Trees of the Eastern Han Dynasty', *Bulletin of the Museum of Far Eastern Antiquities*, no. 66, 1994, pp. 5–115

Erkes 1935 Erkes, E. 'Sung Yü's Chiu-pien', *T'oung Pao*, no. 31, 1935, pp. 363–408

Erkes 1944 Erkes, E. 'Der Hund im alten China', *T'oung Pao*, no. 37, 1944, pp. 186–225

Erkes 1952 Erkes, E. 'Das Problem der Sklaverei in China', *Sitzungsbericht der Sächsischen Akademie der Wissenschaften zu Leipzig*, vol. 100, 1952

Falkenhausen 1990 Falkenhausen, Lothar von. 'Ahnenkult und Grabkult im Staat Qin' in Ledderose and Schlombs 1990, pp. 35–48

Falkenhausen 1991 Falkenhausen, Lothar von. 'Chu Ritual Music' in Thomas Lawton (ed.), *New Perspectives on Chu Culture during the Eastern Zhou Period*, Washington, DC, 1991, pp. 47–106

Falkenhausen 1993 Falkenhausen, Lothar von. *Suspended Music: Chime-bells in the Culture of Bronze Age China*, Berkeley, Los Angeles, Oxford, 1993

Falkenhausen 1994 Falkenhausen, Lothar von. 'Sources of Taoism: Reflections on Archaeological Indicators of Religious Change in Eastern Zhou China', *Taoist Resources*, vol. 5, no. 2, 1994, pp. 1–12

Fan Ye 1971 Fan Ye. *Hou Hanshu*, Beijing, 1971

Fang Dianchun 1991 Fang Dianchun. 'Fuxin, Chahai Xinshiqi shidai yizhi di chubu fajue yu fenxi', *Liaohai wenwu xuekan* 1991.1, pp. 27–34

Fessel 1988 Fessel, K. 'Geschichte' in Goepper 1988, pp. 47–112

Finsterbusch 1952 Finsterbusch, Käte. *Das Verhältnis des Schan-haidjing zur bildenden Kunst*, Berlin, 1952

Finsterbusch 1971 Finsterbusch, Käte. *Verzeichnis und Motivindex der Han-Darstellungen*, vol. 2, Wiesbaden, 1971

Fitzgerald 1965 Fitzgerald, C. L. *China: A Short Cultural History*, London, 1965 (1st edn, 1935)

Fong 1991 Fong, H. M. 'Tomb-Guardian Figurines: Their Evolution and Iconography' in Kuwayama 1991

Franke 1913 Franke, O. *Keng Tschi T'u, Ackerbau und Seidengewinnung in China*, Hamburg, 1913

Franke 1930 Franke, O. *Geschichte des chinesischen Reiches*, vol. 1, Berlin and Leipzig, 1930

Franklin 1983a Franklin, Ursula Martius. 'The Beginnings of Metallurgy in China: A Comparative Approach' in Kuwayama 1983, pp. 94–9

Franklin 1983b Franklin, Ursula Martius. 'On Bronze and Other Metals in Early China' in Keightley 1983, pp. 279–96

Fu Juyou 1986 Fu Juyou. 'Lun Qin Han shiqi de geju boxi jianji geju wenjing', *Kaogu xuebao* 1986.1, pp. 21–42

Fu Qifeng 1985 Fu Qifeng. *Chinese Acrobatics through the Ages*, Beijing, 1985

Fu Tianchou 1985 Fu Tianchou (ed.). *Zhongguo meishu quanji – Diaosu bian, 2, Qin Han diaosu*, Beijing, 1985

Fujieda 1991 Fujieda, A. *Moji no bunkashi*, Tokyo, 1991

Gao Feng and Sun Jianqun 1992 Gao Feng and Sun Jianqun. *Zhongguo dengju jianshi*, Beijing, 1992

Gao Wen 1987 Gao Wen. *Sichuan Handai huaxiangzhuan*, Shanghai, 1987

Gernet 1987 Gernet, Jacques (trans. J. R. Foster). *A History of Chinese Civilization*, Cambridge, 1987 (1st edn, 1982, trans. of *Le Monde chinois*, Paris, 1972)

Gettens 1969 Gettens, Rutherford John. *The Freer Chinese Bronzes, Volume II, Technical Studies*, Washington, DC, 1969

Goepper 1965 Goepper, Roger. 'Kalligraphie' in W. Speiser, R. Goepper, J. Fribourg (eds), *Chinesische Kunst, Malerei, Kalligraphie, Steinabreibungen, Holzschnitte*, Fribourg and Zurich, 1965

Goepper 1988 Goepper, Roger (ed.). *Das Alte China*, Munich, 1988

Goepper 1995 Goepper, Roger (ed.). *Das Alte China: Menschen und Götter im Reich der Mitte*, Munich, 1995

Goffman 1990 Goffman, Erving. *The Presentation of Self in Everyday Life*, London, 1990 (1st edn, 1959; paperback, 1969)

Gombrich 1979 Gombrich, E. H. *The Sense of Order*, Oxford, 1979

Goodall 1979 Goodall, J. A. *Heaven and Earth*, London, 1979

Goodman 1988 Goodman, Nelson. 'How Buildings Mean' in Nelson Goodman and Catherine Z. Elgin, *Reconceptions in Philosophy and Other Arts and Sciences*, Cambridge and Indianapolis, 1988, pp. 31–48

Graham 1989 Graham, Angus. *Disputers of the Tao: Philosophical Argument in Ancient China*, La Salle, 1989

Granet 1934 Granet, M. *La Pensée chinoise*, Paris, 1934

Güntsch 1988 Güntsch, G. *Das Shen-hsien chuan und das Erscheinungsbild eines Hsien*, Frankfurt, Bern, New York, Paris, 1988

Guo Baojun 1964 Guo Baojun. *Junxian Xincun*, Beijing, 1964, pp. 63–6

Guo Dalun and Li Yingfu 1994 Guo Dalun and Li Yingfu. 'Guanghan Sanxingdui yizhi chutu yushiqi di chubu kaocha', *Kaogu yu wenwu* 1994.2, pp. 82–6

Guo Dashun 1989 Guo Dashun. 'Liaoxi guwenhua de xin renshi' in *Qingzhu Su Bingqi kaogu wushiwu zhounian lunwenji*, Beijing, 1989, pp. 203–15

Guo Dashun 1995 Guo Dashun. 'Hongshan and Related Cultures' in Nelson 1995, pp. 21–64

Guo Moruo 1937 Guo Moruo. *Yinqi cuibian*, Tokyo, 1937

Guo Moruo 1978 Guo Moruo. *Jiaguwen heji*, vol. 3, Beijing, 1978

Guo Moruo 1982 Guo Moruo. *Gujiu keci zhi yi kaocha* in *Guo Moruo quanji*, Beijing, 1982, pp. 411–30

Guo Moruo 1991 Guo Moruo. *Shang Zhou guwenzi leizuan*, Beijing, 1991

Guo Zhizhong 1991 Guo Zhizhong *et al.* 'Linxixian Baiyinchanghan yizhi fajue shuyao' in *Neimenggu Dongbuqu kaoguxue wenhua yanjiu wenji*, Haiyang, 1991

Hansford 1957 Hansford, Sidney Howard. *The Seligman Collection of Oriental Art*, vol. 1, London, 1957

Harper 1985 Harper, Donald. 'A Chinese Demonography of the Third Century B.C.', *Harvard Journal of Asiatic Studies*, vol. 45, 1985, pp. 459–98

Harper 1994 Harper, Donald. 'Resurrection in Warring States Popular Religion', *Taoist Resources*, vol. 5, no. 2, 1994, pp. 13–28

Harper forthcoming Harper, Donald. 'Warring States Natural Philosophy and Occult Thought' in Michael Loewe and Edward Shaughnessy (eds), *Cambridge History of China*, forthcoming

Hausman 1989 Hausman, Carl R. *Metaphor and Art, Interactionism and Reference in the Verbal and Nonverbal Arts*, Cambridge, 1989

Hawkes 1985 Hawkes, David. *Ch'u Tz'u. The Songs of the South*, Harmondsworth, 1985 (1st edn, Oxford, 1959)

Hay 1986 Hay, John. *Kernels of Energy, Bones of Earth: The Rock in Chinese Art*, New York, 1986

Hayashi Minao 1969 Hayashi Minao. 'Chūgoku kodai no saigyoku, zuigyoku', *Tōhō gakuhō*, no. 40, 1969, pp. 161–323

Hayashi Minao 1972 Hayashi Minao. 'Seishū jidai gyoku jinzō no ifuku to tōshoku', *Shirin*, vol. 55, no. 11, March 1972, pp. 1–38

Hayashi Minao 1976 Hayashi Minao. *Kandai no bumbutsu*, Kyoto, 1976

Hayashi Minao 1981 Hayashi Minao. 'Ryōsho bunkatekki gyokki', *Hakubutsukan*, 1981.3 (360), pp. 22–34

Hayashi Minao 1990a Hayashi Minao. 'Ryōsho bunka to Daibunkō bunka no zuzō kigō', *Shirin*, vol. 73, no. 5, 1990, pp. 116–34

Hayashi Minao 1990b Hayashi Minao (abridged and adapted by Alexander C. Soper). 'On the Chinese Neolithic Jade *tsung/cong*', *Artibus Asiae*, vol. 50, pts 1/2, 1990, pp. 5–22

Hayashi Minao 1991a Hayashi Minao. 'Chūgoku kodai no ibutsu ni arawasareta 'ki' no zuzō-teki hyōgen', *Tōhō gakuhō*, vol. 61, republished in *Chūgoku kogyoku no kenkyū*, Tokyo, 1991, pp. 269–358

Hayashi Minao 1991b Hayashi Minao. 'Inkyo Fukō-bo shutsudo no gyokki jakkan ni taisuru chūshaku, *Tōhō gakuhō*, vol. 58, republished in *Chūgoku kogyoku no kenkyū*, Tokyo, 1991, pp. 515–76

He Xin 1986 He Xin. *Zhushen de qiyuan*, Beijing, 1986

He Xingliang 1992 He Xingliang. *Zhongguo ziranshen yu ziran chongbai*, Shanghai, 1992

Hebei 1991–3 *Zhongguo yuqi quanji*, vol. 6 (Qing), 1991; vol. 1 (Neolithic), 1992; vol. 2 (Shang and Western Zhou), 1993; vol. 5 (Sui, Tang and Ming), 1993; vol. 3 (Spring and Autumn, Warring States Period), 1993; vol. 4 (Qin, Han and Six Dynasties), 1993, Shijiazhuang, 1991–3

Helms 1988 Helms, Mary W. *Ulysses' Sail, An Ethnographic Odyssey of Power, Knowledge, and Geographical Distance*, Princeton, 1988

Henan 1985 Henan Bowuguan. *Zhongguo Bowuguan Congshu*, vol. 7, Beijing, 1985

Hentze 1967 Hentze, Carl. *Funde in Alt-China: das Welterleben im ältesten China*, Göttingen, 1967

Hervouet 1978 Hervouet, Y. *A Sung Bibliography (Bibliographie des Sung)*, Hong Kong, 1978

Herzer 1963 Herzer, C. 'Das Szu-min yüeh-ling des Ts'ui Shih. Ein Bauernkalender aus der Späteren Han-Zeit', dissertation, University of Hamburg, 1963

Higuchi and Enjōji 1984 Higuchi Takayesu and Enjōji Jiro. *Chūgoku seidoki hyaku sen*, Tokyo, 1984

Hildebrand 1987 Hildebrand, J. *Das Ausländerbild in der Kunst Chinas als Spiegel kultureller Aktivitäten*, Stuttgart, 1987

Ho 1975 Ho Ping-ti. *The Cradle of the East*, Hong Kong, 1975

Höllmann 1986 Höllmann, T. O. *Jinan. Die Chu-Hauptstadt Ying im China der Späteren Zhou-Zeit*, Munich, 1986

Hong Kong 1990 *Chinese Ivories from the Kwan Collection*, Hong Kong, 1990

Hong Kong 1992 *Zhongguo Han Yangling caiyong*, Hong Kong, 1992

Hong Kong 1994a Jiangxi Sheng Bowuguan, Shanghai Bowuguan (eds). *Jiangxi Xin'gan chutu qingtongqi yishu*, Hong Kong, 1994

Hong Kong 1994b Tang Chung (ed.). *Nan Zhongguo ji linjin diqu gu wenhua yanjiu*, Hong Kong, 1994

Hong Kong 1994c Centre for Chinese Archaeology and Art, ICS and The Chinese University of Hong Kong (eds). *Ancient Cultures of South China and Neighbouring Regions*, Hong Kong, 1994

Hsia Nai 1983 Hsia Nai. 'The Classification, Nomenclature and Usage of Shang Dynasty Jades' in Chang Kwang-chih 1986b, pp. 207–36

Hua 1983 Hua Jue-ming. 'The Mass Production of Iron Castings in Ancient China', *Scientific American*, January 1983, pp. 120–8

Huan Kuan 1979 Huan Kuan. *Yantielun jiaozhu zhaji*, Taipei, 1979

Huang Tsui-mei 1992 Huang Tsui-mei. *The Role of Jades in the late Neolithic cultures of ancient China, The case of Liangzhu*, unpublished doctoral dissertation submitted to University of Pittsburgh, Ann Arbor, Michigan, 1992

Huang Xuanpei and Zhang Minghua 1980 Huang Xuanpei and Zhang Minghua. 'Qingpu Xian, Songze yizhi, di erci fajue', *Kaogu xuebao* 1980.1, pp. 29–57

Huang Xuanpei 1987 Huang Xuanpei. 'Luelun woguo Xinshiqi shidai yuqi', *Shanghai Bowuguan jikan*, no. 4, 1987, pp. 150–70

Huang Xuanpei 1988 Huang Xuanpei. *Ritual and Power, Jades of Ancient China*, New York, 1988

Huang Zhanyue 1990 Huang Zhanyue. *Zhongguo gudai de rensheng renxun*, Beijing, 1990

Huayang guozhi Chang Qu (comp.), Liu Lin (ed.). *Huayang guozhi jiaozhu*, Chengdu, 1984

Imperial China 1992 *Imperial China: The Living Past*, exhibition catalogue, Sydney, 1992

James 1991 James, Jean M. 'Images of power, Masks of the Liangzhu culture', *Orientations*, June 1991, pp. 46–55

James 1983 James, Mervyn. 'Ritual, Drama and the Social Body', *Past and Present*, vol. 98, 1983, pp. 3–29

Jan 1977 Jan Yunhua. 'The Silk Manuscripts on Taoism,' *T'oung Pao*, vol. LXIII, 1977, pp. 65–84

Jansen 1994 Jansen, T. 'Die Felsengräber von Mancheng und das Höfische Leben zur Zeit der Westlichen Han-Dynastie (206 v.Chr.-9 n.Chr.)' in Eggebrecht 1994, pp. 85–96

Jin Weinuo 1986 Jin Weinuo (ed.). *Zhongguo meishu quanji – Diaosu bian*, 1, Beijing, 1986

Jin Zutong 1974 Jin Zutong. *Yinqi yizhu, 2 juan*, Taipei, 1974

Ji'nan 1982 *Qufu Luguo Gucheng*, Ji'nan, 1982

Johnson 1981 Johnson, Mark (ed.). *Philosophical Perspectives on Metaphor*, Minneapolis, 1981 (paperback)

Kandai no bijutsu 1975 Osaka Shiritsu Bijutsukan (ed.). *Kandai no bijutsu*, Tokyo, 1975

Kane 1974 Kane, Virginia C. 'The Independent Bronze Industries in the South of China Contemporary with the Shang and Western Chou Dynasties', *Archives of Asian Art*, 28, 1974–5, pp. 77–107

Kane 1982 Kane, Virginia C. 'Aspects of Western Chou Appointment Inscriptions: The Charge, the Gifts, the Response', *Early China*, 8, 1982–3, pp. 14–28

Kao 1985 Kao, Jeffrey Yu-teh. 'The Archaeology of Ancient Chinese Jade, A Case Study from the late Shang period Site of Yinxu', 2 vols, unpublished doctoral dissertation submitted to Harvard University, Ann Arbor, 1985

Kao Chih-hsi 1986 Kao Chih-hsi. 'An Introduction to Shang and Chou Bronze Nao Excavated in South China' in Chang Kwang-chih 1986b, pp. 275–99

Karlgren 1934 Karlgren, Bernard. 'Early Chinese Mirror Inscriptions', *Bulletin of the Museum of Far Eastern Antiquities*, no. 6, 1934, pp. 9–79

Karlgren 1972 Karlgren, Bernard. *Grammata Serica Recensa*, Stockholm, 1972

Keightley 1976 Keightley, David N. 'Late Shang Divination: The Magic-Religious Legacy', *Journal of Thematic Studies*, vol. L, pt 2, pp. 11–34

Keightley 1978 Keightley, David N. *Sources of Shang History: The Oracle-Bone Inscriptions of Bronze Age China*, Berkeley, Los Angeles, London, 1978

Keightley 1983 Keightley, David N. (ed.). *The Origins of Chinese Civilization*, Berkeley, Los Angeles, London, 1983

Kern 1994 Kern, Martin. *Zum Topos 'Zimtbaum' in der chinesischen Literatur*, Stuttgart, 1994

Kerr 1990 Kerr, Rose. *Later Chinese Bronzes*, London, 1990

Kerr 1991 Kerr, Rose. *Chinese Art and Design*, London, 1991

Kesner 1991 Kesner, Ladislav. 'The Taotie reconsidered, Meanings and functions of Shang theriomorphic imagery', *Artibus Asiae*, vol. LI, 1/2, 1991, pp. 29–53

Kesner 1995 Kesner, Ladislav. 'Likeness of No One: (Re)presenting the First Emperor's Army', *Art Bulletin*, vol. LXXVII, 1995, pp. 115–32

Keyser 1979 Keyser, Barbara W. 'Decor Replication in Two Late Chou Bronze *chien*', *Ars Orientalis*, no. 11, 1979, pp. 127–62

Knechtges 1982 Knechtges, David R. (trans. with annotations). *Wen Xuan or Selections of Refined Literature*, vol. 1, Princeton, New Jersey, 1982

Kohn 1992 Kohn, Livia. *Early Chinese Mysticism: Philosophy and Soteriology in the Taoist Religion*, Princeton, New Jersey, 1992 (paperback)

Koizumi and Hamada 1934 Koizumi Akio and Hamada Kosaku. *Rakurō saikyōzuka*, Seoul, 1934

Kominami Ichiro 1974 Kominami Ichiro. 'Seiōbo to shichiseki denshō', *Tōhō gakuhō*, no. 46, 1974, pp. 33–82

Kuhn 1982 Kuhn, Dieter. 'The Silk-Workshops of the Shang Dynasty (16th–11th Century B.C.)' in *Explorations in the History of Science and Technology in China – Collections of Essays on Chinese Literature and History in Honour of the Eightieth Birthday of Dr. Joseph Needham*, Shanghai, 1982

Kuhn 1988a Kuhn, Dieter. 'Hand-Spindle Spinning', *Science and Civilization in China*, vol. v, pt 9, Cambridge, 1988

Kuhn 1988b Kuhn, Dieter. 'Vom Spinnwirtel zum Gusseisen' in Goepper 1988, pp. 249–58

Kuhn 1991 Kuhn, Dieter. *Status und Ritus: das China der Aristokraten von den Anfängen bis zum 10. Jahrhundert nach Christus*, Heidelberg, 1991

Kuhn 1995 Kuhn, Dieter. 'Silk Weaving in Ancient China: From Geometric Figures to Patterns of Pictorial Likeness', *Chinese Science*, vol. 12, 1995, pp. 77–114

Kuhn and von Eschenbach 1992 Kuhn, Dieter and Eschenbach, S. Freiin Ebner von (eds). *Arbeitsmaterialien aus chinesischen Ausgrabungsberichten (1988–1991) zu Gräbern aus der Han- bis Tang-Zeit*, Heidelberg, 1992

Kunstschätze aus China 1980 *Kunstschätze aus China*, exhibition catalogue, Zurich, Berlin, Hildesheim, Cologne, 1980

Kuttner 1990 Kuttner, Fritz A. *The Archaeology of Music in Ancient China: 2000 Years of Acoustical Experimentation, 1400 BC–AD 750*, New York, 1990

Kuwayama 1976 Kuwayama, George. *Ancient Ritual Bronzes of China*, Los Angeles, 1976

Kuwayama 1983 Kuwayama, George (ed.). *The Great Bronze Age of China, A Symposium*, Los Angeles, 1983

Kuwayama 1991 Kuwayama, George (ed.). *Ancient Mortuary Traditions of China, Papers on Chinese Ceramic Funerary Sculpture*, Los Angeles, 1991

Kyoto 1976 'Seishū kimbun no bengi o megutte', *Kōkotsugaku*, no. 11, 1976, pp. 21–68

Lakoff and Johnson 1980 Lakoff, George and Johnson, Mark. *Metaphors We Live By*, Chicago and London, 1980

Lam 1991 Lam, Peter Y. K. *Jades from the Tomb of the King of Nan Yue*, Hong Kong, 1991

Lau 1970 Lau, D. C. (trans.). *Mencius*, London, 1970

Lau 1979 Lau, D. C. (trans.). *The Analects (Lun Yü)*, London, 1979

Laufer 1909 Laufer, B. *Chinese Pottery of the Han Dynasty*, Leiden, 1909

Lawton 1982 Lawton, Thomas. *Chinese Art of the Warring States Period, Change and Continuity, 480–221 BC*, Washington, DC, 1982

Lawton 1987 Lawton, Thomas *et al. Asian Art in the Arthur M. Sackler Gallery*, Washington, DC, 1987

Lawton 1991 Lawton, Thomas (ed.). *New Perspectives on Chu Culture during the Eastern Zhou Period*, Princeton and Washington, DC, 1991

Leach 1969 Leach, Bernard. *A Potter's Book*, Glasgow, 1969

Ledderose 1978 Ledderose, Lothar. 'Some Observations on the Imperial Art Collection in China', *Transactions of the Oriental Ceramic Society*, vol. 43, 1978–9, pp. 33–46

Ledderose 1979 Ledderose, Lothar. *Mi Fu and the Classical Tradition of Chinese Calligraphy*, Princeton, 1979

Ledderose 1992 Ledderose, Lothar. 'Module and Mass Production' in *International Colloquium on Chinese Art History, 1991, Proceedings, Antiquities, Part 1*, Taipei, 1992, pp. 826–47

Ledderose and Schlombs 1990 Ledderose, Lothar and Schlombs, Adele. *Jenseits der Grossen Mauer: Der Erste Kaiser von China und Seine Terrakotta-Armee*, Munich, 1990

Legge 1871 Legge, James. *The She King or the Book of Poetry*, in *The Chinese Classics*, vol. IV, pt 1, Hong Kong and London 1871

Legge 1872 Legge, James. *The Ch'un Ts'ew, with the Tso Chuen* in *The Chinese Classics*, vol. v, Hong Kong and London, 1872

Lewis 1990 Lewis, Mark. *Sanctioned Violence in Early China*, Albany, 1990

Li 1977 Li Chi. *Anyang*, Seattle, 1977

Li Ling forthcoming Li Ling. *An Archaeological Study of Taiyi*, forthcoming

Li Xianguo 1988 Li Xianguo. 'Diaozaozhai yanbi shang de shenshi congbai shi', *Liaowang*, vol. 20, 1988, pp. 30–1

Li Xueqin 1978 Li Xueqin. 'Lun Shi Qiang ji qi yiyi', *Kaogu xuebao* 1978.2, pp. 149–58

Li Xueqin 1979 Li Xueqin. 'Xi Zhou zhong qi qingtongqi de zhong-yao biaochi – Zhouyuan Zhuangbai, Qiangjia liang chu qingtongqi jiaocang de zonghe yanjiu', *Zhongguo Lishi Bowuguan guankan* 1979.1, pp. 29–36

Li Xueqin 1980 Li Xueqin. *The Wonder of Chinese Bronzes*, Beijing, 1980

Li Xueqin 1985a Li Xueqin (trans. K. C. Chang). *Eastern Zhou and Qin Civilizations*, New Haven and London, 1985

Li Xueqin 1985b Li Xueqin. 'Yi Hou Ze *gui* yu Wu guo', *Wenwu* 1985.7, pp. 13–16, 25

Li Xueqin 1985c Li Xueqin. *Zhongguo meishu quanji, gongyi meishu bian, qingtongqi (4)*, Beijing, 1985

Li Xueqin 1986a Li Xueqin. 'Lun Chang'an Huayuancun liang mu qingtongqi', *Wenwu* 1986.1, pp. 32–6

Li Xueqin 1986b Li Xueqin. *Zhongguo meishu quanji, gongyi meishu bian, qingtongqi (2)*, Beijing, 1986

Li Xueqin 1993a Li Xueqin. 'Liangzhu culture and the Shang dynasty *Taotie*', in Whitfield 1993, pp. 56–66

Li Xueqin 1993b Li Xueqin. 'A Neolithic Jade Plaque and Ancient Chinese Cosmology', *National Palace Museum Bulletin*, vol. XXVII, nos 5–6, November–December 1992/January–February 1993

Li Zehou 1992 Li Zehou, K. Pohl and G. Wacker (eds). *Der Weg des Schönen. Wesen und Geschichte der chinesischen Kultur und Ästhetik*, Freiburg, Basel and Vienna, 1992

Lienert 1979 Lienert, Ursula. *Typology of the Ting in the Shang Dynasty. A Tentative Chronology of the Yin-Hsü Period*, 2 vols, Wiesbaden, 1979

Lienert 1980 Lienert, Ursula. *Das Imperium der Han*, Cologne, 1980

Lim 1987 Lim, Lucy (ed.). *Stories from China's Past*, exhibition catalogue, San Francisco, 1987

Lin 1986 Lin Yün. 'A Reexamination of the Relationship between Bronzes of the Shang Culture and of the Northern Zone' in Chang Kwang-chih 1986b, pp. 237–73

Lindqvist 1990 Lindqvist, Cecilia. *China: Empire of the Written Symbol*, London, 1990

Liu Daofan 1984 Liu Daofan. 'Ivory Carving in Ancient China' in *Recent Discoveries in Chinese Archaeology*, Beijing, 1984, pp. 59–60

Loehr 1956 Loehr, Max. *Chinese Bronze Age Weapons – The Werner Jannings Collection in the Chinese National Palace Museum, Peking*, Ann Arbor, 1956

Loehr 1968 Loehr, Max. *Ritual Vessels of Bronze Age China*, New York, 1968

Loehr 1975 Loehr, Max. *Ancient Chinese Jades in the Grenville L. Winthrop Collection*, Cambridge, Mass., 1975

Loewe 1974 Loewe, Michael. *Crisis and Conflict in Han China, 104 BC to AD 9*, London, 1974

Loewe 1977 Loewe, Michael. 'Manuscripts Found Recently in China: A Preliminary Survey', *T'oung Pao*, vol. LXIII, 1977, pp. 98–136

Loewe 1979 Loewe, Michael. *Ways to Paradise: The Chinese Quest for Immortality*, London, 1979

Loewe 1982 Loewe, Michael. *Chinese Ideas of Life and Death: Faith, Myth and Reason in the Han Period*, London, 1982

Loewe 1985 Loewe, Michael. 'Royal Tombs of Zhongshan', *Arts Asiatiques*, vol. XL, 1985, pp. 130–4

Loewe 1993 Loewe, Michael (ed.). *Early Chinese Texts: A Bibliographical Guide*, Berkeley, 1993

London 1935 *Catalogue of the International Exhibition of Chinese Art 1935–6*, London, 1935

London 1984 Watson, William (ed.). *Chinese Ivories from the Shang to the Qing*, London, 1984

Los Angeles 1987 *The Quest for Eternity, Chinese Ceramic Sculptures from the People's Republic of China*, London, 1987

Lu Delin 1986 Lu Delin (ed.). *Luoyang Handai caihua*, Luoyang, 1986

Lu Liancheng and Hu Zhisheng 1988 Lu Liancheng and Hu Zhisheng. *Baoji Yuguo mudi*, 2 vols, Beijing, 1988

Lu Liancheng 1993 Lu Liancheng. 'Chariot and Horse Burials in Ancient China', *Antiquity*, vol. 67, 1993, pp. 824–38

Lubar and Kingery 1993 Lubar, Steven and Kingery, W. David (eds). *History From Things: Essays on Material Culture*, Washington, DC, and London, 1993

Luo Zhenyu 1912 Luo Zhenyu. *Yinxu shuqi qianbian*, Japan, *c.* 1912

Luo Zhenyu 1935 Luo Zhenyu. *Zhen Song Tang jijin tu*, Dalian, 1935

Luo Zhewen 1993 Luo Zhewen. *Kaiser- und Königsgräber der chinesischen Dynastien* (adapted trans. from Chinese by M. Katzenschlager), Beijing, 1993

Luoyang 1990 Luoyang Wenwu Gongzuodui (ed.). *Ancient Treasures of Luoyang 1990*, Beijing, 1990

Lutz 1986 Lutz, A. (ed.). *Dian. Ein versunkenes Königreich in China*, Zurich, 1986

Ma Chengyuan 1986 Ma Chengyuan. *Ancient Chinese Bronzes*, Hong Kong, Oxford, New York, 1986

Mackenzie 1987 Mackenzie, Colin. 'The Chu tradition of wood carving', *Style in the East Asian Tradition*, Colloquies on Art and Archaeology in Asia, no. 14, London, 1987

Mackenzie 1991 Mackenzie, Colin. 'Chu Bronze Works' in Lawton 1991, pp. 107–57

Major 1993 Major, J. S. *Heaven and Earth in Early Han Thought: Chapters Three, Four and Five of the Huainanzi*, New York, 1993

Mao shi 1934 Harvard Yenching Institute Sinological Index Series, supplement no. 9, Beijing, 1934

Marchev 1982 Marchev, R. P. *Musik im alten China*, Zurich, 1982

Mathieu 1983 Mathieu, Rémi. *Étude sur la mythologie et l'ethnologie de la Chine ancienne. Traduction annotée du Shanhai jing*, 2 vols, Paris, 1983

Mende 1988 Mende, E. von. 'Wirtschaft' in Goepper 1988, pp. 149–86

Michaelson 1992 Michaelson, Carol. 'Mass Production and the Development of the Lacquer Industry During the Han Dynasty', *Orientations*, November 1992, pp. 60–5

Miller 1991 Miller, Daniel. *Material Culture and Mass Consumption*, Oxford, 1991

Mizuno 1953 Mizuno Seichi. 'In Shū seidōki hennen no sho mondai,' *Tōhō gakuhō*, no. 23, 1953, pp. 79–134

Mizuno 1959 Mizuno Seiichi. *In Shū seidō to gyoku*, Tokyo, 1959

Mote 1971 Mote, Frederick W. *Intellectual Foundations of China*, New York, 1971

Mou Lingsheng 1992 Mou Lingsheng. *The Coloured Figurines in Yang Ling Mausoleum of Han in China (Zhongguo Han Yangling caiyong)*, Xi'an, 1992

Mou Yongkang 1989 Mou Yongkang. 'Liangzhu yuqi shang shen congbai de tansuo' in *Qingzhu Su Bingqi kaogu wushinian lunwenji*, Beijing, 1989

Müller-Karpe 1979 Müller-Karpe, Hermann. 'Das Grab der Fu Hao von Anyang', *Beiträge zur Allgemeinen und Vergleichenden Archäologie*, vol. 1, 1979, pp. 31–68

Müller-Karpe 1982 Müller-Karpe, Hermann. *Neolithische Siedlungen der Yangshao-Kultur in Nordchina*, Munich, 1982

Munakata 1990 Munakata Kiyohiko (ed.). *Sacred Mountains in Chinese Art*, Urbana-Champaign, 1990

Murray 1983 Murray, Julia, K. 'Neolithic Chinese Jades in the Freer Gallery of Art', *Orientations*, November 1983, pp. 14–22

Murray 1992 Murray, Julia, K. 'The Hangzhou Portraits of Confucius and 72 Disciples (*Shengxian tu*): Art in the Service of Politics', *The Art Bulletin*, vol. 74, March 1992, pp. 7–18

Nanjing 1991 Nanjing Bowuyuan (ed.). *Sichuan Pengshan Handai yanmu*, Nanjing, 1991

Needham 1959 Needham, Joseph. *Science and Civilization in China*, vol. 3, Cambridge, 1959

Needham 1961 Needham, Joseph. *Science and Civilization in China*, vol. 1, Cambridge, 1961

Needham 1965 Needham, Joseph. *Science and Civilization in China*, vol. 4, pt 2, Cambridge, 1965

Needham 1980 Needham, Joseph. *Science and Civilization in China*, Cambridge, vol. 5, pt 4, 1980

Nelson 1995 Nelson, Sarah Milledge (ed.). *The Archaeology of Northeast China beyond the Great Wall*, London, 1995

New York 1980 Wen Fong (ed.). *The Great Bronze Age of China: An Exhibition from the People's Republic of China*, New York, 1980

Nivison 1983 Nivison, David S. 'Western Chou History Reconstructed from Bronze Inscriptions' in Kuwayama 1983, pp. 44–55

Osaka 1993 Osaka Shiritsu Bijutsukan *et al.* (eds). *Chūgoku ōchō no tanjō*, exhibition catalogue, Tokyo, 1993

Owen 1986 Owen, Stephen. *Remembrances: The Experience of the Past in Classical Chinese Literature*, Cambridge, Mass., 1986

Palmgren 1934 Palmgren, Nils. *Kansu Mortuary Urns of the Pan Shan and Ma Chang Groups*, Beijing, 1934

Paludan 1981 Paludan, Ann. *The Imperial Ming Tombs*, New Haven and London, 1981

Paludan 1991 Paludan, Ann. *The Chinese Spirit Road: The Classical Tradition of Stone Tomb Statuary*, New Haven, 1991

Paludan 1994 Paludan, Ann. *Chinese Tomb Figurines*, Hong Kong, 1994

Paris 1984 *Zhongshan: Tombes des Rois Oubliés – Exposition archéologique chinoise du Royaume de Zhongshan*, Paris, 1984

Peerenboom 1993 Peerenboom, R. P. *Law and Morality in Ancient China, The Silk Manuscripts of Huang-Lao*, Albany, 1993

Pinker 1994 Pinker, Steven. *The Language Instinct*, London, 1994

Pirazzoli t'Serstevens 1982 Pirazzoli t'Serstevens, Michèle. *The Han Dynasty*, New York, 1982

Pirazzoli t'Serstevens 1991 Pirazzoli t'Serstevens, Michèle. 'The Art of Dining in the Han Period: Food Vessels from Tomb No. 1 at Mawangdui', *Food and Foodways*, 1991, vol. 4 (3 & 4), pp. 209–19

Pomian 1990 Pomian, Krzysztof (trans. Elizabeth Wiles-Portier). *Collectors and Curiosities, Paris and Venice, 1500–1800*, Cambridge, 1990, pp. 1–64

Powers 1987 Powers, M. J. 'Social Values and Aesthetic Choices in Han Dynasty Sichuan' in Lim 1987, pp. 54–63

Průšek 1971 Průšek, Jaroslav. *Chinese Statelets and the Northern Barbarians in the Period 1400–300 B.C.*, Dordrecht, 1971

Pu Muzhou 1993 Pu Muzhou. *Muzang yu shengsi, Zhongguo gudai zongjia zhi shengsi*, Taiwan, 1993

Qian Yuzhi 1992 Qian Yuzhi. 'Sanxingdui qingtong liren xiang kao' in Sichuan 1992, pp. 50–5

Qiu Pu 1962 Qiu Pu. *Ewenkeren de yuanshi shehui xingtai*, Beijing, 1962

Rawson 1975 Rawson, Jessica M. 'The surface decoration on jades of the Chou and Han dynasties', *Oriental Art*, 21.1, Spring 1975, pp. 36–55

Rawson 1980 Rawson, Jessica M. *Ancient China, Art and Archaeology*, London, 1980

Rawson 1983a Rawson, Jessica M. 'Eccentric Bronzes of the Early Western Zhou', *Transactions of the Oriental Ceramic Society*, vol. 47, 1982–3, pp. 11–32

Rawson 1983b Rawson, Jessica M. (ed.). *The Chinese Bronzes of Yunnan*, London, 1983

Rawson 1984a Rawson, Jessica M. 'Song Silver and its Connections with Ceramics', *Apollo*, July 1984, pp. 18–23

Rawson 1984b Rawson, Jessica M. *Chinese Ornament: The Lotus and the Dragon*, London, 1984

Rawson 1987a Rawson, Jessica M. 'An unusual bronze *you* in the British Museum', *Orientations*, June 1987, pp. 44–9

Rawson 1987b Rawson, Jessica M. *Chinese Bronzes: Art and Ritual*, London, 1987

Rawson 1989a Rawson, Jessica M. 'Chu Influences on the Development of Han Bronze Vessels', *Arts Asiatiques*, vol. XLIV, 1989, pp. 84–99

Rawson 1989b Rawson, Jessica M. 'Statesmen or Barbarians, the Western Zhou as seen through their bronzes', British Academy Albert Reckitt Archaeological Lecture, 19 October 1989, *Proceedings of the British Academy*, LXXV, 1989, pp. 71–95

Rawson 1990 Rawson, Jessica M. *Western Zhou Ritual Bronzes from the Arthur M. Sackler Collections*, 2 vols, Washington, DC, and Cambridge, Mass., 1990

Rawson and Bunker 1990 Rawson, Jessica M. and Bunker, Emma C. *Ancient Chinese and Ordos Bronzes*, Hong Kong, 1990

Rawson 1992a Rawson, Jessica M. 'Shang and Western Zhou Designs in Jade and Bronze' in *International Colloquium on Chinese Art History, 1991, Proceedings, Antiquities, Part 1*, Taipei, 1992, pp. 73–105

Rawson 1992b Rawson, Jessica M. (ed.). *The British Museum Book of Chinese Art*, London, 1992

Rawson 1993a Rawson, Jessica M. 'Late Shang Bronze Design, Meaning and Purpose' in Whitfield 1993, pp. 67–95

Rawson 1993b Rawson, Jessica M. 'Some examples of human or human-like faces on Shang and Western Zhou bronzes', lecture given at the opening of the Sackler Museum, Beijing, 1993 (forthcoming)

Rawson 1993c Rawson, Jessica M. 'The Ancestry of Chinese Bronzes' in Lubar and Kingery 1993, pp. 51–73

Rawson 1993d Rawson, Jessica M. 'Ancient Chinese Ritual Bronzes: the Evidence from Tombs and Hoards of the Shang (*c.* 1500–1050 BC) and Western Zhou (*c.* 1050–771 BC) periods', *Antiquity*, vol. 67, no. 257, December 1993, pp. 805–23

Rawson 1994 Rawson, Jessica M. 'Contact between Southern China and Henan during the Shang Period', *Transactions of the Oriental Ceramic Society*, vol. 57, London, 1994, pp. 1–24

Rawson 1995 Rawson, Jessica M. *Chinese Jade from the Neolithic to the Qing*, London, 1995

Renfrew 1988 Renfrew, Colin. 'Varna and the emergence of wealth in prehistoric Europe' in Arjun Appadurai (ed.), *The Social Life of Things*, Cambridge, 1988, pp. 141–68

Ronan 1978–94 Ronan, Colin. *The Shorter Science and Civilization in China*, 4 vols, Cambridge, 1978, 1981, 1986, 1994

Salmony 1938 Salmony, Alfred. *Carved Jade of Ancient China*, Berkeley, 1938

Salmony 1954 Salmony, Alfred. *Antler and Tongue. An Essay on Ancient Chinese Symbolism and its Implications*, Ascona, 1954

Salmony 1963 Salmony, Alfred. *Chinese Jade through the Wei Dynasty*, New York, 1963

Schafer 1963 Schafer, Edward H. 'Mineral Imagery in the Paradise Poems of Kuan Hsiu', *Asia Major*, vol. 10, 1963, pp. 73–102

Schipper 1965 Schipper, Kristopher M. *L'empereur Wou des Han dans la légende taoiste: Han Wou-ti Nei-tchouan*, Paris, 1965

Schipper 1978 Schipper, Kristopher M. 'The Taoist Body', *History of Religions*, vol. 17, 1978, pp. 355–86

Schlombs 1990 Schlombs, A. 'Die Herstellung der Terrakotta-Armee' in Ledderose and Schlombs 1990, pp. 88–97

Schlombs 1991 Schlombs, A. 'Guanghan. Die Entdeckung einer versunkenen Metropole der Shang-Zeit (16.-11. Jh.v.Chr.) in Westchina', *Kölner Museums-Bulletin*, vol. 4, 1991, pp. 18–25

Schmidt-Glintzer 1990 Schmidt-Glintzer, H. 'Qin Shihuangdi. Der Erste Gottkaiser von China' in Ledderose and Schlombs 1990, pp. 58–65

Scott and Hutt 1987 Scott, Rosemary E. and Graham Hutt. *Style in the East Asian Tradition*, Colloquies on Art and Archaeology in Asia, no. 14, London, 1987

Seidel 1982 Seidel, Anna. 'Tokens of Immortality in Han Graves' (with appendix by Marc Kalinowski), *Numen*, vol. XXIX, fasc. 1, July 1982, pp. 79–122

Seidel 1983 Seidel, Anna. 'Treasures and Taoist Sacraments: Taoist roots in the Apocrypha' in Strickmann 1983, pp. 291–371

Seidel 1984 Seidel, Anna. 'Taoist Messianism', *Numen*, vol. XXXI, fasc. 2, December 1984, pp. 161–98

Seidel 1987 Seidel, Anna. 'Traces of Han Religion in Funerary Texts Found in Tombs' in Akizuki Kan'ei (ed.), *Dokyō to shōkyō bunka*, Tokyo, 1987, pp. 678–714

Shaanxi 1990 Shaanxi Sheng Bowuguan (ed.). *Han Tang sichou zhi lu wenwu jinghua*, Hong Kong, 1990

Shanghai 1964 *Shanghai Bowuguan cang qingtongqi*, 2 vols, Shanghai, 1964

Shanghai 1992 Shanghai Museum and Hong Kong Urban Council. *Gems of Liangzhu culture from the Shanghai Museum*, Hong Kong, 1992

Shanghai Museum 1993 Shanghai Museum. *Catalogue of exhibition at Tokyo National Museum, Aichi Prefectural Museum of Art and Fukuoka Art Museum*, Tokyo, 1993

Shanxi 1994a Shanxi Sheng Kaogu Yanjiusuo (ed.). *Shanxi Sheng Kaogu Xuehui lunwenji*, vol. 2, Taiyuan, 1994

Shanxi 1994b Shanxi Sheng Kaogu Yanjiusuo (ed.). *San Jin kaogu*, vol. 1, Taiyuan, 1994

Shanxi 1994c Shanxi Sheng Kaogu Yanjiusuo (ed.). *Shanxi kaogu sishinian*, Taiyuan, 1994

Shapin 1994 Shapin, Steven. *A Social History of Truth, Civility and Science in 17th Century England*, Chicago, 1994

Shaughnessy 1988 Shaughnessy, Edward L. 'Historical Perspectives on the Introduction of the Chariot into China', *Harvard Journal of Asiatic Studies*, vol. 48, 1988, pp. 189–237

Shaughnessy 1991 Shaughnessy, Edward L. *Sources of Western Zhou History: Inscribed Bronze Vessels*, Berkeley, Los Angeles, London, 1991

Shen Congwen 1992 Shen Congwen. *Zhongguo gudai fuzhuang yanjiu*, Hong Kong, 1992

Shima 1967 Shima Kunio. *Inkyo bokuji sōrui*, Tokyo, 1967

Shimonaka 1954 Shimonaka Yasaburo *et al.* (eds). *Shodō zenshū*, vol. 1, Tokyo, 1954

Sichuan n.d. Sichuansheng Bowuguan (ed.). *Ba-Shu qingtongqi*, Chengdu and Macao, n.d.

Sichuan 1989 *Guanghan Sanxingdui yizhi yanjiu zhuanji*, special issue of *Sichuan Wenwu*, 1989

Sichuan 1992 *Sanxingdui gu Shu wenhua yanjiu zhuanji*, special issue of *Sichuan Wenwu*, 1992

Sima Qian 1959 Sima Qian. *Shiji*, Beijing, 1959

Singapore 1990 Empress Place (ed.). *Treasures from the Han*, exhibition catalogue, Singapore, 1990

Singapore 1993 Empress Place (ed.). *War and Ritual: Treasures from the Warring States 475–221 B.C.*, Singapore, 1993

Sirén 1938 Sirén, O. *et al. Studies in Chinese Art and Some Indian Influences*, London, 1938

Sirén 1942 Sirén, O. *Kinas Konst under Tre Artusenden*, Stockholm, 1942

Smith 1981 Smith, Cyril Stanley. *A Search for Structure: Selected Essays on Science, Art, and History*, Cambridge, Mass., 1981

So 1993 So, Jenny F. 'A Hongshan Jade Pendant in the Freer Gallery of Art', *Orientations*, May 1993, pp. 87–92

So 1995 So, Jenny. *Eastern Zhou Ritual Bronzes from the Arthur M. Sackler Collections*, Washington, DC, 1995

Song Zhaolin 1983a Song Zhaolin. 'Yuanshide shengyu xinyang', *Shijian yanjiu* 1983.1, pp. 131–9

Song Zhaolin 1983b Song Zhaolin. *Zhongguo yuanshi shehui shi*, Beijing, 1983

Song Zhaolin 1989 Song Zhaolin. *Wu yu wushu*, Chengdu, 1989

Speiser 1965 Speiser, W. *Lackkunst in Ostasien*, Baden-Baden, 1965

Steele 1966 Steele, J. (trans.). *The I-Li*, Taipei, 1966 (1st edn, London, 1917)

Strickmann 1977 Strickmann, Michel. 'The Mao Shan Revelations: Taoism and the Aristocracy', *T'oung Pao*, no. 63, 1977, pp. 1–64

Strickmann 1983 Strickmann, Michel (ed.) *Tantric and Taoist Studies in Honour of R. A. Stein*, vol. 2, *Mélanges Chinois et Bouddhiques*, vol. XXI, Brussels, 1983

Sturman 1988 Sturman, Peter C. 'Celestial Journey: Meditations on (and in) Han dynasty Painted Pots at the Metropolitan Museum of Art', *Orientations*, May 1988, pp. 54–67

Su Bingqi 1994 Su Bingqi. *Huaren – Long de chuanren – Zhongguoren: kaogu xungen ji*, Shenyang, 1994

Sun Ji 1991 Sun Ji. *Handai wuzhi wenhua ziliao tushuo*, Beijing, 1991

Sun Ji 1994 Sun Ji. 'Xian Qin, Han, Jin yaodai yong jin yin daikou', *Wenwu* 1994.1, pp. 50–64

Sun Sen 1987 Sun Sen. *Xia Shang shigao*, Beijing, 1987

Sun Zhixin 1993 Sun Zhixin. 'The Liangzhu Culture, its Discovery and its Jades', *Early China*, vol. 18, 1993, pp. 1–40

Sung Ying-hsing 1966 Sung Ying-hsing (trans. E-Tu Zen Sun and

Shiou Chuan Sun). *T'ien-kung K'ai-wu, Chinese Technology in the Seventeenth Century*, University Park, Pennsylvania, and London, 1966

Taipei 1967 National Palace Museum (ed.). *Chinese Cultural Art Treasures 1967*, 4th edn, Taipei, 1967

Taipei 1992a *International Colloquium on Chinese Art History, 1991, Proceedings*, 2 vols, Taipei, 1992

Taipei 1992b Wenwu Jiaoliu Zhongxin and Zhanwang Wenjiao Jijinhui (eds). *Dalu guwu zhenbaozhan*, Taipei, 1992

Takayasu Higuchi 1979 Takayasu Higuchi. *Kokyō*, 2 vols, Tokyo, 1979

Tang Lan 1981 Tang Lan. *Yinxu wenzi ji*, Beijing, 1981

Teng Shu-p'ing 1986 Teng Shu-p'ing. 'Gudai yuqi shang qiyi wenshi de yanjiu', *Gugong xueshu jikan*, vol. 4, no. 1, 1986, pp. 1–57

Teng Shu-p'ing 1990 Teng Shu-p'ing. 'Gu yu xin quan (2) – liuqi yu liurui', *Gugong wenwu yuekan*, vol. 8, no. 1, issue no. 86, 1990, pp. 118–31

Teng Shu-p'ing 1992a Teng Shu-p'ing. *Guoli Gugong Bowuyuan cang Xinshiqi shidai yuqi tulu – Neolithic Jades in the Collection of the National Palace Museum*, Taipei, 1992

Teng Shu-p'ing 1992b Teng Shu-p'ing. ' The mystery of the markings on jades of the Liang-chu culture', *National Palace Museum Bulletin*, vol. XXVII, nos 5–6, November/December 1992–January/February 1993

Thorp 1981–2 Thorp, Robert L. ' The Sui Xian Tomb: Re-thinking the Fifth Century', *Artibus Asiae*, vol. XLIII, pts 1/2, 1981–2, pp. 67–92

Thorp 1982 Thorp, Robert L. ' The Date of Tomb 5 at Yinxu, Anyang', *Artibus Asiae*, vol. XLIII, pt 3, 1982, pp. 239–46

Thorp 1983 Thorp, Robert L. 'Origins of Chinese Architectural Style: The Earliest Plans and Building Types,' *Archives of Asian Art*, no. 36, 1983, pp. 22–39

Thorp 1988a Thorp, Robert L. *Son of Heaven, Imperial Arts of China*, Seattle, 1988

Thorp 1988b Thorp, Robert L. ' The Archaeology of Style at Anyang: Tomb 5 in Context', *Archives of Ancient Art*, vol. XLI, 1988, pp. 47–69

Thorp 1991 Thorp, Robert. 'Mountain Tombs and Jade Burial Suits: Preparations for Eternity in the Western Han' in Kuwayama 1991, pp. 26–39

Thote 1991 Thote, Alain. ' The Double Coffin of Leigudun Tomb No. 1: Iconographic Sources and Related Problems' in Lawton 1991, pp. 23–46

Thote 1993 Thote, Alain. 'Aspects of the Serpent on Eastern Zhou Bronzes and Lacquerware' in Whitfield 1993, pp. 150–60

Thote 1995 Thote, Alain. 'De quelques décors au serpent sur les bronzes rituels du royaume de Chu' in Jean-Pierre Diény (ed.), *Hommage à Kwong Hing Foon: études d'histoire culturelle de la Chine*, Paris, 1995

Tianjin 1989 Zhang Nairen, Tian Guanglin and Wang Huide (eds). *Liaohai qiguan*, Tianjin, 1989

Tianjin 1993 Tianjinshi Yishu Bowuguan (ed.). *Tianjinshi yishuguan cangyu*, Hong Kong, 1993

Till 1980 Till, B. 'Some observations on Stone Winged Chimeras at Ancient Chinese Tomb Sites', *Artibus Asiae*, vol. XL, pt 4, 1980, pp. 261–81

Timmerman 1986 Timmerman, I. *Die Seide Chinas. Eine Kulturgeschichte am seidenen Faden*, Cologne, 1986

Tokyo 1973 Tokyo Kokuritsu Hakubutsukan *et al.* (eds). *Archaeolo-*
gical Treasures Excavated in the People's Republic of China 1973, Tokyo, 1973

Tokyo 1981 Tokyo Kokuritsu Hakubutsukan (ed.). *Chūsan ōkoku bumbutsu ten*, Tokyo, 1981

Tokyo 1992 *Sō Kō Itsu bo*, Tokyo, 1992

Tong Enzheng 1987 Tong Enzheng. 'Shi lun wo guo cong dongbei zhi xinan de biandi banyuexing wenhua zhuanbodai' in *Wenwu Chubanshe chengli sanshi zhounian jinian – wenwu yu kaogu lunji*, Beijing, 1987, pp. 17–43

Trigger 1978 Trigger, Bruce G. *Time and Traditions, Essays in Archaeological Interpretation*, Edinburgh, 1978

Trigger 1989 Trigger, Bruce G. *A History of Archaeological Thought*, Cambridge, 1989

Tsien Tsuen-hsiun 1962 Tsien Tsuen-hsiun. *Written on Bamboo and Silk: The Beginnings of Chinese Books and Inscriptions*, Chicago and London, 1962

Umehara 1964 Umehara Sueji. *Inkyō*, Tokyo, 1964

Venice 1983 *7000 Years of Chinese Civilisation: Chinese art and archaeology from the Neolithic Period to the Han Dynasty*, exhibition catalogue, Milan, 1983

Vienna 1974 Österreichisches Museum für Angewandte Kunst (ed.). *Archäologische Funde der Volksrepublik China*, Vienna, 1974

Wagner 1992 Wagner, M. 'Die Motive der bemalten neolithischen Keramik Chinas. Ein auf stilkritischen Analysen beruhender und in Typologien geordneter Bildatlas zur Sino-Archäologie', unpublished dissertation, University of Leipzig, 1992

Wagner 1994 Wagner, M. 'Jade – Der edle Stein für die Elite' in Eggebrecht 1994, pp. 96–104

Waley 1954 Waley, Arthur. *The Book of Songs*, London, 1954

Waley-Cohen 1984 Waley-Cohen, Joanna (trans.). *The Lacquers of the Mawangdui Tomb* (translated from the sections dealing with the lacquer finds in *Changsha Mawangdui yihao Hanmu*, Beijing, 1976), *Oriental Ceramic Society Translations*, no. 11, London, 1984

Walton 1993 Walton, Kendall L. *Mimesis as Make-believe, on the Foundations of the Representational Arts*, Cambridge, Mass., and London, 1993 (paperback; 1st edn, 1990)

Wang Binghua 1990 Wang Binghua. *Xinjiang Tianshan shenshi congbai yanhua*, Beijing, 1990

Wang Hongyuan 1993 Wang Hongyuan. *The Origins of Chinese Characters*, Beijing, 1993

Wang Kefen 1989 Wang Kefen. *Zhongguo wudao fazhanshi*, Shanghai, 1989

Wang Tao 1990 Wang Tao. 'A Textual Investigation of the Taotie' in Whitfield 1993, pp. 102–18

Wang Xu and Wang Yarong 1993 Wang Xu and Wang Yarong. 'Guanghan chutu qingtong liren xiang fushi guanjian', *Wenwu* 1993.9, pp. 60–8

Wang Zhongshu 1982 Wang Zhongshu. *Han Civilisation*, New Haven, 1982

Watson 1961 Watson, Burton. *Records of the Grand Historian of China*, translated from the *Shih chi* of Ssu-ma Ch'ien, vol. 2, *The Age of the Emperor Wu, 140 – c. 100 BC*, pt 1, 'The Treatise on the Feng and Shan Sacrifices', New York and London, 1961, pp. 13–69

Watson 1993 Watson, Burton (trans.). *Records of the Grand Historian: Qin Dynasty*, Hong Kong, 1993

Watson 1971 Watson, William. *Cultural Frontiers in Ancient East Asia*, Edinburgh, 1971

Watson 1973 Watson, William. *The Genius of China: An Exhibition of Archaeological Finds of the People's Republic of China*, London, 1973

Watt 1988–9 Watt, James. 'Neolithic Jade Carving in China', *Transactions of the Oriental Ceramic Society*, vol. 53, 1988–9, pp. 11–26

Weber 1968 Weber, Charles D. *Chinese Pictorial Bronze Vessels of the Late Chou Period*, Ascona, 1968

Wei Zhengjin 1993 Wei Zhengjin. 'Yingpanshan guwenhua yizhi' in *Jinling shengyi daquan*, Nanjing, 1993, pp. 169–72

Welch and Seidel 1979 Welch, Holmes and Seidel, Anna (eds). *Facets of Taoism*, New Haven, 1979

Wen Guang and Jing Zhichun 1992 Wen Guang and Jing Zhichun. 'Chinese Neolithic Jade, A Preliminary Geoarchaeological Study', *Geoarchaeology, An International Journal*, vol. 7, no. 3, pp. 251–75

White 1934 White, W. *Tombs of Old Lo-yang*, Shanghai, 1934

White and Bunker 1994 White, Julia and Bunker, Emma C. *Adornment for Eternity: Status and Rank in Chinese Ornament*, Denver and Hong Kong, 1994

Whitfield 1993 Whitfield, Roderick (ed.). *The Problem of Meaning in Early Chinese Ritual Bronzes*, Colloquies on Art and Archaeology in Asia, no. 15, London, 1993

Wilhelm 1923 Wilhelm, Richard. *Dschuang Dsi*, Jena, 1923

Wilhelm 1929 Wilhelm, Richard. *Frühling und Herbst des Lü Bu We*, Jena, 1929

Wilhelm 1930 Wilhelm, Richard. *Li Gi, Das Buch der Sitte*, Jena, 1930

Wong Yanchong 1988 Wong Yanchong 1988. 'Bronze Mirror Art of the Han-Dynasty', *Orientations*, December 1988, pp. 42–53

Wu 1963 Wu, Nelson I. *Chinese and Indian Architecture*, New York, 1963

Wu Hung 1984 Wu Hung. 'The Sanpan Shan Chariot Ornament and the Xiangrui Design in Western Han Art', *Archives of Asian Art*, vol. xxxvii, 1984, pp. 38–59

Wu Hung 1985 Wu Hung. 'Bird motifs in Eastern Yi art', *Orientations*, October 1985, pp. 30–41

Wu Hung 1987 Wu Hung. 'Myths and Legends in Han Funerary Art' in Lim 1987, pp. 72–82

Wu Hung 1988 Wu Hung. 'From Temple to Tomb: Ancient Chinese Art and Religion in Transition', *Early China*, vol. 13, 1988, pp. 78–115

Wu Hung 1989 Wu Hung. *The Wu Liang Shrine: The Ideology of Early Chinese Pictorial Art*, Stanford, 1989

Wu Hung 1990 Wu Hung. 'A Great Beginning, Ancient Chinese Jades and the origin of ritual art' in Wu Hung and Brian Morgan, *Chinese Jades from the Mu-Fei Collection*, London, 1990

Wu Hung 1992 Wu Hung. 'Art in a Ritual Context: Rethinking Mawangdui', *Early China*, vol. 17, 1992, pp. 111–44

Wu Hung 1994 Wu Hung. 'Beyond the "Great Boundary": Funerary Narratives in the Cangshan Tomb' in John Hay (ed.), *Boundaries in China*, London, 1994

Wu Hung 1995 Wu Hung. 'Princes of jade revisited: Han material symbolism as observed in Mancheng tomb finds', paper forthcoming in Percival David Foundation of Chinese Art, Colloquies on Art and Archaeology in Asia, no. 18, London

Wu Shan 1982 Wu Shan. *Zhongguo xinshiqi shidai taoqi zhungshi yishu*, Beijing, 1982

Wu Shan 1988 Wu Shan (ed.). *Zhongguo gongyi meishu da cidian*, Nanjing, 1988

Wu Tanghai 1994 Wu Tanghai. *Renshi gu yu: gudai yuqi zhizuo yu xingzhi*, Taipei, 1994

Wu Zhongbi 1982 Wu Zhongbi. *Jiangling Fenghuangshan 168-hao mu Xi Han gushi yanjiu*, Beijing, 1982

Xia Nai 1983 see **Hsia Nai 1983**

Xiao Kangda 1992 Xiao Kangda. *Handai lewu baixi yishu yanjiu*, Beijing, 1992

Xing Runchuan and Tang Yunming 1984 Xing Runchuan and Tang Yunming. 'Archaeological Evidence for Ancient Wine Making' in *Recent Discoveries in Chinese Archaeology*, Beijing, 1984, pp. 56–8

Xu Naixiang and Cui Yanxun 1987 Xu Naixiang and Cui Yanxun. *Shuolong*, Beijing, 1987

Xu Shen 1981 Xu Shen (ed.). *Shuowen jiezi zhu*, with annotations by Duan Yucai (1735–1815), Shanghai, 1981

Xu Zhengcai 1991 Xu Zhengcai (ed.). *Jiangling chutu wenwu jingpin*, Jingzhou, 1991

Xu Zongyuan 1964 Xu Zongyuan. *Diwang shiji jicun*, Beijing, 1964

Yan Wenming 1989 Yan Wenming. *Yangshao wenhua yanjiu*, Beijing, 1989

Yang Hsien-yi and Gladys Yang 1979 Yang Hsien-yi and Gladys Yang. *Selections from the Records of the Historian, by Sima Qian*, Beijing, 1979

Yang Jianfang 1987 Yang Jianfang. *Jade Carving in Chinese Archaeology*, vol. 1, Hong Kong, 1987

Yang Kuan 1985 Yang Kuan. *Zhongguo gudai lingqin zhidushi yanjiu*, Shanghai, 1985

Yang Meili 1993 Yang Meili. 'Xibi langgan hupo longsheji bixie chu qunxiong', *Gugong wenwu yuekan*, no. 122, May 1993, pp. 44–51

Yang Meili 1994 Yang Meili. 'Xuanzi you huan: qi yi zai Zeng shang: gudai xibei diqu di huanxing yu, shiqi xilie zhi si – lianhuanxing yuqi yu xibei diqu di yuqi qiege', *Gugong wenwu yuekan*, no. 137, August 1994, pp. 14–33

Yang Meili 1995 Yang Meili. *A Catalogue of the National Palace Museum's Special Exhibition of Circular Jade*, Taipei, 1995

Yang Xiaoneng 1988a Yang Xiaoneng. *Zhongguo yuanshi diaosu yishu*, Hong Kong, 1988

Yang Xiaoneng 1988b Yang Xiaoneng. *Zhongguo Xia Shang diaosu yishu*, Hong Kong, 1988

Yang Xiaowu 1992 Yang Xiaowu. 'Qiantan Sanxingdui chutu jinmian tongtouxiang de xiufu gongyi' in Sichuan 1992, pp. 93–6

Yang Xizhang and Yang Baocheng 1986 Yang Xizhang and Yang Baocheng. 'Shangdai de qingtongyue' in Beijing 1986a, vol. 1, pp. 128–38

Yao Qinde 1991 Yao Qinde (intro. Hsio-Yen Shih, trans. Vivian Ho). 'Spring and Autumn Period Jades from the State of Wu', *Orientations*, October 1991, pp. 47–52

Yoshikai Masato 1994 Yoshikai Masato. 'Lun "T" zi yuhuan' in Hong Kong 1994b, pp. 255–68

You Rende 1981 You Rende. 'Shangdai yudiao longwen di zaoxing yu wenshi yanjiu', *Wenwu* 1981.8, pp. 56–60

You Rende 1986 You Rende. 'Shangdai yuniao yu Shangdai shehui', *Kaogu yu wenwu* 1986.2, pp. 51–60

Yü Yingshih 1964–5 Yü Yingshih. 'Life and Immortality in the Mind of Han China', *Harvard Journal of Asiatic Studies*, vol. 25, 1964–5, pp. 80–122

Yü Yingshih 1987 Yü Yingshih. 'O Soul, Come Back! A Study in the Changing Conceptions of the Soul and Afterlife in Pre-Buddhist China', *Harvard Journal of Asiatic Studies*, vol. 47, no. 2, December 1987, pp. 363–95

Yuan Ke 1991 Yuan Ke (ed.). *Shanhaijing quanyi*, Guizhou, 1991

Yuan Zhongyi 1990 Yuan Zhongyi. *Qin Shihuang ling bingmayong yanjiu*, Beijing, 1990

Zach 1958 Zach, Erwin von. *Die Chinesische Anthologie*, Cambridge, Mass., 1958

Zhang Changshou 1987 Zhang Changshou. 'Ji Fengxi xin faxian di shoumian yushi', *Kaogu* 1987.5, pp. 470–3, 469

Zhang Minghua 1989 Zhang Minghua. 'Liangzhu yuqi yanjiu', *Kaogu* 1989.7, pp. 624–35

Zhang Nairen 1989 Zhang Nairen *et al*. 'Zhongguo de weinasi' in Tianjin 1989

Zhang Xiaoling 1992 Zhang Xiaoling. *Zhongguo yuanshi yishu jingshen*, Chongqing, 1992

Zhang Xiying 1992 Zhang Xiying. 'Xinshiqi shidai de wushi ji Wu wenhua yicun', *Bowuguan yanjiu* 1992.1

Zhang Xiying 1994 Zhang Xiying. 'Zhongguo zongjiao yishu suyuan', *Bowuguan yanjiu* 1994.2

Zhang Xuezheng 1980 Zhang Xuezheng *et al*. 'Tan Majiayao, Banshan, Machang leixing de fenqi he xianghu guanxi' in *Zhongguo kaogu xuehui diyici nianhui lunwen ji 1979*, Beijing, 1980, pp. 50–71

Zhang Xuqiu 1992 Zhang Xuqiu. *Changjiang zhongyou xinshiqi shidai wenhua gailun*, Wuhan, 1992

Zhang Zhengming 1987 Zhang Zhengming. *Chu wenhuashi*, Shanghai, 1987

Zhao Guohua 1987 Zhao Guohua. 'Bagua fuhao yuanshi shuzi yiyi de xin tansuo', *Zhexue yanjiu* 1987.6, pp. 45–59

Zhao Guohua 1990 Zhao Guohua. *Shengzhi chongbai wenhualun*, Beijing, 1990

Zhao Qingfang 1989 Zhao Qingfang (trans. Harold Mok). 'On *bi* and *cong*', *Orientations*, May 1989, pp. 78–82

Zhejiang 1990 Zhejiang Sheng Wenwu Kaogu Yanjiusuo, Shanghai Shi Wenwu Guanli Weiyuanhui, Nanjing Bowuyuan (eds). *Liangzhu wenhua yuqi*, Beijing, 1990

Zhou Nanquan 1993 Zhou Nanquan. *Gu yuqi*, Shanghai, 1993

Zhou Xibao 1984 Zhou Xibao. *Zhongguo gudai fushishi*, Beijing, 1984

Zhou Xun and Gao Chunming 1984 Zhou Xun and Gao Chunming. *Zhongguo fushi wuqian nian*, Hong Kong, 1984

Zhou Xun and Gao Chunming 1988 Zhou Xun and Gao Chunming. *5000 Jahre chinesische Mode*, Tübingen, 1988

Zhou Xun and Gao Chunming 1991 Zhou Xun and Gao Chunming. *Zhongguo lidai funü zhuangshi*, Shanghai, 1991

Zhu Tianshun 1982 Zhu Tianshun. *Zhongguo gudai zongjiao chutan*, Shanghai, 1982

INDEX

Figures in italics refer to illustrations.